Theorizing Diaspora

KeyWorks in Cultural Studies

As cultural studies powers ahead to new intellectual horizons, it becomes increasingly important to chart the discipline's controversial history. This is the object of an exciting new series, KeyWorks in Cultural Studies. By showcasing the best that has been thought and written on the leading themes and topics constituting the discipline, KeyWorks in Cultural Studies provides an invaluable genealogy for students striving to better understand the contested space in which cultural studies takes place and is practiced.

Theorizing Diaspora

A Reader

Edited by

Jana Evans Braziel and Anita Mannur

Blackwell
Publishing

Editorial material and organization © 2003 by Blackwell Publishing Ltd

350 Main Street, Malden, MA 02148-5018, USA
108 Cowley Road, Oxford OX4 1JF, UK
550 Swanston Street, Carlton South, Melbourne, Victoria 3053, Australia
Kurfürstendamm 57, 10707 Berlin, Germany

First published 2003 by Blackwell Publishing Ltd

Library of Congress Cataloging-in-Publication Data

Theorizing diaspora : a reader / edited by Jana Evans Braziel and Anita
Mannur.
    p.   cm. – (Keyworks in cultural studies ; 6)
Includes bibliographical references and index.
    ISBN 0-631-23391-1 (hardcover : alk. paper) – ISBN 0-631-23392-X
(pbk. : alk. paper)
    1. Emigration and immigration – History – 20th century.   2. Popula-
tion geography – History – 20th century.   3. Refugees – History – 20th
century.   I. Braziel, Jana Evans, 1967–   II. Mannur, Anita.   III. Series.
    JV6032 .T44 2003
    304.8 – dc21

                                                                    2002006549

A catalogue record for this title is available from the British Library.

Set in 10 on 12 pt Galliard
by SNP Best-set Typesetter Ltd., Hong Kong
Printed and bound in the United Kingdom
by MPG Books Ltd, Bodmin, Cornwall

For further information on
Blackwell Publishing, visit our website:
http://www.blackwellpublishing.com

Contents

Acknowledgments

This project began three years ago in a copy shop in Amherst, Massachusetts. The two of us were frantically trying to photocopy articles about diaspora to put on reserve for a course reader. As we rushed to collate the articles that we had found useful in our own attempts to theorize diaspora, the question as to why these articles had not been collected in a single volume came up. Following our own desire to see a volume that would collect the tenor and trajectory of diaspora studies, we embarked on this project.

For sustaining us through this long process, we owe a debt of thanks to many individuals. First and foremost, we would like to thank Jayne Fargnoli and Annie Lenth at Blackwell Publishing for their expertise and guidance through the publication process. Thanks to the anonymous reviewers for their helpful comments on the editors' introduction; to Greg Horvath, Dale Hudson, and Carolyn Porter, for graciously and expediently providing meticulous comments on our introduction – thanks! And thanks to Jack Messenger for his copy-editing assistance.

We are grateful for the support and encouragement of our colleagues at the University of Massachusetts Amherst, University of Wisconsin La Crosse, Harvard University, and the Massachusetts Institute of Technology. We are also immensely grateful to a group of fine scholars who co-presented their research with us at a seminar during the 2000 conference of the American Comparative Literature Association at Yale University. Thanks to all who participated, especially Grant Farred, Radhika Gajjala, Neil Hartlen, Shu-Chen Huang, Rajeev Patke, Zeynep Kilic Ozgen, and Benzi Zhang.

Anita Mannur's Personal Acknowledgments

Thanks to my parents, Shobana and Hanumant Mannur for their unwavering love and support of my academic pursuits. They named me to fit into any culture in the world and without them I would not have the intellectual and emotional resources necessary to think about what it means to inhabit numerous locations as a diasporic individual. I am also grateful to a number of incredibly intelligent and wonderful friends, mentors, and colleagues for their continued support. Maeve Adams, Anne Ciecko, David Eng, Liz Fitzpatrick, Neil Hartlen, Dale Hudson, David Lenson, Ignacio López-Vicuña, Sanda Mayzaw Lwin, Luís Madureira, Sunaina Maira, Cathy Portuges, R. Radhakrishnan, Jennifer Rodgers, Jonathan Sadow, B. K. Tuon, Radhika Wakankar, and Leeta White – thank you! And to Jana, for always believing in the power of collaborative work: I am immensely grateful.

Jana Evans Braziel's Personal Acknowledgments

Thanks, first and foremost, to Anita Mannur, whose persistence and intellectual rigor never ceases to astonish me: I owe a debt of gratitude. I am also extremely grateful to the colleagues, close friends, and family members who have offered advice, mentorship, support, laughter, and even a few pots of coffee (*when needed!*). Thanks to all my colleagues and all my students in the Comparative Literature and Women's Studies Departments at the University of Massachusetts and in the English Department at the University of Wisconsin La Crosse, particularly those who engaged me in critical conversations about issues of diaspora, transnational feminist thought, and migration, while challenging my ideas about these issues. Special thanks are owed to Leila Ahmed, Arlene Avakian, Brenda Bethman, Briankle Chang, Alex Deschamps, Ann Ferguson, Monika Giacoppe, Shu-Chen Huang, Sara Lennox, David Lenson, Jeannine Marks, Bushra Mohammed, Nancy Patteson, Elizabeth Petroff, Catherine Portuges, Jennifer Rodgers, Carolyn Ruszala, Robert Schwartzwald, Meher Singh, and Paula Straile. For intellectual conversation and friendship, I also want to thank Neil Hartlen, Susan Crutchfield, Sonja Simonson Schrag, Joseph Young, and Jim Braziel. Thanks, finally, to my family for teaching me about life and love.

For permission to reprint the essays included in this anthology, we gratefully acknowledge the following:
Arjun Appadurai for permission to reprint "Disjuncture and Difference in the Global Cultural Economy." *Public Culture* 2.2 (1990): 1–24.
Harvard University Press for permission to reprint Paul Gilroy's "The Black Atlantic as a Counterculture of Modernity." In *The Black Atlantic: Modernity and Double Consciousness*. Cambridge, MA: Harvard University Press, 1993, 1–40.

The University of Chicago Press for permission to reprint Daniel Boyarin and Jonathan Boyarin's "Diaspora: Generation and the Ground of Jewish Identity." *Critical Inquiry* 19.4 (1993): 693–725.

South End Press for permission to reprint R. Radhakrishnan's "Ethnicity in an Age of Diaspora." In *The State of Asian America*, ed. Karin Aguilar-San Juan. Boston, MA: South End Press, 1994, 219–33.

The University of Toronto Press for permission to reprint Lisa Lowe's "Heterogeneity, Hybridity, Multiplicity: Marking Asian American Differences." In *Diaspora: A Journal of Transnational Studies* 1.1 (spring 1991): 24–44.

Indiana University Press for permission to reprint Rey Chow's "Against the Lures of Diaspora: Minority Discourse, Chinese Women, and Intellectual Hegemony." In *Writing Diaspora: Tactics of Intervention*. Bloomington: Indiana University Press, 1993, 99–119.

Routledge for permission to reprint Jayne O. Ifekwunigwe's "Returning(s): Relocating the Critical Feminist Auto-Ethnographer." In *Scattered Belongings: Cultural Paradoxes of "Race," Nation and Gender*. London and New York: Routledge, 1999, 29–49.

Duke University Press for permission to reprint Martin F. Manalansan IV's "In the Shadows of Stonewall: Examining Gay Transnational Politics and the Diasporic Dilemma." In *The Politics of Culture in the Shadow of Capital*, ed. Lisa Lowe and David Lloyd. Duke University Press, 1997, 485–505; and Gayatri Gopinath's "Nostalgia, Desire, Diaspora: South Asian Sexualities in Motion." *Positions* 5.2 (1997): 467–89.

Lawrence and Wishart for permission to reprint Stuart Hall's essay "Cultural Identity and Diaspora." In *Identity: Community, Culture, Difference*, ed. Jonathan Rutherford. London: Lawrence and Wishart, 1990, 222–37.

MIT Press for permission to reprint Kobena Mercer's "Diaspora Culture and the Dialogic Imagination." In *Blackframes: Critical Perspectives on Black Independent Cinema*, ed. M. Cham and C. Watkins. Cambridge, MA: MIT Press, 1988, 50–61.

Every effort has been made to trace copyright holders and to obtain their permission for the use of copyright material. We apologize for any errors or omissions in the above list and would be grateful if notified of any corrections that should be incorporated in future reprints or editions of this book.

Nation, Migration, Globalization: Points of Contention in Diaspora Studies

Jana Evans Braziel and Anita Mannur

India always exists off the turnpikes of America.

Agha Shahid Ali

I have seen Cubans everywhere, scattered from Tierra del Fuego to Iceland
... We have taken root where exile threw us ...

Virgil Suarez

Diaspora, Paul Gilroy reminds us, "is an ancient word" (1994: 207), but as the poetic lines of Agha Shahid Ali and Virgil Suarez reveal, its new currencies in globalist discourses confound the once (presumed to be) clearly demarcated parameters of geography, national identity, and belonging. Etymologically derived from the Greek term *diasperien*, from *dia-*, "across" and *-sperien*, "to sow or scatter seeds," diaspora can perhaps be seen as a naming of the other which has historically referred to displaced communities of people who have been dislocated from their native homeland through the movements of migration, immigration, or exile. First used in the *Septuagint*, the Greek translation of the Hebrew scriptures explicitly intended for the Hellenic Jewish communities in Alexandria (circa 3rd century BCE) to describe the Jews living in exile from the homeland of Palestine, diaspora suggests a dislocation from the nation-state or geographical location of origin and a relocation in one or more nation-states, territories, or countries.[1] The term "diaspora," then, has religious significance and pervaded medieval rabbinical writings on the Jewish diaspora, to describe the plight of Jews living outside of Palestine.

Another early historical reference is the Black African diaspora, beginning in the sixteenth century with the slave trade, forcibly exporting West Africans out of their native lands and dispersing them into the "New World" – parts of North America, South America, the Caribbean and elsewhere that slave labor was exploited – through the Middle Passage. These early historical references reveal that diaspora is not always voluntary.[2] The movement of people across the globe in the early modern period resulted in conquests, genocides, and the trade of spices, sugar, and slaves. The Middle Passage marks one trajectory of this triangulated form of circulation – raw resources for goods for peoples – inhumanely buying and selling manufactured products for human lives. Some scholars estimate that as many as 12 million West Africans were sold into slavery and forcibly exiled to the "New World" during the almost 400-year period of legalized slavery which began in 1502 (when Ferdinand and Isabella allowed Nicholas de Ovando, the Spanish governor of Hispaniola, to import African slaves to the island) and ended in the mid-nineteenth century (Britain legally abolished slavery in 1833, but slavery continued in the British Caribbean until 1834; Spain and Portugal illegalized slavery in 1840, although Portuguese ships continued to illegally import slaves into its South American colonies until the late nineteenth century; and slavery was abolished in the US in 1865). This early transatlantic African diaspora resulted in numerous fractured diasporas in the late nineteenth century and throughout the twentieth century, as Black Africans migrated from south to north in North America and across the Western hemisphere – from Port au Prince to Montréal, from Kingston to New York – and from west to east across the Atlantic ocean again – from Trinidad to London and elsewhere. Diaspora, in the rapidly changing world we now inhabit, speaks to diverse groups of displaced persons and communities moving across the globe – from Kuala Lumpur to Sydney, Harare to Toronto, Paris to Marrakesh, Budapest to Santo Domingo, or even Calcutta to Tijuana, just as earlier in the twentieth century it mapped the movements of Palestinian refugees from Jerusalem to Amman or Beirut, and Pakistani refugees from Karachi to Dar es Salaam.

Theorizing Diaspora(s)

In the last decade, theorizations of diaspora have emerged in area studies, ethnic studies, and cultural studies as a major site of contestation. Since the journal *Diaspora: A Journal of Transnational Studies* was inaugurated in 1991, debates over the theoretical, cultural, and historical resonances of the term have proliferated in academic journals devoted to ethnic, national, and (trans)national concerns. A glance through recent academic journals reveals an increasing preoccupation with theorizations and problematizations of diaspora and nation. The explosion in various fields – literature, sociology, anthropology, film studies, queer theory, area studies, ethnic studies – in work about diaspora makes it difficult to ascertain how and why the term is being deployed in critical scholarship. It is often used as a catch-all phrase to speak of and for all movements, however privileged, and for all dislocations, even symbolic ones. Following the lead of the theorists included in this collection, we caution, therefore, against the uncritical, unreflexive application of the term "diaspora" to any and all contexts of global displacement and movement; some forms of travel are tourism, and every attempt to mark movements as necessarily disenfranchising become imperialist gestures.[3]

What do we mean by diaspora? How is diaspora historicized and politicized, and how does it connect with ideas of nationalism, transnationalism, or transmigration? In thinking through the category of diaspora and its link to geopolitical entities such as nation-states, it is thus crucial to consider the important role of nation formation and constitution during the post-World War II era. While cultural and literary critics have been increasingly concerned with how to rethink concepts of nationhood and national identity, such critical analyses should also interrogate contemporary forms of movement, displacement, and dislocation – from travel to exile. Indeed, these questions are inextricably linked to a theorization of diaspora. Mass migration movements, the multiple waves of political refugees seeking asylum in other countries, the reconfiguration of nation-states, particularly in Central Europe and the Balkan states, demand that the concept of nationhood take account of the specific geopolitical circumstances that precipitate the movement of people and communities in the late twentieth and early twenty-first centuries.

We suggest that *theorizing* diaspora offers critical spaces for thinking about the discordant movements of modernity, the massive migrations that have defined this century – from the late colonial period through the decolonization era into the twenty-first century. Theorizations of diaspora need not, and should not, be divorced from historical and cultural specificity. Diasporic traversals question the rigidities of identity itself – religious, ethnic, gendered, national; yet this diasporic movement marks not a postmodern turn from history, but a nomadic turn in which the very parameters of specific historical moments are embodied and – as diaspora itself suggests – are scattered and regrouped into new points of becoming.

The selections from the increasing corpus of critical writings on diaspora included in *Theorizing Diaspora* do not merely reiterate different theories about national community and diaspora, but revisit some of the crucial theoretical writings on diaspora and nation, inquiring why diaspora has become such an important category of critical analysis in the social sciences, literature, and the humanities. Mediating between different theorizations of diaspora, this volume asks how we can understand the widescale dispersal and migration movements that were emblematic of the twentieth century. Comparatively examining some of the theoretical arguments that have acquired an almost canonical status in studies of diaspora, nationalism, and transnationalism, this volume offers strategies for rethinking the idea of national community to respond more explicitly to the question: why is diaspora studies important? Why is it accorded so much importance now? In addition to historicizing different migrations and modern paths of displacement, this volume also historicizes the variant movements of migration and diaspora studies.

Once conceptualized as an exilic or nostalgic dislocation from homeland, diaspora has attained new epistemological, political, and identitarian resonances as its points of reference proliferate. The term "diaspora" has been increasingly used by anthropologists, literary theorists, and cultural critics to describe the mass migrations and displacements of the second half of the twentieth century, particularly in reference to independence movements in formerly colonized areas, waves of refugees fleeing war-torn states, and fluxes of economic migration in the post-World War II era. *Diaspora, diasporic,* and *diaspora-ization* (Stuart Hall) are contested terms, the meanings and multiple referents of which are currently being theorized and debated. The theorists anthologized here – as well as scholars engaging in dialogues about migrant subjects[4] or migratory subjectivities[5] – are all important voices in the ongoing dialogue surrounding the field of diaspora studies.

Most recent theorizations of diaspora, notably the essays collected here, have been marked by the ambiguities of the term diaspora itself – a term which literally (and on an historical level, negatively) denotes communities of people dislocated from their native homelands through migration, immigration, or exile as a consequence of colonial expansion, but etymologically suggests the (more positive) fertility of dispersion, dissemination, and the scattering of seeds. For example, Paul Gilroy remains critical of earlier critical formations of the African diaspora that see all African diasporic individuals everywhere – scattered across several continents – as linked by a common heritage, history, and racial descent; for Gilroy, such African diasporic conceptions homogenize difference and form the kind of "ethnic absolutism" of which he is so critical in *The Black Atlantic*. Like the critical terms *rhizome, créole, creolization, hybridity, heterogeneity, métis* and *métissage*, then, diaspora has emerged as an internal critique of the binarisms (colonizer/ colonized; white/black; West/East) that circulated and found currency within colonial discourse and that persist even within some spheres of postcolonial studies: or as Gilroy critiques, Africa vs. Europe, or alternately, Africa vs. America.

Speaking to different communities than postcolonies,[6] recent theorizations of diaspora also seek to represent (and problematize) the lived experiences (in all their ambivalences, contradictions, migrations, and multiple
traversals) of people whose lives have unfolded in myriad diasporic communities across the globe. Diasporic subjects are marked by hybridity and
heterogeneity – cultural, linguistic, ethnic, national – and these subjects are
defined by a traversal of the boundaries demarcating nation and diaspora.
For Hall, the diaspora experience "is defined, not by essence or purity, but
by the recognition of a necessary heterogeneity and diversity; by a conception of identity which lives in and through, not despite, difference; by hybridity." For Gilroy, "the politics of transfiguration" that diaspora necessitates
"strives in pursuit of the sublime, struggling to repeat the unrepeatable;
to present the unrepresentable." For other scholars, this hybridity opens
diasporic subjectivity to a liminal, dialogic space wherein identity is negotiated (Clifford, Gilroy, Hall, Mercer, Ifekwunigwe, Radhakrishnan). Kobena
Mercer theorizes a diasporic "critical dialogism" that challenges "the monologic exclusivity on which dominant versions of national identity and collective belonging are based"; this critical dialogism, according to Mercer,
allows for a "powerfully *syncretic* dynamic, which critically appropriates
elements from the master-codes of the dominant culture and *creolizes* them,
disarticulating given signs and rearticulating their symbolic meaning
otherwise." Thus, diasporic subjects experience double (and even plural)
identifications that are constitutive of hybrid forms of identity (Chow,
Gopinath, Ifekwunigwe, Manalansan); hybrid national (and transnational)
identities are positioned with other identity categories and severed from an
essentialized, nativist identity that is affiliated with constructions of the
nation or homeland.

Diaspora does not, however, transcend differences of race, class, gender,
and sexuality, as one scholar has suggested,[7] nor can diaspora stand alone as
an epistemological or historical category of analysis, separate and distinct
from these interrelated categories. More complexly, diasporic scholars have
suggested innovative and nuanced ways of thinking across the once-
demarcated terrains of identity and exploring the imbrications of ethnic and
national categories, while offering insights into the cultural constructions of
identity in relation to nationality, diaspora, race, gender, and sexuality; of
course, class inflects, if not haunts, the formation of all of these categories.
To that end, class disrupts and complicates – often in productive ways – the
intersections of race, gender, and sexuality.

Diaspora has been theorized from many diverse points of departure –
East Asian, South Asian, Southeast Asian, Asian Pacific, Caribbean, South
American, Latin American, African, and Central European. Recent uses of
the term move from essentialist notions of homeland, national or ethnic

identity, and geographical location to deployments of diaspora conceptualized in terms of hybridity, *métissage*, or heterogeneity. After all, a Cap-Haïtien diasporic living in Miami may embrace both Haiti and the US, and more flexible or diasporic notions of citizenship are needed to probe the multiple belongings created in diaspora, as both Michel Laguerre (1998) and Aihwa Ong (1999) note. By addressing the conditions that allow and oblige people to inhabit more than one of these national spaces, theorizations of diaspora have acquired an increasingly important space within critical discourse on race, ethnicity, nation, and identity.

Scholars of the Jewish diaspora and the African diaspora, seen most clearly in the contributions of Black British Cultural Studies, are also rethinking earlier notions of diaspora as grounded in the fixed or metaphysical–geographical foundations of home, identity, and exile. Such models privilege the geographical, political, cultural, and subjective spaces of the home-nation as an authentic space of belonging and civic participation, while devaluing and bastardizing the states of displacement or dislocation, rendering them inauthentic places of residence.

While diasporic studies has emerged as an important new field of study, it is not without its critics. Theorizations of diaspora have been hotly contested and critiqued. The term "diaspora" has been critiqued as being theoretically celebrated, while methodologically indistinct and ahistorical. Some scholars, arguing that diaspora enters into a semantic field with other terms and terrains, such as those of exile, migrant, immigrant, and globalization, have asserted that diasporic communities are paragons of the transnationalist moment;[8] other critics have resisted and critiqued such celebratory models for thinking diaspora, noting that such celebrations are often ahistorical and apolitical, failing to note the different contexts allowing or prohibiting movement globally (and even locally). For example, Bruce Robbins (1995) offers a close reading of four journals – *Diaspora, boundary 2, Social Text,* and *Public Culture* – that have "broken new ground in stimulating and supporting work in the international area, the nonspecialist area beyond area studies, and each of them sees the work it publishes as in some senses adversarial" (p. 97). In his analysis he describes *Diaspora* as "one of the four journals which has gone furthest – though never without qualification – toward celebrating transnational mobility and the hybridity that results from it as simple and sufficient goods in themselves" (p. 98). While Robbins's description of *Diaspora* as a journal that "celebrates transnational mobility" is itself somewhat problematic, the article importantly asks: how and why do reputed academic journals contribute to and also map out the terrain of intellectual engagement centering around the question of nation formation and migration within a transnational frame? And how do these journals valorize certain types of theorizations of nation – specifically those centered on global mobility – over others?[9]

In its multiple uses, as Robbins astutely notes, the term "diaspora" has occasionally been used in an ahistorical and uncritical manner that fails to attend to the historical conditions that produce diasporic subjectivities. Analogous to the problematic use of the term *border* within branches of area and ethnic studies in general, the term "diaspora" risks losing specificity and critical merit if it is deemed to speak for all movements and migrations between nations, within nations, between cities, within cities *ad infinitum*. While not losing sight of this important point, our objective is to examine, within an interdisciplinary frame, both the historical phenomena of migrations and diasporas and how these movements also inflect identity formation in relation to race, ethnicity, gender, and sexuality. If we are to take the lessons of interdisciplinarity seriously, it is also incumbent on us to examine how work in ethnic studies, communication studies, area studies, and cultural studies, as well as sociology and anthropology, provides us with the tools to understand the lived experiences of diasporic subjects.

Why Diaspora Studies Now?

In response to this question, we propose two important premises upon which to ground the urgency of theorizing diaspora. First, diaspora forces us to rethink the rubrics of nation and nationalism, while refiguring the relations of citizens and nation-states. Second, diaspora offers myriad, dislocated sites of contestation to the hegemonic, homogenizing forces of globalization.

Diaspora forces us to rethink the rubrics of nation and nationalism, while refiguring the relations of citizens and nation-states

In the last century, under the pressure of monumental transnationalist and global shifts (economically, politically, geographically), the nation as a political ideal and as a state form has undergone significant transformation, if not massive ideological erosion. The shaping of national identities occurs within many discursive frames – juridical, political, civic, economic, and literary. Such deterritorializations of nationalism and nation-states, however, do not place us within a decisively postnationalist world. Diaspora has been loosely associated with other terms, particularly transnationalism, to describe the disjunctures and fractured conditions of late modernity; however, diaspora needs to be extricated from such loose associations and its historical and theoretical specificities made clear. While diaspora may be accurately described as transnationalist, it is not synonymous with transnationalism. Transnationalism may be defined as the flow of people, ideas, goods, and capital across national territories in a way that undermines nationality and nationalism as discrete categories of identification, economic organization, and political constitution. We differentiate diaspora from transnationalism, however, in that diaspora refers specifically to the movement – forced or voluntary – of people from one or more nation-states to another. Transnationalism speaks to larger, more impersonal forces – specifically, those of globalization and global capitalism. Where diaspora addresses the migrations and displacements of subjects, transnationalism also includes the movements of information through cybernetics, as well as the traffic in goods, products, and capital across geopolitical terrains through multinational corporations. While diaspora may be regarded as concomitant with transnationalism, or even in some cases consequent of transnationalist forces, it may not be reduced to such macroeconomic and technological flows. It remains, above all, a human phenomenon – lived and experienced.

Part of the value (and necessity) of thinking about different diasporas in transnational settings is that it offers an alternative paradigm for national (or multinational, transnational, and even postnational) identification. Where diaspora and diasporic persons are often considered imitations of the real citizens in the home state, theories of diaspora and transnationalism since the 1990s have offered ways out of the trappings of this hierarchical construct of nation and diaspora. Within some early scholarship grounded in more traditional foundations of nation, exile, and identity, diaspora stands in a hierarchically subordinate relation to nation or homeland, regarded as "the bastard child of the nation – disavowed, inauthentic, illegitimate, and impoverished imitation of the originary culture."[10] These theorizations also create new configurations of nation and diaspora. For Hall, the Caribbean is triply traversed by a *Présence Africaine, Présence Européenne,* and a *Présence Américaine,* as well as the multiple cultural striations of Indian, Chinese, and Middle Eastern influences and the erased presences (through decimation and genocide) of the Arawak, the Carib, and other indigenous Amerindians; for Gopinath, diaspora can "be seen as part of the nation itself," and this destabilized border "allows the nation to be rewritten into the diaspora."[11]

Established generations of diasporic populations across the globe – Jewish, African, Chinese, Japanese – have been grappling with these questions. Future generations descended wholly, or in part, from immigrants from South Asia; economic and political refugees from Haiti, Southeast Asia, Eastern Europe will all have to grapple with similar questions as youth of these ethnicities are born and raised in diasporic contexts and enter into adulthood.[12] How will their memories of the homeland, marked by ambivalence and contradiction, operate? How will they relate to the cultural heritage of their parents? Will they reject aspects of the home country culture? Will they embrace other aspects? What types of alliances will they seek to establish? To fruitfully analyze such questions and problematic dynamics, diaspora studies will need to move beyond theorizing how diasporic identities are constructed and consolidated and must ask, how are these diasporic identities practiced, lived, and experienced?

In such contexts, prevailing metaphors applied to the diasporic individual or diasporic communities must be rigorously interrogated. Janus, the figure from the Greek pantheon whose gaze is simultaneously directed both forward and backward, suggests a certain temporality; the figure at once looks to the future and the past. Indeed this is a seductive metaphor for the immigrant, exile, refugee, or expatriate; but how useful is this metaphor in light of the fact that hybridity, heterogeneity, and multiplicity (to evoke Lisa Lowe's influential essay) characterize the situation of many diasporic communities and individuals? As in the case of Haitian, Cuban, Vietnamese, and Khmer refugees who emigrate under complicated, deeply painful and troubling circumstances, what happens when one cannot or does not want to look back for political or economic reasons?

What happens when future generations do not know how to look back, or as Karin Aguilar-San Juan notes, if looking back means looking back to a place *within* the United States where they spent their childhood and not to some primordial beginning in the home country?[13] Khojah Ismaili Muslim diasporic communities in East Africa, the Caribbean, and North America that emigrated under the leadership of Aga Khan III in the nineteenth century from Kutch, Sindh, Katiawar, and Gujarat do not necessarily accord much importance to connections with South Asia, making questions of looking back to India as a homeland irrelevant, or at best, inappropriate.[14] Or, as one of our undergraduate students interjected during a class discussion about homeland in relation to the Jewish diaspora: "Where, Brooklyn?"

For Vietnamese refugees – the thousands who evacuated Vietnam with American troops after the fall of Saigon in 1975, and for the nearly 2 million Southeast Asian refugees who fled Vietnam, Laos, and Cambodia between 1976 and 1979 – the possibility for a nostalgic return to the homeland is complicated by war, military alliances, anti-communist sentiments, and the psychic and physical brutalities suffered during the war and after. For the Amerasian children of the Vietnam War (culturally, nationally, and genealogically disinherited from their country of birth, and often ambivalent toward their country of adoption), the double-gaze of here/home is one of skeptical resistance with the signified references of here and home unclear at best. As Vietnamese American author Christian Nguyen Langworthy writes in the poem "In this Country Revised," "you fall into dust / as Amerasians without / documented names – / traceless."[15]

In contrast, exiles of the Haitian diaspora frequently hoped for return, despite the brutality of the Duvaliers and the Tonton Macoutes, or even in the years after 1986 (when Jean-Claude Duvalier himself was exiled) as the country still suffered under the Macoutes, while seeking to restore greater equality to the Haitian people. Indeed, the territorial configuration of the Haitian homeland cartographically and legislatively includes its citizens in diaspora, with the diaspora being designated the *10ᵉ Département* of Haiti.[16] Such movements, however – *from home to here to where?* – remain haunted by an uncertain relation to origin and place. For Dany Laferrière, a Haitian–Québécois writer (who now migrates between Montréal and Miami), returning home is an ambivalent move: "I've been waiting a long time for this moment: to be able to sit down at my work table (a wobbly little table underneath a mango tree, at the rear of the yard) and speak calmly of Haiti, at length. Better yet: to speak of Haiti in Haiti." These words, the opening line of a novel written on returning to Haiti after a twenty-year absence, a novel entitled *Pays sans chapeau* (*Down Among the Dead Men*), do not unambiguously suggest the comforts of home, but also evoke the memories and violence of flight: "I'm at home with this music of green flies working on the body of a dead dog, a few meters past the mango tree. I'm at home with this mob tearing itself to bits like mad dogs . . . In Port au Prince, silence exists between one o'clock and three o'clock in the morning."[17] War refugees are not the only types of diasporic subjects ambivalent about "looking back"; other migrants with complex motivations for emigrating and troubled relocations in new countries also experience such apprehension.

Diaspora offers myriad, dislocated sites of contestation to the hegemonic, homogenizing forces of globalization

In the context of late modernity or late capitalism, capital has gone global; and while distinctions need to be made between diaspora as an epistemological and historical category of analysis and other related (however inaccurately) terms such as globalization and global capitalism, clearly some diasporic zones are located (at least partially) within the movements and mechanisms of global capitalist forces. With the signing of intercontinental trade agreements such as NAFTA and GATT, and the formation of transnational alliances such as the European Union, we have entered a period of historical globalization wherein multinational corporations export industry and manufacturing jobs, economic migrants stay home and migrate, and the international division of labor more sharply divides *those who have* and *those who have not*, even as it simultaneously rigidifies and erodes First World/Third World economic divisions, creating "first-world zones" in formerly "developing" countries and "third-world zones" in supposed "First World" nations. As the World Trade Organization negotiates financial treaties globally, environmental, labor, and anarchist protests in the US (Seattle, Washington DC, New York), Italy, Switzerland, and elsewhere resist such globalization and global capitalism locally. The boundaries of local/global, like those of nation/diaspora, are no longer so clearly distinguishable.

Diaspora and diasporic movement, then, must be examined within the contexts of global capitalism. For example, economic migrants such as Thai sex workers who relocate to Japan in order to secure more viable economic futures live in the volatile and precarious relations of nation, diasporic location, political disenfranchisement, and capitalist underclass. Many such sex workers travel to Japan on tourist visas and never return to Thailand for socioeconomic reasons.[18] As economic migrants who maintain financial and emotive links by sending money to their families in Thailand, the threat of deportation is particularly strong. Going back – psychically or physically – has markedly different valences for economic migrants such as the Thai sex workers, as well as for sex workers in many (though not all) settings.[19] Often, diasporic sex workers support their families at home, creating a diasporic–economic context in which these women are trapped by the pressures of family, nation, and economic necessity.[20] This form of sexual–economic migration defines only one of the economic situations of diasporic zones within the mixed zones of global capitalism.

Diasporas are frequently marked by the flows that are transhuman or transmigrant – flows that are ideological, financial, political, and national. Sun Yat Sen and Yasser Arafat, as one scholar notes, are important sources of transnational capital,[21] and such transhuman flows demand a rethinking of diasporic-*scapes* in relation to ideologies of nationalism, transnationalism, and global capital. In theorizing future trajectories of diaspora and diaspora studies, it will be crucial to schematically analyze the role of cybertechnology and the World Wide Web within such ideological and capitalistic formations: how, for example, do supporters of specific organizations such as the PLO (Palestine Liberation Organization) and LTTE (Liberation Tigers of Tamil Eelam), who are committed to positing a different version of the homeland, use cyberspace to promote alternative visions of the home and the homeland, while also moving capital across such divides? How does their presence on the World Wide Web allow for faster or easier transnational flows of money? At such a level the neat demarcations of local capital and global capitalism become blurred, as do micropolitical actions and choices within an international or transnational frame.

We are in a unique historical moment wherein different diasporic trajectories intersect and overlap. The accumulation of political, sociological, anthropological, historical, and literary scholarship on diasporic communities from Africa, the Caribbean, South Asia, Southeast Asia, and elsewhere – as exhibited in the Select Bibliography included at the end of this volume – creates fertile sites from which to theorize and problematize diaspora. Theorizations of diaspora, however, must emerge from this base of scholarship, historically grounded in different diasporic locations, rather than purely postmodern theoretical abstractions of displacement and movement. Heeding Caren Kaplan's caveat in *Questions of Travel* against overly abstract theorizations of diaspora that are not historically located, Anita Mannur has compiled the select bibliography as a means of facilitating future work in the field of diaspora studies.

Theorizing Diaspora: A Reader

By mapping the trajectory of diaspora studies since the early 1990s, *Theorizing Diaspora* hopes to contribute to future diasporic paths and theorizations of the multiple migratory subjectivities lived in diaspora. As one of the only collections devoted exclusively to diaspora as a theoretical term, *Theorizing Diaspora* comprises the critical forays and multiple theoretical shifts in contemporary theorizations of diaspora in its multiple valences – ideological, social, cultural, national, transnational, and postnational – and establishes new terrains for the field of diaspora studies. *Theorizing Diaspora: A Reader* collects the tenor and trajectories of these critical debates, offering readers a selection of disparate and challenging ideas on diaspora.

Although numerous books addressing the historical perspectives of the Jewish and Black African diasporas, and increasingly, the South Asian diaspora, have been published, theoretical perspectives on diaspora developing within the rubric of postcolonial theory are less established. *Theorizing Diaspora* complements and builds on the work of these scholars and theorists. The unique contribution of this text is that it anthologizes many of the most influential voices discussing diasporic communities and conceptualizing diaspora as an emergent theoretical space. It presents in one volume the divergent strains of multiple diasporas – Jewish, Black African, Chinese, South Asian, Filipino, and Caribbean – and collects several key essays that contribute to the ongoing dialogue on diaspora, transnationalism, and migrant subjectivity. While there are certainly other diasporic contexts and communities that could be included in this volume, our aim was not to simply provide a smorgasbord of all contexts, and the selection has been informed by our own intellectual and personal interests in Caribbean, African, South Asian, and Asian American diasporas. Written by anthropologists, literary theorists, and cultural critics trained in the humanities and social sciences, primarily in North America and Britain, all of the essays included here have been previously published. Essays by renowned scholars are paired with more recent essays that are fast becoming crucial for critics interested in rethinking nationhood, citizenship, and ethnicity in non-hierarchical, non-heteronormative, and non-patriarchal forms. All noted articles have substantially shaped the trajectory of diaspora studies, marking multinational and interdisciplinary theorizations of diaspora and reflecting the methods, methodologies, and perspectives of scholars in anthropology, cultural studies, ethnic studies, gender studies, literary studies, film and performative studies, postcolonial theory, queer theory, and other disciplines.

The book is organized into four thematic sections: *Part One: Modernity, Globalism, and Diaspora; Part Two: Ethnicity, Identity, and Diaspora; Part Three: Sexuality, Gender, and Diaspora; and Part Four: Cultural Production and Diaspora.* These sections are not meant, however, to establish rigid boundaries between the essays, as many of the thematic concerns are overlapping. Part One probes the economic, political, and cultural relations of diaspora and globalization as phenomena defining modernity; it includes Paul Gilroy's "The Black Atlantic" and Arjun Appadurai's "Disjuncture and Difference in the Global Cultural Economy." Part Two includes three essays that explore the subjective terrains of diaspora and migration and examine diaspora in relation to social constructions of ethnicity; in these essays, Daniel Boyarin and Jonathan Boyarin, R. Radhakrishnan, and Lisa Lowe demonstrate how notions of ethnicity and ethnic identity are fluid constructs that vary according to location. For example, Radhakrishnan examines Indian identity in diaspora in the US, and Lowe examines the fractured notions of the political construct "Asian American." Boyarin and Boyarin displace the Israeli homeland as an exclusive space for locating identity, reinscribing it onto filiation and generations of Jewish diasporic subjects. In Part Three Rey Chow, Jayne O. Ifekwunigwe, and Martin F. Manalansan IV all suggest the ways in which gender and sexuality inflect diasporic formations. Chow cautions against celebratory notions of diaspora that do not address the roles of class and women in modern forms of movement. Ifekwunigwe deploys auto-ethnography as a feminist methodology for examining the lives of diasporic women, including herself, and she explores autobiography as a critical lens through which to complicate border crossings (gendered, racialized, nationalized). Manalansan troubles the nationalist framework of queer alliances (and histories) in the US, exploring how both certain historical points of reference (for example, Stonewall) and sexual categories (being "out") do not necessarily cohere for diasporic queer subjects. In Part Four essays by Stuart Hall, Kobena Mercer, and Gayatri Gopinath consider the cultural aspects of diaspora and diasporic communities in film, literature, and identity politics. Both Hall and Mercer use Black British cultural productions (film, specifically) to examine changing notions of blackness and identity within a diasporic context; Gopinath analyzes the heteronormative implications of nation and diaspora, as well as the ethnocentric implications of sexual identities and queer politics in literary and filmic media. We conclude the book with a postscript that examines the role of cyberscapes (and its interfacing of diasporas) in shaping some future diasporic paths.

Future Diasporic Paths

In the postnational world that we see emerging, diaspora runs with, and not against, the grain of identity, movement and reproduction . . . Many people find themselves exiles without really having moved very far – Croats in Bosnia, Hindus in Kashmir, Muslims in India. Yet others find themselves in patterns of repeat migration. Indians who went to East Africa in the nineteenth and early twentieth centuries found themselves pushed out of Uganda, Kenya and Tanzania in the 1980s to find fresh travails and opportunities in England and the United States, and they are now considering returning to East Africa. Similarly, Chinese from Hong Kong who are buying real estate in Vancouver, Gujarati traders from Uganda opening motels in New Jersey and newspaper kiosks in New York City, and Sikh cabdrivers in Chicago and Philadelphia are all examples of a new sort of world in which diaspora is the order of things and settled ways of life are increasingly hard to find. The United States, always in its self-perception a land of immigrants, finds itself awash in these global diasporas, no longer a closed space for the melting pot to work its magic, but yet another diasporic switching point.[22]

To think of the United States as just "another diasporic switching point," as Appadurai does, rather than as the teleological end to which all the world aspires, is a refreshingly different and necessary intervention into theorizations of diaspora. To theorize living in the United States, or the West, as a mark of arrival is intensely problematic on numerous levels. Part of the value of using a framework (such as the one provided by Appadurai or other theorists of diaspora who grapple with the problematic issue of discerning a specific point of origin) is that it offers a way to theorize nationhood and belonging as a process always in change and always mediated by issues of class, ethnicity, gender, and sexuality. As we have entered into a new millennium, insisting that a nation is defined by its geopolitical boundaries is inherently reductive, exclusionary, and problematic; at the same time, we cannot ignore the very real ways in which communities are legally and politically bounded by nation-states and their (often multiple) movements across such borders, especially in the wake of September 11, 2001. People, capital, and information increasingly cross borders, challenging the notion that a national community is necessarily bounded by its geographic borders; but at the same time, these border crossings are informed by issues of class, race, and citizenship. What, for example, does it mean for a white English-speaking American female citizen to cross the US–Canada border, and what does it mean for a Pakistani American woman who wears *hijab*, or for a young Sikh American man crossing the same border to visit relatives on the other side? Although it is true that not everyone can cross borders with ease, and while it is also true that not everyone necessarily wants to traverse borders, it is also true that for reasons of necessity and sometimes choice, people do cross borders and see their lives unfolding in diasporic settings.

Important distinctions still need to be made, then, between the political risks entailed in different forms of movement and migration, as well as between transnationalism (which can describe NGOs, multinational corporations, and dissident political organizations, as well as individuals) and diaspora (which is a human phenomenon). Scholars and theorists need to probe important questions related to diaspora: How, for example, do constructions of nation, diaspora, and transnation differ for different transmigrational groups – exiles, refugees, immigrants, and migrants? How are voluntary diasporic subjects different from those whose lives have been mapped by exile, refugee camps, mass migration, and economic immigration? What are the subjective, psychological, and social dimensions of diaspora and other modern forms of geographical displacements and dislocations? What are the disjunctures – geopolitical, psychosocial, class and gender based – in these contemporary forms of mass movement? How is transnationalism invested in the movements of global capitalism, whereas diaspora remains a distinctly human – albeit intensely political – or transmigratory, phenomenon? How, if at all, is diaspora striated by the transnational movements of global capital? How are these movements further striated and complicated by – as Appadurai's taxonomy of modern *scapes* (ethnoscapes, mediascapes, technoscapes, financescapes, and ideoscapes) suggests – the multiple, intercontinental movements of ideology, information, and capital online? In other words, how is diaspora being remapped through cyberscape interfacing?

What, then, will be the course of future trajectories of diasporic studies? What paths remain to be explored in theorizations of diaspora, particularly those that interrogate the classist, racist, heterosexist, and gendered foundations of nations, nation-states, and even of diaspora? What different types of communities and identitarian forms will be imagined and created as a result of these shifts? Some scholars even suggest that such movements will force redefinition of citizenship, arguing for models of flexible, diasporic, and even nomadic citizenship.[23] We end by posing specific questions that interrogate the foundations and the imbricated constructions of nationality, national identity, citizenry, and diasporic or migrant subjects.

First, how are geopolitical territories defined in relation to a people or *demos* that require "imported" foreigners as internal–external others (whether in the ancient Greek city-state or *polis* where the enslaved were predominantly migrant metic laborers – or in the "New World" where African slaves and Asian "coolies" were "imported" through the first and second Middle Passages; or in the contemporary transnationalist and geovirtual – if also politically real – terrains of global capitalism where the demarcated spaces of First and Third Worlds are reterritorialized, less as discrete national and continental borders and more as first- and third-world zones that traverse territories or nation-states and map the interstitial, international, and interpenetrating zones of enterprise and impoverishment)? How are boundaries predicated not merely on a geographical and political outside (i.e., other foreign territories), but also on the internal presence of non-citizen classes, such as immigrants, economic migrants, exiles, refugees, and illegal aliens?

Second, how are geopolitical boundaries and territorial identities predicated not merely on internal exclusion (as posed in the previous question), but also on constitutive forms of externalizing exclusion (such as forced economic migration, imposed or political exile, evacuation of refugees, and deportation of illegal aliens)? These constitutive forces of territorialization may be seen in mythic or literary accounts (as well as historical ones), such as Polyphemus's Cyclopian extraterritoriality, the forced exile of diasporic Jews from medieval Christian and European cities, and Dante's political–religious ostracization from Florence in the fourteenth century, to cite only a few well-known premodern examples.[24] (Post)modern correlates are mapped in the oceanic crossings of Haitian and Vietnamese refugees, or *les «boat peuples» vietnamiennes et haïtiennes*, and South Asians fleeing Uganda, Tanzania, and other parts of East Africa, as well as the many other migrants who have moved in transnationalist patterns across the globe.

Third, how do odyssey, sojourn, and travel differ from migration, diaspora, and exile, in that the former constitute forms of territorial conquest or "exploration," while the latter mark lines of deterritorialization, dispossession, and displacement from territory, custom, protectorship, and citizenry? How do these differing and fluctuating movements map out hegemonic power relations of country, colony, state, and diaspora?

Fourth, how are these internal–external and constitutive forces of territorialization supportive of economic or class structures within given territories? For example, the African slave trade bolstered economic progress in the United States (especially the "cotton" South), Brazil, Argentina, the West Indies, and West African territories. Another early example is the spice and labor trades between England, India, and China, wherein economic laborers were brought to sustain the cane and cotton industries in the British-colonized Caribbean in the post-slavery period (from 1834 on). Or how economic migrants from Southern Europe and East Asia sustained the post-Emancipation economies of Brazil and the United States. Contemporary examples include economic migrants who move across the globe seeking work, but more significantly, the late global capital migration of multinational corporations to the source of cheap labor, seeking to keep costs low and to maximize their profit margins.

Finally, we end with our own caveat: in the wake of September 11, 2001, it is imperative that we ignore neither the question of national belonging and citizenship, nor how the ways in which academics must theorize diaspora have been altered. While it has never been advisable to use diaspora as a means of celebrating border traversals, it is even more pressing now to think about just how difficult it has become for certain individuals to cross borders. Diaspora studies, in this context, will have to rethink the contours of citizenship, migration, and belonging globally.

The migratory spaces traversed by migrants or refugees in a few decades mark diasporic zones that deterritorialize and reterritorialize the increasingly blurred borders of nations and nation-states.[25] Such deterritorializations are not without risks of and propulsions toward reterritorialization, however, as Caren Kaplan suggests.[26] The above questions are a response, in part, to Kaplan's call for more studies interrogating the discursive, political, and economic forces of territorialization and reterritorialization, and our questions formulate new parameters for historicized diasporic scholarship that addresses the intersectionalities and fissures of identity, whether those of race, ethnicity, gender, or sexuality.

Many questions still need to be addressed with regard to diaspora and diasporic communities: What is gained in theorizations of diaspora as a general framework for understanding the fractures of modernity and the disjunctures within notions of citizenship, nationality, and even capital? How are the myriad waves of transnational migration in the late twentieth century part of the regulatory flows of global capitalism? How do these migrations form and deform modern *scapes* as hybrid discursive and political spaces created through disjunct and contradictory discourses around the issues of globalization, economic migration, political exile, and nomadic citizenships? If the structuring forces of capitalism (however disjunct) were implicated with those of colonialism (however hybrid), and if the deterritorializing movements of anti-colonialist sentiment and early decolonization emerged concomitantly with the revolutionary, anti-capitalist destratifications of Marxian social systems and state communist regimes, how and to what extent are the transnational fluctuations of diasporas and diasporized nation-states inextricable from the neocolonialist reterritorializations of global capitalism (such as free trade agreements, world financial markets, and the international divisions of labor, production, and profit)?

These earlier geopolitical, systemic, and ideological shifts (those of colonialism/capitalism and decolonization/communism) resulted in world migrations: settler migrations from colonial empire to colony; economic migrations from "third-world" zones to "first-world" countries; militaristic and imperialist (i.e., Superpower) occupations of and coups in war-torn territories (from Eastern Europe to Southeast Asia); and Cold War waves of political refugees fleeing homelands (in Vietnam, Cuba, Haiti, Algeria, Guatemala, Afghanistan, and elsewhere) and seeking asylum across the globe. The last century was defined by innumerable border crossings, crossings that destabilized the boundaries of nations and states, even as it bore witness to Holocaust, apartheid, the resurgences of ethnic nationalisms, as in Rwanda and the Balkan states, marked (and marred) by the brutal excesses and inhuman violations of ethnic cleansing.

In this cacophonous and interkinetic moment of late capitalism, spawning micropolitical and macrocapital reterritorializations economically and culturally on a worldwide level, the proliferations of cyber-information and technocapital virtually render the concept of border anachronistic; and yet, as age-old systems are deterritorialized, others emerge, reterritorialize, and establish new borders, however transient or *dromic*, as Paul Virilio claims. What do these fluxes promise or portend for future diasporic or transnationalist spaces? Where will we locate the time, speed, and movement of diasporas in the new century? Within or outside of the boundaries of deterritorialized nation-states? Or simply beyond such archaic constructions? As we have entered into the new millennium, such space-times and movement-trajectories are yet to be(come).

Perhaps, instead of us crossing borders, the borders (multiple and virtual vectors of energy, power, desire, and capital) will cross and crisscross, deterritorialize and reterritorialize us. Perhaps, as Jerry Herron suggests, we will no longer go to the border: the border will (be)come to us.[27]

Notes

1   See Durham Peters (1999: 23).
2   As Kaplan affirms, many may not know where *home is* in order to *stay there*: "For many of us there is no possibility of staying at home in the conventional sense – that is, the world has changed to the point that those domestic, national, or marked spaces no longer exist" (p. 7).
3   See Kaplan (1996) and Puar (1994).
4   Ganguly (1992).
5   Davies (1994).
6   We use the term *postcolonies*, not to monolithically homogenize the experiences of colonized spaces of the various European and American empires, but to distinguish it from other types of migrant communities. In this regard, there are multiple gradations of "decolonization" and autonomy, as well as conflicting and emergent neocolonial narratives within nation-states, both "Western" and "non-Western."
7   Urgo (1995).
8   Tölölyan (1996).
9   Robbins (1995).
10 Gopinath (1995).
11 Ibid.
12 See Maira (2002) and Danticat (2001).
13 In her influential essay, "Going Home: Enacting Justice in Queer Asian America," Aguilar-San Juan (1998) thoughtfully meditates on how to talk about home. Noting that there is no place that she really calls home, she writes: "I was born in Boston but eventually left for Providence. I recently moved to southern California, which has always fascinated me. To go westward, is for an Asian American, to go home, in the sense that many Asian Americans have family in California, in Washington state, or farther west in Hawai'i. But my immediate family is scattered around the midwest" (p. 25). Her own story thus maps out a network of myriad affiliations that complicates the notion that there exists a fixed point of origin to which one can nostalgically harken back.
14 Kassam-Remtulla isolates numerous possible reasons for emigration. Although many Ismailis "left in search of better economic opportunities as traders and merchants in East Africa . . . they also left for many other reasons including famine, unemployment, religious persecution and political instability."
15 Langworthy, "In this Country Revised," from *The Geography of War* (Oklahoma City: Cooper House Publishing, 1995) 17. See also Tran, Truong and Truong Khoi (1998).
16 Adolphe (1995).
17 Laferrière (1996); translation by Homel (1997).
18 Watenabe (1998).
19 In the same collection, *Global Sex Workers: Rights, Resistance and Redefinition*, also see Anarfi and Kempadoo for specific analyses of gender, migration, and sex work in different global contexts.

20   Wijers (1998: 75).
21   See Tölölyan (1991, 1996).
22   Appadurai (1996: 171).
23   See the following: Ong (1999); Laguerre (1998); Joseph (1999).
24   See Said (1984).
25   On this problematic, see Schiller, Basch, and Blanc-Szanton (1992).
26   Kaplan (1996).
27   Herron (1993).

References

Adolphe, Carlo. "La diaspora haïtienne dans le 10e département: Un monde haïtien américaine." *Le Nouvelliste*, January 10, 1995.

Aguilar-San Juan, Karin. "Going Home: Enacting Justice in Queer Asian America." *Q&A: Queer in Asian America*. Ed. David Eng and Alice V. Hom. Philadelphia, PA: Temple University Press, 1998. 25–40.

Ali, Agha Shahid. *A Nostalgist's Map of America*. New York: W. W. Norton, 1991.

Anarfi, John K. "Ghanaian Women and Prostitution in Cote D'Ivoire." *Global Sex Workers: Rights, Resistance and Redefinition*. Ed. Kamala Kempadoo and Jo Doezema. New York: Routledge, 1998. 104–13.

Appadurai, Arjun. *Modernity at Large: Cultural Dimensions of Globalization*. Minneapolis: University of Minnesota Press, 1996.

Danticat, Edwidge, ed. *The Butterfly's Way: Voices from the Haitian Dyaspora in the United States*. New York: SoHo, 2001.

Davies, Carole Boyce. "Introduction: Migratory Subjectivities." *Black Women, Writing and Identity*. New York: Routledge, 1994.

Durham Peters, John. "Exile, Nomadism and Diaspora: The Stakes of Mobility in the Western Canon." *Home, Exile, Homeland: Film, Media and the Politics of Place*. Ed. Hamid S. Naficy. London: Routledge, 1999. 17–44.

Ganguly, Keya. "Migrant Identities, Personal Memory and the Construction of Self-hood." *Cultural Studies* 6.1 (1992): 27–50.

Gilroy, Paul. *The Black Atlantic: Modernity and Double Consciousness*. Cambridge, MA: Harvard University Press, 1993.

——"Diaspora." *Paragraph* 17.1 (March 1994): 207–12.

Gopinath, Gayatri. " 'Bombay, U.K., Yuba City': Bhangra Music and the Engendering of Diaspora." *Diaspora* 4.3 (1995): 303–22.

——"On Fire." *GLQ* 4.4 (1998): 631–6.

Herron, Jerry. *After Culture: Detroit and the Humiliation of History*. Detroit, MI: Wayne State University Press, 1993.

Joseph, May. *Nomadic Identities: The Performance of Citizenship*. Minneapolis: University of Minnesota Press, 1999.

Kaplan, Caren. *Questions of Travel: Postmodern Discourses of Displacement*. Durham, NC: Duke University Press, 1996.

Kassam-Remtulla, Aly. "History, Diaspora and 'Homelands'." *(Dis)placing Khojahs: Forging Identities, Revitalizing Islam and Crafting Global Ismailism.* Honors Thesis: Stanford University, 2000. First Ismaili Electronic Library and Database. Date accessed: September 3, 2001. Date updated: March 15, 1999. ⟨http://ismaili.net/~heritage/Source/1121b/02.html⟩

—— "Global Ismailism: Rethinking Diaspora, Nation and Religion." *(Dis)placing Khojahs: Forging Identities, Revitalizing Islam and Crafting Global Ismailism.* Honors Thesis: Stanford University, 2000. First Ismaili Electronic Library and Database. Date accessed: September 3, 2001. Date updated: March 15, 1999. ⟨http://ismaili.net/~heritage/Source/1121b/05.html⟩

Kempadoo, Kamala. "The Migrant Tightrope: Experiences from the Caribbean." *Global Sex Workers: Rights, Resistance and Redefinition.* Ed. Kamala Kempadoo and Jo Doezema. New York: Routledge, 1998. 124–38.

Laferrière, Dany. *Pays sans chapeau.* Montréal: Lanctôt Éditeur, 1996.

——*Down Among the Dead Men.* Trans. David Homel. Toronto: Douglas & McIntyre, 1997.

Laguerre, Michel S. *Diasporic Citizenship: Haitian Americans in Transnational America.* New York: St. Martin's Press, 1998.

Lavie, Smadar and Ted Swedenburg. "Introduction: Displacement, Diaspora, and Geographies of Identity." *Displacement, Diaspora, and Geographies of Identity.* Ed. Smadar Lavie and Ted Swedenburg. Durham, NC: Duke University Press, 1996. 1–25.

Maira, Sunaina. *Desis in the House: Indian American Culture in New York City.* Philadelphia, PA: Temple University Press, 2002.

Nguyen Langworthy, Christian. "In this Country Revised." *The Geography of War.* Oklahoma City, OK: Cooper House Publishing, 1995.

Ong, Aihwa. *Flexible Citizenship: The Cultural Logics of Transnationality.* Durham, NC: Duke University Press, 1999.

Puar, Jasbir K. "Writing My Way 'Home': Traveling South Asian Bodies and Diasporic Journeys." *Socialist Review* 24.2 (1994): 75–108.

Robbins, Bruce. "Some Versions of U.S. Internationalism." *Social Text* 45 (1995): 97–123.

Said, Edward. "Reflections on Exile." *Granta* 13 (August 1984).

Schiller, Nina Glick, Linda Basch, and Cristina Blanc-Szanton, eds. *Towards a Transnational Perspective on Migration: Race, Class, Ethnicity and Nationalism Reconsidered.* New York: New York Academy of Sciences, 1992.

Suarez, Virgil. "The Culture of Leaving: Balsero Dreams." *Hopscotch: A Cultural Review* 2.2 (2000): 2–13.

Tölölyan, Khachig. "The Nation-State and its Others: In Lieu of a Preface." *Diaspora* 1.1 (1991): 3–7.

—— "Rethinking Diaspora(s): Stateless Power in the Transnational Moment." *Diaspora* 5.1 (1996): 3–35.

Tran, Barbara, Monique T. D. Truong, and Luu Truong Khoi, eds. *Watermark: Vietnamese American Poetry and Prose.* New York: Asian American Writers' Workshop, 1998.

Urgo, Joseph R. *Willa Cather and the Myth of American Migration.* Urbana: University of Illinois Press, 1995.

Virilio, Paul. *The Virilio Reader*. Ed. James Der Derian; trans. Michael Degener and Lauren Osepchuk. Oxford: Blackwell, 1998.

Watenabe, Sakoto. "From Thailand to Japan: Migrant Sex Workers as Autonomous Subjects." *Global Sex Workers: Rights, Resistance and Redefinition*. Ed. Kamala Kempadoo and Jo Doezema. New York: Routledge, 1998. 114–23.

Wijers, Marjan. "Women, Labor and Migration: The Position of Trafficked Women and Strategies for Support." *Global Sex Workers: Rights, Resistance and Redefinition*. Ed. Kamala Kempadoo and Jo Doezema. New York: Routledge, 1998.

Part I

Modernity, Globalism, and Diaspora

1

Disjuncture and Difference in the Global Cultural Economy

Arjun Appadurai

Arjun Appadurai's important essay argues against the notion that relationships in the new global cultural economy can be reduced to a simple center–periphery model. Focusing on migration, diaspora, and the movements of peoples and capital around the world, the essay provides a framework for thinking about how various global cultural flows have fundamentally altered the nature of the global cultural economy. Building on Benedict Anderson's work on the role of print capitalism and imagination in creating imagined national communities, this essay explores how new imagined worlds have become a vital part of the global economy.

Appadurai describes five different types of imagined world landscapes that help explain the nature of this "new" global economy: *ethnoscapes* (people who move between nations, such as tourists, immigrants, exiles, guestworkers, and refugees), *technoscapes* (technology, often linked to multinational corporations), *financescapes* (global capital, currency markets, stock exchanges), *mediascapes* (electronic and new media), and *ideoscapes* (official state ideologies and counter-ideologies).

By describing these imagined worlds that traverse the borders of the nation-state, Appadurai offers a critical vocabulary to discuss specialized types of economic and social domination without naively celebrating border crossings and traversals. These imagined worlds, Appadurai argues, are increasingly present in the contemporary world. By foregrounding their presence, it becomes possible to reflect on how communities are forged transnationally, across nation-states through networks of diaspora, migration, technology, electronic media, ideologies, and global capital. In an era of globalization and mass migration, increasingly mediated by electronic media, Appadurai argues that it is difficult to believe in the supremacy of the nation-state.

Recognizing that not everyone travels, migrates, or crosses borders, he suggests that few people in the world do not know of someone who has traveled to different locations in the world. Foregrounding the importance of theorizing the role of the imagination and the ways that people and capital move around the world, Appadurai helps to establish a new trajectory in diaspora studies that grapples with the links between nationalism, diaspora, cultural processes, and globalization in a postcolonial moment.

It takes only the merest acquaintance with the facts of the modern world to note that it is now an interactive system in a sense which is strikingly new.[1] Historians and sociologists, especially those concerned with translocal processes (Hodgson 1974) and with the world systems associated with capitalism (Abu-Lughod 1989; Braudel 1981–4; Curtin 1984; Wallerstein 1974; Wolf 1982), have long been aware that the world has been a congeries of large-scale interactions for many centuries. Yet today's world involves interactions of a new order and intensity. Cultural transactions between social groups in the past have generally been restricted, sometimes by the facts of geography and ecology, and at other times by active resistance to interactions with the Other (as in China for much of its history and in Japan before the Meiji Restoration). Where there have been sustained cultural transactions across large parts of the globe, they have usually involved the long-distance journey of commodities (and of the merchants most concerned with them) and of travelers and explorers of every type (Helms 1988; Schafer 1963). The two main forces for sustained cultural interaction before this century have been warfare (and the large-scale political systems sometimes generated by it) and religions of conversion, which have sometimes, as in the case of Islam, taken warfare as one of the legitimate instruments of their expansion. Thus, between travelers and merchants, pilgrims and conquerors, the world has seen much long-distance (and long-term) cultural traffic. This much seems self-evident.

But few will deny that given the problems of time, distance, and limited technologies for the command of resources across vast spaces, cultural dealings between socially and spatially separated groups have until the last few centuries been bridged at great cost and sustained over time only with great effort. The forces of cultural gravity seemed always to pull away from the formation of large-scale ecumenes, whether religious, commercial or political, towards smaller-scale accretions of intimacy and interest.

Sometime in the last few centuries the nature of this gravitational field seems to have changed. Partly due to the spirit of the expansion of Western maritime interests after 1500, and partly because of the relatively autonomous developments of large and aggressive social formations in the Americas (such as the Aztecs and the Incas); in Eurasia (such as the Mongols, and their descendants, the Mughals and Ottomans); in island Southeast Asia (such as the Buginese); and in the kingdoms of precolonial Africa (such as

Dahomey), an overlapping set of ecumenes began to emerge, in which congeries of money, commerce, conquest, and migration began to create durable cross-societal bonds. This process was accelerated by the technology transfers and accelerations of the late eighteenth and nineteenth centuries (e.g., Bayly 1989), which created complex colonial orders centered on European capitals and spread throughout the non-European world. This complex and overlapping set of Euro-colonial worlds (first Spanish and Portuguese, later principally English, French, and Dutch) set the basis for a permanent traffic in ideas of peoplehood and selfhood which created the imagined communities (Anderson 1983) of recent nationalisms throughout the world.

With what Benedict Anderson has called "print capitalism," a new power was unleashed in the world, the power of mass literacy and its attendant large-scale production of projects of ethnic affinity that were remarkably free of the need for face-to-face communication or even of indirect communication between persons and groups. The act of reading things together set the stage for movements based on a paradox: the paradox of constructed primordialism. There is, of course, a great deal else that is involved in the story of colonialism and of its dialectically generated nationalisms (Chatterjee 1986), but the issue of constructed ethnicities is surely a crucial strand in this tale.

But the revolution of print capitalism, and the cultural affinities and dialogues unleashed by it, were only modest precursors to the world we live in now. For in the last century there has been a technological explosion, largely in the domain of transportation and information, which makes the interactions of a print-dominated world seem as hard-won and as easily erased as the print revolution made earlier forms of cultural traffic appear. For with the advent of the steamship, the automobile and the airplane, the camera, the computer and the telephone, we have entered into an altogether new condition of neighborliness, even with those most distant from ourselves. Marshall McLuhan, among others, sought to theorize about this world as a global village, but theories such as McLuhan's appear to have overestimated the communitarian implications of the new media order. We are now aware that with media, each time we are tempted to speak of the "global village," we must be reminded that media create communities with "no sense of place" (Meyrowitz 1985). The world we live in now seems rhizomic (Deleuze and Guattari 1987), even schizophrenic, calling for theories of rootlessness, alienation, and psychological distance between individuals and groups, on the one hand, and fantasies (or nightmares) of electronic propinquity on the other. Here we are close to the central problematic of cultural processes in today's world.

Thus, the curiosity which recently drove Pico Iyer to Asia (1988) is in some ways the product of a confusion between some ineffable McDonaldization of the world and the much subtler play of indigenous trajectories of desire and fear with global flows of people and things. Indeed Iyer's own impressions are testimony to the fact that, if *a* global cultural system is emerging, it is filled with ironies and resistances, sometimes camouflaged as passivity and a bottomless appetite in the Asian world for things Western.

Iyer's own account of the uncanny Philippine affinity for American popular music is rich testimony to the global culture of the "hyperreal," for somehow Philippine renditions of American popular songs are both more widespread in the Philippines, and more disturbingly faithful to their originals, than they are in the United States today. An entire nation seems to have learned to mimic Kenny Rogers and the Lennon sisters, like a vast Asian Motown chorus. But Americanization is certainly a pallid term to apply to such a situation, for not only are there more Filipinos singing perfect renditions of some American songs (often from the American past) than there are Americans doing so, there is, of course, the fact that the rest of their lives is not in complete synchrony with the referential world which first gave birth to these songs.

In a further, globalizing twist on what Jameson (1989) has recently called "nostalgia for the present," these Filipinos look back to a world they have never lost. This is one of the central ironies of the politics of global cultural flows, especially in the arena of entertainment and leisure. It plays havoc with the hegemony of Euro-chronology. American nostalgia feeds on Filipino desire represented as a hyper-competent reproduction. Here we have nostalgia without memory. The paradox, of course, has its explanations, and they are historical; unpacked, they lay bare the story of the American missionization and political rape of the Philippines, one result of which has been the creation of a nation of make-believe Americans, who tolerated for so long a leading lady who played the piano while the slums of Manila expanded and decayed. Perhaps the most radical postmodernists would argue that this is hardly surprising, since in the peculiar chronicities of late capitalism, pastiche and nostalgia are central modes of image production and reception. Americans themselves are hardly in the present any more as they stumble into the mega-technologies of the twenty-first century garbed in the film noir scenarios of sixties "chills," fifties diners, forties clothing, thirties houses, twenties dances, and so on *ad infinitum*.

As far as the United States is concerned, one might suggest that the issue is no longer one of nostalgia but of a social *imaginaire* built largely around reruns. Jameson (1983) was bold to link the politics of nostalgia to the postmodern commodity sensibility and surely he was right. The drug wars in Colombia recapitulate the tropical sweat of Vietnam, with Ollie North and his succession of masks—Jimmy Stewart concealing John Wayne concealing Spiro Agnew and all of them transmogrifying into Sylvester Stallone who wins in Afghanistan—thus simultaneously fulfilling the secret American envy of Soviet imperialism and the rerun (this time with a happy ending) of the Vietnam War. The Rolling Stones, approaching their fifties, gyrate before eighteen year-olds who do not appear to need the machinery of nostalgia to be sold on their parents' heroes. Paul McCartney is selling the Beatles to a new audience by hitching his oblique nostalgia to their desire for the new that smacks of the old. *Dragnet* is back in nineties drag, and so is *Adam-12*, not to speak of *Batman* and *Mission Impossible*, all dressed up technologically but remarkably faithful to the atmospherics of their originals.

The past is now not a land to return to in a simple politics of memory. It has become a synchronic warehouse of cultural scenarios, a kind of temporal central casting, to which recourse can be had as appropriate, depending on the movie to be made, the scene to be enacted, the hostages to be rescued. All this is par for the course, if you follow Baudrillard or Lyotard into a world of signs wholly unmoored from their social signifiers (all the world's a Disneyland). But I would like to suggest that the apparent increasing substitutability of whole periods and postures for one another, in the cultural styles of advanced capitalism, is tied to larger global forces, which have done much to show Americans that the past is usually another country. If your present is their future (as in much modernization theory and in many self-satisfied tourist fantasies), and their future is your past (as in the case of the Philippine virtuosos of American popular music), then your own past can be made to appear as simply a normalized modality of your present. Thus, although some anthropologists may continue to relegate their Others to temporal spaces that they do not themselves occupy (Fabian 1983), post-industrial cultural productions have entered a post-nostalgic phase.

The crucial point, however, is that the United States is no longer the puppeteer of a world system of images, but is only one node of a complex transnational construction of imaginary landscapes. The world we live in today is characterized by a new role for the imagination in social life. To grasp this new role, we need to bring together: the old idea of images, especially mechanically produced images (in the Frankfurt School sense); the idea of the imagined community (in Anderson's sense); and the French idea of the imaginary (*imaginaire*) as a constructed landscape of collective aspirations, which is no more and no less real than the collective representations of Emile Durkheim, now mediated through the complex prism of modern media.

The image, the imagined, the imaginary—these are all terms which direct us to something critical and new in global cultural processes: *the imagination as a social practice*. No longer mere fantasy (opium for the masses whose real work is elsewhere), no longer simple escape (from a world defined principally by more concrete purposes and structures), no longer elite pastime (thus not relevant to the lives of ordinary people), and no longer mere con-templation (irrelevant for new forms of desire and subjectivity), the imagi-nation has become an organized field of social practices, a form of work (both in the sense of labor and of culturally organized practice) and a form of nego-tiation between sites of agency ("individuals") and globally defined fields of possibility. It is this unleashing of the imagination which links the play of pastiche (in some settings) to the terror and coercion of states and their com-petitors. The imagination is now central to all forms of agency, is itself a social fact, and is the key component of the new global order. But to make this claim meaningful, it is necessary to address some other issues.

Homogenization and Heterogenization

The central problem of today's global interactions is the tension between cultural homogenization and cultural heterogenization. A vast array of empirical facts could be brought to bear on the side of the homogenization argument, and much of it has come from the left end of the spectrum of media studies (Hamelink 1983; Mattelart 1983; Schiller 1976), and some from other perspectives (Gans 1985; Iyer 1988). Most often, the homogenization argument subspeciates into either an argument about Americanization, or an argument about commoditization, and very often the two arguments are closely linked. What these arguments fail to consider is that at least as rapidly as forces from various metropolises are brought into new societies they tend to become indigenized in one or another way: this is true of music and housing styles as much as it is true of science and ter-rorism, spectacles and constitutions. The dynamics of such indigenization have just begun to be explored systemically (Barber 1987; Feld 1988; Hannerz 1987, 1989; Ivy 1988; Nicoll 1989; Yoshimoto 1989), and much more needs to be done. But it is worth noticing that for the people of Irian Jaya, Indonesianization may be more worrisome than Americanization, as Japanization may be for Koreans, Indianization for Sri Lankans, Vietnamization for the Cambodians, Russianization for the people of Soviet Armenia and the Baltic Republics. Such a list of alternative fears to Americanization could be greatly expanded, but it is not a shapeless inventory: for polities of smaller scale, there is always a fear of cultural absorp-tion by polities of larger scale, especially those that are nearby. One man's imagined community is another man's political prison.

  This scalar dynamic, which has widespread global manifestations, is also tied to the relationship between nations and states, to which I shall return later. For the moment let us note that the simplification of these many forces (and fears) of homogenization can also be exploited by nation-states in relation to their own minorities, by posing global commoditization (or capitalism, or some other such external enemy) as more real than the threat of its own hegemonic strategies.

The new global cultural economy has to be seen as a complex, over-lapping, disjunctive order, which cannot any longer be understood in terms of existing center–periphery models (even those which might account for multiple centers and peripheries). Nor is it susceptible to simple models of push and pull (in terms of migration theory), or of surpluses and deficits (as in traditional models of balance of trade), or of consumers and producers (as in most neo-Marxist theories of development). Even the most complex and flexible theories of global development which have come out of the Marxist tradition (Amin 1980; Mandel 1978; Wallerstein 1974; Wolf 1982) are inadequately quirky and have failed to come to terms with what Lash and Urry (1987) have called disorganized capitalism. The complexity of the current global economy has to do with certain fundamental disjunctures between economy, culture, and politics which we have only begun to theorize.[2]

I propose that an elementary framework for exploring such disjunctures is to look at the relationship between five dimensions of global cultural flow which can be termed: (a) ethnoscapes; (b) mediascapes; (c) technoscapes; (d) financescapes; and (e) ideoscapes.[3] The suffix -scape allows us to point to the fluid, irregular shapes of these landscapes, shapes which characterize international capital as deeply as they do international clothing styles. These terms with the common suffix -scape also indicate that these are not objec-tively given relations which look the same from every angle of vision, but rather that they are deeply perspectival constructs, inflected by the historical, linguistic, and political situatedness of different sorts of actors: nation-states, multinationals, diasporic communities, as well as subnational groupings and movements (whether religious, political, or economic), and even intimate face-to-face groups, such as villages, neighborhoods, and families. Indeed, the individual actor is the last locus of this perspectival set of landscapes, for these landscapes are eventually navigated by agents who both experience and constitute larger formations, in part by their own sense of what these landscapes offer.

These landscapes thus are the building blocks of what (extending Benedict Anderson) I would like to call *imagined worlds*, that is, the multiple worlds which are constituted by the historically situated imaginations of persons and groups spread around the globe (Appadurai: 1996). An impor-tant fact of the world we live in today is that many persons on the globe live in such imagined worlds (and not just in imagined communities) and thus are able to contest and sometimes even subvert the imagined worlds of the official mind and of the entrepreneurial mentality that surround them.

By *ethnoscape* I mean the landscape of persons who constitute the shifting world in which we live: tourists, immigrants, refugees, exiles, guest-workers, and other moving groups and persons constitute an essential feature of the world and appear to affect the politics of (and between) nations to a hitherto unprecedented degree. This is not to say that there are no relatively stable communities and networks, of kinship, of friendship, of work and of leisure, as well as of birth, residence, and other filiative forms. But it is to say that the warp of these stabilities is everywhere shot through with the woof of human motion, as more persons and groups deal with the realities of having to move or the fantasies of wanting to move. What is more, both these realities as well as these fantasies now function on larger scales, as men and women from villages in India think not just of moving to Poona or Madras, but of moving to Dubai and Houston, and refugees from Sri Lanka find themselves in South India as well as in Switzerland, just as the Hmong are driven to London as well as to Philadelphia. And as international capital shifts its needs, as production and technology generate different needs, as nation-states shift their policies on refugee populations, these moving groups can never afford to let their imaginations rest too long, even if they wish to.

By *technoscape* I mean the global configuration, also ever fluid, of technology, and of the fact that technology, both high and low, both mechanical and informational, now moves at high speeds across various kinds of previously impervious boundaries. Many countries now are the roots of multinational enterprise: a huge steel complex in Libya may involve interests from India, China, Russia, and Japan, providing different components of new technological configurations. The odd distribution of technologies, and thus the peculiarities of these technoscapes, are increasingly driven not by any obvious economies of scale, of political control, or of market rationality, but by increasingly complex relationships between money flows, political possibilities, and the availability of both unskilled and highly skilled labor. So, while India exports waiters and chauffeurs to Dubai and Sharjah, it also exports software engineers to the United States—indentured briefly to Tata-Burroughs or the World Bank, then laundered through the State Department to become wealthy resident aliens, who are in turn objects of seductive messages to invest their money and know-how in federal and state projects in India.

The global economy can still be described in terms of traditional indicators (as the World Bank continues to do) and studied in terms of traditional comparisons (as in Project Link at the University of Pennsylvania), but the complicated technoscapes (and the shifting ethnoscapes) which underlie these indicators and comparisons are further out of the reach of the queen of the social sciences than ever before. How is one to make a meaningful comparison of wages in Japan and the United States or of real estate costs in New York and Tokyo, without taking sophisticated account of the very complex fiscal and investment flows that link the two economies through a global grid of currency speculation and capital transfer?

Thus it is useful to speak as well of *financescapes*, since the disposition of global capital is now a more mysterious, rapid, and difficult landscape to follow than ever before, as currency markets, national stock exchanges, and commodity speculations move mega-monies through national turnstiles at blinding speed, with vast absolute implications for small differences in percentage points and time units. But the critical point is that the global relationship between ethnoscapes, technoscapes, and financescapes is deeply disjunctive and profoundly unpredictable, since each of these landscapes is subject to its own constraints and incentives (some political, some informational, and some techno-environmental), at the same time as each acts as a constraint and a parameter for movements in the others. Thus, even an elementary model of global political economy must take into account the deeply disjunctive relationships between human movement, technological flow, and financial transfers.

Further refracting these disjunctures (which hardly form a simple, mechanical global infrastructure in any case) are what I call *mediascapes* and *ideoscapes*, though the latter two are closely related landscapes of images. Mediascapes refer both to the distribution of the electronic capabilities to produce and disseminate information (newspapers, magazines, television stations, and film production studios), which are now available to a growing number of private and public interests throughout the world, and to the images of the world created by these media. These images of the world involve many complicated inflections, depending on their mode (documentary or entertainment), their hardware (electronic or pre-electronic), their audiences (local, national, or transnational), and the interests of those who own and control them. What is most important about these mediascapes is that they provide (especially in their television, film, and cassette forms) large and complex repertoires of images, narratives, and ethnoscapes to viewers throughout the world, in which the world of commodities and the world of news and politics are profoundly mixed. What this means is that many audiences throughout the world experience the media themselves as a complicated and interconnected repertoire of print, celluloid, electronic screens, and billboards. The lines between the realistic and the fictional landscapes they see are blurred, so that the further away these audiences are from the direct experiences of metropolitan life, the more likely they are to construct imagined worlds which are chimerical, aesthetic, even fantastic objects, particularly if assessed by the criteria of some other perspective, some other imagined world.

Mediascapes, whether produced by private or state interests, tend to be image-centered, narrative-based accounts of strips of reality, and what they offer to those who experience and transform them is a series of elements (such as characters, plots, and textual forms) out of which scripts can be formed of imagined lives, their own as well as those of others living in other places. These scripts can and do get disaggregated into complex sets of metaphors by which people live (Lakoff and Johnson 1980) as they help to constitute narratives of the Other and proto-narratives of possible lives, fantasies which could become prolegomena to the desire for acquisition and movement.

Ideoscapes are also concatenations of images, but they are often directly political and frequently have to do with the ideologies of states and the counter-ideologies of movements explicitly oriented to capturing state power or a piece of it. These ideoscapes are composed of elements of the Enlightenment worldview, which consists of a concatenation of ideas, terms, and images, including "freedom," "welfare," "rights," "sovereignty," "representation," and the master-term "democracy." The master-narrative of the Enlightenment (and its many variants in England, France, and the United States) was constructed with a certain internal logic and presupposed a certain relationship between reading, representation, and the public sphere (for the dynamics of this process in the early history of the United States, see Warner: in press). But their diaspora across the world, especially since the nineteenth century, has loosened the internal coherence that held these terms and images together in a Euro-American master-narrative and provided instead a loosely structured synopticon of politics, in which different nation-states, as part of their evolution, have organized their political cultures around different keywords (e.g., Williams 1976).

As a result of the differential diaspora of these keywords, the political narratives that govern communication between elites and followings in different parts of the world involve problems of both a semantic and a pragmatic nature: semantic to the extent that words (and their lexical equivalents) require careful translation from context to context in their global movements; and pragmatic to the extent that the use of these words by political actors and their audiences may be subject to very different sets of contextual conventions that mediate their translation into public politics. Such conventions are not only matters of the nature of political rhetoric (viz., what does the aging Chinese leadership mean when it refers to the dangers of hooliganism? What does the South Korean leadership mean when it speaks of discipline as the key to democratic industrial growth?).

These conventions also involve the far more subtle question of what sets of communicative genres are valued in what way (newspapers versus cinema, for example) and what sorts of pragmatic genre conventions govern the collective readings of different kinds of text. So, while an Indian audience may be attentive to the resonances of a political speech in terms of some keywords and phrases reminiscent of Hindi cinema, a Korean audience may respond to the subtle codings of Buddhist or neo-Confucian rhetorical strategy encoded in a political document. The very relationship of reading to hearing and seeing may vary in important ways that determine the morphology of these different ideoscapes as they shape themselves in different national and transnational contexts. This globally variable synaesthesia has hardly even been noted, but it demands urgent analysis. Thus democracy has clearly become a master-term, with powerful echoes from Haiti and Poland to the Soviet Union and China, but it sits at the center of a variety of ideoscapes (composed of distinctive pragmatic configurations of rough trans-lations of other central terms from the vocabulary of the Enlightenment). This creates ever new terminological kaleidoscopes, as states (and the groups that seek to capture them) seek to pacify populations whose own ethnoscapes are in motion and whose mediascapes may create severe problems for the ideoscapes with which they are presented. The fluidity of ideoscapes is com-plicated in particular by the growing diasporas (both voluntary and invol-untary) of intellectuals who continuously inject new meaning-streams into the discourse of democracy in different parts of the world.

This extended terminological discussion of the five terms I have coined sets the basis for a tentative formulation about the conditions under which current global flows occur: *they occur in and through the growing disjunctures between ethnoscapes, technoscapes, financescapes, mediascapes, and ideoscapes.* This formulation, the core of my model of global cultural flow, needs some explanation. First, people, machinery, money, images, and ideas now follow increasingly non-isomorphic paths; of course, at all periods in human history, there have been some disjunctures between the flows of these things, but the sheer speed, scale, and volume of each of these flows is now so great that the disjunctures have become central to the politics of global culture. The Japanese are notoriously hospitable to ideas and are stereotyped as inclined to export (all) and import (some) goods, but they are also notoriously closed to immigration, like the Swiss, the Swedes, and the Saudis. Yet the Swiss and Saudis accept populations of guestworkers, thus creating labor diasporas of Turks, Italians, and other circum-Mediterranean groups. Some such guest-worker groups maintain continuous contact with their home nations, like the Turks, but others, like high-level South Asian migrants, tend to desire lives in their new homes, raising anew the problem of reproduction in a deterritorialized context.

Deterritorialization, in general, is one of the central forces of the modern world, since it brings laboring populations into the lower-class sectors and spaces of relatively wealthy societies, while sometimes creating exaggerated and intensified senses of criticism or attachment to politics in the home state. Deterritorialization, whether of Hindus, Sikhs, Palestinians, or Ukrainians, is now at the core of a variety of global fundamentalisms, including Islamic and Hindu fundamentalism. In the Hindu case, for example (Appadurai and Breckenridge: forthcoming), it is clear that the overseas movement of Indians has been exploited by a variety of interests both within and outside India to create a complicated network of finances and religious identifications, in which the problem of cultural reproduction for Hindus abroad has become tied to the politics of Hindu fundamentalism at home.

At the same time, deterritorialization creates new markets for film companies, art impresarios, and travel agencies, who thrive on the need of the deterritorialized population for contact with its homeland. Naturally, these invented homelands, that constitute the mediascapes of deterritorialized groups, can often become sufficiently fantastic and one-sided that they provide the material for new ideoscapes in which ethnic conflicts can begin to erupt. The creation of Khalistan, an invented homeland of the deterritorialized Sikh population of England, Canada, and the United States, is one example of the bloody potential in such mediascapes, as they interact with the internal colonialisms (e.g., Hechter 1974) of the nation-state. The West Bank, Namibia, and Eritrea are other theatres for the enactment of the bloody negotiation between existing nation-states and various deterritorialized groupings.

The idea of deterritorialization may also be applied to money and finance, as money managers seek the best markets for their investments, independent of national boundaries. In turn, these movements of monies are the basis of new kinds of conflict, as Los Angelenos worry about the Japanese buying up their city, and people in Bombay worry about the rich Arabs from the Gulf States who have not only transformed the price of mangos in Bombay, but have also substantially altered the profile of hotels, restaurants, and other services in the eyes of the local population, just as they continue to do in London. Yet most residents of Bombay are ambivalent about the Arab presence there, for the flip side of their presence is the absence of friends and kinsmen earning big money in the Middle East and bringing back both money and luxury commodities to Bombay and other cities in India. Such commodities transform consumer taste in these cities and often end up smuggled through air and sea ports and peddled in the gray markets of Bombay's streets. In these gray markets some members of Bombay's middle classes and of its lumpenproletariat can buy some of these goods, ranging from cartons of Marlboro cigarettes, to Old Spice shaving cream and tapes of Madonna. Similar gray routes, often subsidized by the moonlighting activities of sailors, diplomats, and airline stewardesses who get to move in and out of the country regularly, keep the gray markets of Bombay, Madras, and Calcutta filled with goods not only from the West, but also from the Middle East, Hong Kong, and Singapore.

It is in this fertile ground of deterritorialization, in which money, commodities, and persons are involved in ceaselessly chasing each other around the world, that the mediascapes and ideoscapes of the modern world find their fractured and fragmented counterpart. For the ideas and images produced by mass media often are only partial guides to the goods and experiences that deterritorialized populations transfer to one another. In Mira Nair's brilliant film *India Cabaret* we see the multiple loops of this fractured deterritorialization as young women, barely competent in Bombay's metropolitan glitz, come to seek their fortunes as cabaret dancers and prostitutes in Bombay, entertaining men in clubs with dance formats derived wholly from the prurient dance sequences of Hindi films. These scenes cater in turn to ideas about Western and foreign women and their "looseness," while they provide tawdry career alibis for these women. Some of these women come from Kerala, where cabaret clubs and the pornographic film industry have blossomed, partly in response to the purses and tastes of Keralites returned from the Middle East, where their diasporic lives away from women distort their very sense of what the relations between men and women might be. These tragedies of displacement could certainly be replayed in a more detailed analysis of the relations between the Japanese and German sex tours to Thailand and the tragedies of the sex trade in Bangkok, and in other similar loops which tie together fantasies about the Other, the conveniences and seductions of travel, the economics of global trade, and the brutal mobility fantasies that dominate gender politics in many parts of Asia and the world at large.

While far more could be said about the cultural politics of deterritorialization and the larger sociology of displacement that it expresses, it is appropriate at this juncture to bring in the role of the nation-state in the disjunctive global economy of culture today. The relationship between states and nations is everywhere an embattled one. It is possible to say that in many societies, the nation and the state have become one another's projects. That is, while nations (or more properly groups with ideas about nationhood) seek to capture or coopt states and state power, states simultaneously seek to capture and monopolize ideas about nationhood (Baruah 1986; Chatterjee 1986; Nandy 1989). In general, separatist transnational movements, including those which have included terror in their methods, exemplify nations in search of states: Sikhs, Tamil Sri Lankans, Basques, Moros, Québécois, each of these represent imagined communities which seek to create states of their own or carve pieces out of existing states. States, on the other hand, are everywhere seeking to monopolize the moral resources of community, either by flatly claiming perfect coevality between nation and state, or by systematically museumizing and representing all the groups within them in a variety of heritage politics that seems remarkably uniform throughout the world (Handler 1988; Herzfeld 1982; McQueen 1988).

Here, national and international mediascapes are exploited by nation-states to pacify separatists or even the potential fissiparousness of all ideas of difference. Typically, contemporary nation-states do this by exercising taxonomic control over difference, by creating various kinds of international spectacle to domesticate difference, and by seducing small groups with the fantasy of self-display on some sort of global or cosmopolitan stage. One important new feature of global cultural politics, tied to the disjunctive relationships between the various landscapes discussed earlier, is that state and nation are at each other's throats, and the hyphen that links them is now less an icon of conjuncture than an index of disjuncture. This disjunctive relationship between nation and state has two levels: at the level of any given nation-state, it means that there is a battle of the imagination, with state and nation seeking to cannibalize one another. Here is the seed-bed of brutal separatisms, majoritarianisms that seem to have appeared from nowhere, and micro-identities that have become political projects within the nation-state. At another level, this disjunctive relationship is deeply entangled with the global disjunctures discussed throughout this essay: ideas of nationhood appear to be steadily increasing in scale and regularly crossing existing state boundaries; sometimes, as with the Kurds, because previous identities stretched across vast national spaces, or, as with the Tamils in Sri Lanka, the dormant threads of a transnational diaspora have been activated to ignite the micropolitics of a nation-state.

In discussing the cultural politics that have subverted the hyphen that links the nation to the state, it is especially important not to forget its mooring in the irregularities that now characterize disorganized capital (Kothari 1989; Lash and Urry 1987). It is because labor, finance, and technology are now so widely separated that the volatilities that underlie movements for nation-hood (as large as transnational Islam on the one hand, or as small as the movement of the Gurkhas for a separate state in the northeast of India) grind against the vulnerabilities that characterize the relationships between states. States find themselves pressed to stay "open" by the forces of media, tech-nology, and travel that have fueled consumerism throughout the world and have increased the craving, even in the non-Western world, for new com-modities and spectacles. On the other hand, these very cravings can become caught up in new ethnoscapes, mediascapes, and eventually, ideoscapes, such as democracy in China, that the state cannot tolerate as threats to its own control over ideas of nationhood and peoplehood. States throughout the world are under siege, especially where contests over the ideoscapes of democracy are fierce and fundamental, and where there are radical disjunc-tures between ideoscapes and technoscapes (as in the case of very small coun-tries that lack contemporary technologies of production and information); or between ideoscapes and financescapes (as in countries such as Mexico or Brazil, where international lending influences national politics to a very large degree); or between ideoscapes and ethnoscapes (as in Beirut, where diasporic, local, and translocal filiations are suicidally at battle); or between ideoscapes and mediascapes (as in many countries in the Middle East and Asia), where the lifestyles represented on both national and international TV and cinema completely overwhelm and undermine the rhetoric of national politics: in the Indian case, the myth of the law-breaking hero has emerged to mediate this naked struggle between the pieties and the realities of Indian politics, which has grown increasingly brutalized and corrupt (Vachani 1989).

The transnational movement of the martial arts, particularly through Asia, as mediated by the Hollywood and Hong Kong film industries (Zarilli: forthcoming) is a rich illustration of the ways in which long-standing martial arts traditions, reformulated to meet the fantasies of contemporary (sometimes lumpen) youth populations, create new cultures of masculinity and violence, which are in turn the fuel for increased violence in national and international politics. Such violence is in turn the spur to an increasingly rapid and amoral arms trade which penetrates the entire world. The worldwide spread of the AK-47 and the Uzi, in films, in corporate and state security, in terror, and in police and military activity, is a reminder that apparently simple technical uniformities often conceal an increasingly complex set of loops, linking images of violence to aspirations for community in some imagined world.

Returning then to the ethnoscapes with which I began, the central paradox of ethnic politics in today's world is that primordia (whether of language or skin color or neighborhood or kinship) have become globalized. That is, sentiments whose greatest force is in their ability to ignite intimacy into a political sentiment and turn locality into a staging ground for identity, have become spread over vast and irregular spaces as groups move, yet stay linked to one another through sophisticated media capabilities. This is not to deny that such primordia are often the product of invented traditions (Hobsbawm and Ranger 1983) or retrospective affiliations, but to emphasize that because of the disjunctive and unstable interplay of commerce, media, national policies, and consumer fantasies, ethnicity, once a genie contained in the bottle of some sort of locality (however large), has now become a global force, forever slipping in and through the cracks between states and borders.

But the relationship between the cultural and economic levels of this new set of global disjunctures is not a simple one-way street in which the terms of global cultural politics are set wholly by, or confined wholly within, the vicissitudes of international flows of technology, labor, and finance, demanding only a modest modification of existing neo-Marxist models of uneven development and state formation. There is a deeper change, itself driven by the disjunctures between all the landscapes I have discussed, and constituted by their continuously fluid and uncertain interplay, which concerns the relationship between production and consumption in today's global economy. Here I begin with Marx's famous (and often mined) view of the fetishism of the commodity and suggest that this fetishism has been replaced in the world at large (now seeing the world as one, large, interactive system, composed of many complex subsystems) by two mutually supportive descendants, the first of which I call production fetishism, and the second of which I call the fetishism of the consumer.

By production fetishism I mean an illusion created by contemporary transnational production loci, which masks translocal capital, transnational earning-flows, global management and often faraway workers (engaged in various kinds of high-tech putting-out operations) in the idiom and spectacle of local (sometimes even worker) control, national productivity, and territorial sovereignty. To the extent that various kinds of Free Trade Zones have become the models for production at large, especially of high-tech commodities, production has itself become a fetish, masking not social relations as such, but the relations of production, which are increasingly transnational. The locality (both in the sense of the local factory or site of production and in the extended sense of the nation-state) becomes a fetish which disguises the globally dispersed forces that actually drive the production process. This generates alienation (in Marx's sense) twice intensified, for its social sense is now compounded by a complicated spatial dynamic which is increasingly global.

As for the fetishism of the consumer, I mean to indicate here that the consumer has been transformed, through commodity flows (and the mediascapes, especially of advertising, that accompany them), into a sign, both in Baudrillard's sense of a simulacrum which only asymptotically approaches the form of a real social agent; and in the sense of a mask for the real seat of agency, which is not the consumer but the producer and the many forces that constitute production. Global advertising is the key technology for the worldwide dissemination of a plethora of creative and culturally well-chosen ideas of consumer agency. These images of agency are increasingly distortions of a world of merchandising so subtle that the consumer is consistently helped to believe that he or she is an actor, where in fact he or she is at best a chooser.

The globalization of culture is not the same as its homogenization, but globalization involves the use of a variety of instruments of homogenization (armaments, advertising techniques, language hegemonies, and clothing styles) which are absorbed into local political and cultural economies, only to be repatriated as heterogeneous dialogues of national sovereignty, free enterprise, and fundamentalism in which the state plays an increasingly delicate role: too much openness to global flows, and the nation-state is threatened by revolt – the China syndrome; too little, and the state exits the international stage, as Burma, Albania, and North Korea in various ways have done. In general, the state has become the arbitrager of this *repatriation of difference* (in the form of goods, signs, slogans, and styles). But this repatriation or export of the designs and commodities of difference continuously exacerbates the internal politics of majoritarianism and homogenization, which is most frequently played out in debates over heritage.

Thus the central feature of global culture today is politics of the mutual effort of sameness and difference to cannibalize one another and thus to proclaim their successful hijacking of the twin Enlightenment ideals of the triumphantly universal and the resiliently particular. This mutual cannibalization shows its ugly face in riots, in refugee flows, in state-sponsored torture, and in ethnocide (with or without state support). Its brighter side is the expansion of many individual horizons of hope and fantasy, in the global spread of oral rehydration therapy and other low-tech instruments of well-being, in the susceptibility even of South Africa to the force of global opinion, in the inability of the Polish state to repress its own working classes, and in the growth of a wide range of progressive, transnational alliances. Examples of both sorts could be multiplied. The critical point is that both sides of the coin of global cultural process today are products of the infinitely varied mutual contest of sameness and difference on a stage characterized by radical disjunctures between different sorts of global flows and the uncertain landscapes created in and through these disjunctures.

The Work of Reproduction in an Age of Mechanical Art

I have inverted the key terms of the title of Walter Benjamin's famous essay (1969; orig. 1936) to return this rather high-flying discussion to a more manageable level. There is a classic human problem which will not disappear however much global cultural processes might change their dynamics, and this is the problem today typically discussed under the rubric of reproduction (and traditionally referred to in terms of the transmission of culture). In either case, the question is as follows: how do small groups, especially families, the classical loci of socialization, deal with these new global realities as they seek to reproduce themselves, and in so doing, as it were by accident, reproduce cultural forms themselves? In traditional anthropological terms this could be phrased as the problem of enculturation in a period of rapid culture change. So the problem is hardly novel. But it does take on some novel dimensions under the global conditions discussed so far in this essay.

In the first place, the sort of transgenerational stability of knowledge which was presupposed in most theories of enculturation (or, in slightly broader terms, of socialization) can no longer be assumed. As families move to new locations, or as children move before older generations, or as grown sons and daughters return from time spent in strange parts of the world, family relationships can become volatile, as new commodity patterns are negotiated, debts and obligations are recalibrated, and rumors and fantasies about the new setting are maneuvered into existing repertoires of knowledge and practice. Often, global labor diasporas involve immense strains on marriages in general and on women in particular, as marriages become the meeting points of historical patterns of socialization and new ideas of proper behavior. Generations easily divide, as ideas about property, propriety, and collective obligation wither under the siege of distance and time. Most important of all, the work of cultural reproduction in new settings is profoundly complicated by the politics of representing a family as "normal" (particularly for the young) to neighbors and peers in the new setting. All this is, of course, not new to the cultural study of immigration.

What is new is that this is a world in which both points of departure and points of arrival are in cultural flux, and thus the search for steady points of reference, as critical life-choices are made, can be very difficult. It is in this atmosphere that the invention of tradition (and of ethnicity, kinship, and other identity-markers) can become slippery, as the search for certainties is regularly frustrated by the fluidities of transnational communication. As group pasts become increasingly parts of museums, exhibits, and collections, both in national and transnational spectacles, culture becomes less what Bourdieu would have called a *habitus* (a tacit realm of reproducible practices and dispositions) and more an arena for conscious choice, justification, and representation, the latter often to multiple and spatially dislocated audiences.

The task of cultural reproduction, even in its most intimate arenas, such as husband–wife and parent–child relations, becomes both politicized and exposed to the traumas of deterritorialization as family members pool and negotiate their mutual understandings and aspirations in sometimes fractured spatial arrangements. At larger levels, such as community, neighborhood, and territory, this politicization is often the emotional fuel for more explicitly violent politics of identity, just as these larger politics sometimes penetrate and ignite domestic politics. When, for example, two offspring in a household split with their father on a key matter of political identification in a transnational setting, preexisting localized norms carry little force. Thus a son who has joined the Hezbollah group in Lebanon may no longer get along with parents or siblings who are affiliated with Amal or some other branch of Shi'i ethnic political identity in Lebanon. Women in particular bear the brunt of this sort of friction, for they become pawns in the heritage politics of the household, and are often subject to the abuse and violence of men who are themselves torn about the relation between heritage and opportunity in shifting spatial and political formations.

The pains of cultural reproduction in a disjunctive global world are, of course, not eased by the effects of mechanical art (or mass media, if you will), since these media afford powerful resources for counter-nodes of identity which youth can project against parental wishes or desires. At larger levels of organization there can be many forms of cultural politics within displaced populations (whether of refugees or of voluntary immigrants), all of which are inflected in important ways by media (and the mediascapes and ideoscapes they offer). A central link between the fragilities of cultural reproduction and the role of the mass media in today's world is the politics of gender and of violence. As fantasies of gendered violence dominate the B-grade film industries that blanket the world, they both reflect and refine gendered violence at home and in the streets, as young men (in particular) come to be torn between the macho politics of self-assertion in contexts where they are frequently denied real agency, and women are forced to enter the labor force in new ways on the one hand, and continue the maintenance of familial heritage on the other. Thus the honor of women becomes not just an armature of stable (if inhuman) systems of cultural reproduction, but a new arena for the formation of sexual identity and family politics, as men and women face new pressures at work, and new fantasies of leisure.

Since both work and leisure have lost none of their gendered qualities in this new global order, but have acquired ever subtler fetishized representations, the honor of women becomes increasingly a surrogate for the identity of embattled communities of males, while their women, in reality, have to negotiate increasingly harsh conditions of work at home and in the non-domestic workplace. In short, deterritorialized communities and displaced populations, however much they may enjoy the fruits of new kinds of earning and new dispositions of capital and technology, have to play out the desires and fantasies of these new ethnoscapes, while striving to reproduce the family-as-microcosm of culture. As the shapes of cultures grow themselves less bounded and tacit, more fluid and politicized, the work of cultural reproduction becomes a daily hazard. Far more could, and should, be said about the work of reproduction in an age of mechanical art: the preceding discussion was meant to indicate the contours of the problems that a new, globally informed theory of cultural reproduction will have to face.

Shape and Process in Global Cultural Formations

The deliberations of the arguments that I have made so far constitute the bare bones of an approach to a general theory of global cultural processes. Focusing on disjunctures, I have employed a set of terms (ethnoscape, financescape, technoscape, mediascape, and ideoscape) to stress different streams or flows along which cultural material may be seen to be moving across national boundaries. I have also sought to exemplify the ways in which these various flows (or landscapes, from the stabilizing perspectives of any given imagined world) are in fundamental disjuncture with respect to one another. What further steps can we take towards a general theory of global cultural processes, based on these proposals?

The first is to note that our very models of cultural shape will have to alter, as configurations of people, place, and heritage lose all semblance of isomorphism. Recent work in anthropology has done much to free us of the shackles of highly localized, boundary-oriented, holistic, primordialist images of cultural form and substance (Appadurai: in press; Hannerz 1989; Marcus and Fisher 1986; Thornton 1988). But not very much has been put in their place, except somewhat larger if less mechanical versions of these images, as in Wolf's work on the relationship of Europe to the rest of the world. What I would like to propose is that we begin to think of the configuration of cultural forms in today's world as fundamentally fractal; that is, as possessing no Euclidean boundaries, structures, or regularities. Second, I would suggest that these cultural forms, which we should strive to represent as fully fractal, are also overlapping, in ways that have been discussed only in pure mathematics (in set theory for example) and in biology (in the language of polythetic classifications). Thus we need to combine a fractal metaphor for the shape of cultures (in the plural) with a polythetic account of their overlaps and resemblances. Without this latter step, we shall remain enmired in comparative work which relies on the clear separation of the entities to be compared before serious comparison can begin. How are we to compare fractally shaped cultural forms which are also polythetically overlapping in their coverage of terrestrial space?

Finally, in order for the theory of global cultural interactions predicated on disjunctive flows to have any force greater than that of a mechanical metaphor, it will have to move into something like a human version of the theory that some scientists are calling "chaos theory." That is, we will need to ask how these complex, overlapping, fractal shapes constitute not a simple, stable (even if large-scale) system, but to ask what its dynamics are: Why do ethnic riots occur when and where they do? Why do states wither at greater rates in some places and times rather than others? Why do some countries flout conventions of international debt repayment with so much less apparent worry than others? How are international arms flows driving ethnic battles and genocides? Why are some states exiting the global stage while others are clamoring to get in? Why do key events occur at a certain point in a certain place rather than in others? These are, of course, the great traditional questions of causality, contingency, and prediction in the human sciences, but in a world of disjunctive global flows it is perhaps important to start asking them in a way that relies on images of flow and uncertainty, hence "chaos," rather than on older images of order, stability, and systemacity. Otherwise, we will have gone far towards a theory of global cultural systems but thrown out "process" in the bargain. And that would make these notes part of a journey towards the kind of illusion of order that we can no longer afford to impose on a world that is so transparently volatile.

Whatever the directions in which we can push these macro-metaphors (fractals, polythetic classifications, and chaos), we need to ask one other old-fashioned question out of the Marxist paradigm: is there some pre-given order to the relative determining force of these global flows? Since I have postulated the dynamics of global cultural systems as driven by the relationship between flows of persons, technologies, finance, information, and ideology, can we speak of some structural–causal order linking these flows, by analogy to the role of the economic order in one version of the Marxist paradigm? Can we speak of some of these flows as being, for *a priori* structural or historical reasons, always prior to and formative of other flows? My own hypothesis, which can only be tentative at this point, is that the relationship of these various flows to one another, as they constellate into particular events and social forms, will be radically context-dependent. Thus, while labor flows and their loops with financial flows between Kerala and the Middle East may account for the shape of media flows and ideoscapes in Kerala, the reverse may be true of Silicon Valley in California, where intense specialization in a special technological sector (computers) and specific flows of capital may well profoundly determine the shape that ethnoscapes, ideoscapes, and mediascapes may take.

This does not mean that the causal–historical relationship between these various flows is random or meaninglessly contingent, but that our current theories of cultural "chaos" are insufficiently developed to be even parsimonious models, at this point, much less to be predictive theories, the golden fleeces of one kind of social science. What I have sought to provide in this essay is a reasonably economical technical vocabulary and a rudimentary model of disjunctive flows, from which something like a decent global analysis might emerge. Without some such analysis, it will be difficult to construct what John Hinkson calls a "social theory of postmodernity" that is adequately global.

Notes

1   A shorter version of this essay appeared in *Theory, Culture and Society,* Vol. 7, Nos. 2 and 3, June 1990. The current version has benefited from discussion and

suggestions at the Seminar on "Post-Colonial National Identities" at the Institute for Advanced Study in Princeton.

2   One major exception is Fredric Jameson, whose work on the relationship between postmodernism and late capitalism has, in many ways, inspired this essay. However, the debate between Jameson and Ahmad in *Social Text* shows that the creation of a globalizing Marxist narrative, in cultural matters, is difficult territory indeed. My own effort, in this context, is to begin a restructuring of the Marxist narrative (by stressing lags and disjunctures) that many Marxists might find abhorrent. Such a restructuring has to avoid the dangers of obliterating difference within the third world, of eliding the social referent (as some French postmodernists seem inclined to do), and of retaining the narrative authority of the Marxist tradition, in favor of greater attention to global fragmentation, uncertainty, and difference.

3   These ideas are argued more fully in a book I am currently working on, tentatively entitled *Imploding Worlds: Imagination and Disjuncture in the Global Cultural Economy*. [*Editors' note*: This published book title was *Modernity at Large: Cultural Dimensions of Globalization* (1996)]

References

Abu-Lughod, J. *Before European Hegemony: The World System AD 1250–1350*. New York: Oxford University Press, 1989.

Ahmad, A. "Jameson's Rhetoric of Otherness and the 'National Allegory'." *Social Text* 17 (1987): 3–25.

Amin, S. *Class and Nation: Historically and in the Current Crisis*. New York: Monthly Review Press, 1980.

Anderson, B. *Imagined Communities: Reflections on the Origin and Spread of Nationalism*. London: Verso, 1983.

Appadurai, A. "Global Ethnoscapes: Notes and Queries for a Transnational Anthropology." *Interventions: Anthropologies of the Present*. Ed. R. G. Fox (in press).

—— *Modernity at Large: Cultural Dimensions of Globalization*. Minneapolis: University of Minnesota Press, 1996.

Appadurai, A. and C. A. Breckenridge. *A Transnational Culture in the Making: The Asian Indian Diaspora in the United States*. London: Berg (forthcoming).

Barber, K. "Popular Arts in Africa." *African Studies Review* 30.3 (September 1987): 1–78.

Baruah, S. "Immigration, Ethnic Conflict and Political Turmoil, Assam 1979–1985." *Asian Survey* 26.11 (November 1986): 1184–206.

Bayly, C. *Imperial Meridian: The British Empire and The World, 1780–1830*. London: Longman, 1989.

Benjamin, W. "The Work of Art in the Age of Mechanical Reproduction." *Illuminations*. Ed. H. Arendt; trans. H. Zohn. New York: Schocken Books, 1969. 217–51.

Braudel, F. *Civilization and Capitalism, 15th–18th Century* (3 vols.). London: Collins, 1981–4.

Chatterjee, P. *Nationalist Thought and the Colonial World: A Derivative Discourse.* London: Zed Books, 1986.

Curtin, P. *Cross-Cultural Trade in World History.* Cambridge: Cambridge University Press 1984.

Deleuze, G. and F. Guattari. *A Thousand Plateaus: Capitalism and Schizophrenia.* Trans. B. Massumi. Minneapolis: University of Minnesota Press, 1987.

Fabian, I. *Time and the Other: How Anthropology Makes Its Object.* New York: Columbia University Press, 1983.

Feld, S. "Notes on World Beat." *Public Culture* 1.1 (1988): 31–7.

Gans, E. *The End of Culture: Toward a Generative Anthropology.* Berkeley: University of California Press, 1985.

Hamelink, C. *Cultural Autonomy in Global Communications.* New York: Longman, 1983.

Handler, R. *Nationalism and the Politics of Culture in Quebec.* Madison: University of Wisconsin Press, 1988.

Hannerz, U. "The World in Creolization." *Africa* 57.4 (1987): 546–59.

—— "Notes on the Global Ecumene." *Public Culture* 1.2 (spring 1989): 66–75.

Hechter, M. *Internal Colonialism: The Celtic Fringe in British National Development, 1536–1966.* Berkeley: University of California Press, 1974.

Helms, M. W. *Ulysses' Sail: An Ethnographic Odyssey of Power, Knowledge, and Geographical Distance.* Princeton, NJ: Princeton University Press, 1988.

Herzfeld, M. *Ours Once More: Folklore, Ideology and the Making of Modern Greece.* Austin: University of Texas Press, 1982.

Hobsbawm, E. and T. Ranger, eds. *The Invention of Tradition.* New York: Columbia University Press, 1983.

Hodgson, M. *The Venture of Islam: Conscience and History in a World Civilization.* Chicago, IL: University of Chicago Press, 1974.

Ivy, M. "Tradition and Difference in the Japanese Mass Media." *Public Culture* 1.1 (1988): 21–9.

Iyer, P. *Video Night in Kathmandu.* New York: Knopf, 1988.

Jameson, F. "Postmodernism and Consumer Society." *The Anti-Aesthetic: Essays on Postmodern Culture.* Ed. H. Foster. Port Townsend, WA: Bay Press, 1983. 111–25.

—— "Third World Literature in the Era of Multi-National Capitalism." *Social Text* 15 (fall 1986): 65–88.

—— "Nostalgia for the Present." *South Atlantic Quarterly* 88.2 (spring 1989): 517–37.

Kothari, R. *State Against Democracy: In Search of Humane Governance.* New York: New Horizons, 1989.

Lakoff, G. and M. Johnson *Metaphors We Live By.* Chicago, IL: University of Chicago Press, 1980.

Lash, S. and J. Urry. *The End of Organized Capitalism.* Madison: University of Wisconsin Press, 1987.

McQueen, H. "The Australian Stamp: Image, Design and Ideology." *Arena* 84 (spring 1988): 78–96.

Mandel, E. *Late Capitalism.* London: Verso, 1978.

Marcus, G. and M. Fisher. *Anthropology As Cultural Critique: An Experimental Moment in the Human Sciences.* Chicago, IL: University of Chicago Press, 1986.

Mattelart, A. *Transnationals and Third World: The Struggle for Culture.* South Hadley, MA: Bergin and Garvey, 1983.

Meyrowitz, J. *No Sense of Place: The Impact of Electronic Media on Social Behavior.* New York: Oxford University Press, 1985.

Nandy, A. "The Political Culture of the Indian State." *Daedalus* 118.4 (1989): 1–26.

Nicoll, F. "My Trip to Alice." *Criticism, Heresy and Interpretation* (CHAI) 3 (1989): 21–32.

Schafer, E. *Golden Peaches of Samarkand: A Study of T'ang Exotics.* Berkeley: University of California Press, 1963.

Schiller, H. *Communication and Cultural Domination.* White Plains, NY: International Arts and Sciences, 1976.

Thornton, R. "The Rhetoric of Ethnographic Holism." *Cultural Anthropology* 3.3 (August 1988): 285–303.

Vachani, L. "Narrative, Pleasure and Ideology in the Hindi Film: An Analysis of the Outsider Formula." M.A. Thesis, Annenberg School of Communication, University of Pennsylvania, 1989.

Wallerstein, I. *The Modern World-System* (2 vols.). New York: Academic Press, 1974.

Warner, M. *The Letters of the Republic: Publication and the Public Sphere.* Cambridge, MA: Harvard University Press (in press).

Williams, R. *Keywords.* New York: Oxford University Press, 1976.

Wolf, E. *Europe and the People Without History.* Berkeley: University of California Press, 1982.

Yoshimoto, M. "The Postmodern and Mass Images in Japan." *Public Culture* 1.2 (1989): 8–25.

Zarilli, P. "Repositioning the Body: An Indian Martial Art and its Pan-Asian Publics." *Producing the Postcolonial: Trajectories to Public Culture in India.* Ed. C. A. Breckenridge (forthcoming). [Published as *Consuming Modernity: Public Culture in a South Asian World.* Minneapolis: University of Minnesota Press, 1995.]

2

The Black Atlantic as a Counterculture of Modernity

Paul Gilroy

In this essay Paul Gilroy deploys cultural studies methods to examine black cultural production and to disrupt contemporary forms of *cultural nationalism* which, according to Gilroy,"present immutable, ethnic differences as an absolute break in the histories and experiences of 'black' and 'white' people." For Gilroy, these forms of cultural nationalism are grounded within rigid beliefs about "ethnic absolutism."

Moving away from nationalist and essentialist models of cultural production, Gilroy posits the "black Atlantic" as a transnational space of traversal, cultural exchange, production, and belonging, and demonstrates how well-known black individuals in Africa, Britain, the Caribbean, and the US (such as Phyllis Wheatley, Olaudah Equiano, Martin Delaney, W. E. B. Du Bois, C. L. R. James, George Padmore, Richard Wright, and others) have charted diasporic paths across this transnational terrain that spans several continents.

In the movements of modernity (colonialist expansion, genocide, slavery, indenture), Gilroy argues, the ship is a *chronotope* that marks the temporalities and fissures of the modern world; because European settlers and traders were not "sealed off hermetically" from the Native American, African, and Asian people they exterminated, colonized, enslaved, and indentured, the "black Atlantic" (as a cultural *contact zone*) forms a counterculture to modernity.

This is an edited version of Gilroy's essay: [. . .] indicates where text has been omitted.

> *We who are homeless – Among Europeans today there is no lack of those who are entitled to call themselves homeless in a distinctive and honourable sense . . . We children of the future, how could we be at home in this today? We feel disfavour for all ideals that might lead one to feel at home even in this fragile, broken time of transition; as for "realities," we do not believe that they will last. The ice that still supports people today has become*

very thin; the wind that brings the thaw is blowing; we ourselves who are homeless constitute a force that breaks open ice and other all too thin "realities."

Nietzsche

On the notion of modernity. *It is a vexed question. Is not every era "modern" in relation to the preceding one? It seems that at least one of the components of "our" modernity is the spread of the awareness we have of it. The awareness of our awareness (the double, the second degree) is our source of strength and our torment.*

Edouard Glissant

Striving to be both European and black requires some specific forms of double consciousness. By saying this I do not mean to suggest that taking on either or both of these unfinished identities necessarily exhausts the subjective resources of any particular individual. However, where racist, nationalist, or ethnically absolutist discourses orchestrate political relationships so that these identities appear to be mutually exclusive, occupying the space between them or trying to demonstrate their continuity has been viewed as a provocative and even oppositional act of political insubordination.

The contemporary black English, like the Anglo-Africans of earlier generations, and perhaps like all blacks in the West, stand between (at least) two great cultural assemblages, both of which have mutated through the course of the modern world that formed them and assumed new configurations. At present, they remain locked symbiotically in an antagonistic relationship marked out by the symbolism of colors which adds to the central Manichean dynamic – black and white. These colors support a special rhetoric that has grown to be associated with a language of nationality and national belonging as well as the languages of "race" and ethnic identity.

Though largely ignored by recent debates over modernity and its discontents, these ideas about nationality, ethnicity, authenticity, and cultural integrity are characteristically modern phenomena that have profound implications for cultural criticism and cultural history. They crystallized with the revolutionary transformations of the West at the end of the eighteenth and the beginning of the nineteenth centuries and involved novel typologies and modes of identification. Any shift towards a postmodern condition should not, however, mean that the conspicuous power of these modern subjectivities and the movements they articulated has been left behind. Their power has, if anything, grown, and their ubiquity as a means to make political sense of the world is currently unparalleled by the languages of class and socialism by which they once appeared to have been surpassed. My concern here is less with explaining their longevity and enduring appeal than with exploring some of the special political problems that arise from the fatal junction of the concept of nationality with the concept of culture and the affinities and affiliations which link the blacks of the West to one of their adoptive, parental cultures: the intellectual heritage of the West since the Enlightenment. I have become fascinated with how successive generations of black intellectuals have understood this connection and how they have projected it in their writing and speaking in pursuit of freedom, citizenship, and social and political autonomy.

If this appears to be little more than a roundabout way of saying that the reflexive cultures and consciousness of the European settlers and those of the Africans they enslaved, the "Indians" they slaughtered, and the Asians they indentured were not, even in situations of the most extreme brutality, sealed off hermetically from each other, then so be it. This seems as though it ought to be an obvious and self-evident observation, but its stark character has been systematically obscured by commentators from all sides of political opinion. Regardless of their affiliation to the right, left, or center, groups have fallen back on the idea of cultural nationalism, on the overintegrated conceptions of culture which present immutable, ethnic differences as an absolute break in the histories and experiences of "black" and "white" people. Against this choice stands another, more difficult option: the theorization of creolization, *métissage*, *mestizaje*, and hybridity. From the viewpoint of ethnic absolutism, this would be a litany of pollution and impurity. These terms are rather unsatisfactory ways of naming the processes of cultural mutation and restless (dis)continuity that exceed racial discourse and avoid capture by its agents.

[. . .]

My concerns at this stage are primarily conceptual: I have tried to address the continuing lure of ethnic absolutisms in cultural criticism produced both by blacks and by whites. In particular, this chapter seeks to explore the special relationships between "race," culture, nationality, and ethnicity which have a bearing on the histories and political cultures of Britain's black citizens. I have argued elsewhere that the cultures of this group have been produced in a syncretic pattern in which the styles and forms of the Caribbean, the United States, and Africa have been reworked and reinscribed in the novel context of modern Britain's own untidy ensemble of regional and class-oriented conflicts. Rather than make the invigorating flux of those mongrel cultural forms my focal concern here, I want instead to look at broader questions of ethnic identity that have contributed to the scholarship and the political strategies that Britain's black settlers have generated and to the underlying sense of England as a cohesive cultural community against which their self-conception has so often been defined. Here the ideas of nation, nationality, national belonging, and nationalism are paramount. They are extensively supported by a clutch of rhetorical strategies that can be named "cultural insiderism."[1] The essential trademark of cultural insiderism which also supplies the key to its popularity is an absolute sense of ethnic difference. This is maximized so that it distinguishes people from one another and at the same time acquires an incontestable priority over all other dimensions of their social and historical experience, cultures, and identities. Characteristically, these claims are associated with the idea of national belonging or the aspiration to nationality and other more local but equivalent forms of cultural kinship. The range and complexity of these ideas in English cultural life defies simple summary or exposition. However, the forms of cultural insiderism they sanction typically construct the nation as an ethnically homogeneous object and invoke ethnicity a second time in the hermeneutic procedures deployed to make sense of its distinctive cultural content.

The intellectual seam in which English cultural studies has positioned itself—through innovative work in the fields of social history and literary criticism—can be indicted here. The statist modalities of Marxist analysis that view modes of material production and political domination as exclusively *national* entities are only one source of this problem. Another factor, more evasive but nonetheless potent for its intangible ubiquity, is a quiet cultural nationalism which pervades the work of some radical thinkers. This crypto-nationalism means that they are often disinclined to consider the cross-catalytic or transverse dynamics of racial politics as a significant element in the formation and reproduction of English national identities. These formations are treated as if they spring, fully formed, from their own special viscera.

My search for resources with which to comprehend the doubleness and cultural intermixture that distinguish the experience of black Britons in contemporary Europe required me to seek inspiration from other sources and, in effect, to make an intellectual journey across the Atlantic. In black America's histories of cultural and political debate and organization I found another, second perspective with which to orient my own position. Here too the lure of ethnic particularism and nationalism has provided an ever-present danger. But that narrowness of vision which is content with the merely national has also been challenged from within that black community by thinkers who were prepared to renounce the easy claims of African-American exceptionalism in favor of a global, coalitional politics in which anti-imperialism and anti-racism might be seen to interact if not to fuse.

[. . .] I have settled on the image of ships in motion across the spaces between Europe, America, Africa, and the Caribbean as a central organizing symbol for this enterprise and as my starting point. The image of the ship – a living, microcultural, micropolitical system in motion – is especially important for historical and theoretical reasons that I hope will become clearer

below. Ships immediately focus attention on the Middle Passage, on the various projects for redemptive return to an African homeland, on the circulation of ideas and activists as well as the movement of key cultural and political artifacts: tracts, books, gramophone records, and choirs.
[. . .]

Cultural Studies in Black and White

Any satisfaction to be experienced from the recent spectacular growth of cultural studies as an academic project should not obscure its conspicuous problems with ethnocentrism and nationalism. Understanding these difficulties might commence with a critical evaluation of the ways in which notions of ethnicity have been mobilized, often by default rather than design, as part of the distinctive hermeneutics of cultural studies or with the unthinking assumption that cultures always flow into patterns congruent with the borders of essentially homogeneous nation-states. The marketing and inevitable reification of cultural studies as a discrete academic subject also has what might be called a secondary ethnic aspect. The project of cultural studies is a more or less attractive candidate for institutionalization according to the ethnic garb in which it appears. The question of whose cultures are being studied is therefore an important one, as is the issue of where the instruments which will make that study possible are going to come from. In these circumstances it is hard not to wonder how much of the recent international enthusiasm for cultural studies is generated by its profound associations with England and ideas of Englishness. This possibility can be used as a point of entry into consideration of the ethnohistorical specificity of the discourse of cultural studies itself.

Looking at cultural studies from an ethnohistorical perspective requires more than just noting its association with English literature, history, and New Left politics. It necessitates constructing an account of the borrowings made by these English initiatives from wider, modern, European traditions of thinking about culture, and at every stage examining the place which these cultural perspectives provide for the images of their racialized[2] others as objects of knowledge, power, and cultural criticism. It is imperative, though very hard, to combine thinking about these issues with consideration of the pressing need to get black cultural expressions, analyses, and histories taken seriously in academic circles, rather than assigned via the idea of "race relations" to sociology and thence abandoned to the elephants' graveyard to which intractable policy issues go to await their expiry. These two important conversations pull in different directions and sometimes threaten to cancel each other out, but it is the struggle to have blacks perceived as agents, as people with cognitive capacities and even with an intellectual history – attributes denied by modern racism – that is for me the primary reason for writing. [. . .] It provides a valuable warrant for questioning some of the ways in which ethnicity is appealed to in the English idioms of cultural theory and history, and in the scholarly productions of black America. Understanding the political culture of blacks in Britain demands close attention to both these traditions. [. . .]

Histories of cultural studies seldom acknowledge how the politically radical and openly interventionist aspirations found in the best of its scholarship are already articulated to black cultural history and theory. These links are rarely seen or accorded any significance. In England the work of figures like C. L. R. James and Stuart Hall offers a wealth of both symbols and concrete evidence for the practical links between these critical political projects. In the United States the work of interventionist scholars like bell hooks and Cornel West as well as that of more orthodox academics like Henry Louis Gates, Jr., Houston A. Baker, Jr., Anthony Appiah, and Hazel Carby, points to similar convergences. The position of these thinkers in the contested "contact zones"[3] between cultures and histories is not, however, as exceptional as it might appear at first. We shall see below that successive generations of black intellectuals (especially those whose lives, like James's, crisscrossed the Atlantic Ocean) noted this intercultural positionality and accorded it a special significance before launching their distinct modes of cultural and political critique. They were often urged on in their labor by the brutal absurdity of racial classification that derives from and also celebrates racially exclusive conceptions of national identity from which blacks were excluded as either non-humans or non-citizens. I shall try to show that their marginal endeavors point to some new analytic possibilities with a general significance far beyond the well-policed borders of black particularity. For example, this body of work offers intermediate concepts, lodged between the local and the global, which have a wider applicability in cultural history and politics precisely because they offer an alternative to the nationalist focus which dominates cultural criticism. [. . .]

Getting beyond these national and nationalistic perspectives has become essential for two additional reasons. The first arises from the urgent obligation to reevaluate the significance of the modern nation-state as a political, economic, and cultural unit. Neither political nor economic structures of domination are still simply coextensive with national borders. This has a special significance in contemporary Europe, where new political and economic relations are being created seemingly day by day, but it is a worldwide phenomenon with significant consequences for the relationship between the politics of information and the practices of capital accumulation. Its effects underpin more recognizably political changes like the growing centrality of transnational ecological movements which, through their insistence on the association of sustainability and justice, do so much to shift the moral and scientific precepts on which the modern separation of politics and ethics was built. The second reason relates to the tragic popularity of ideas about the integrity and purity of cultures. In particular, it concerns the relationship between nationality and ethnicity. This too currently has a special force in Europe, but it is also reflected directly in the postcolonial histories and complex, transcultural, political trajectories of Britain's black settlers.

What might be called the peculiarity of the black English requires attention to the intermixture of a variety of distinct cultural forms. Previously separated political and intellectual traditions converged and, in their coming together, overdetermined the process of black Britain's social and historical formation. This blending is misunderstood if it is conceived in simple ethnic terms, but right and left, racist and anti-racist, black and white tacitly share a view of it as little more than a collision between fully formed and mutually exclusive cultural communities. This has become the dominant view where black history and culture are perceived, like black settlers themselves, as an illegitimate intrusion into a vision of authentic British national life that, prior to their arrival, was as stable and as peaceful as it was ethnically undifferentiated. [. . .] However, though it arises from present rather than past conditions, contemporary British racism bears the imprint of the past in many ways. The especially crude and reductive notions of culture that form the substance of racial politics today are clearly associated with an older discourse of racial and ethnic difference which is everywhere entangled in the history of the idea of culture in the modern West. This history has itself become hotly contested since debates about multiculturalism, cultural pluralism, and the responses to them that are sometimes dismissively called "political correctness" arrived to query the ease and speed with which European particularisms are still being translated into absolute, universal standards for human achievement, norms, and aspirations.

It is significant that prior to the consolidation of scientific racism in the nineteenth century,[4] the term "race" was used very much in the way that the word "culture" is used today. But in the attempts to differentiate the true, the good, and the beautiful which characterize the junction point of capitalism, industrialization, and political democracy and give substance to the discourse of Western modernity, it is important to appreciate that scientists did not monopolize either the image of the black or the emergent concept of biologically based racial difference. As far as the future of cultural studies is concerned, it should be equally important that both were centrally employed in those European attempts to think through beauty, taste, and aesthetic judgment that are the precursors of contemporary cultural criticism.

Tracing the racial signs from which the discourse of cultural value was constructed, and their conditions of existence in relation to European aesthetics and philosophy, as well as European science, can contribute much to an ethnohistorical reading of the aspirations of Western modernity as a whole and to the critique of Enlightenment assumptions in particular. It is certainly the case that ideas about "race," ethnicity, and nationality form an important seam of continuity linking English cultural studies with one of its sources of inspiration – the doctrines of modern European aesthetics that are consistently configured by the appeal to national and often racial particularity.[5]

This is not the place to go deeply into the broader dimensions of this intellectual inheritance. Valuable work has already been done by Sander Gilman,[6] Henry Louis Gates, Jr.,[7] and others on the history and role of the image of the black in the discussions which found modern cultural axiology; Gilman points out usefully that the figure of the black appears in different forms in the aesthetics of Hegel, Schopenhauer, and Nietzsche (among others) as a marker for moments of cultural relativism and to support the production of aesthetic judgments of a supposedly universal character to differentiate, for example, between authentic music and, as Hegel puts it, "the most detestable noise." Gates emphasizes a complex genealogy in which ambiguities in Montesquieu's discussion of slavery prompt responses in Hume that can be related, in turn, to philosophical debates over the nature of beauty and sublimity found in the work of Burke and Kant. Critical evaluation of these representations of blackness might also be connected to the controversies over the place of racism and anti-Semitism in the work of Enlightenment figures like Kant and Voltaire.[8] [. . .] Nor should important inquiries into the contiguity of racialized reason and unreasonable racism be dismissed as trivial matters. These issues go to the heart of contemporary debates about what constitutes the canon of Western civilization and how this precious legacy should be taught.

In these embattled circumstances it is regrettable that questions of "race" and representation have been so regularly banished from orthodox histories of Western aesthetic judgment, taste, and cultural value.[9] There is a plea here that further inquiries should be made into precisely how discussions of "race," beauty, ethnicity, and culture have contributed to the critical thinking that eventually gave rise to cultural studies. The use of the concept of fetishism in Marxism and psychoanalytic studies is one obvious means to open up this problem.[10] The emphatically national character ascribed to the concept of modes of production (cultural and otherwise) is another fundamental question which demonstrates the ethnohistorical specificity of dominant approaches to cultural politics, social movements, and oppositional consciousnesses.

These general issues appear in a specific form in the distinctive English idioms of cultural reflection. Here too, the moral and political problem of slavery loomed large, not least because it was once recognized as *internal* to the structure of Western civilization and appeared as a central political and philosophical concept in the emergent discourse of modern English cultural uniqueness.[11] Notions of the primitive and the civilized which had been integral to premodern understanding of "ethnic" differences became fundamental cognitive and aesthetic markers in the processes which generated a constellation of subject positions in which Englishness, Christianity, and other ethnic and racialized attributes would finally give way to the dislocating dazzle of "whiteness."[12] A small but telling insight into this can be found in Edmund Burke's discussion of the sublime, which has achieved a certain currency lately. He makes elaborate use of the association of darkness with blackness, linking them to the skin of a real, live black woman. Seeing her produces a sublime feeling of terror in a boy whose sight has been restored to him by a surgical operation.

> Perhaps it may appear on enquiry, that blackness and darkness are in some degree painful by their natural operation, independent of any associations whatever. I must observe that the ideas of blackness and darkness are much the same; and they differ only in this, that blackness is a more confined idea.
>
> Mr Cheselden has given us a very curious story of a boy who had been born blind, and continued so until he was thirteen or fourteen years old; he was then couched for a cataract, by which operation he received his sight . . . Cheselden tells us that the first time the boy saw a black object, it gave him great uneasiness; and that some time after, upon accidentally seeing a negro woman, he was struck with great horror at the sight.[13]

Burke, who opposed slavery and argued for its gradual abolition, stands at the doorway of the tradition of inquiry mapped by Raymond Williams which is also the infrastructure on which much of English cultural studies came to be founded. This origin is part of the explanation of how some of the contemporary manifestations of this tradition lapse into what can only be called a morbid celebration of England and Englishness. These modes of subjectivity and identification acquire a renewed political charge in the post-imperial history that saw black settlers from Britain's colonies take up their citizenship rights as subjects in the United Kingdom. The entry of blacks into national life was itself a powerful factor contributing to the circumstances in which the formation of both cultural studies and New Left politics became possible. It indexes the profound transformations of British social and cultural life in the 1950s and stands, again usually unacknowledged, at the heart of laments for a more human scale of social living that seemed no longer practicable after the 1939–45 war.

The convoluted history of black settlement need not be recapitulated here. One recent fragment from it, the struggle over Salman Rushdie's book *The Satanic Verses*, is sufficient to demonstrate that racialized conflict over the meaning of English culture is still very much alive and to show that these antagonisms have become enmeshed in a second series of struggles in which Enlightenment assumptions about culture, cultural value, and aesthetics go on being tested by those who do not accept them as universal moral standards. These conflicts are, in a sense, the outcome of a distinct historical period in which a new, ethnically absolute and culturalist racism was produced. It would explain the burning of books on English streets as manifestations of irreducible cultural differences that signposted the path to domestic racial catastrophe. This new racism was generated in part by the move towards a political discourse which aligned "race" closely with the idea of national belonging and which stressed complex cultural difference rather than simple biological hierarchy. These strange conflicts emerged in circumstances where blackness and Englishness appeared suddenly to be mutually exclusive attributes and where the conspicuous antagonism between them proceeded on the terrain of culture, not that of politics. Whatever view of Rushdie one holds, his fate offers another small, but significant omen of the extent to which the almost metaphysical values of England and Englishness are currently being contested through their connection to "race" and ethnicity. His experiences are also a reminder of the difficulties involved in attempts to construct a more pluralistic, postcolonial sense of British culture and national identity. In this context, locating and answering the nationalism if not the racism and ethnocentrism of English cultural studies has itself become a directly political issue.

Returning to the imperial figures who supplied Raymond Williams with the raw material for his own brilliant critical reconstruction of English intellectual life is instructive. Apart from Burke, Thomas Carlyle, John Ruskin, Charles Kingsley, and the rest of Williams's cast of worthy characters can become valuable not simply in attempts to purge cultural studies of its doggedly ethnocentric focus, but in the more ambitious and more useful task of actively reshaping contemporary England by reinterpreting the cultural core of its supposedly authentic national life. In the work of reinterpretation and reconstruction, reinscription and relocation required to transform England and Englishness, discussion of the cleavage in the Victorian intelligentsia around the response to Governor Eyre's handling of the Morant Bay Rebellion in Jamaica in 1865 is likely to be prominent.[14] Like the English responses to the 1857 uprising in India examined by Jenny Sharpe,[15] it may well turn out to be a much more formative moment than has so far been appreciated. Morant Bay is doubly significant because it represents an instance of metropolitan, internal conflict that emanates directly from an external colonial experience. These crises in imperial power demonstrate their continuity. It is part of my argument that this inside/outside relationship should be recognized as a more powerful, more complex, and more contested element in the historical, social, and cultural memory of our glorious nation than has previously been supposed.

I am suggesting that even the laudable, radical varieties of English cultural sensibility examined by Williams and celebrated by Edward Thompson and others were not produced spontaneously from their own internal and intrinsic dynamics. The fact that some of the most potent conceptions of Englishness have been constructed by alien outsiders like Carlyle, Swift, Scott, or Eliot should augment the note of caution sounded here. The most heroic, subaltern English nationalisms and countercultural patriotisms are perhaps better understood as having been generated in a complex pattern of antagonistic relationships with the supranational and imperial world for which the ideas of "race," nationality, and national culture provide the primary (though not the only) indices. This approach would obviously bring William Blake's work into a rather different focus from that supplied by orthodox cultural history, and, as Peter Linebaugh has suggested, this overdue reassessment can be readily complemented by charting the long-neglected involvement of black slaves and their descendants in the radical history of our country in general and its working-class movements in particular.[16] Olaudah Equiano, whose involvement in the beginnings of organized working-class politics is now being widely recognized; the anarchist, Jacobin, ultra-radical, and Methodist heretic Robert Wedderburn; William Davidson, son of Jamaica's attorney general, hanged for his role in the Cato Street conspiracy to blow up the British cabinet in 1819;[17] and the Chartist William Cuffay are only the most urgent, obvious candidates for rehabilitation. Their lives offer invaluable means of seeing how thinking with and through the discourses and the imagery of "race" appears in the core rather than at the fringes of English political life. Davidson's speech from the scaffold before being subject to the last public decapitation in England is, for example, one moving appropriation of the rights of dissident freeborn Englishmen that is not widely read today.

Of this infamous trio, Wedderburn is perhaps the best known, thanks to the efforts of Peter Linebaugh and Iain McCalman.[18] The child of a slave dealer, James Wedderburn, and a slave woman, Robert was brought up by a Kingston conjure woman who acted as an agent for smugglers. He migrated to London at the age of seventeen in 1778. There, having published a number of disreputable ultra-radical tracts as part of his subversive political labors, he presented himself as a living embodiment of the horrors of slavery in a debating chapel in Hopkins Street near the Haymarket, where he preached a version of chiliastic anarchism based on the teachings of Thomas Spence and infused with deliberate blasphemy. In one of the debates held in his "ruinous hayloft with 200 persons of the lowest description," Wedderburn defended the inherent rights of the Caribbean slave to slay his master, promising to write home and "tell them to murder their masters as soon as they please." After this occasion he was tried and acquitted on a charge of blasphemy after persuading the jury that he had not been uttering sedition but merely practicing the "true and infallible genius of prophetic skill."[19]

It is particularly significant for the direction of my overall argument that both Wedderburn and his sometime associate Davidson had been sailors, moving to and fro between nations, crossing borders in modern machines that were themselves microsystems of linguistic and political hybridity. Their relationship to the sea may turn out to be especially important for both the early politics and poetics of the black Atlantic world that I wish to counterpose against the narrow nationalism of so much English historiography. Wedderburn served in the Royal Navy and as a privateer, while Davidson, who ran away to sea instead of studying law, was pressed into naval service on two subsequent occasions. Davidson inhabited the same ultra-radical subculture as Wedderburn and was an active participant in the Marylebone Reading Society, a radical body formed in 1819 after the Peterloo massacre. He is known to have acted as the custodian of their black flag, which significantly bore a skull and crossbones with the legend "Let us die like men and not be sold as slaves," at an open-air meeting in Smithfield later that year.[20] The precise details of how radical ideologies articulated the culture of the London poor before the institution of the factory system to the insubordinate maritime culture of pirates and other pre-industrial workers of the world will have to await the innovative labors of Peter Linebaugh and Marcus Rediker.[21] However, it has been estimated that at the end of the eighteenth century a quarter of the British navy was composed of Africans for whom the experience of slavery was a powerful orientation to the ideologies of liberty and justice. Looking for similar patterns on the other side of the Atlantic network, we can locate Crispus Attucks at the head of his "motley rabble of saucy boys, negroes, mulattoes, Irish teagues and outlandish jack tars"[22] and can track Denmark Vesey sailing the Caribbean and picking up inspirational stories of the Haitian revolution (one of his co-conspirators testified that he had said they would "not spare one white skin alive for this was the plan they pursued in San Domingo").[23] There is also the shining example of Frederick Douglass, whose autobiographies reveal that he learnt of freedom in the North from Irish sailors while working as a ship's caulker in Baltimore. He had less to say about the embarrassing fact that the vessels he readied for the ocean – Baltimore Clippers – were slavers, the fastest ships in the world and the only craft capable of outrunning the British blockade. Douglass, who played a neglected role in English anti-slavery activity, escaped from bondage disguised as a sailor and put this success down to his ability to "talk sailor like an old salt."[24] These are only a few of the nineteenth-century examples. The involvement of Marcus Garvey, George Padmore, Claude McKay, and Langston Hughes with ships and sailors lends additional support to Linebaugh's prescient suggestion that "the ship remained perhaps the most important conduit of Pan-African communication before the appearance of the long-playing record."[25]

Ships and other maritime scenes have a special place in the work of J. M. W. Turner, an artist whose pictures represent, in the view of many contemporary critics, the pinnacle of achievement in the English school in painting. Any visitor to London will testify to the importance of the Clore Gallery as a national institution and of the place of Turner's art as an enduring expression of the very essence of English civilization. Turner was secured on the summit of critical appreciation by John Ruskin, who, as we have seen, occupies a special place in Williams's constellation of great Englishmen. Turner's celebrated picture of a slave ship[26] throwing overboard its dead and dying as a storm comes on was exhibited at the Royal Academy to coincide with the world anti-slavery convention held in London in 1840. The picture, owned by Ruskin for some twenty-eight years, was rather more than an answer to the absentee Caribbean landlords who had commissioned its creator to record the tainted splendor of their country houses, which, as Patrick Wright has eloquently demonstrated, became an important signifier of the contemporary, ruralist distillate of national life.[27] It offered a powerful protest against the direction and moral tone of English politics. This was made explicit in an epigraph Turner took from his own poetry and which has itself retained a political inflection: "Hope, hope, fallacious hope where is thy market now?" Three years after his extensive involvement in the campaign to defend Governor Eyre,[28] Ruskin put the slave ship painting up for sale at Christie's. It is said that he had begun to find it too painful to live with. No buyer was found at that time, and he sold the picture to an American three years later. The painting has remained in the United States ever since. Its exile in Boston is yet another pointer towards the shape of the Atlantic as a system of cultural exchanges. It is more important, though, to draw attention to Ruskin's inability to discuss the picture except in terms of what it revealed about the aesthetics of painting water. He relegated the information that the vessel was a slave ship to a footnote in the first volume of *Modern Painters*.[29]

In spite of lapses like this, the New Left heirs to the aesthetic and cultural tradition in which Turner and Ruskin stand compounded and reproduced its nationalism and its ethnocentrism by denying imaginary, invented Englishness any external referents whatsoever. England ceaselessly gives birth to itself, seemingly from Britannia's head. The political affiliations and cultural preferences of this New Left group amplified these problems. They are most visible and most intense in the radical historiography that supplied a counterpart to Williams's subtle literary reflections. For all their enthusiasm for the work of C. L. R. James, the influential British Communist Party's historians' group is culpable here.[30] Their predilections for the image of the freeborn Englishman and the dream of socialism in one country that framed their work are both to be found wanting when it comes to nationalism. This uncomfortable pairing can be traced through the work of Edward Thompson and Eric Hobsbawm, visionary writers who contributed so much to the strong foundations of English cultural studies and who share a non-reductive Marxian approach to economic, social, and cultural history in which the nation – understood as a stable receptacle for counter-hegemonic class struggle – is the primary focus. These problems within English cultural studies form at its junction point with practical politics and instantiate wider difficulties with nationalism and with the discursive slippage or connotative resonance between "race," ethnicity, and nation.

Similar problems appear in rather different form in African-American letters where an equally volkish popular cultural nationalism is featured in the work of several generations of radical scholars and an equal number of not so radical ones. We will see below that absolutist conceptions of cultural difference allied to a culturalist understanding of "race" and ethnicity can be found in this location too.

In opposition to both of these nationalist or ethnically absolute approaches, I want to develop the suggestion that cultural historians could take the Atlantic as one single, complex unit of analysis in their discussions of the modern world and use it to produce an explicitly transnational and intercultural perspective.[31] Apart from the confrontation with English historiography and literary history this entails a challenge to the ways in which black American cultural and political histories have so far been conceived. I want to suggest that much of the precious intellectual legacy claimed by African-American intellectuals as the substance of their particularity is in fact only partly their absolute ethnic property. No less than in the case of the English New Left, the idea of the black Atlantic can be used to show that there are other claims to it which can be based on the structure of the African diaspora into the Western hemisphere. A concern with the Atlantic as a cultural and political system has been forced on black historiography and intellectual history by the economic and historical matrix in which plantation slavery – "capitalism with its clothes off" – was one special moment. The fractal patterns of cultural and political exchange and transformation that we try and specify through manifestly inadequate theoretical terms like creolization and syncretism indicate how both ethnicities and political cultures have been made anew in ways that are significant not simply for the peoples of the Caribbean but for Europe, for Africa, especially Liberia and Sierra Leone, and of course, for black America.

It bears repetition that Britain's black settler communities have forged a compound culture from disparate sources. Elements of political sensibility and cultural expression transmitted from black America over a long period of time have been reaccentuated in Britain. They are central, though no longer dominant, within the increasingly novel configurations that characterize another newer black vernacular culture. This is not content to be either dependent upon or simply imitative of the African diaspora cultures of America and the Caribbean. The rise and rise of Jazzie B and Soul II Soul at the turn of the last decade constituted one valuable sign of this new assertive mood. North London's Funki Dreds, whose name itself projects a newly hybridized identity, have projected the distinct culture and rhythm of life of black Britain outwards into the world. Their song "Keep On Moving" was notable for having been produced in England by the children of Caribbean settlers and then remixed in a (Jamaican) dub format in the United States by Teddy Riley, an African American. It included segments or samples of music taken from American and Jamaican records by the JBs and Mikey Dread respectively. This formal unity of diverse cultural elements was more than just a powerful symbol. It encapsulated the playful diasporic intimacy that has been a marked feature of transnational black Atlantic creativity. The record and its extraordinary popularity enacted the ties of affiliation and affect which articulated the discontinuous histories of black settlers in the new world. The fundamental injunction to "Keep On Moving" also expressed the restlessness of spirit which makes that diaspora culture vital. The contemporary black arts movement in film, visual arts, and theatre as well as music, which provided the background to this musical release, have created a new topography of loyalty and identity in which the structures and presuppositions of the nation-state have been left behind because they are seen to be outmoded. It is important to remember that these recent black Atlantic phenomena may not be as novel as their digital encoding via the transnational force of north London's Soul II Soul suggests. Columbus's pilot, Pedro Nino, was also an African. The history of the black Atlantic since then, continually crisscrossed by the movements of black people – not only as commodities but engaged in various struggles towards emancipation, autonomy, and citizenship – provides a means to reexamine the problems of nationality, location, identity, and historical memory. They all emerge from it with special clarity if we contrast the national, nationalistic, and ethnically absolute paradigms of cultural criticism to be found in England and America with those hidden expressions, both residual and emergent, that attempt to be global or outer-national in nature. These traditions have supported countercultures of modernity that touched the workers' movement but are not reducible to it. They supplied important foundations on which it could build.

Turner's extraordinary painting of the slave ship remains a useful image not only for its self-conscious moral power and the striking way that it aims directly for the sublime in its invocation of racial terror, commerce, and England's ethico-political degeneration. It should be emphasized that ships were the living means by which the points within that Atlantic world were joined. They were mobile elements that stood for the shifting spaces in between the fixed places that they connected.[32] Accordingly they need to be thought of as cultural and political units rather than abstract embodiments of the triangular trade. They were something more – a means to conduct political dissent and possibly a distinct mode of cultural production. The ship provides a chance to explore the articulations between the discontinuous histories of England's ports, its interfaces with the wider world.[33] Ships also refer us back to the Middle Passage, to the half-remembered micropolitics of the slave trade and its relationship to both industrialization and modernization. As it were, getting on board promises a means to reconceptualize the orthodox relationship between modernity and what passes for its prehistory. It provides a different sense of where modernity might itself be thought to begin in the constitutive relationships with outsiders that both found and temper a self-conscious sense of Western civilization.[34] For all these reasons, the ship is the first of the novel chronotopes presupposed by my attempts to rethink modernity via the history of the black Atlantic and the African diaspora into the Western hemisphere.

In the venturesome spirit proposed by James Clifford in his influential work on traveling culture,[35] I want to consider the impact that this outernational, transcultural reconceptualization might have on the political and cultural history of black Americans and that of blacks in Europe. In recent history this will certainly mean reevaluating Garvey and Garveyism, pan-Africanism, and Black Power as hemispheric if not global phenomena. In periodizing modern black politics it will require fresh thinking about the importance of Haiti and its revolution for the development of African-American political thought and movements of resistance. From the European side it will no doubt be necessary to reconsider Frederick Douglass's relationship to English and Scottish radicalisms and to meditate on the significance of William Wells Brown's five years in Europe as a fugitive slave, on Alexander Crummell's living and studying in Cambridge, and upon Martin Delany's experiences at the London congress of the International Statistical Congress in 1860.[36] It will require comprehension of such difficult and complex questions as W. E. B. Du Bois's childhood interest in Bismarck, his investment in modeling his dress and moustache on that of Kaiser Wilhelm II, his likely thoughts while sitting in Heinrich Von Treitschke's seminars,[37] and the use his tragic heroes make of European culture.

Notable black American travelers, from the poet Phyllis Wheatley onwards, went to Europe and had their perceptions of America and racial domination shifted as a result of their experiences there. This had important consequences for their understanding of racial identities. The radical journalist and political organizer Ida B. Wells is typical, describing her productive times in England as like "being born again in a new condition."[38] Lucy Parsons is a more problematic figure in the political history of black America,[39] but how might her encounters with William Morris, Annie Besant, and Peter Kropotkin impact upon a rewriting of the history of English radicalism? What of Nella Larsen's relationship to Denmark, where George Padmore was held in jail during the early 1930s and which was also the home base of his banned paper the *Negro Worker*, circulated across the world by its supporters in the Colonial Seamen's Association?[40] What of Sarah Parker Remond's work as a medical practitioner in Italy and the life of Edmonia Lewis, the sculptor, who made her home in Rome?[41] What effects did living in Paris have upon Anna Cooper, Jessie Fauset, Gwendolyn Bennett,[42] and Lois Maillou Jones?

It would appear that there are large questions raised about the direction and character of black culture and art if we take the powerful effects of even temporary experiences of exile, relocation, and displacement into account. How, for example, was the course of the black vernacular art of jazz changed by what happened to Quincy Jones in Sweden and Donald Byrd in Paris? This is especially interesting because both men played powerful roles in the remaking of jazz as a popular form in the early 1970s. Byrd describes his sense of Europe's appeal as something that grew out of the view of Canada he developed as a young man growing up in Detroit:

> That's why Europe was so important to me. Living across the river from Canada as a kid, I used to go down and sit and look at Windsor, Ontario. Windsor represented Europe to me. That was the rest of the world that was foreign to me. So I always had a feeling for the foreign, the European thing, because Canada was right there. We used to go to Canada. For black people, you see, Canada was a place that treated you better than America, the North. For my father Detroit was better than the South, to me born in the North, Canada was better. At least that was what I thought. Later on I found out otherwise, but anyway, Canada represented for me something foreign, exotic, that was not the United States.[43]

Richard Wright's life in exile . . . has been written off as a betrayal of his authenticity and as a process of seduction by philosophical traditions supposedly outside his narrow ethnic compass,[44] . . . an exemplary instance of how the politics of location and the politics of identity get inscribed in analyses of black culture. [. . .] They are all potential candidates for inclusion in the latest African-American cultural canon, a canon that is conditional on and possibly required by the academic packaging of black cultural studies.[45] [. . .] Du Bois's travel experiences raise in the sharpest possible form a question common to the lives of almost all these figures who begin as African Americans or Caribbean people and are then changed into something else

which evades those specific labels and with them all fixed notions of nationality and national identity. Whether their experience of exile is enforced or chosen, temporary or permanent, these intellectuals and activists, writers, speakers, poets, and artists repeatedly articulate a desire to escape the restrictive bonds of ethnicity, national identification, and sometimes even "race" itself. Some speak, like Wells and Wright, in terms of the rebirth that Europe offered them. Whether they dissolved their African-American sensibility into an explicitly pan-Africanist discourse or political commitment, their relationship to the land of their birth and their ethnic political constituency was absolutely transformed. The specificity of the modern political and cultural formation I want to call the black Atlantic can be defined, on one level, through this desire to transcend both the structures of the nation-state and the constraints of ethnicity and national particularity. These desires are relevant to understanding political organizing and cultural criticism. They have always sat uneasily alongside the strategic choices forced on black movements and individuals embedded in national political cultures and nation-states in America, the Caribbean, and Europe.
[. . .]

Black Politics and Modernity

[. . .] The problem of weighing the claims of national identity against other contrasting varieties of subjectivity and identification has a special place in the intellectual history of blacks in the West. Du Bois's concept of double consciousness [. . .] is only the best-known resolution of a familiar problem which points towards the core dynamic of racial oppression as well as the fundamental antinomy of diaspora blacks. How has this doubleness, what Richard Wright calls the dreadful objectivity[46] which follows from being both inside and outside the West, affected the conduct of political movements against racial oppression and towards black autonomy? Are the inescapable pluralities involved in the movements of black peoples, in Africa and in exile, ever to be synchronized? How would these struggles be periodized in relation to modernity: the fatal intermediation of capitalism, industrialization, and a new conception of political democracy? Does posing these questions in this way signify anything more than the reluctant intellectual affiliation of diaspora blacks to an approach which mistakenly attempts a premature totalization of infinite struggles, an approach which itself has deep and problematic roots within the ambiguous intellectual traditions of the European Enlightenment which have, at different moments, been both a lifeline and a fetter?

[Martin] Delany's work has provided some powerful evidence to show that the intellectual heritage of Euro-American modernity determined and possibly still determines the manner in which nationality is understood within black political discourse. In particular, this legacy conditions the continuing aspiration to acquire a supposedly authentic, natural, and stable "rooted" identity. This invariant identity is in turn the premise of a thinking "racial" self that is both socialized and unified by its connection with other kindred souls encountered usually, though not always, within the fortified frontiers of those discrete ethnic cultures which also happen to coincide with the contours of a sovereign nation-state that guarantees their continuity.

Consider for a moment the looseness with which the term "black nationalism" is used both by its advocates and by skeptics. Why is a more refined political language for dealing with these crucial issues of identity, kinship, generation, affect, and affiliation such a long time coming? A small but telling example can be drawn from the case of Edouard Glissant, who has contributed so much to the emergence of a creole counter-discourse that can answer the alchemy of nationalisms. Discussion of these problems suffers when his translator excises Glissant's references to the work of Deleuze and Guattari from the English edition of his 1981 book *Le Discours antillais,*[47] presumably because to acknowledge this exchange would somehow violate the aura of Caribbean authenticity that is a desirable frame around the work. This typical refusal to accept the complicity and syncretic interdependency of black and white thinkers has recently become associated with a second difficulty: the overintegrated conceptions of pure and homogeneous culture which mean that black political struggles are construed as somehow automatically *expressive* of the national or ethnic differences with which they are associated.

This overintegrated sense of cultural and ethnic particularity is very popular today, and blacks do not monopolize it. It masks the arbitrariness of its own political choices in the morally charged language of ethnic absolutism and this poses additional dangers because it overlooks the development and change of black political ideologies and ignores the restless, recombinant qualities of the black Atlantic's affirmative political cultures. The political project forged by thinkers like Delany in the difficult journey from slave ship to citizenship is in danger of being wrecked by the seemingly insoluble conflict between two distinct but currently symbiotic perspectives. They can be loosely identified as the essentialist and the pluralist standpoints, though they are in fact two different varieties of essentialism: one ontological, the other strategic. The antagonistic relationship between these two outlooks has been especially intense in discussions of black art and cultural criticism. The ontological essentialist view has often been characterized by a brute pan-Africanism. It has proved unable to specify precisely where the highly prized but doggedly evasive essence of black artistic and political sensibility is currently located, but that is no obstacle to its popular circulation.

This perspective sees the black intellectual and artist as a leader. Where it pronounces on cultural matters, it is often allied to a realist approach to aesthetic value that minimizes the substantive political and philosophical issues involved in the processes of artistic representation. Its absolutist conception of ethnic cultures can be identified by the way in which it registers uncomprehending disappointment with the actual cultural choices and patterns of the mass of black people. It has little to say about the profane, contaminated world of black popular culture and looks instead for an artistic practice that can disabuse the mass of black people of the illusions into which they have been seduced by their condition of exile and unthinking consumption of inappropriate cultural objects like the wrong hair-care products, pop music, and Western clothing. The community is felt to be on the wrong road, and it is the intellectual's job to give them a new direction, firstly by recovering and then by donating the racial awareness that the masses seem to lack.

This perspective currently confronts a pluralistic position which affirms blackness as an open signifier and seeks to celebrate complex representations of a black particularity that is *internally* divided: by class, sexuality, gender, age, ethnicity, economics, and political consciousness. There is no unitary idea of black community here, and the authoritarian tendencies of those who would police black cultural expression in the name of their own particular history or priorities are rightly repudiated. The ontologically grounded essentialism is replaced by a libertarian, strategic alternative: the cultural saturnalia which attends the end of innocent notions of the essential black subject.[48] Here, the polyphonic qualities of black cultural expression form the main aesthetic consideration and there is often an uneasy but exhilarating fusion of modernist and populist techniques and styles. From this perspective, the achievements of popular black cultural forms like music are a constant source of inspiration. They are prized for their implicit warning against the pitfalls of artistic conceit. The difficulty with this second tendency is that in leaving racial essentialism behind by viewing "race" itself as a social and cultural construction, it has been insufficiently alive to the lingering power of specifically racialized forms of power and subordination.

Each outlook compensates for the obvious weaknesses in the other camp, but so far there has been little open and explicit debate between them. Their conflict, initially formulated in debates over black aesthetics and cultural production,[49] is valuable as a preliminary guide to some of the dilemmas faced by cultural and intellectual *historians* of the modern, Western, African diaspora. The problems it raises become acute, particularly for those who seek to comprehend cultural developments and political resistances which have had scant regard for either modern borders or premodern frontiers. At its worst, the lazy, casual invocation of cultural insiderism which frequently characterizes the ontological essentialist view is nothing more than a symptom of the growing cleavages *within* the black communities. There, uneasy spokespeople of the black elite – some of them professional cultural commentators, artists, writers, painters, and filmmakers as well as political leaders – have fabricated a volkish outlook as an expression of their own contradictory position. This neonationalism seems out of tune with the spirit of the novel Africentric garb in which it appears before us today. It incorporates commentary on the special needs and desires of the relatively privileged castes within black communities, but its most consistent trademark is the persistent mystification of that group's increasingly problematic relationships with the black poor, who, after all, supply the elite with a dubious entitlement to speak on behalf of the phantom constituency of black people in general. The idea of blacks as a national or protonational group with its own hermetically enclosed culture plays a key role in this mystification, and, though seldom overtly named, the misplaced idea of a national interest gets invoked as a means to silence dissent and censor political debate when the incoherences and inconsistencies of Africalogical discourse are put on display.

These problems take on a specific aspect in Britain, which currently lacks anything that can be credibly called a black bourgeoisie. However, they are not confined to this country and they cannot be overlooked. The idea of nationality and the assumptions of cultural absolutism come together in other ways.[50] It should be emphasised that, where the archeology of black critical knowledges enters the academy, it currently involves the construction of canons which seems to be proceeding on an exclusively *national* basis – African American, Anglophone Caribbean, and so on. This is not an oblique plea for the legitimacy of an equally distinctive black English or British cultural inventory. If it seems indelicate to ask who the formation of such canons might serve, then the related question of where the impulse to formalize and codify elements of our cultural heritage in this particular pattern comes from may be a better one to pursue. Is this impulse towards cultural protectionism the most cruel trick which the West can play upon its dissident affiliates? The same problem of the status enjoyed by national boundaries in the writing of cultural history is evident in recent debates over hip hop culture, the powerful expressive medium of America's urban black poor which has created a global youth movement of considerable significance. The musical components of hip hop are a hybrid form nurtured by the social relations of the South Bronx where Jamaican sound-system culture was transplanted during the 1970s and put down new roots. In conjunction with specific technological innovations, this routed and rerooted Caribbean culture set in train a process that was to transform black America's sense of itself and a large portion of the popular music industry as well. Here we have to ask how a form which flaunts and glories in its own malleability as well as its transnational character becomes interpreted as an expression of some authentic

African-American essence? How can rap be discussed as if it sprang intact from the entrails of the blues?[51] Another way of approaching this would be to ask what is it about black America's writing elite which means that they need to claim this diasporic cultural form in such an assertively nationalist way?[52]

An additional, and possibly more profound, area of political difficulty comes into view when the voguish language of absolute cultural difference associated with the ontological essentialist standpoint provides an embarrassing link between the practice of blacks who comprehend racial politics through it and the activities of their foresworn opponents – the ethnic absolutists of the racist right – who approach the complex dynamics of race, nationality, and ethnicity through a similar set of pseudo-precise, culturalist equations. This unlikely convergence is part of the history of hip hop because black music is so often the principal symbol of racial authenticity. Analyzing it leads rapidly and directly back to the status of nationality and national cultures in a postmodern world where nation-states are being eclipsed by a new economy of power that accords national citizenship and national boundaries a new significance. In seeking to account for the controversy over hip hop's origins we also have to explore how the absolutist and exclusivist approach to the relationship between "race," ethnicity, and culture places those who claim to be able to resolve the relationship between the supposedly incommensurable discourses characteristic of different racial groups, in command of the cultural resources of their own group as a whole. Intellectuals can claim this vanguard position by virtue of an ability to translate from one culture to another, mediating decisive oppositions along the way. It matters little whether the black communities involved are conceived as entire and self-sustaining nations or as protonational collectivities.

No less than their predecessor Martin Delany, today's black intellectuals have persistently succumbed to the lure of those romantic conceptions of "race," "people," and "nation" which place themselves, rather than the people they supposedly represent, in charge of the strategies for nation building, state formation, and racial uplift. This point underscores the fact that the status of nationality and the precise weight we should attach to the conspicuous differences of language, culture, and identity which divide the blacks of the diaspora from one another, let alone from Africans, are unresolved within the political culture that promises to bring the disparate peoples of the black Atlantic world together one day. Furthermore, the dependence of those black intellectuals who have tried to deal with these matters on theoretical reflections derived from the canon of occidental modernity – from Herder to Von Trietschke and beyond – is surely salient. W. E. B. Du Bois's work will be explored below as a site of this affiliation. The case of his 1888 Fisk graduation address on Bismarck provides a preliminary example. Reflecting on it some years later in *Dusk of Dawn* he wrote: "Bismarck was my hero. He made a nation out of a mass of bickering peoples. He had dominated the whole development with his strength until he crowned an emperor at Versailles. This foreshadowed in my mind the kind of thing that American Negroes must do, marching forward with strength and determination under trained leadership."[53] This model of national development has a special appeal to the bickering peoples of the black Atlantic diaspora. It is an integral component of their responses to modern racism and directly inspired their efforts to construct nation-states on African soil and elsewhere. The idea of nationality occupies a central, if shifting place in the work of Alexander Crummell, Edward Blyden, Martin Delany, and Frederick Douglass. This important group of post-Enlightenment men, whose lives and political sensibilities can ironically be defined through the persistent crisscrossing of national boundaries, often seems to share the decidedly Hegelian belief that the combination of Christianity and a nation-state represents the overcoming of all antinomies.

The themes of nationality, exile, and cultural affiliation accentuate the inescapable fragmentation and differentiation of the black subject. This fragmentation has recently been compounded further by the questions of gender, sexuality, and male domination which have been made unavoidable by the struggles of black women and the voices of black gay men and lesbians. I cannot attempt to resolve these tensions here, but the dimension of social and political differentiation to which they refer provides a frame for what follows. As indices of differentiation they are especially important because the intracommunal antagonisms which appear between the local and immediate levels of our struggles and their hemispheric and global dynamics can only grow. Black voices from within the overdeveloped countries may be able to go on resonating in harmony with those produced from inside Africa or they may, with varying degrees of reluctance, turn away from the global project of black advancement once the symbolic and political, if not the material and economic, liberation of Southern Africa is completed.

[. . .] The history and significance of these musics are consistently overlooked by black writers for two reasons: because they exceed the frameworks of national or ethnocentric analysis with which we have been too easily satisfied, and because talking seriously about the politics and aesthetics of black vernacular cultures demands an embarrassing confrontation with substantive intraracial differences that make the easy essentialism from which most critical judgments are constructed simply untenable. As these internal divisions have grown, the price of that embarrassment has been an aching silence.

To break that silence, I want to argue that black musical expression has played a role in reproducing what Zygmunt Bauman has called a distinctive counterculture of modernity.[54] I will use a brief consideration of black musical development to move beyond an understanding of cultural processes which, as I have already suggested, is currently torn between seeing them either as the expression of an essential, unchanging, sovereign racial self or as the effluent from a constituted subjectivity that emerges contingently from the endless play of racial signification. This is usually conceived solely in terms of the inappropriate model which *textuality* provides. The vitality and complexity of this musical culture offers a means to get beyond the related oppositions between essentialists and pseudo-pluralists on the one hand and between totalizing conceptions of tradition, modernity, and postmodernity on the other. It also provides a model of performance which can supplement and partially displace concern with textuality.

Black music's obstinate and consistent commitment to the idea of a better future is a puzzle to which the enforced separation of slaves from literacy and their compensatory refinement of musical art supplies less than half an answer. The power of music in developing black struggles by communicating information, organizing consciousness, and testing out or deploying the forms of subjectivity which are required by political agency, whether individual or collective, defensive or transformational, demands attention to both the formal attributes of this expressive culture and its distinctive *moral* basis. The formal qualities of this music are becoming better known,[55] and I want to concentrate instead on the moral aspects and in particular on the disjunction between the ethical value of the music and its status as an ethnic sign.

In the simplest possible terms, by posing the world as it is against the world as the racially subordinated would like it to be, this musical culture supplies a great deal of the courage required to go on living in the present. It is both produced by and expressive of that "transvaluation of all values" precipitated by the history of racial terror in the new world. It contains a theodicy but moves beyond it, because the profane dimensions of that racial terror made theodicy impossible.[56] I have considered its distinctive critique of capitalist social relations elsewhere.[57] Here, because I want to show that its critical edge includes but also surpasses anti-capitalism, it is necessary to draw out some of the inner philosophical dynamics of this counterculture and to explore the connection between its normative character and its utopian aspirations. These are interrelated and even inseparable from each other and from the critique of racial capitalism[58] that these expressive cultures construct but also surpass. Comprehending them necessitates an analysis of the lyrical content and the forms of musical expression as well as the often hidden social relations in which these deeply encoded oppositional practices are created and consumed. The issue of normative content focuses attention on what might be called the politics of fulfillment:[59] the notion that a future society will be able to realize the social and political promise that present society has left unaccomplished. Reflecting the foundational semantic position of the Bible, this is a discursive mode of communication. Though by no means literal, it can be grasped through what is said, shouted, screamed, or sung. The politics of fulfillment practiced by the descendants of slaves demands, as Delany did, that bourgeois civil society live up to the promises of its own rhetoric. It creates a medium in which demands for goals like non-racialized justice and rational organization of the productive processes can be expressed. It is immanent within modernity and is no less a valuable element of modernity's counter-discourse for being consistently ignored.

The issue of how utopias are conceived is more complex, not least because they strive continually to move beyond the grasp of the merely linguistic, textual, and discursive. The invocation of utopia references what, following Seyla Benhabib's suggestive lead, I propose to call the politics of transfiguration. This emphasizes the emergence of qualitatively new desires, social relations, and modes of association within the racial community of interpretation and resistance *and* between that group and its erstwhile oppressors. It points specifically to the formation of a community of needs and solidarity which is magically made audible in the music itself and palpable in the social relations of its cultural utility and reproduction. Created under the very nose of the overseers, the utopian desires which fuel the complementary politics of transfiguration must be invoked by other, more deliberately opaque means. This politics exists on a lower frequency where it is played, danced, and acted, as well as sung and sung about, because words, even words stretched by melisma and supplemented or mutated by the screams which still index the conspicuous power of the slave sublime, will never be enough to communicate its unsayable claims to truth. The wilfully damaged signs which betray the resolutely utopian politics of transfiguration therefore partially transcend modernity, constructing both an imaginary anti-modern past and a postmodern yet-to-come. This is not a counter-discourse but a counterculture that defiantly reconstructs its own critical, intellectual, and moral genealogy in a partially hidden public sphere of its own. The politics of transfiguration therefore reveals the hidden internal fissures in the concept of modernity. The bounds of politics are extended precisely because this tradition of expression refuses to accept that the political is a readily separable domain. Its basic desire is to conjure up and enact the new modes of friendship, happiness, and solidarity that are consequent on the overcoming of the racial oppression on which modernity and its antinomy of rational, Western progress as excessive barbarity relied. Thus the vernacular arts of the children of slaves give rise to a verdict on the role of art which is strikingly in harmony with Adorno's reflections on the dynamics of European artistic expression in the wake of Auschwitz: "Art's Utopia, the counterfactual yet-

to-come, is draped in black. It goes on being a recollection of the possible
with a critical edge against the real; it is a kind of imaginary restitution of
that catastrophe, which is world history; it is a freedom which did not pass
under the spell of necessity and which may well not come to pass ever at
all."[60] These sibling dimensions of black sensibility, the politics of fulfillment
and the politics of transfiguration, are not coextensive. There are significant
tensions between them, but they are closely associated in the vernacular cultures of the black Atlantic diaspora. [. . .] The politics of fulfillment is mostly
content to play occidental rationality at its own game. It necessitates a
hermeneutic orientation that can assimilate the semiotic, verbal, and textual.
The politics of transfiguration strives in pursuit of the sublime, struggling to
repeat the unrepeatable, to present the unpresentable. Its rather different
hermeneutic focus pushes towards the mimetic, dramatic, and performative.

It seems especially significant that the cultural expressions which these
musics allow us to map out do not seek to exclude problems of inequality
or to make the achievement of racial justice an exclusively abstract matter.
Their grounded ethics offers, among other things, a continuous commentary on the systematic and pervasive relations of domination that supply its
conditions of existence. Their grounded aesthetics is never separated off into
an autonomous realm where familiar political rules cannot be applied and
where, as Salman Rushdie memorably puts it, "the little room of literature"[61]
can continue to enjoy its special privileges as a heroic resource for the well-
heeled adversaries of liberal capitalism.

I am proposing, then, that we reread and rethink this expressive counterculture not simply as a succession of literary tropes and genres, but as a philosophical discourse which refuses the modern, occidental separation of ethics
and aesthetics, culture and politics. The traditional teaching of ethics and
politics – practical philosophy – came to an end some time ago, even if its
death agonies were prolonged. This tradition had maintained the idea that a
good life for the individual and the problem of the best social and political
order for the collectivity could be discerned by rational means. Though it is
seldom acknowledged even now, this tradition lost its exclusive claim to
rationality partly through the way that slavery became internal to Western
civilization and through the obvious complicity which both plantation slavery
and colonial regimes revealed between rationality and the practice of racial
terror. Not perceiving its residual condition, blacks in the West eavesdropped
on and then took over a fundamental question from the intellectual obses-
sions of their enlightened rulers. Their progress from the status of slaves to
the status of citizens led them to inquire into what the best possible forms of
social and political existence might be. The memory of slavery, actively preserved as a living intellectual resource in their expressive political culture,
helped them to generate a new set of answers to this inquiry. They had to

fight – often through their spirituality – to hold on to the unity of ethics and politics sundered from each other by modernity's insistence that the true, the good, and the beautiful had distinct origins and belong to different domains of knowledge. First slavery itself and then their memory of it induced many of them to query the foundational moves of modern philosophy and social thought, whether they came from the natural rights theorists who sought to distinguish between the spheres of morality and legality, the idealists who wanted to emancipate politics from morals so that it could become a sphere of strategic action, or the political economists of the bourgeoisie who first formulated the separation of economic activity from both ethics and politics. The brutal excesses of the slave plantation supplied a set of moral and political responses to each of these attempts. [. . .] This subculture often appears to be the intuitive expression of some racial essence but is in fact an elementary historical acquisition produced from the viscera of an alternative body of cultural and political expression that considers the world critically from the point of view of its emancipatory transformation. In the future it will become a place which is capable of satisfying the (redefined) needs of human beings that will emerge once the violence – epistemic and concrete – of racial typology is at an end. Reason is thus reunited with the happiness and freedom of individuals and the reign of justice within the collectivity.

I have already implied that there is a degree of convergence here with other projects towards a critical theory of society, particularly Marxism. However, where lived crisis and systemic crisis come together, Marxism allocates priority to the latter while the memory of slavery insists on the priority of the former. Their convergence is also undercut by the simple fact that in the critical thought of blacks in the West, social self-creation through labor is not the center-piece of emancipatory hopes. For the descendants of slaves, work signifies only servitude, misery, and subordination. Artistic expression, expanded beyond recognition from the grudging gifts offered by the masters as a token substitute for freedom from bondage, therefore becomes the means towards both individual self-fashioning and communal liberation. Poiesis and poetics begin to coexist in novel forms – autobiographical writing, special and uniquely creative ways of manipulating spoken language, and, above all, the music. All three have overflowed from the containers that the modern nation-state provides for them.

Notes

1   Werner Sollors, *Beyond Ethnicity* (New York and Oxford: Oxford University Press, 1986).
     [. . .]

2   The concept of racialization is developed by Frantz Fanon in his essay "On National Culture" in *The Wretched of the Earth* (Harmondsworth: Penguin Books, 1967), pp. 170–1. See also Robert Miles, *Racism* (New York and London: Routledge, 1989), pp. 73–7.

3   Mary Louise Pratt, *Imperial Eyes* (London and New York: Routledge, 1992).

4   Nancy Stepan, *The Idea of Race in Science: Great Britain, 1800–1960* (Basingstoke: Macmillan, 1982); Michael Banton, *Racial Theories* (Cambridge: Cambridge University Press, 1987).

5   George Mosse, *Nationalism and Sexuality: Middle-Class Morality and Sexual Norms in Modern Europe* (Madison and London: University of Wisconsin Press, 1985). Reinhold Grimm and Jost Hermand, eds., *Blacks and German Culture* (Madison and London: University of Wisconsin Press, 1986).

6   Sander Gilman, *On Blackness Without Blacks* (Boston, MA: G. K. Hall, 1982).

7   See Henry Louis Gates, Jr., "The History and Theory of Afro-American Literary Criticism, 1773–1831: The Arts, Aesthetic Theory and the Nature of the African" (doctoral thesis, Clare College, Cambridge University, 1978); David Brion Davis, *The Problem of Slavery in Western Culture* (Ithaca, NY: Cornell University Press, 1970) and *The Problem of Slavery in the Age of Revolution* (Ithaca, NY: Cornell University Press, 1975); and Eva Beatrice Dykes, *The Negro in English Romantic Thought; or A Study of Sympathy for the Oppressed* (Washington, DC: Associated Publishers, 1942).

8   Leon Poliakov, *The Aryan Myth* (London: Sussex University Press, 1974), ch. 8, and "Racism from the Enlightenment to the Age of Imperialism," in Robert Ross, ed., *Racism and Colonialism: Essays on Ideology and Social Structure* (The Hague: Martinus Nijhoff, 1982); Richard Popkin, "The Philosophical Basis of Eighteenth Century Racism," in *Studies in Eighteenth Century Culture*, vol. 3: *Racism in the Eighteenth Century* (Cleveland and London: Case Western Reserve University Press, 1973); Harry Bracken, "Philosophy and Racism," *Philosophia* 8, nos. 2–3, November 1978. In some respects this pioneering work foreshadows the debates about Heidegger's fascism.

9   Hugh Honour's contribution to the DeMenil Foundation Project, *The Representation of the Black in Western Art* (London and Cambridge, MA: Harvard University Press, 1989), is a welcome exception to this amnesia.

10 W. Pietz, "The Problem of the Fetish, I," *Res* 9 (spring 1985).

11 Robin Blackburn, *The Overthrow of Colonial Slavery, 1776–1848* (London and New York: Verso, 1988).

12 Winthrop D. Jordan, *White over Black* (New York: W. W. Norton, 1977).

13 Edmund Burke, *A Philosophical Enquiry into the Origin of Our Ideas of the Sublime and the Beautiful,* ed. James T. Boulton (Oxford: Blackwell, 1987).

14 Catherine Hall, *White, Male and Middle Class* (Cambridge: Polity Press, 1992).

15 Jenny Sharpe, "The Unspeakable Limits of Rape: Colonial Violence and Counter-Insurgency," *Genders,* no. 10 (spring 1991): 25–46, and "Figures of Colonial Resistance," *Modern Fiction Studies* 35, no. 1 (spring 1989).

16 Peter Linebaugh, "All the Atlantic Mountains Shook," *Labour/Le Travailleur* 10 (autumn 1982): 87–121.

17 Peter Fryer, *Staying Power* (London: Pluto Press, 1980), p. 219.

18   *The Horrors of Slavery and Other Writings by Robert Wedderburn,* ed. Iain McCalman (Edinburgh: Edinburgh University Press, 1992).

19   Iain McCalman, "Anti-Slavery and Ultra Radicalism in Early Nineteenth-Century England: The Case of Robert Wedderburn," *Slavery and Abolition* 7 (1986).

20   Fryer, *Staying Power,* p. 216. Public Records Office, London: PRO Ho 44/5/202, PRO Ho 42/199.

21   Their article "The Many Headed Hydra," *Journal of Historical Sociology* 3, no. 3 (September 1990): 225–53, gives a foretaste of these arguments.

22   John Adams quoted by Linebaugh in "Atlantic Mountains," p. 112.

23   Alfred N. Hunt, *Haiti's Influence on Antebellum America* (Baton Rouge and London: Louisiana State University Press, 1988), p. 119.

24   Douglass's own account of this is best set out in Frederick Douglass, *Life and Times of Frederick Douglass* (New York: Macmillan, 1962), p. 199. See also Philip M. Hammmer, "Great Britain, the United States and the Negro Seamen's Acts" and "British Consuls and the Negro Seamen's Acts, 1850–1860," *Journal of Southern History* 1 (1935): 3–28, 138–68. Introduced after Denmark Vesey's rebellion, these interesting pieces of legislation required free black sailors to be jailed while their ships were in dock as a way of minimizing the political contagion their presence in the ports was bound to transmit.

25   Linebaugh, "Atlantic Mountains," p. 119.

26   Paul Gilroy, "Art of Darkness, Black Art and the Problem of Belonging to England," *Third Text* 10 (1990). A very different interpretation of Turner's painting is given in Albert Boime's *The Art of Exclusion: Representing Blacks in the Nineteenth Century* (London: Thames and Hudson, 1990).

27   Patrick Wright, *On Living in an Old Country* (London: Verso, 1985).

28   Bernard Semmel, *Jamaican Blood and the Victorian Conscience* (Westport, CT: Greenwood Press, 1976). See also Gillian Workman, "Thomas Carlyle and the Governor Eyre Controversy," *Victorian Studies* 18, no. 1 (1974): 77–102.

29   Vol. 1, sec. 5, ch. 3, sec. 39. W. E. B. Du Bois reprinted this commentary while he was editor of *The Crisis*; see vol. 15 (1918): 239.

30   Eric Hobsbawm, "The Historians' Group of the Communist Party," in M. Cornforth, ed., *Essays in Honour of A. L. Morton* (Atlantic Highlands, NJ: Humanities Press, 1979).

31   Linebaugh, "Atlantic Mountains." This is also the strategy pursued by Marcus Rediker in his brilliant book *Between the Devil and the Deep Blue Sea* (Cambridge: Cambridge University Press, 1987).

32   "A space exists when one takes into consideration vectors of direction, velocities, and time variables. Thus space is composed of intersections of mobile elements. It is in a sense articulated by the ensemble of movements deployed within it." Michel de Certeau, *The Practice of Everyday Life* (Berkeley and London: University of California Press, 1984), p. 117.

33   See Michael Cohn and Michael K. Platzer, *Black Men of the Sea* (New York: Dodd, Mead, 1978). I have been heavily reliant on George Francis Dow's anthology *Slave Ships and Slaving,* publication no. 15 of the Marine Research Society (1927; rpt. Cambridge, MD: Cornell Maritime Press, 1968), which

includes extracts from valuable eighteenth and nineteenth-century material. On England, I have found the anonymously published study *Liverpool and Slavery* (Liverpool: A. Bowker and Sons, 1884) to be very valuable. Memoirs produced by black sea captains also point to a number of new intercultural and transcultural research problems. Captain Harry Dean's *The Pedro Gorino: The Adventures of a Negro Sea Captain in Africa and on the Seven Seas in His attempts to Found an Ethiopian Empire* (Boston and New York: Houghton Mifflin, 1929) contains interesting material on the practical politics of pan-Africanism that go unrecorded elsewhere. Captain Hugh Mulzac's autobiography, *A Star to Steer By* (New York: International Publishers, 1963), includes valuable observations on the role of ships in the Garvey movement. Some pointers towards what a black Atlantic rereading of the history of Rastafari might involve are to be found in Robert A. Hill's important essay which accentuates complex post-slavery relations between Jamaica and Africa: "Dread History: Leonard P. Howell and Millenarian Visions in Early Rastafari Religions in Jamaica," *Epoché: Journal of the History of Religions at UCLA* 9 (1981): 30–71.

34   Stephen Greenblatt, *Marvellous Possessions* (Oxford: Oxford University Press, 1992). See also Pratt, *Imperial Eyes.*

35   James T. Clifford, "Travelling Cultures," in *Cultural Studies,* ed. Lawrence Grossberg et al. (New York and London: Routledge, 1992), and "Notes on Theory and Travel," *Inscriptions* 5 (1989).

36   *Manchester Weekly Advertiser*, July 21, 1860; *Punch*, July 28, 1860; *Morning Star*, July 18, 1860; and F. A. Rollin, *Life and Public Services of Martin R. Delany* (Boston, MA: Lee and Shepard, 1868), p. 102.

37   Peter Winzen, "Treitschke's Influence on the Rise of Imperialist and Anti-British Nationalism in Germany," in P. Kennedy and A. Nicholls, eds., *Nationalist and Racialist Movements in Britain and Germany before 1914* (Basingstoke: Macmillan, 1981).

38   Ida B. Wells quoted in Vron Ware, *Beyond the Pale: White Women, Racism, and History* (London and New York: Verso, 1992), p. 177.

39   Carolyn Ashbaugh, *Lucy Parsons: American Revolutionary* (Chicago, IL: Charles H. Kerr, 1976). I must thank Tommy Lott for this reference.

40   Frank Hooker, *Black Revolutionary: George Padmore's Path from Communism to Pan-Africanism* (London: Pall Mall Library of African Affairs, 1967).

41   William S. McFeely, *Frederick Douglass* (New York: W. W. Norton, 1991), p. 329.

42   Michel Fabre, *Black American Writers in France, 1840–1980* (Urbana and Chicago: University of Illinois Press, 1991).

43   Ursula Broschke Davis, *Paris without Regret* (Iowa City: University of Iowa Press, 1986), p. 102.

44   I challenge this view in chapter 5. [*Editors' note*: Gilroy refers to chapter 5 of *The Black Atlantic.*]

45   Some of the problems associated with this strategy have been discussed by Cornel West in "Minority Discourse and the Pitfalls of Canon Formation," *Yale Journal of Criticism* 1, no. 1 (fall 1987): 193–201.
[. . .]

46 This phrase is taken from Wright's novel *The Outsider* (New York: Harper and Row, 1953), p. 129. In his book of essays, *White Man Listen!* (Garden City, NY: Anchor Books, 1964), he employs the phrase "dual existence" to map the same terrain. See chapter 5 below. [*Editors' note*: Gilroy refers to chapter 5 of *The Black Atlantic.*]

47 Edouard Glissant, *Le Discours antillais* (Paris: Editions du Seuil, 1981).

48 Stuart Hall, "New Ethnicities," in K. Mercer, ed., *Black Film: British Cinema* (London: ICA Documents 7, 1988), p. 28.

49 See *Ten.8* 2, no. 3 (1992), issue entitled *The Critical Decade*.

50 Etienne Balibar and Immanuel Wallerstein, *Race, Nation, Class* (London and New York: Verso, 1991).

51 Nelson George, *The Death of Rhythm and Blues* (London: Omnibus, 1988).

52 I should emphasize that it is the assimilation of these cultural forms to an unthinking notion of nationality which is the object of my critique here. Of course, certain cultural forms become articulated with sets of social and political forces over long periods of time. These forms may be played with and lived with as though they were natural emblems of racial and ethnic particularity. This may even be an essential defensive attribute of the interpretive communities involved. However, the notion of nationality cannot be borrowed as a ready-made means to make sense of the special dynamics of this process.

53 W. E. B. Du Bois, *Dusk of Dawn*, in *Dubois Writings* (New York: Library of America, 1986), p. 577.

54 Zygmunt Bauman, "The Left as the Counterculture of Modernity," *Telos* 70 (winter 1986–7): 81–93.

55 Anthony Jackson's dazzling exposition of James Jamerson's bass style is, in my view, indicative of the type of detailed critical work which needs to be done on the form and dynamics of black musical creativity. His remarks on Jamerson's use of harmonic and rhythmic ambiguity and selective employment of dissonance were especially helpful. To say that the book from which it is taken has been geared to the needs of the performing musician rather than the cultural historian is to indict the current state of cultural history rather than the work of Jackson and his collaborator Dr. Licks. See "An Appreciation of the Style," in Dr. Licks, ed., *Standing in the Shadows of Motown* (Detroit, MI: Hal Leonard, 1989).

56 I am thinking here both of Wright's tantalizing discussion of the Dozens in the essay on the "Literary Tradition of the Negro in the United States" in *White Man Listen!* and also of Levinas's remarks on useless suffering in another context: "useless and unjustifiable suffering [are] exposed and displayed . . . without any shadow of a consoling theodicy." See "Useless Suffering," in R. Bernasconi and D. Wood, eds., *The Provocation of Levinas* (London: Routledge, 1988). Jon Michael Spencer's thoughtful but fervently Christian discussion of what he calls the Theodicy of the Blues is also relevant here. See *The Theology of American Popular Music,* a special issue of *Black Sacred Music* 3, no. 2 (Durham, NC: Duke University Press, fall 1989). I do not have space to develop my critique of Spencer here.

57 *There Ain't No Black in the Union Jack: The Cultural Politics of Race and Nation* (London: Hutchinson, 1987), ch. 5.

58   Cedric Robinson, *Black Marxism* (London: Zed Press, 1982).
59   This concept and its pairing with the politics of transfiguration have been adapted from their deployment in Seyla Benhabib's inspiring book *Critique, Norm and Utopia* (New York: Columbia University Press, 1987).
60   T. W. Adorno, *Aesthetic Theory* (London: Routledge, 1984), p. 196.
61   Salman Rushdie, *Is Nothing Sacred?* The Herbert Read Memorial Lecture 1990 (Cambridge: Granta, 1990), p. 16.

Additional Readings on Modernity, Globalism, and Diaspora

Anthias, Flora. "Beyond Unities of Identity in High Modernity." *Identities: Global Studies in Culture and Power*. 6.1 (1999): 121–44.

Appadurai, Arjun. *Modernity at Large: Cultural Dimensions of Globalization*. Minneapolis: University of Minnesota Press, 1996.

Beyer, Peter. "The City and Beyond as Dialogue: Negotiating Religious Authenticity in Global Society." *Social Compass*. 45.1 (1998): 67–79.

Cochran, Terry. "The Emergence of Global Contemporaneity." *Diaspora*. 5.1 (1996): 119–40.

Cohen, Robin. *Global Diasporas: An Introduction*. Seattle: University of Washington Press, 1997.

Dirlik, Arif. "The Postcolonial Aura: Third World Criticism in the Age of Global Capitalism." *Critical Inquiry* 20.2 (1994): 328–56.

Gilroy, Paul. "It Ain't Where You're From, It's Where You're At: The Dialectics of Diasporic Identification." *Third Text* 13 (winter 1991): 3–16.

—— *The Black Atlantic: Modernity and Double Consciousness*. Cambridge, MA: Harvard University Press, 1993.

Green, Charles. *Globalization and Survival in the Black Diaspora: The New Urban Challenge*. Albany: State University of New York Press, 1997.

Grosfoguel, R. and Hector Cordero-Guzman. "International Migration in a Global Context: Recent Approaches to Migration Theory." *Diaspora* 7.3 (1998): 351–68.

Hanchard, Michael. "Identity, Meaning and the African-American." *Social Text* 24 (1990): 31–42.

—— "Racial Consciousness and Afro-Diasporic Experiences: Antonio Gramsci Reconsidered." *Socialism and Democracy* 3 (1991): 83–106.

—— "Afro-Modernity: Temporality, Politics and the African Diaspora." *Public Culture* 11.1 (1999): 245–68.

Harper, T. N. "Globalism and the Pursuit of Authenticity: The Making of a Diasporic Public Sphere in Singapore." *Sojourn: Journal of Social Issues in Southeast Asia* 12.2 (1997): 261–92.

Humphrey, Michael. "Globalization and Arab Diasporic Identities: The Australian Arab Case." *Bulletin of the Royal Institute for Inter Faith Studies* 2.1 (2000): 141–58.

Jain, Ravindra K. "Indian Diaspora, Globalization and Multiculturalism: A Cultural Analysis." *Contributions to Indian Sociology* 32.2 (1998): 337–60.

Jusdanis, Gregory. "Culture, Culture, Everywhere: The Swell of Globalization Theory." *Diaspora* 5.1 (1996): 141–61.

Kaiwar, Vasant and Sucheta Mazumdar, eds. *South Asia and the New Globalization.* Boulder, CO: Westview Press, in press.

Kearney, M. "The Local and the Global: The Anthropology of Globalization and Transnationalism." *Annual Review of Anthropology* 24 (1995): 547–65.

Lazarus, Neil. "Is Counterculture of Modernity a Theory of Modernity?" *Diaspora* 4.3 (1995): 323–39.

Muthyale, John. "Reworlding America: The Globalization of American Studies." *Cultural Critique* 47.1 (2001): 99–122.

Nelson, Diane M. "Maya Hackers and the Cyberspatialized Nation-State: Modernity, Ethnostalgia and a Lizard Queen in Guatemala." *Cultural Anthropology* 11.3 (1996): 287–308.

Nurse, Keith. "Globalization and Trinidad Carnival: Diaspora, Hybridity and Identity in Global Culture." *Cultural Studies* 13.4 (1999): 661–90.

Ong, Aihwa and Donald M. Nonini, eds. *Ungrounded Empires: The Cultural Politics of Modern Chinese Transnationalism.* New York: Routledge, 1997.

—— *Flexible Citizenship: The Cultural Logics of Transnationality.* Durham, NC: Duke University Press, 1999.

Sadowski-Smith, Claudia. "US Border Theory, Globalization, and Ethnonationalisms in Post-Wall Eastern Europe." *Diaspora* 8.1 (1999): 3–22.

Smith, Michael Pete. "Transnational Migration and the Globalization of Grassroots Movements." *Social Text* 39 (1994): 15–34.

Werbner, Pnina. "Global Pathways: Working Class Cosmopolitans and the Creation of Transnational Ethnic Worlds." *Social Anthropology* 7.1 (1999): 17–35.

Wong, Lloyd L. "Globalization and Transnational Migration: A Study of Recent Chinese Capitalist Migration from the Asian Pacific to Canada." *International Sociology* 12.3 (1997): 329–51.

Part II

Ethnicity, Identity, and Diaspora

3

Diaspora: Generation and the Ground of Jewish Identity

Daniel Boyarin and Jonathan Boyarin

In this essay Daniel Boyarin and Jonathan Boyarin explore the political implications of current theological and critical understandings of Jewish group identity. Exploring texts from the Letters of Paul to rabbinical Jewish texts and contemporary critical theory, the essay explores how to define Jewish identity by emphasizing generational rather than geographic links. In examining how the "Jew" has allegorically come to represent or to occupy the position of being that causes discord and disorder in the Christian polity, the authors ask whether it is possible to imagine kinship being organized around a shared spirit, rather than a shared ancestor.

De-emphasizing the importance of geography, the authors explore why it is important to articulate a Jewish political subject other than that offered by the Zionist vision. They argue against the idea that geography is the only source of connection for identity, suggesting instead that generational links offer alternative ways to construct more open and flexible versions of Jewish identity. Wary of Zionist state practices, or the belief that redemption is gained by securing land for a Jewish state, the authors suggest that diaspora, rather than the model of national self-determination, offers a vision of identity that might be utopic, but one that is also strong and free of persecution for all.

The essay concludes by presenting a version of Jewish identity that asks how memory, history, family, and practice might be more significant factors determining Jewish identity than the claim to be indigenous and/or to belong to certain spaces and land without denying the fundamentally important ways that people are connected to the land. Suggesting that diaspora offers important lessons for those interested in thinking about how cultures survive, they argue that mixing is itself not bad; in fact, intermixing enables certain cultural practices and ideas to persist. Arguing that the idea of diaspora, rather than the idea of monotheism, might be the single most important contribution of Judaism, Daniel and Jonathan Boyarin conclude that the Jewish diaspora offers a vision of a disaggregated identity. Because it is not a genealogical, religious, or nationally bounded set of practices, it can in fact survive and thrive in a diasporized setting.

> *In the field of rational analysis, a feeling of recognized kinship is more desirable than nationalism.*
>
> *Gayatri Chakravorty Spivak*[1]

Group identity has been constructed traditionally in two ways. It has been figured on the one hand as the product of a common genealogical origin and, on the other, as produced by a common geographical origin. The first has a strongly pejorative value in current writing – having become tainted with the name *race* and thus racism – while the second has a generally positive ring. One of the reasons for this split in values is undoubtedly the unfortunate usages to which the term and concept of race in the sense of genotype has been put in Europe since early modern times.[2] Another source, however, of our cultural disdain for genealogy as a value is undoubtedly the sustained attack on it that lies at the fountainhead of Christendom, the Letters of Paul. In this essay we would like to interrogate the Pauline sources of Western discourse about generation, space, and identity, along with the rabbinic Jewish counter-discourse around these terms. We will trace this fault line into the present as well, confronting claims of "pure theory" with our own discourses of critically grounded identity, speaking about paradoxes of individual and collective identity with reference to Jean-François Lyotard, Jean-Luc Nancy, and Walter Benn Michaels.

I

פּאָולוט איז געווען רער ערשטער קאָלשעוויק
[Paul was the first Bolshevik.]

Hillel Kempinsky[3]

In early patristic writings and again in many quarters since the mid-nineteenth century, Paul's project has been understood as one of universalizing the Torah, breaking through the "particularism" of the Jewish religion. Galatians 3:26–9 is taken as the moral center of Paul's work: "For as many of you as were baptized into Christ have put on Christ [saying]: 'There is neither Jew nor Greek; there is neither slave nor free-man; there is no male and female. For you are all one in Christ Jesus.' If, however, you belong to Christ, then you are Abraham's offspring, heirs according to the promise."

Paul cites the baptismal formula that the Galatians themselves recited or heard recited at the time of their baptism: "There is neither Jew nor Greek."[4] He interprets the text, and thus baptism itself, in the following fashion. The rite consists of a new birth that is understood as substituting an allegorical genealogy for a literal one. In Christ, that is, in baptism, all the differences that mark off one body from another as Jew or Greek (circumcision is considered a "natural" mark of the Jew (Romans 2:27)), male or female, slave or free, are effaced, for in the Spirit such marks do not exist.

Accordingly, if one belongs to Christ, then one participates in the allegorical meaning of the promise to the "seed of Abraham," an allegorical meaning of genealogy that is already hinted at in the biblical text itself, when it said that in "Abraham all nations would be blessed" (Genesis 12:3) and even more when it interpreted his name as "Father to many nations" (Genesis 17:5). The individual body itself is replaced by its allegorical referent, the body of Christ of which all the baptized are part.[5] This is what the "putting-on" of Christ means, which is certainly a reference to the topos of the body as a garment.[6] Paul is the vehicle of a certain distrust of corporeality that is characteristic of Christian culture as well as of the Western critique of ethnicity, since his text is the material base of much of the discourse on ethnicity in Christian culture. Things of the body are less important than things of the spirit. The physical connection of common descent from Abraham and the embodied practices with which that genealogy is marked off as difference are rejected in favor of a connection between people based on individual recreation and entry *de novo* into a community of common belief. Charles Mopsik has recently glossed the cultural effect of Paul's works as "the persistence of a split opened two millennia ago by the ideological victory over one part of the inhabited world of the Christian conception of carnal relation – and of carnal filiation – as separate from spiritual life and devalued in relation to it."[7]

In his authentic passion to find a place for the Gentiles in the Torah's scheme of things and the brilliance of the radically dualist and allegorical hermeneutic that he developed to accomplish this purpose, Paul had (almost against his will) sown the seeds for a Christian discourse that would completely deprive Jewish ethnic, cultural specificity of any positive value and indeed turn it into a "curse" in the eyes of Gentile Christians.[8] Elizabeth Castelli has focused most sharply on the extent to which the drive for sameness was constitutive of Pauline discourse by analyzing the function of imitation and its political effects in his letters:

> the language of imitation, with its concomitant tension between the drive toward sameness and the inherent hierarchy of the mimetic relationship, masks the will to power which one finds in Pauline discourse. Paul's appropriation of

the discourse of mimesis is a powerful rhetorical move, because this language identifies the fundamental values of wholeness and unity with Paul's own privileged position vis-à-vis the gospel, the early Christian communities he founded and supervises, and Christ himself. *Here is precisely where he makes his coercive move. To stand for anything other than what the apostle stands for is to articulate for oneself a place of difference, which has already implicitly been associated with discord and disorder.* To stand in a position of difference is to stand in opposition, therefore, to the gospel, the community, and Christ.[9]

Castelli describes the personal will to power implicit in the Pauline rhetorical drive toward sameness. The same analysis can be applied, however, to the politics of group relations even after the apostle's death. We suggest that as Paul gradually became not an embattled apostle for one kind of Christianity contending with others but the source of Christianity *tout court*, and as so-called pagans faded from the scene, the function of those who "stand in a position of difference" came to be filled almost exclusively in the discourse by the Jews, and the "coercive move" toward sameness came to be directed at the Jews.[10] The place of difference increasingly becomes the Jewish place, and thus the Jew becomes the very sign of discord and disorder in the Christian polity. That this is so can be shown from the fact that as other "differences" appear on the medieval European scene (the Lollards, for example), they are figured in literature as "Jews."

It is, however, important to emphasize that Paul is not "anti-Semitic" or even anti-Jewish. From his perspective the drive toward sameness was precisely to be understood as the fulfillment of Judaism, for "true" Jewishness was not an affair of descent "according to the flesh" (Galatians 4:21–31); nor was it an affair of practice according to the flesh, like circumcision (Romans 2:28–9).[11] True Jewishness lay, according to Paul, precisely in renunciation of difference and entry into the one body of Christ. Anyone at all can be Jewish, and those who "call themselves Jews" are not necessarily Jewish at all.

This double reading of the sign *Jew* by Paul as both signifier of unruly difference and symbol of universalism has had fateful consequences for the Jews in the Christian West. Once Paul succeeded, "real Jews" ended up being only a trope. They have remained such for European discourse down to the present and even in the writings of leftists whose work is *explicitly* opposed to anti-Semitism – and even in the writings of Jews. Although well intentioned, any such allegorization of *Jew* is problematic in the extreme for the way that it deprives those who have historically grounded identities in those material signifiers of the power to speak for themselves and remain different. In this sense the "progressive" idealization of *Jew* and *woman*, or more usually, *Jew* and *Woman*, ultimately deprives difference of the right to be different.

II

Sometimes the reference to the allegorized Jew is implicit or made in passing; in other recent works it is an explicit and central trope. An example of the former is contained in Jean-Luc Nancy's recent *The Inoperative Community*. Nancy's central problem in that work is to formulate a notion of community that will not violate the standard of non-coercion. That standard holds that community is "the compearance (*comparution*) of singular beings." For Nancy, such singularity and the simultaneity that is a condition of it appear to imply an evacuation of history and memory. So many brutalities, so many violations of any notion of humanly responsible community have been carried out in the name of solidary collectives supposed to have obtained in the past, that Nancy seems to have renounced any possible recourse to memory in his attempt to think through the possibility of there ever being community without coercion. Of there ever *being*: the only community that does not betray the hope invested in that word, Nancy argues, is one that resists any kind of stable existence.[12]

The problem is that Nancy has in fact attempted a generalized model of community as *non-being*. Hence any already existing "community" is out of consideration by its very existence, relegated through philosophical necessity to a world we have lost or that never existed. Following Nancy's rhetoric, the only possible residues of that lost world are false community appearing as a serial, undifferentiated collective in the same analytic category as the fascist mass or, alternatively, an assemblage of unrelated individuals. The individual in turn "is merely the residue of the experience of the dissolution of community," and furthermore, "the true consciousness of the loss of community is Christian" (*IC*: 3, 10).

Although Nancy is silent on the relations among history, memory, and community, he considers at some length the apparently tortured relation between "myth" and community. For Nancy, myth – that necessary fiction that grounds the insistent specialness of the existent communal group – is an irreducible component of community and at the same time is necessarily pernicious in its effects. Therefore Nancy asserts a search not for the eradication of myth but rather for its "interruption": "The interruption of myth is therefore also, necessarily, the interruption of community" (*IC*: 57). In a footnote, Nancy elaborates on a comment made in 1984 by Maurice Blanchot:

> "The Jews incarnate . . . the refusal of myths, the abandonment of idols, the recognition of an ethical order that manifests itself in respect for the law. What Hitler wants to annihilate in the Jew, in the 'myth of the Jew,' is precisely man freed from myth." This is another way of showing where and when myth was

definitively interrupted. I would add this: "man freed from myth" belongs henceforth to a community that it is incumbent upon us to let come, to let write itself. (*IC*: 162 n. 40)

We want to press, in a sense by literalizing, the opening offered here. The quote from Blanchot seems ambiguous if not contradictory: do the Jews literally "incarnate the refusal of myths," or is that one of Hitler's myths? Let us first pursue the first reading, which is both the more flattering and the more dangerous. This reading would tell us that community without myth was once the special possession of the Jews. Nancy's "addition" would then explore the consequences of the release of that secret to "us" as a result of the genocide. What else, after all, can *henceforth* mean? We deeply respect the fact that this and other work of Nancy's is explicitly motivated by the desire to understand and "unwork" the complicity between philosophy and twentieth-century violence.[13] Nancy would doubtless be horrified and/or furious at the suggestion that his rhetoric is complicit in perpetuating the cultural annihilation of the Jew, yet it seems clear that this is one potential accomplishment of his further allegorization of Blanchot. *That which the Jew represented before "he" was annihilated is that which "we" must let come, must let write itself.* The word *henceforth* indeed implies that the secret of freedom from myth has passed from the Jews to a community that does not exist, that is only imaginable in and by theory. The secret becomes potentially available to all who await a second coming of this sacrificed Jew. We insist that this plausible yet "uncharitable" reading cannot be stretched to an accusation of anti-Judaism. On the contrary, it is clear that Nancy and thinkers like him are committed to a sympathetic philosophical comprehension of the existence and annihilation of the Jews. Our claim is rather that within the thought of philosophers such as Nancy lies a blindness to the particularity of Jewish difference that is itself part of a relentless penchant for allegorizing all "difference" into a univocal discourse.

Now let us pursue the alternate reading of Blanchot, and of Nancy's gloss. Its implications are both more modest and more conducive to our project. According to this second reading of Blanchot, the Jews' freedom from myth was primarily, if not exclusively, significant as a myth that murderously irritated Hitler. Nancy would then be saying not that "we" have inherited the secret of the Jews but rather that it is incumbent upon us – the pronoun this time not excluding in any way Jews living after the Nazi genocide – to assume the challenge of the myth of freedom from myth, to let come a community that is free from myth. We will suggest below that living Jews may have a particular contribution to make to that general effort, especially in the experience of Diaspora that has constrained Jews to create forms of community that do not rely on one of the most potent and dangerous myths – the myth of autochthony.

The critical text that has gone furthest in employing "the jew" as an allegorical trope for otherness is Jean-François Lyotard's recent *Heidegger and "the jews."* The title tells the story: *Heidegger* gets a capital *H*, but *the jews* are in lowercase. This is done, as the back cover blurb explains, "to represent the outsiders, the nonconformists: the artists, anarchists, blacks, homeless, Arabs, etc. – and the Jews."[14] The Jews are doubtless chosen as exemplary both because the voices of some Jews are so prominent in European modernism and because of the enormous challenge of Nazi genocide to Enlightenment thought. But the name as used here is *essentially* a generic term standing for the other. And indeed Lyotard's book is all about the danger of forgetting that one ("one" in a position of relative power, that is) has always already forgotten the Other.

But why does Lyotard feel free to appropriate the name *the jews*? What does it mean for David Carroll, the author of the introduction to the English translation of Lyotard's book, to write in reference to Lyotard's citation of "Freud, Benjamin, Adorno, Arendt, Celan" that "these are ultimately 'the jews' we all have to read and even in some sense to become, 'the jews' we always already are but have forgotten we are, 'the jews' that Heidegger forgets at great cost for his thinking and writing" (*H*: xxiv)?

What Lyotard refuses to forget, remembering the negative example of Heidegger, is not so much upper- *or* lowercase Jews as Christian European crimes against humanity. In other words, Lyotard takes history seriously as an implication of philosophy, doubtless a vital exercise. This sketch of a critique, therefore, is not intended as an exposé of Lyotard but as a further implication of the universalizing, allegorizing traditions of Hellenistic philosophy as absorbed in Christian culture.

Lyotard basically repeats Sartre's thesis about the production of the Jew by the anti-Semite: "What is most real about real Jews is that Europe, in any case, does not know what to do with them: Christians demand their conversion; monarchs expel them; republics assimilate them; Nazis exterminate them. 'The jews' are the object of a dismissal with which Jews, in particular, are afflicted in reality" (*H*: 3). Let us pause at the first words here and test a paraphrase. How would it work if a man or a woman said, "What is most real about real women is that men continually try to dominate them"? The condescension of Lyotard's statement immediately becomes evident.

It would have been quite different if Lyotard had written rather: "What matters most to me here about those usually called 'Jews' is that Europe does not know what to do with them." There is no gainsaying the power of his insight. Europe indeed does not know what to do with "real Jews." But what of European philosophy? Is Lyotard not Europe here? Might we not fairly say, "Europe does not know what to do with them," "philosophers allegorize them," and so on? To which one might comment that in doing so, they continue another particularly Christian practice with regard to up-percase Jews, one that begins with Paul.

Here we can see more analytically what is wrong with Carroll's rhetoric about us all becoming once again "the jews we always already are but have forgotten we are." We must resist the seduction of these sentiments, for like Paul's writing they deny, they *spiritualize* history. For some contemporary critics – indeed, those most profoundly concerned with the lessons of the encounter between Jewish identity and European self-adequation – it seems that the real Jew is the non-Jewish Jew. What does this say about the "reality" of those Jews – most of those who call themselves Jews, of course, are the untheorized, unphilosophical, unspiritualized Jews – who would think the phrase "non-Jewish Jew" to be nonsense? Is it politically correct, that is, ethical, to "forget" them and to fashion an imaginary dialogue with the other who is, in fact, the already sanctioned, official model of the "non-Jewish Jew," the Franz Kafkas and Walter Benjamins? For as we know, the vast majority of the Nazis' Jewish victims were unredeemed, "real" Jews.[15]

Against this incipient critique stands precisely the force implicit in Lyotard's act of allegorizing the name *jew*. Radiating out from the sun of philosophy, remembering the other by writing the "jew," Lyotard challenges all those who would fetishize their particular difference, insisting that we learn how to imagine ourselves as blacks, as Arabs, as homeless, as Indians. This is a political challenge, but Lyotard does not suggest how those who are themselves "real Jews" could respond to it. Indeed, he explains that one reason for his avoidance of the proper noun, of the uppercase "Jews," is to make clear that he is not discussing a particularly Jewish political subject, which he identifies as Zionism (*IC*: 3). We want to insist in response to Lyotard that there is a loss and a danger either in allegorizing away real, uppercase Jews or in regarding them primarily as a problem for Europe. Our claim entails in turn a responsibility to help articulate a Jewish political subject "other" than that of Zionism, which in fundamental ways merely reproduces the exclusivist syndromes of European nationalism. Zionism itself is predicated on a myth of autochthony. We will suggest that a Jewish subject position founded on generational connection and its attendant anamnestic responsibilities and pleasures affords the possibility of a flexible and non-hermetic critical Jewish identity.

III

In a recent essay, Walter Benn Michaels criticizes the notion of a cultural retentionism that is not "race"-based. His text is of extraordinary theoretical importance for the analysis of both the ancient dialectic between Paul and the rabbis on the status of Jewish ethnicity, as well as for the current debate over ethnicity and multiculturalism in the United States. Michaels argues that all conceptions of cultural ethnicity are dependent on prior and often unacknowledged notions of race. In a series of examples, including the work on African-American culture of anthropologist Melville Herskovits and a novel of Oliver La Farge, Michaels argues that although they insist they are only talking about culture and not something that is biologically innate, they nevertheless assume that someone who does not "have" the culture of his or her "People" is in some sense lacking something and that the lack can be repaired.[16] Michaels questions this assumption: if they do not already observe the practices of that culture, in what sense other than "racial" can it be said to be theirs? His conclusion is: "This is not to say, of course, that all accounts of cultural identity require a racial component; it is only to say that the accounts of cultural identity that do any cultural work require a racial component" ("RC": 682). By this Michaels means that one is already either doing "Navajo things" or not. If one is doing them, then there is no cultural work to be done; they are one's culture already. If one is not already doing them, then it can only make sense to call them one's culture that one ought to be doing on the basis of an assumed or imputed biological identity as Navajo. He concludes that "the modern concept of culture is not, in other words, a critique of racism; it is a form of racism" (p. 683).

Michaels's argument that any identification of culture with ethnicity is logically dependent on a genealogical connection for it to work at all seems correct. Yet by glossing as "racist" all claims for group identity based on genealogy (whatever the posture of that genealogy, rhetorical or biological, might be), he inscribes a particular ideology as natural. The residue of Michaels's critique of genealogically based identity as "racist" is a radically individualist, voluntaristic, and attenuated notion of something that can only with difficulty be called "identity." This valorization of any kind of elective and affective connection between people over against the claims of physical kinship is deeply embedded in the Platonic value system Europe has largely inherited from Paul. In opposition to a traditional Jewish culture, which, in virtually all of its varieties, considered literal descent from Abraham and thus physical kinship as of supreme value in establishing identity, Paul preached kinship in the spirit as the mark of identity. Secondly, where other Jewish groups insisted on the value of doing traditional Jewish things – the Law – as the practice of Jewish identity, Paul asserted the doing of new things, "better" things, baptism for instance, as the marker of Christian identity. Both of these moves are, moreover, crucially founded on the hierarchical dualism of spirit and flesh, with anything having to do with flesh implicitly and explicitly devalued.

The attenuation of memory in Michaels's residual account of identity is shown by his remarks on Herskovits. Herskovits had argued that African practices were retained by house slaves who had been acculturated into the white culture through a process of "reabsorption" of "Africanisms." To this Michaels reacts, "if you were trained as a house slave, why would absorbing Africanisms count as reabsorbing them?" ("RC": 679). The function of this claim for Herskovits, as Michaels correctly argues, is precisely to avoid the necessity for assuming any "innate endowment" of cultural traits in order to bolster his argument for the African component of African-American culture. At this point, however, Michaels jumps from here to the following:

> To make what *they* did part of *your* past, there must be some prior assumption of identity between you and them, and this assumption is as racial to Herskovits as it is in Cullen or La Farge. The things the African Negro used to do count as the American Negro's past only because both the African and the American are "the Negro." Herskovits's anti-racist culturalism can only be articulated through a commitment to racial identity. ("RC": 680)

Indeed. But this demonstration, repeated over and over in Michaels's essay, does not in any way imply that cultural practices are "innately endowed," as racialist (and racist) theories of cultural differentiation had been wont to do before the intervention of culturalists like Franz Boas and his followers, whose work, as we have said, had been largely accomplished by the 1920s.[17]

Let us think for a moment how Herskovits's "house slaves" might have come to feel a sense of identity with the field slaves who had not been acculturated to the white norm. First of all, they might indeed have managed to *remember* – simply not forget – that their immediate ancestors had been Africans in Africa. Secondly, their bodies were marked as being different from the other people doing "white" things. Third, they shared a slave status with the field hands. Fourth, the notion of complete separation followed by reestablished contact is a pure fiction. Much more plausible would be a model of acculturation whereby these house slaves had been exposed to the culture of the other slaves that they had partially forgotten during the process of (presumably) early childhood "acculturation" to the house culture and that indeed they might reabsorb as adults.

Identity is not only reinvented, as Michaels would have it; it is at least partially given for different people in different ways and intensities. Bodies are marked as different and often as negatively different to the dominant cultural system, thus producing a dissonance or gap between one's practices and affects. Partly assimilated, partly repressed, early childhood acculturation reasserts itself as a sense of dissonance, or guilt, as well. Contact with other people who share the name of a given identity and seem to feel organically connected to a community can produce a sense of nostalgia even in one who has never been near the things that that community does. Michaels obscures all of this by eliding racism – the idea of an innate capacity or tendency for certain practices – and generation understood as a kinship with other people who happen to do certain things. Versions of this same argument can be constructed for all of Michaels's deconstructions of culturalism.[18]

Michaels's text thus implicitly inscribes as natural another characteristically Protestant theme, a radical individualism, in which a person sufficiently makes her- or himself. For Michaels, apparently belonging to a culture cannot determine a life trajectory. There can be no "mark of identity that transcends one's actual practices and experiences . . . The fact . . . that something belongs to our culture, cannot count as a motive for our doing it since, if it *does* belong to our culture we *already* do it and if we don't do it (if we've stopped or haven't yet started doing it) it doesn't belong to our culture" ("RC": 681 n. 36, 682–3). Does this apply to children? Is there no model of *learning* or *transmission* here? What happens if we substitute *language* for *culture*? Should we say that it is racist to speak of teaching children "their language" because "their language" is what they know already, so there is no reason for parents to speak a different language than that of the majority to small children in order that they will know "their" native language as well as the dominant one? What about a thirteen-year-old child whom we have allowed until now to concentrate on learning the language/culture of the dominant group? Is it racist to send him or her to a school to learn "our" language? What about a thirty-year-old long-lost cousin who wants to reconnect with his or her "roots"? Michaels's individualism allows him to slip in the problematic pronoun *our*, which he employs in fact to mean not only each and everyone of us, separately, but – as this quote shows – each and everyone of us separately from any possible identity with ourselves yesterday or tomorrow because that would be to prescribe in a racist way what "our" identity is, separately from anything that happened before we, as particular organisms, were born.

Male Jewish circumcision provides a particularly sharp disruption of Michaels's statement that no "mark of identity . . . transcends one's actual practices and experiences," for it certainly can be a mark that transcends one's actual practices and (at least remembered) experiences, yet it is a mark that can reassert itself, and often enough does, as a demand (almost a compulsion) to reconnect, relearn, reabsorb, and reinvent the doing of Jewish things.[19] Indeed, one could understand circumcision precisely as the cultural construction of a genealogical differentiation, as a diacritic that symbolizes the biological status of Jewishness – not in the sense of a biological difference between Jews and others but in the sense of the biological connection that filiation provides. Further evidence that this connection has nothing to do with racism *per se* is the fact that one not Jewish can indeed adopt Jewish identity by taking on Jewish practices and through symbolic rebirth (and for men, physical marking) as a member of the Jewish People. It is thus not quite as obvious as Michaels claims it to be that a New York Jew cannot become a Mashpee Indian ("RC": 680 n. 36). Certainly a Mashpee Indian can become a Jew. Those Jewish subcultures that do promulgate racist or quasi-racist notions of Jewishness have great theological difficulty with conversion and ultimately retreat to the same kind of dualism of bodies and souls that characterizes Paul.

More revealingly, however, the convert's name is changed to "ben Avraham" or "bas Avraham," son or daughter of Abraham. The convert is adopted into the family and assigned a new "genealogical" identity, but because Abraham is the first convert in Jewish tradition, converts are his descendants in that sense as well. There is thus a sense in which the convert becomes the ideal type of the Jew. We not only do these things because we are this thing, but we are this thing because we do these things.

Michaels also marginalizes the political dimensions of cultural retention and loss: "Without race, losing our culture can mean no more than doing things differently from the way we now do them and preserving our culture can mean no more than doing things the same – the melodrama of assimilation disappears" ("RC": 685). He allows only that "the situation is entirely different with respect to compulsory assimilation; what puts the pathos back is precisely the element of compulsion" ("RC": 685 n. 41). However, as Michaels surely knows, power operates in many ways other than the exercise of actual compulsion. Ideological state apparatuses and discourses all press mightily on different identities to assimilate to the dominant culture. The pathos of notions such as assimilation, cultural demise, and cultural survival grows precisely out of the ways in which they are embedded in political processes of domination and exploitation. The insistence on the value of bodily connection and embodied practice that is emblematic of Judaism since Paul thus has significant critical power *vis-à-vis* the isolating and disembodying direction of Western idealist philosophies.

IV

This feeling of identity between self and body, which, naturally, has nothing in common with popular materialism, will therefore never allow those who wish to begin with it to rediscover, in the depths of this unity, the duality of a free spirit that struggles against the body to which it is chained. On the contrary, for such people, the whole of the spirit's essence lies in the fact that it is chained to the body. To separate the spirit from the concrete forms with which it is already involved is to betray the originality of the very feeling from which it is appropriate to begin.[20]

Levinas's statement here is extremely significant. If, as he claims, writing in 1934, the philosophy of Hitlerism is a reaction to German idealism with its disembodied notions of universal spirit, then we have a startling and troubling analogy with the reaction of rabbinic Judaism to similar philosophical developments in the rabbis' world, a reaction that also rejected the notion of "the duality of a free spirit that struggles against the body to which it is chained." Levinas argues that the philosophy of Hitlerism consists precisely of a struggle against this flight from the body so characteristic of Western culture, a protest against the disgust with corporeality that makes one ashamed of having parents, genealogical connections, or a native country. Like white cells gone wild and destroying healthy tissue, this reaction turned into the most destructive horror that human beings have ever invented. With a terrifying irony, then, the rabbinic reaction against dualism in late antiquity bears strong analogies to this modern one. If Lyotard continues Paul, does Heidegger continue the rabbis?

The reaction against such idealism and disembodiment in "the philosophy of Hitlerism" produced the worst violence that human beings have ever perpetrated against each other, but Judaism, in a similar reaction, did not. The most violent practice that rabbinic Judaism ever developed *vis-à-vis* its Others was spitting on the floor in the synagogue or walking around the block to avoid passing a pagan or Christian place of worship. Something else was needed for the potential negative implications of the culture to become actualized. That necessity is power over others. Particularism plus power yields tribal warfare or fascism.

Christianity plus power has also yielded horror. If particularism plus power tends toward fascism, then universalism plus power produces imperialism and cultural annihilation as well as, all too often, actual genocide of those who refuse to conform. Our thesis is that Judaism and Christianity, as two different hermeneutic systems for reading the Bible, generate two diametrically opposed and mirror-image forms of racism – and also two dialectical possibilities of anti-racism.[21] The genius of Christianity is its concern for all the peoples of the world; the genius of Judaism is its ability to leave other people alone.[22] And the evils of the two systems are the precise obverse of these genii. The genies all too easily become demons. Christian universalism, even at its most liberal and benevolent, has been a powerful force for coercive discourses of sameness, denying, as we have seen, the rights of Jews, women, and others to retain their difference. As Etienne Balibar has brilliantly realized, this universalism is indeed a racism:

This leads us to direct our attention towards a historical fact that is even more difficult to admit and yet crucial, taking into consideration the French national form of racist traditions. There is, no doubt, a specifically French brand of the doctrines of Aryanism, anthropometry and biological geneticism, but the true "French ideology" is not to be found in these: it lies rather in the idea that the culture of the "land of the Rights of Man" has been entrusted with a universal mission to educate the human race. There corresponds to this mission a practice of assimilating dominated populations and a consequent need to differentiate and rank individuals or groups in terms of their greater or lesser aptitude for – or resistance to – assimilation. It was this simultaneously subtle and crushing form of exclusion/inclusion which was deployed in the process of colonization and the strictly French (or "democratic") variant of the "White man's burden."[23]

Thus paradoxically and tragically, at the very heart of those most truly progressive discourses of Europe, including Marxism, the inability to accommodate difference provides a fatal flaw. This inability was characteristic of German liberalism, as Marc Shell points out,[24] and still persists in the United States of today in such "liberal" expressions as "too Jewish."[25] Shell documents such notions in the discourse of the contemporary Russian ideologue Igor Sharevich, who argues that Jews must abandon their difference if they wish to be full citizens of Russia.[26] The paradox in such discourse is that nearly always, as Shell emphasizes, the justification for coercing Jews to become Christian Russian citizens of the world is the alleged intolerance of the Jews. The parallels between this modern liberal discourse and that of Paul seem obvious.

The rabbis' insistence on the centrality of peoplehood can thus be read as a necessary critique of Paul, for if the Pauline move had within it the possibility of breaking out of the tribal allegiances and commitments to one's own family, as it were, it also contains the seeds of an imperialist and colonizing missionary practice. The very emphasis on a universalism expressed as the concern for all of the families of the world turns very rapidly (if not necessarily) into a doctrine that they must all become part of our family of the spirit with all of the horrifying practices against Jews and other Others that Christian Europe produced. The doctrine of the Apostle of the Free Spirit can be diverted, even perverted, to a doctrine of enslaving and torturing bodies. Paul had indeed written, with notorious ambiguity, "For though absent in body I am present in spirit, and if present I have already pronounced judgment in the name of the Lord Jesus on the man who has [lived with his father's wife]. When you are assembled and my spirit is present, with the power of our Lord Jesus, you are to deliver this man to Satan for the destruction of the flesh, that his spirit may be saved in the day of the Lord Jesus" (1 Corinthians 5:3–5). It is surely Paul's own sense of self, divided into body and spirit so that this spirit can be where his body is not – and he means this literally – that permits him to suggest (if that is what is meant) and his followers to practice torturing and killing bodies to save the souls. As Henri Baudet has remarked concerning late fifteenth-century Portugal, "although the bodies of Negroes might be held captive, this very fact made it possible for their souls to achieve true freedom through conversion to Christianity. And so the enslavement of Negroes took on a kind of missionary aspect. It was in keeping that christened Negro slaves should enjoy certain small privileges above their fellows."[27] Disdain for the bodies of others combined with concern for the souls can thus be even more devastating than neglect. From the retrospective position of a world that has, at the end of the second Christian millennium, become thoroughly interdependent, each one of these options is intolerable.

Critics of Zionism, both Arab and others, along with both Jewish and non-Jewish anti-Semites, have often sought to portray Jewish culture as essentially racist. This foundational racism is traced to the Hebrew Bible and is described as the transparent meaning of that document. Critics who are otherwise fully committed to constructionist and historicist accounts of meaning and practice abandon this commitment when it comes to the Hebrew Bible – assuming that the Bible is, in fact and in essence, that which it has been read to be and authorizes univocally that which it has been taken to authorize. Frederick Turner writes: "But the distinctions raised in the covenant between religion and idolatry are like some visitation of the khamsin to wilderness peoples as yet unsuspected, dark clouds over Africa, the Americas, the Far East, until finally even the remotest islands and jungle enclaves are struck by fire and sword and by the subtler weapon of conversion-by-ridicule (Deuteronomy 2:34; 7:2; 20:16–18, Joshua 6:17–21)."[28] The historically and materially defined local practices of a culture far away and long ago are made here "naturally" responsible (like the khamsin, the Middle Eastern Santa Ana) for the colonial practices of cultures entirely other to it simply because those later cultures used those practices as their authorization.[29] One effect of this sudden dehistoricization of hermeneutics has been an exoneration of European Christian society that has been, after all, the religious hegemonic system for virtually all of the imperialist, racist, and even genocidal societies of the West, but not, of course, Judaism. There were no Jewish missionaries in the remote islands and jungle enclaves. It is not the Hebrew Bible that impels the "Societies for the Propagation" but rather Pauline rhetoric like "For as in Adam all men died, so in Christ all men shall be made alive" (1 Corinthians 15:22). Jews and Jewish culture will have to answer for the evil that we do (especially to the Palestinians), but it is absurd for "the Jews" to be implicated in practices in which they had no part and indeed have had no part even until now: forced conversion, deculturation, genocide.[30] Even the primitive command to wipe out the peoples of Canaan was limited by the Bible itself to those particular people in that particular place, and thus declared no longer applicable by the rabbis of the Talmud.[31] It is precisely the very literalism of rabbinic/midrashic hermeneutics that prevented a typological "application" of this command to other groups. It should be clearly recognized, then, that the attempt of the integrationist Zionist Gush Emunim movement to refigure the Palestinians as Amalek and to reactivate the genocidal commandment is a radical act of religious revisionism and not in any way a continuation of historical rabbinic Judaism.

Does this mean that rabbinic Judaism *qua* ideology is innocent of either ethnocentric or supremacist tenets? Certainly not. What it argues is rather that Jewish racism, like the racism of other peoples, is a facultative and dispensible aspect of the cultural system, not one that is necessary for its preservation or essential to its nature. Perhaps the primary function for a critical construction of cultural (or racial or gender or sexual) identity is to construct it in ways that purge it of its elements of domination and oppression. Some, however, would argue that this is an impossible project not because of the nature of Jewishness but because any group identity is oppressive, unless it is oppressed.

In a recent Marxian analysis of both race and racism, Balibar has argued that "racism" has two dissymmetrical aspects. On the one hand, it constitutes a dominating community with practices, discursive and otherwise, that are "articulated around stigmata of otherness (name, skin color, religious practices)." It also constitutes, however, "the way in which, as a mirror image, individuals and collectives that are prey to racism (its 'objects') find themselves constrained to see themselves as a community." Balibar further argues that destruction of racism implies the "internal decomposition of the community created by racism," by which he means the dominating community, as is clear from his analogy to the overcoming of sexism that will involve "the break-up of the community of 'males'" ("I". 18). This is, however, for us the crucial point, for the question is, obviously, if overcoming sexism involves the breaking up of the community of males, does it necessarily imply the breaking up of the community of females? And does this, then, not entail a breaking up of community, *tout court*? Putting it another way, are we not simply imposing a more coercive universal? On the other hand, if indeed the very existence of the dominant group is dependent on domination, if identity is always formed in a master–slave relationship, is the price not too high? What we wish to struggle for, theoretically, is a notion of identity in which there are only slaves but no masters, that is, an alternative to the model of self-determination, which is, after all, in itself a Western, imperialist imposition on the rest of the world. We propose Diaspora as a theoretical and historical model to replace national self-determination.[32] To be sure, this would be an idealized Diaspora generalized from those situations in Jewish history when Jews were both relatively free from persecution and yet constituted by strong identity – those situations, moreover, within which Promethean Jewish creativity was not antithetical, indeed was synergistic with a general cultural activity. Another way of making the same point would be to insist that there are material and social conditions in which cultural identity, difference, will not produce even what Balibar, after P. A. Taguieff, has called "differentialist racism," that is,

> a racism whose dominant theme is not biological heredity but the insurmountability of cultural differences, a racism which, at first sight, does not postulate the superiority of certain groups or peoples in relation to others but "only" the harmfulness of abolishing frontiers, the incompatibility of life-styles and traditions; in short, it is what P. A. Taguieff has rightly called a *differentialist racism.* ("I": 21)

To our understanding, it would be an appropriate goal to articulate a theory and practice of identity that would simultaneously respect the irreducibility and the positive value of cultural differences, address the harmfulness, not of abolishing frontiers but of dissolution of uniqueness, and encourage the mutual fructification of different life-styles and traditions. We do not think, moreover, that such possibilities are merely utopian. We would certainly claim that there have been historical situations in which they obtained without perfect success in this radically imperfect world. The solution of Zionism – that is, Jewish state hegemony, except insofar as it represented an emergency and temporary rescue operation – seems to us the subversion of Jewish culture and not its culmination. It represents the substitution of a European, Western cultural–political formation for a traditional Jewish one that has been based on a sharing, at best, of political power with others and that takes on entirely other meanings when combined with political hegemony.

Let us begin with two concrete examples. Jewish resistance to assimilation and annihilation within conditions of Diaspora, to which we will return below, generated such practices as communal charity in the areas of education, feeding, providing for the sick, and caring for Jewish prisoners, to the virtual exclusion of others. While this meant at least that those others were not subjected to attempts to Judaize them – that is, they were tolerated, and not only by default of lack of Jewish power – it also meant that Jewish resources were not devoted to the welfare of humanity at large but only to one family. Within Israel, where power is concentrated almost exclusively in Jewish hands, this discursive practice has become a monstrosity whereby an egregiously disproportionate measure of the resources of the state is devoted to the welfare of only one segment of the population. A further and some-what more subtle and symbolic example is the following. That very practice mentioned above, the symbolic expression of contempt for places of worship of others, becomes darkly ominous when it is combined with temporal power and domination – that is, when Jews have power over places of worship belonging to others. It is this factor that has allowed the Israelis to turn the central Mosque of Beersheba into a museum of the Negev and to let the Muslim cemetery of that city to fall into ruins.[33] Insistence on ethnic spe-ciality, when it is extended over a particular piece of land, will inevitably produce a discourse not unlike the Inquisition in many of its effects. The archives of the Israeli General Security Services will one day prove this claim eminently, although already we "know" the truth.

We are not comparing Israeli practice to Nazism, for that would occlude more than it reveals and would obscure the real, imminent danger of its becoming the case in the future; the use of *Lebensraum* rhetoric on the part of mainstream Israeli politicians and the ascent to respectability and a certain degree of power of fascist parties in Israel certainly provide portents of this happening. Our argument is rather for an as yet unrealized but necessary theoretical compatability between Zionist ideology and the fascism of state ethnicity. Capturing Judaism in a state transforms entirely the meanings of its social practices. Practices that in Diaspora have one meaning – for example, caring for the feeding and housing of Jews and not "others" – have entirely different meanings under political hegemony. E. P. Sanders has gotten this just right:

> More important is the evidence that points to Jewish pride in separatism. Chris-tian scholars habitually discuss the question under the implied heading "What was wrong with Judaism that Christianity corrected?" Exclusivism is consid-ered to be bad, and the finding that Jews were to some degree separatist fills many with righteous pride. We shall all agree that exclusivism is bad when prac-ticed by the dominant group. Things look different if one thinks of minority groups that are trying to maintain their own identity. I have never felt that the strict Amish are iniquitous, and I do not think that, in assessing Jewish sepa-ratism in the Diaspora, we are dealing with a moral issue. (The moral issue would be the treatment of Gentiles in Palestine during periods of Jewish ascen-dancy. How well were the biblical laws to love the resident alien [Leviticus 19:33–4] observed?)[34]

The inequities – and worse – in Israeli political, economic, and social prac-tice are not aberrations but inevitable consequences of the inappropriate application of a form of discourse from one historical situation to another.

For those of us who are equally committed to social justice and collective Jewish existence, some other formation must be constituted. We suggest that an Israel that reimports diasporic consciousness – a consciousness of a Jewish collective as one sharing space with others, devoid of exclusivist and dominating power – is the only Israel that could answer Paul's, Lyotard's, and Nancy's call for a species-wide care without eradicating cultural difference.[35] Reversing A. B. Yehoshua's famous pronouncement that only in a condition of political hegemony is moral responsibility mobilized, we would argue that the only moral path would be the renunciation of Jewish hegemony *qua* Jewish hegemony.[36] This would involve first of all complete separation of religion from state, but even more than that the revocation of the Law of Return and such cultural, discursive practices that code the state as a Jewish state and not a multinational and multicultural one. The dream of a place that is ours founders on the rock of realization that there are Others there just as there are Others in Poland, Morocco, and Ethiopia. Any notion, then, of redemption through Land must either be infinitely deferred (as the Neturei Karta understands so well) or become a moral monster. Either Israel must entirely divest itself of the language of race and become truly a state that is equally for all of its citizens and collectives, or the Jews must divest themselves of their claim to space. Race and space together form a deadly discourse.

Genealogy and *territorialism* have been the problematic and necessary (if not essential) terms around which Jewish identity has revolved. In Jewish history, however, these terms are more obviously at odds with each other than in synergy. This allows a formulation of Jewish identity not as a proud resting place (hence not as a form of integrism or nativism) but as a perpetual, creative, diasporic tension. In the final section of this essay, then, we would like to begin to articulate a notion of Jewish identity that recuperates its genealogical moment – family, history, memory, and practice – while it problematizes claims to autochthony and indigenousness as the material base of Jewish identity.

V

The Tanak and other sources of Judaism reveal certain ideas concerning The Land that reflect, or are parallel to, primitive Semitic, other Near Eastern, and, indeed, widespread conceptions about the significance of their land to a particular people. Israel is represented as the center of the Earth . . . The religious man desires to live as near to this sacred space as possible and comes to regard it, the place of his abode, his own land, as the center of the world. (I: p. 1; see also p. 87)

There are two diametrically opposed moments in the Jewish discourse of the Land. On the one hand, it is crucial to recognize that the Jewish conception of the Land of Israel is similar to the discourse of the Land of many (if not nearly all) "indigenous" peoples of the world. Somehow the Jews have managed to retain a sense of being rooted somewhere in the world through twenty centuries of exile from that someplace (organic metaphors are not out of place in this discourse, for they are used within the tradition itself).

It is profoundly disturbing to hear Jewish attachment to the Land decried as regressive in the same discursive situations in which the attachment of native Americans or Australians to their particular rocks, trees, and deserts is celebrated as an organic connection to the Earth that "we" have lost.[37] The uncritical valorization of indigenousness (and particularly the confusion between political indigenousness and mystified autochthony) must come under critique, without wishing, however, to deny the rights of native Americans, Australians, and Palestinians to their lands precisely on the basis of real, unmysterious political claims. If, on the other hand, Jews are to give up hegemony over the Land, this does not mean that the profundity of our attachment to the Land can be denied. This also must have a political expression in the present, in the provision of the possibility for Jews to live a Jewish life in a Palestine not dominated by one ethnic group or another.

On the other hand, the biblical story is not one of autochthony but one of always already coming from somewhere else. As Davies has so very well understood, the concept of a divine promise to give this land that is the land of Others to His People Israel is the sign of a bad conscience for having deprived the Other's of their Land (see I: pp. 11–12).[38] Thus at the same time that one vitally important strain of expression within biblical religion promotes a sense of organic, "natural" connectedness between this People and this Land – a settlement in the Land – in another sense or in a counter-strain, Israelite and Jewish religion is perpetually an unsettlement of the very notion of autochthony.

Traditional Jewish attachment to the Land, whether biblical or post-biblical, thus provides a self-critique as well as a critique of identities based on notions of autochthony. Some myths about "the tree over there from which the first man sprung," along with European nationalist myths about Atlantis,[39] have been allowed to harden into a confusion of "indigenous" (the people who belong here, whose land this rightfully is – a political claim, founded on present and recently past political realities) and "autochthonous" (the people who were never anywhere else but here and have a natural right to this land). The Jewish narrative of the Land has the power of insisting on the connection without myths of autochthony, while other narratives, including the Zionist one, have repressed memories of coming from somewhere else. The confusion between indigenousness and autochthony is of the same kind as the confusion in Michaels's text between any kind of genealogically based racism belonging to a people and modern scientific racism.

These very conflations are complicitous with a set of mystifications within which nationalist ideologies subsist. Harry Berger argues that "the alienation of social constructions of divinity and cosmos by conquest groups resembles the alienation of socially constructed kinship and status terms from domestic kin groups to corporate descent groups – in anthropological jargon, from the ego-centered kinship system of families to the more patently fictional ancestor-centered system of lineages."[40] Distinguishing between forms of "weak transcendence" and "strong transcendence," Berger argues that "family membership illustrates weak kinship; tribal membership, strong kinship." Strong transcendence is more aggressive because it is more embattled and does more ideological work, that is, according to Berger, serves to justify land control. "Status that depends on land is generally more precarious and alienable than status inscribed on the body; mobile subsistence economies tend to conceptualize status in terms of the signifying indices of the body–indices of gender, age, and kinship–rather than of more conspicuously artificial constructions, and are closer to the weak end of the weak-to-strong scale" ("L": 121). The place of the first of these alienations can, however, be taken by the alienation of a socially constructed connection to a land by myths of autochthony and the unique belonging of this land to a people, an alienation that can serve the interest of conquerors, as easily as by the transcendental legitimation of kings. Thus if Berger, following Walter Brueggemann, contrasts two covenants, one the Mosaic, which rejects "the imperial gods of a totalitarian and hierarchic social order" ("L": 123), and one, the Davidic, which enthrones precisely those gods as the one God, we could just as well contrast two trajectories, the one toward autochthony and the one against it, in the same way. The first would support the rule of Israelite kings over territory; the second would serve to oppose it.[41]

> The dialectical struggle between anti-royalism and royalism persists throughout the course and formative career of the Old Testament as its structuring force. It sets the tent against the house, nomadism against agriculture, the wilderness against Canaan, wandering and exile against settlement, diaspora against the political integrity of a settled state. ("L": 123)

Our argument, then, is that a vision of Jewish history and identity that valorizes the second half of each of these binary systems and sees the first as only a disease constitutes not a continuation of Jewish culture but its final betrayal.

Berger, however, has also implicated "ancestor-centered systems of lineages" as ideological mystifications in the service of the state power of conquest groups while we have held up such an organization as one feasible component of an alternative to statism. Empirically, tribal organization, with its concomitant myths of the eponymous ancestor, is nearly emblematic of nomadic peoples. Berger's own discourse, however, is inconsistent here, for only a page later he will refer to the premonarchic period of Israel ("roughly from 1250 to 1000 BC") as a sociological experiment in "the rejection of strong transcendence in favor of a less coercive and somewhat weaker alternative, the tribal system that cuts across both local allegiances and stratificational discontinuities" ("L": 123). Thus Berger first puts tribalism on the side of "strong transcendence" and then on the side of "weak." Against Berger's first claim on this point and in favor of his second, we would argue that talk of the eponymous ancestors, of the patriarchs, is conspicuously less prominent in the "Davidic" texts of the settlement than in the "Mosaic" texts of the wandering. As Berger himself writes, David "tried to displace the loyalties and solidarity of kinship ties from clans and tribes to the national dynasty" ("L": 124). We suggest that descent from a common ancestor is rather an extension of family kinship and not its antithesis and thus on the side of wilderness and not on the side of Canaan. Even the myth of descent from common ancestry belongs rather to the semantic field of status through the body and not to the semantic field of status through land. Diaspora, in historical Judaism, can be interpreted then as the later analogue to nomadism in the earlier set of material conditions and thus as a continuation of the sociological experiment that the Davidic monarchy symbolically overturns.[42] With the rabbinic "invention" of Diaspora, the radical experiment of Moses was advanced. The forms of identification typical of nomads, those marks of status in the body, remained, then, crucial to this formation. Race is here on the side of the radicals; space, on the other hand, belongs to the despots.

One modernist story of Israel, the Israeli Declaration of Independence, begins with an imaginary autochthony – "In the Land of Israel this people came into existence" – and ends with the triumphant return of the People to their natural Land, making them "re-autochthonized," "like all of the nations." Israeli state power, deprived of the option of self-legitimation through appeal to a divine king, discovered autochthony as a powerful replacement. An alternative story of Israel, closer, it would seem, to the readings of the Judaism lived for two thousand years, begins with a people forever unconnected with a particular land, a people that calls into question the idea that a people must have a land in order to be a people. "The Land of Israel was not the birthplace of the Jewish people, which did not emerge there (as most peoples have on their own soil). On the contrary it had to enter its own Land from without; there is a sense in which Israel was born in exile. Abraham had to leave his own land to go to the Promised Land: the father of Jewry was deterritorialized" (T: 63).[43] In this view, the stories of Israel's conquest of the Land, whether under Abraham, Joshua, or even more prominently under David, are always stories that are compromised with a sense of failure of mission even more than they are stories of the accomplishment of mission, and the internal critique within the Tanakh (Hebrew Bible) itself, the dissident voice that is nearly always present, does not let us forget this either. Davies also brings into absolutely clear focus a prophetic discourse of preference for "exile" over rootedness in the Land (together with a persistent hope of eschatological restoration), a prophetic discourse that has been totally occluded in modern Zionist ideological representations of the Bible and of Jewish history but was pivotal in the rabbinic ideology (see *T*: 15–19).

The rabbis produced their cultural formation within conditions of Diaspora, and we would argue that their particular discourse of ethnocentricity is ethically appropriate only when the cultural identity is an embattled (or, at any rate, non-hegemonic) minority. The point is not that the Land was devalued by the rabbis but that they renounced it until the final redemption; in an unredeemed world, temporal dominion and ethnic particularity are impossibly compromised. Davies phrases the position just right when he says: "It was its ability to detach its loyalty from 'place,' while nonetheless retaining 'place' in its memory, that enabled Pharisaism to transcend the loss of its Land" (*T*: 69).[44] Our only addition would be to argue that this displacement of loyalty from place to memory of place was necessary not only to transcend the loss of the Land but to enable the loss of the Land. Political possession of the Land most threatened the possibility of continued Jewish cultural practice and difference. Given the choice between an ethnocentricity that would not seek domination over others and a seeking of political domination that would necessarily have led either to a dilution of distinctiveness, tribal warfare, or fascism, the Rabbis chose ethnocentricity. Zionism is thus a subversion of rabbinic Judaism, and it is no wonder that until World War II Zionism was a secular movement to which very few religious Jews adhered, seeing it as a human arrogation of a work that only God should or could perform.[45] This is, moreover, the basis, even to this day, for the anti-Zionist ideology of such groups as Neturei Karta.

The dialectic between Paul and the rabbis can be recuperated for cultural critique. When Christianity is the hegemonic power in Europe and the United States, the resistance of Jews to being universalized can be a critical force and model for the resistance of all peoples to being Europeanized out of particular bodily existence. When, however, an ethnocentric Judaism becomes a temporal, hegemonic political force, it becomes absolutely, vitally necessary to accept Paul's critical challenge – although not his universalizing, disembodying solution – and to develop an equally passionate concern for all human beings. We, including religious Jews – perhaps especially religious Jews – must take seriously the theological dimension of Paul's challenge. How could the God of all the world have such a disproportionate care and concern for only a small part of his world? And yet, obviously, we cannot even conceive of accepting Paul's solution of dissolving into a universal human essence, even one that would not be Christian but truly humanist and universal, even if such an entity could really exist.[46] Somewhere in this dialectic a synthesis must be found, one that will allow for stubborn hanging-on to ethnic, cultural specificity but in a context of deeply felt and enacted human solidarity. For that synthesis, Diaspora provides a model, and only in conditions of Diaspora can such a resolution be even attempted. Within the conditions of Diaspora, many Jews discovered that their well-being was absolutely dependent on principles of respect for difference, indeed that, as the radical slogan goes, "no one is free until all are free." Absolute devotion to the maintenance of Jewish culture and the historical memory was not inconsistent with devotion to radical causes of human liberation; there were Yiddish-speaking and Judeo-Arabic-speaking groups of Marxists and anarchists, and some even retained a commitment to historical Jewish religious practice.[47] The "chosenness" of the Jews becomes, when seen in this light, not a warrant for racism but precisely an antidote to racism. This is a Judaism that mobilizes the critical forces within the Bible and the Jewish tradition rather than mobilizing the repressive and racist forces that also subsist there and that we are not denying.

Within conditions of Diaspora, tendencies toward nativism were also materially discouraged. Diaspora culture and identity allows (and has historically allowed in the best circumstances, such as in Muslim Spain) for a complex continuation of Jewish cultural creativity and identity at the same time that the same people participate fully in the common cultural life of their surroundings. The same figure, a Nagid, an Ibn Gabirol, or a Maimonides, can be simultaneously the vehicle of the preservation of traditions and of the mixing of cultures. This was the case not only in Muslim Spain, nor even only outside of the Land. The rabbis in Diaspora in their own Land also produced a phenomenon of renewal of Jewish traditional culture at the same time that they were very well acquainted with and an integral part of the circumambient late antique culture. Diasporic cultural identity teaches us that cultures are not preserved by being protected from "mixing" but probably can only continue to exist as a product of such mixing. Cultures, as well as identities, are constantly being remade. While this is true of all cultures, diasporic Jewish culture lays it bare because of the impossibility of a natural association between this people and a particular land – thus the impossibility of seeing Jewish culture as a self-enclosed, bounded phenomenon. The critical force of this dissociation among people, language, culture, and land has been an enormous threat to cultural nativisms and integrisms, a threat that is one of the sources of anti-Semitism and perhaps one of the reasons that Europe has been much more prey to this evil than the Middle East. In other words, diasporic identity is a disaggregated identity.

Jewishness disrupts the very categories of identity because it is not national, not genealogical, not religious, but all of these in dialectical tension with one another. When liberal Arabs and some Jews claim that the Jews of the Middle East are Arab Jews, we concur and think that Zionist ideology occludes something very significant when it seeks to obscure this point. The production of an ideology of a pure Jewish cultural essence that has been debased by Diaspora seems neither historically nor ethically correct. "Diasporized," that is, disaggregated, identity allows the early medieval scholar Rabbi Sa'adya to be an Egyptian Arab who happens to be Jewish and also a Jew who happens to be an Egyptian Arab. Both of these contradictory propositions must be held together. Similarly, we suggest that a diasporized gender identity is possible and positive. Being a woman is some kind of special being, and there are aspects of life and practice that insist on and celebrate that speciality. But this does not imply a fixing or freezing of all practice and performance of gender identity into one set of parameters. Human beings are divided into men and women for certain purposes, but that does not tell the whole story of their bodily identity. Rather than the dualism of gendered bodies and universal souls, or Jewish/Greek bodies and universal souls – the dualism that the Western tradition offers – we can substitute partially Jewish, partially Greek bodies, bodies that are sometimes gendered and sometimes not. It is this idea that we are calling diasporized identity.

Crucial to this construction of Jewish history and identity is the simple fact, often consciously or unconsciously suppressed, that Diaspora is not the forced product of war and destruction – taking place after the downfall of Judea – but that already in the centuries before this downfall, the majority of Jews lived voluntarily outside of the Land.[48] Moreover, given a choice between domination by a "foreign" power who would allow them to keep the Torah undisturbed and domination by a "Jewish" authority who would interfere with religious life, the Pharisees and their successors the rabbis generally chose the former (see *T*: 68).[49]

The story we would tell of Jewish history has three stages. In the first stage, we find a people – call it a tribe – not very different in certain respects from peoples in similar material conditions all over the world, a people like most others that regards itself as special among humanity, indeed as the People, and its land as preeminently wonderful among lands, the Land. This is, of course, an oversimplification because this "tribe" never quite dwelled alone and never regarded itself as autochthonous in its Land. In the second stage, this form of life increasingly becomes untenable, morally and politically, because the "tribe" is in cultural, social, and political contact with other people. This is, roughly speaking, the Hellenistic period, culminating in the crises of the first century, of which we have read Paul as an integral part. Various solutions to this problem were eventually adopted. Pauline

Christianity is one; so perhaps is the retreat to Qumran, while the Pharisaic rabbis "invented" Diaspora, even in the Land, as the solution to this cultural dilemma.

The third stage is diasporic existence. The rabbinic answer to Paul's challenge was to renounce any possibility of domination over Others by being perpetually out of power:

> Just as with seeing the return in terms of the restoration of political rights, seeing it in terms of redemption has certain consequences. If the return were an act of divine intervention, it could not be engineered or forced by political or any other human means: to do so would be impious. That coming was best served by waiting in obedience for it: *men of violence would not avail to bring it in.* The rabbinic aloofness to messianic claimants sprang not only from the history of disillusionment with such, but from this underlying, deeply engrained attitude. It can be claimed that under the main rabbinic tradition Judaism condemned itself to powerlessness. But recognition of powerlessness (rather than a frustrating, futile, and tragic resistance) was effective in preserving Judaism in a very hostile Christendom, and therefore had its own brand of "power." (*T:* 82)

As before, our impulse is only slightly to change the nuance of Davies's marvelously precise reading. The renunciation (not merely "recognition") of temporal power was to our minds precisely the most powerful mode of preservation of difference and, therefore, the most effective kind of resistance. The Neturei Karta, to this day, refuse to visit the Western Wall, the holiest place in Judaism, without PLO "visas" because it was taken by violence.

This response has much to teach us. We want to propose a privileging of Diaspora, a dissociation of ethnicities and political hegemonies as the only social structure that even begins to make possible a maintenance of cultural identity in a world grown thoroughly and inextricably interdependent. Indeed, we would suggest that Diaspora, and not monotheism, may be the most important contribution that Judaism has to make to the world, although we would not deny the positive role that monotheism has played in making Diaspora possible.[50] Assimilating the lesson of Diaspora, namely that peoples and lands are not naturally and organically connected, could help prevent bloodshed such as that occurring in Eastern Europe today.[51] In Eastern Europe at the turn of the century, the Jewish Workers' Bund, a mass socialist organization, had developed a model for national–cultural autonomy not based on territorial ethnic states. That program was effectively marginalized by the Bolsheviks and the Zionists. Diaspora can teach us that it is possible for a people to maintain its distinctive culture, its difference, without controlling land, *a fortiori* without controlling other people or developing a need to dispossess them of their lands. Thus the response of rabbinic Judaism to the challenge of universalism that Paul, among others, raised against what was becoming, at the end of one millennium and the beginning of the next, increasingly an inappropriate doctrine of specialness in an already interdependent world may provide some of the pieces to the puzzle of how humanity can survive as another millennium draws to a close with no messiah on the horizon. The renunciation of difference seems both an impoverishment of human life and an inevitable harbinger of oppression. Yet the renunciation of sovereignty (justified by discourses of autochthony, indigenousness, and territorial self-determination), combined with a fierce tenacity in holding onto cultural identity, might well have something to offer to a world in which these two forces, together, kill thousands daily.

Appendix: Statement of the Neturei Karta[52]

We the Neturei Karta (Guardians of the City-Jerusalem), presently numbering in the tens of thousands, are comprised of the descendants of the pioneer Jews who settled in the Holy Land over a hundred years before the establishment of the Zionist State. Their sole motive was to serve G–d, and they had neither political aspirations nor any desire to exploit the local population in order to attain statehood.

Our mission, in the capacity of Palestinian advisers in this round of the Middle East Peace Conference, is to concern ourselves with the safeguarding of the interests of the Palestinian Jews and the entire Jewish nation. The Jewish people are charged by divine oath not to seek independence and cast off the yoke of exile which G–d decreed, as a result of not abiding by the conditions under which G–d granted them the Holy Land. We repeat constantly in our prayers, "since we sinned, we were therefore exiled from our land." G–d promised to gather in the exiled Jews through His messiah. This is one of the principles of the Jewish faith. The Zionist rebelled against this divine decree of exile by taking the land away from its indigenous inhabitants and established their state. Thus are the Jewish people being exposed to the divine retribution set down in the Talmud. "I will make your flesh prey as the deer and the antelope of the forest" (Song of Songs 2:7). Our advice to the negotiating contingent of the Palestinian delegation will remain within the framework of Jewish theology.

Zionist schoolings dictate a doctrine of labeling the indigenous Palestinian population "enemies" in order to sanction their expansionist policies. Judaism teaches that the Jew and non-Jew are to coexist in a cordial and good neighbor relationship. We Palestinian Jews have no desire to expand our places of residence and occupy our neighbors' lands, but only to live alongside non-Jewish Palestinians, just as Jews live throughout the world, in peace and tranquility.

The enmity and animosity toward the non-Jewish population, taught to the Zionist faithful, is already boomeranging. King Solomon in Parables 27:19 describes reality "as one's image is reflected in water: so one's heart toward his fellow man" – so an enemy's heart is reflected in his adversary's heart. The Intifada is "exhibit A" to this King Solomon gem of wisdom. We hope and pray that this face-to-face meeting with imagined adversaries will undo the false image created and that both Jew and Arab in Palestine can once again live as good neighbors as was the life of yesteryear, under a rule chosen by the indigenous residents of the Holy Land – thus conforming with G–d's plan for the Holy Land.

Inchallah![53]

Notes

Some of the material in this essay is taken from the final chapter of Daniel Boyarin's forthcoming book, *A Radical Jew: Paul and the Politics of Identity*. Other material is from Jonathan Boyarin's "Der Yiddisher Isenter; or What Is a Minyan?" and Jonathan Boyarin and Greg Sarris, "Jews and Native Americans as Living Voice and Absent Other," presented at the MLA convention, December 1991. We wish to thank Harry Berger, Jr., Stephen Greenblatt, and Steven Knapp, none of whom necessarily agrees (and one of whom necessarily disagrees) with the claims being made but all of whom made vitally significant interventions. All biblical translations are our own.

1   Gayatri Chakravorty Spivak, "Acting Bits/Identity Talk," *Critical Inquiry* 18 (summer 1992): 773. Paradoxically, Spivak means "recognized kinship" and even "family resemblance" that have nothing to do with genealogy, thus inscribing herself inevitably in a Pauline descent according to the spirit. Perhaps "in the field of rational analysis" is meant exactly as an ironic – or even satiric – distancing from that field.

2   It was not, of course, always used that way. Symptomatic perhaps of this shift is the following statement from Dio Cassius: "I do not know the origin of this name [Jews], but it is applied to all men, even foreigners, who follow their customs. This race is found among Romans" (quoted in John Gager, *The Origins of Anti-Semitism: Attitudes toward Judaism in Pagan and Christian Antiquity* [New York, 1983]: 91). We see from this quotation that race once had much suppler and more complex connections with genealogy, cultural praxis, and identity than it has in our parlance.

3   Oral communication to Jonathan Boyarin. Hillel Kempinsky ז״ל was the archivist at the YIVO Center in New York.

4   See Dennis Ronald Macdonald, *There Is No Male and Female: The Fate of a Dominical Saying in Paul and Gnosticism* (Philadelphia, 1987) and the classic

paper by Wayne A. Meeks, "The Image of the Androgyne: Some Uses of a Symbol in Earliest Christianity," *History of Religions* 13 (February 1974): 165–208.

5   The parallel citation of the formula in 1 Corinthians 12:13 makes this even more explicit: For in one spirit we were all baptized into one body.

6   As in the dominical saying identified plausibly by Macdonald as the source of the baptismal formula itself: "when ye trample on the garment of shame, when the Two become One, and Male with Female neither male nor female." See also Jonathan Z. Smith, "The Garments of Shame," *History of Religions* 5 (winter 1966): 217–38.

7   Charles Mopsik, "The Body of Engenderment in the Hebrew Bible, the Rabbinic Tradition and the Kabbalah," in *Fragments for a History of the Human Body*, ed. Michel Feher (New York, 1989): 49.

8   This is not to deny the radically progressive intent nor even the radically progressive effect of Paul's utterance. Indeed, one of the larger points of Daniel Boyarin's forthcoming book *A Radical Jew: Paul and the Politics of Identity* is to show precisely that ideals of universal human equality that have given rise to the French Revolution, the emancipation of slaves, and the feminist movement also flow from the fountainhead of Galatians 3:28–39. For the nonce, see Daniel Boyarin, "Paul and the Genealogy of Gender," *Representations* 41 (winter 1993), in which this argument is expressly made. As Boyarin writes there:

> In any case, if on the one hand, Wire points to the devastating history of male oppression of women in the name of Paul, one can also cite at least a nascent discourse and real history of chastity as female autonomy also carried out in his name in what is, after all, the Acts of Paul and Thekla for notable example. Similarly with regard to the parallel issue of slavery. Philemon has been used (maybe misused) as a text in the service of slavery. It is just as true, however, that Galatians 3:28 has been mobilized in anti-slavery discourses. The failure of consistency here does not involve Paul's aspirations but his achievements. Others who come after may indeed be able to put into practice that which in Paul is fraught with contradiction. I think that the ultimate elimination of slavery in all of the Christian world is an eloquent case in point, although it took nearly two thousand years for Paul's vision to be realized here. (pp. 32–3 n. 91)

Indeed, if anything, the ultimate point of the present essay is that the progressive elements of that Western universalism that we are locating in Paul are inescapably bound up in their very problematic coerciveness. If, as Etienne Balibar argues (see n. 23 below), the very discourse of "the Rights of Man" provides the form for a particularly French racism, this does not mean that the world would be better off not having had those principles articulated.

9   Elizabeth A. Castelli, *Imitating Paul: A Discourse of Power* (Louisville, KY, 1991), p. 87; emphasis added.

10   At least until new "pagans" were discovered in the early modern period.

11 For a full discussion, see Daniel Boyarin, "'This We Know to Be the Carnal Israel': Circumcision and the Erotic Life of God and Israel," *Critical Inquiry* 18 (spring 1992): 474–506.

12 Jean-Luc Nancy, *The Inoperative Community*, trans. Peter Connor et al., ed. Connor (Minneapolis, MN, 1991), p. 58; hereafter abbreviated *IC*.

13 See Philippe Lacoue-Labarthe and Nancy, "The Nazi Myth," trans. Brian Holmes, *Critical Inquiry* 16 (winter 1990): 291–312.

14 Jean-François Lyotard, *Heidegger and "the jews,"* trans. Andreas Michel and Mark S. Roberts (Minneapolis, MN, 1990); hereafter abbreviated *H*.

15 Lest there be confusion, we of course endorse Isaac Deutscher's actual point that modern Jewish radicals who do not practice the Jewish religion neverthe-less can represent an appropriate way of enacting Jewishness in the contemporary world. See Isaac Deutscher, *The Non-Jewish Jew and Other Essays* (New York, 1968).

16 Walter Benn Michaels, "Race into Culture: A Critical Genealogy of Cultural Identity," *Critical Inquiry* 18 (summer 1992): 679–80; hereafter abbreviated "RC."

17 For W. E. B. Du Bois on this, see Anthony Appiah, "The Uncompleted Argument: Du Bois and the Illusion of Race," *Critical Inquiry* 12 (autumn 1985): 30–2.

18 We do mean deconstruction precisely in the technical sense in which one of the terms of a binary distinction, in this case between race and culture, is shown to be dependent on that which it seeks to exclude. Once again, Michaels has indeed shown the weakness of notions of "culture" dependent on their assumption of binary opposition to a pernicious and discredited account of race.

19 See the analysis of the function of Daniel Deronda's circumcision in Sander Gilman, "'I'm Down on Whores': Race and Gender in Victorian London," in *Anatomy of Racism*, ed. David Theo Goldberg (Minneapolis, MN, 1990), pp. 162–3.

20 Emmanuel Levinas, "Reflections on the Philosophy of Hitlerism" (1934), trans. Sean Hand, *Critical Inquiry* 17 (autumn 1990): 68–9.

21 Etienne Balibar, in a quite different historical context, writes: "In fact racism figures *both* on the side of the universal and the particular." Etienne Balibar, "Racism and Nationalism," trans. Chris Turner, in Balibar and Immanuel Wallerstein, *Race, Nation, Class: Ambiguous Identities* [London, 1991]: 54.

22 Paula Fredriksen cites abundant evidence to the effect that in antiquity Jews permitted Gentiles to attend the synagogue without conversion and even if they continued to worship idols! See her *From Jesus to Christ: The Origins of the New Testament Images of Jesus* (New Haven, CT, 1988), pp. 149–51.

23 Balibar, "Is There a 'Neo-Racism'?" in *Race, Nation, Class*, p. 24; hereafter abbreviated "I." To be sure, there are those who would locate the origins of this "universal mission to educate the human race" in the "imperialist" monotheism of the Hebrew Bible, and ultimately, of course, the Hebraic and Hellenic sources of Christianity cannot be neatly separated out. There are aspects of both the Israelite history and of the prophetic discourse that could give rise to such a reading. Rabbinic Judaism and Christianity – in their relation to peo-

plehood and universalism – are interpreted by us, in a sense, as mutual thesis and antithesis within the biblical system. See further discussion below, as well as our reach for a synthesis.

24   "Moses Mendelssohn in his *Jerusalem* tried to steer the ideology of a universalist Enlightenment . . . away from what he took to be its probably inevitable course towards barbarism . . . In the Germany of his day Jews were pressured to renounce their faith in return for civil equality and union with the Christian majority. The pressure was kindly, but it was also a form of intolerance towards non-kin." Marc Shell, "Marranos (Pigs), or From Coexistence to Toleration," *Critical Inquiry* 17 (winter 1991): 331.

25   On this point see Gilman, *The Jew's Body* (New York, 1991), pp. 25–7. At Oxford University, the Centre for Advanced Hebrew Studies holds its dinners on Friday night (even though many of its participants cannot, therefore, attend) because "we are not a Jewish institution; we are an Oxford institution." This is, we submit, an example of the internalization of the racist demand for universalism.

26   See Shell, "Marranos (Pigs)," p. 332 n. 84.

27   Henri Baudet, *Paradise on Earth: Some Thoughts on European Images of Non-European Man*, trans. Elizabeth Wentholt (New Haven, CT, 1965), p. 30. In California certain missionaries had thousands of Indian babies killed so that their souls would be saved before their bodies could sin.

28   Frederick Turner, *Beyond Geography: The Western Spirit against the Wilderness* (New York, 1980), p. 45. In his book *Storm from Paradise: The Politics of Jewish Memory* (Minneapolis, MN, 1992), p. 134 n. 13, Jonathan Boyarin has provided a summary critique of Turner's book. See also on this theme Regina Schwartz, "Monotheism, Violence, and Identity," in *Religion and Literature*, ed. Mark Krupnick (forthcoming).

29   A particularly extreme and explicit version of this naturalizing and dehistoricizing move *vis-à-vis* biblical hermeneutics is found in Donald Harman Akenson, *God's Peoples: Covenant and Land in South Africa, Israel, and Ulster* (Ithaca, NY, 1992), who writes, "For certain societies, in certain eras of their development, the scriptures have acted culturally and socially in the same way the human genetic code operates physiologically. That is, this great code has, in some degree, directly determined what people would believe and what they would think and what they would do" (p. 9).

30   See Shell, "Marranos (Pigs)," for the argument that Jewish reluctance to convert others is built into the system and not merely a result of later material and historical conditions. We think, however, that Shell underestimates the potential for grounding racist thought in other aspects of biblical discourse.

31   See Jonathan Boyarin, "Reading Exodus into History," *New Literary History* 23 (summer 1992): 523–54.

32   To the extent that this diasporic existence is an actual historical entity, we ourselves are not prey to the charge of "allegorizing" the Jew. It may be fairly suggested, however, that the model is so idealized as to be in itself an allegory.

33   A highly ingenuous, or more likely egregiously disingenuous, claim by Abba Eban is given the lie in every page of Israeli history, particularly the last ones.

Beersheba may have been "virtually empty," but that is little consolation to the Bedouin who were and continue to be dispossessed there and in its environs. And the refugees in camps in Gaza, as well as the still-visible ruins of their villages, would certainly dispute the claim that Arab populations had avoided "the land of the Philistines in the coastal plain . . . because of insalubrious conditions" (Abba Eban, letter to W. D. Davies, in Davies, *The Territorial Dimension of Judaism* (1982; Minneapolis, MN, 1992), p. 76; hereafter abbreviated *T*).

34   E. P. Sanders, "Jewish Association with Gentiles and Galatians 2:11–14," in *The Conversation Continues: Studies in Paul and John in Honor of Louis Martyn*, ed. Robert T. Fortna and Beverly R. Gaventa (Nashville, TN, 1990), p. 181.

35   See Jonathan Boyarin, "Palestine and Jewish History," ch. 7 of *Storm from Paradise*.

36   Shell argues, following Spinoza, that temporal power is necessary for toleration ("Marranos (Pigs)," p. 328 n. 75). We are suggesting the opposite, that only conditions in which power is shared among religions and ethnicities will allow for difference with common caring.

37   An aboriginal Australian recently began her lecture at a conference with greetings from her people to the indigenous people of the United States, of whom there were two representatives in the audience and whom she addressed by name. Much of her lecture consisted of a critique of the rootlessness of Europeans. Daniel Boyarin had a sense of being trapped in a double bind, for if the Jews are the indigenous people of the Land of Israel, as Zionism claims, then the Palestinians are indigenous nowhere, but if the Palestinians are the indigenous people of Palestine, then Jews are indigenous nowhere. He had painfully renounced the possibility of realizing his very strong feeling of connection to the Land (this connection having been coopted by the state) in favor of what he and Jonathan Boyarin take to be the only possible end to violence and movement toward justice. Are we now to be condemned as people who have lost their roots?

38   Davies remarks that this sense of "bad conscience" can be found in texts as late as the first century BCE. We think he underestimates this. The classical midrash on Genesis, Bereshith Rabba, a product of the fourth and fifth centuries CE, begins with the question, "Why does the Torah open with the creation of the world?" It answers, "So that when the Nations will call Israel robbers for their theft of the Land, they will be able to point to the Torah and say: God created the earth and can dispose of it at his will!" (our translation).

39   See Pierre Vidal-Naquet, "Atlantis and the Nations," trans. Janet Lloyd, *Critical Inquiry* 18 (winter 1992): 300–26.

40   Harry Berger, Jr., "The Lie of the Land: The Text beyond Canaan," *Representations* 25 (winter 1989): 121; hereafter abbreviated "L."

41   For an even more nuanced reading of tensions within the Davidic stories themselves, see Schwartz, "Nations and Nationalism: Adultery in the House of David," *Critical Inquiry* 19 (autumn 1992): 142. Schwartz's forthcoming book will deal with many of the themes of identity in the Bible that this essay is treating, albeit with quite different methods and often with quite different results.

42   It is important to emphasize that this analysis is indifferent to the historical question of whether there were nomadic Israelite tribes to begin with or the thesis (made most famous by the work of Norman K. Gottwald, *The Tribes of Yahweh: A Sociology of the Religion of Liberated Israel*, 1250–1050 BCE (Maryknoll, NY, 1979)) that ascribes them to a "retribalization" process taking place among "native" Canaanites. For a discussion of this thesis, see "L," pp. 131–2. For our purposes, the representations of the tribes as nomadic and the ideological investments in that representation are indifferent to the "actual" history.

43   Also: "The desert is, therefore, the place of revelation and of the constitution of 'Israel' as a people; there she was elected" (*T*: 39). Davies's book is remarkable for many reasons, one of which is surely the way that while it intends to be a defense and explanation of Zionism as a deeply rooted Jewish movement, it consistently and honestly documents the factors in the tradition that are in tension with such a view.

44   We think that Davies occasionally seems to lose his grip on his own great insight by confusing ethnic identity with political possession (see *T*: 90–1 n. 10). The same mixture appears also when he associates, it seems, deterritorialization and deculturation (p. 93). It is made clear when he writes: "At the same time the age-long engagement of Judaism with The Land in religious terms indicates that ethnicity and religion . . . are finally inseparable in Judaism" (p. 97). We certainly agree that ethnicity and religion are inseparable in Judaism, but we fail to see the necessary connection between ethnicity, religion, and territoriality. Moreover, a people can be on their land without this landedness being expressed in the form of a nation-state, and landedness can be shared in the same place with others who feel equally attached to the same land. This is the solution of the Neturei Karta, who live, after all, in Jerusalem but do not seek political hegemony over it.

45   Davies states that "for religious Jews, we must conclude, The Land is ultimately inseparable from the state of Israel, however much the actualities of history have demanded their distinction" (*T*: 51). Yet clearly many religious Jews have not felt that way at all. Although we do not deny entirely the theological bona fides of religious Zionism as one option for modern Jewish religious thought, the fact that they are the historical "winners" in an ideological struggle should not blind us to the fact that their option was, until only recently, just one option for religious Jews, and a very contested one at that. Even the theological "patron saint" of religious Zionists, the holy Rabbi Loewe (Mahara"I) of Prague, who, as Davies points out, "understood the nature and role of nations to be ordained by God, part of the natural order," and that "nations were intended to cohere rather than be scattered"; even he held that "reestablishment of a Jewish state should be left to God" (*T*: 33). Rabbi Nahman of Bratslav's desire to touch any part of the Land and then immediately return to Poland hardly bespeaks a proto-Zionism either (ibid.). Davies nuances his own statement when he remarks: "Zionism cannot be equated with a reaffirmation of the eternal relation of The Land, the people, and the Deity, except with the most cautious reservations, since it is more the expression of nationalism than of Judaism" (*T*: 64). Davies is right, however, in his claim that J. J. Petuchowski's statement – that there can

be a "full-blooded Judaism which is in no need to hope and to pray for a messianic return to Palestine" (J. J. Petuchowski, "Diaspora Judaism – An Abnormality?" *Judaism* 9 (1960): 27) – is missing something vital about historical Jewish tradition. The desire, the longing for unity, coherence, and groundedness in the utopian future of the messianic age is, as Davies eminently demonstrates, virtually inseparable from historical Judaism (*T:* 66). There is surely a "territorial theological tradition." At issue rather is its status in pre-messianic praxis.

46   Judith Butler asks "How is it that we might ground a theory or politics in a speech situation or subject position which is 'universal' when the very category of the universal has only begun to be exposed for its own highly ethnocentric biases?" Judith Butler, "Contingent Foundations: Feminism and the Question of 'Postmodernism,'" *Praxis International* 11 (July 1991): 153.

47   Lenin's minister of justice, I. N. Steinberg, was an orthodox Jew.

48   Davies is one scholar who does not suppress this fact but forthrightly faces it. See *T:* 65.

49   Once again, the Neturei Karta, in their deference to Palestinian political claims on the Land of Israel, are, it seems, on solid historical ground.

50   Sidra Ezrahi has recently argued that monotheism and Diaspora are inextricably intertwined (oral communication with Daniel Boyarin).

51   Our point is not to reallegorize the Jew as wanderer but simply to point to certain aspects of the concrete realities of Jewish history as a possible, vital, positive contribution to human political culture in general. The implicitly normative call on other Jews to participate in our image of Jewishness is, we admit, ambivalent and potentially coercive, but how could it be otherwise? Even coercions can be ranked.

52   This statement was made by the Palestinian Jewish (Neturei Karta) members of the Palestinian delegation to the Middle East Peace Conference in Washington, DC, 1992, and has been translated here from the New York Yiddish weekly *Di yidishe vokhnshrift*, September 4, 1992. We are not including this statement with our essay in order to advance Neturei Karta as an organization, nor are we members of Neturei Karta, some of whose policies we are in sympathy with and others of which we find violently objectionable. We include it because we consider it to be eloquent evidence of the kind of radical political rhetoric available within a highly traditional diasporic Jewish framework and in particular for its insight into what could be called the construction of the demonized Other.

53   The word is the traditional Muslim prayer, "May it be God's [Allah's] will."

4

Ethnicity in an Age of Diaspora

R. Radhakrishnan

Interweaving personal history, literary criticism, and commentaries on the contemporary political scene in India, R. Radhakrishnan's important essay carefully
navigates through a series of questions that enable us to theorize how different generations of Indians living in the diaspora can understand their ethnic and
national backgrounds. The essay argues that ethnicity is always in a state of flux;
far from being static, unchanging, and immutable, Radhakrishnan suggests that
understandings of ethnicity are always context-specific, so that, for instance,
being Indian-American, in a hyphenated sense, is completely different from
being Indian.

 The essay also explores how different generations living in diaspora can
understand each other. Cautioning against an essentialist definition of the
"nation" that would always privilege the experiences of those who have
spent time in India, the essay makes a distinction between possessing information and knowledge about India and having an emotional investment in India,
ultimately suggesting that everyone can lay claim to the former. The essay
grapples with the concept of "authenticity" and why it occupies such a central
role in the diasporan imaginary. While Radhakrishnan critiques any practices
that appear to "sanction ignorance" of history, he also suggests that the experiences of both younger and older generations in the diaspora can be enriched
by understanding different histories and that identities are always open to
change.

My eleven-year-old son asks me, "Am I Indian or American?" The question
excites me, and I think of the not-too-distant future when we will discuss
the works of Salman Rushdie, Toni Morrison, Amitav Ghosh, Jamaica
Kincaid, Bessie Head, Amy Tan, Maxine Hong Kingston, and many others
who have agonized over the question of identity through their multivalent
narratives. I tell him he is *both* and offer him brief and down-to-earth

definitions of ethnicity and how it relates to nationality and citizenship. He
follows me closely and says, "Yeah, Dad [or he might have said "Appa"], I
am both," and a slight inflection in his voice underscores the word "both,"
as his two hands make a symmetrical gesture on either side of his body. I am
persuaded, for I have seen him express deep indignation and frustration
when friends, peers, teachers, and coaches mispronounce his name in cava-
lier fashion. He pursues the matter with a passion bordering on the peda-
gogical, until his name comes out correctly on alien lips. I have also heard
him narrate to his "mainstream" friends stories from the *Ramayana* and the
Mahabharatha with an infectious enthusiasm for local detail, and negotiate
nuances of place and time with great sensitivity. My son comes back to me
and asks, "But you and Amma [or did he say "Mom"?] are not US citizens?"
I tell him that we are Indian citizens who live here as resident aliens. "Oh,
yes, I remember we have different passports," he says and walks away.

At a recent Deepavali (a significant Hindu religious festival) get together
of the local India Association (well before the horrendous destruction of the
Babri Masjid by Hindu zealots), I listen to an elderly Indian man explain to
a group of young first-generation Indian-American children the festival's significance. He goes on and on about the contemporary significance of Lord
Krishna, who has promised to return to the world in human form during
times of crisis to punish the wicked and protect the good. During this lecture
I hear not a word to distinguish Hindu identity from Indian identity, not a
word about present-day communal violence in India in the name of Hindu
fundamentalism, and not even an oblique mention of the ongoing crisis in
Ayodhya. In a sense, these egregious oversights and omissions do not matter,
for the first-generation American kids, the intended recipients of this ethnic
lesson, hardly pay attention: they sleep, run around, or chatter among themselves, their mouths full of popcorn. I do not know whether I am more angry
with the elderly gentleman for his disingenuous ethnic narrative or with the
younger generation, who in their putative assimilation do not seem to care
about ethnic origins.

I begin with these two episodes because they exemplify a number of issues
and tensions that inform ethnicity. I imagine that the main problem that
intrigued my son was this: How could *someone* be both *one* and something
other? How could the unity of identity have more than one face or name? If
my son is both Indian and American, which *one* is he really? Which is the
real self and which the other? How do these two selves coexist and how do
they weld into one identity? How is ethnic identity related to national identity? Is this relationship hierarchically structured, such that the "national" is
supposed to subsume and transcend ethnic identity, or does this relationship
produce a hyphenated identity, such as African-American, Asian-American,

and so forth, where the hyphen marks a dialogic and non-hierarchic conjuncture? What if identity is exclusively ethnic and not national at all? Could such an identity survive (during these days of bloody "ethnic cleansing") and be legitimate, or would society construe this as a non-viable "difference," that is, experientially authentic but not deserving of hegemony?

The Indian gentleman's address to his audience of first-generation Indian-Americans raises several insidious and potentially harmful conflicts. First it uses religious (Hindu) identity to empower Indian ethnicity in the United States, which then masquerades as Indian nationalism. What does the appeal to "roots and origins" mean in this context, and what is it intended to achieve? Is ethnicity a mere flavor, an ancient smell to be relived as nostalgia? Is it a kind of superficial blanket to be worn over the substantive US identity? Or is Indianness being advocated as a basic immutable form of being that triumphs over changes, travels, and dislocations?

The narrative of ethnicity in the United States might run like this. During the initial phase, immigrants suppress ethnicity in the name of pragmatism and opportunism. To be successful in the New World, they must actively assimilate and, therefore, hide their distinct ethnicity. This phase, similar to the Booker T. Washington era in African-American history, gives way to a Du Boisian period that refuses to subsume political, civil, and moral revolutions under mere strategies of economic betterment. In the call for total revolution that follows, immigrants reassert ethnicity in all its autonomy. The third phase seeks the hyphenated integration of ethnic identity with national identity under conditions that do not privilege the "national" at the expense of the "ethnic." We must keep in mind that in the United States the renaming of ethnic identity in national terms produces a preposterous effect. Take the case of the Indian immigrant. Her naturalization into American citizenship simultaneously minoritizes her identity. She is now reborn as an ethnic minority American citizen.

Is this empowerment or marginalization? This new American citizen must think of her Indian self as an ethnic self that defers to her nationalized American status. The culturally and politically hegemonic Indian identity is now a mere qualifier: "ethnic." Does this transformation suggest that identities and ethnicities are not a matter of fixed and stable selves but rather the results and products of fortuitous travels and recontextualizations? Could this mean that how identity relates to place is itself the expression of a shifting equilibrium? If ethnic identity is a strategic response to a shifting sense of time and place, how is it possible to have a theory of ethnic identity posited on the principle of a natural and native self? Is ethnicity nothing but, to use the familiar formula, what ethnicity does? Is ethnic selfhood an end in itself, or is it a necessary but determinate phase to be left behind when the time is right to inaugurate the "post-ethnic"? With some of these general concerns in mind, I would now like to address the Indian diaspora in the United States.

This chapter began with a scenario both filial and pedagogic. The child asks a question or expresses some doubt or anxiety and the parent resolves the problem. The parent brings together two kinds of authority: the authority of a parent to transmit and sustain a certain pattern generationally and the authority of a teacher based on knowledge and information. Thus, in my response to my son, "You are both," I was articulating myself as teacher as well as parent. But how do I (as a parent) know that I know? Do I have an answer by virtue of my parenthood, or does the answer have a pedagogic authority that has nothing to do with being a parent? In other words, how is my act of speaking for my daughter or son different from a teacher speaking for a student? Is knowledge *natural* or is it a questioning of origins? In either case, is there room for the student's own self-expression? How are we to decide whether or not the "conscious" knowledge of the teacher and the "natural" knowledge of the parent are relevant in the historical instance of the child/student?

Let's look at yet another episode as a counterpoint to my teacherly episode with my son. During the last few years, I have talked and listened to a number of young, gifted Indian children of the diaspora who, like my son, were born here and are thus "natural" American citizens. I was startled when they told me that they had grown up with a strong sense of being exclusively Indian, and the reason was that they had experienced little during their growing years that held out promise of first-class American citizenship. Most of them felt they could not escape being *marked* as different by virtue of their skin color, their family background, and other ethnic and unassimilated traits. Many of them recited the reality of a double life, the ethnic private life and the "American" public life, with very little mediation between the two. For example, they talked about being the targets of racial slurs and racialized sexist slurs, and they remembered not receiving the total understanding of their parents who did not quite "get it." Sure, the parents understood the situation in an academic and abstract way and would respond with the fierce rhetoric of civil rights and anti-racism, but the fact was that the parents had not gone through similar experiences during their childhoods. Although the home country is indeed replete with its own divisions, phobias, and complexes, the racial line of color is not one of them. Thus, if the formulaic justification of parental wisdom is that the parent "has been there before," the formula does not apply here. Is the prescriptive wisdom of "you are both" relevant?

Within the diaspora, how should the two generations address each other? I would suggest for starters that we candidly admit that learning and knowledge, particularly in the diaspora, can only be a two-way street. The problem here is more acute than the unavoidable "generation gap" between students/young adults and teachers/parents. The tensions between the old and new homes create the problem of divided allegiances that the two generations experience differently. The very organicity of the family and the community, displaced by travel and relocation, must be renegotiated and redefined. The two generations have different starting points and different givens. This phenomenon of historical rupture within the "same" community demands careful and rigorous analysis. The older generation cannot afford to invoke India in an authoritarian mode to resolve problems in the diaspora, and the younger generation would be ill-advised to indulge in a spree of forgetfulness about "where they have come from." It is vital that the two generations empathize and desire to understand and appreciate patterns of experience not their own.

What does "being Indian" mean in the United States? How can one be and live Indian without losing clout and leverage as Americans? How can one transform the so-called mainstream American identity into the image of the many ethnicities that constitute it? We should not pretend we are living in some idealized "little India" and not in the United States. As Maxine Hong Kingston demonstrates painfully in *The Woman Warrior*, both the home country and the country of residence could become mere "ghostly" locations, and the result can only be a double depoliticization. For example, the anguish in her book is *relational*; it is not exclusively about China or the United States. The home country is not "real" in its own terms and yet it is real enough to impede Americanization, and the "present home" is materially real and yet not real enough to feel authentic. Whereas at home one could be just Indian or Chinese, here one is constrained to become Chinese-, Indian-, or Asian-American. This leads us to the question: Is the "Indian" in Indian and the "Indian" in Indian-American the same and therefore interchangeable? Which of the two is authentic, and which merely strategic or reactive? To what extent does the "old country" function as a framework and regulate our transplanted identities within the diaspora? Should the old country be revered as a pregiven absolute, or is it all right to invent the old country itself in response to our contemporary location? Furthermore, whose interpretation of India is correct: the older generation's or that of the younger; the insider's version or the diasporan?

These questions emphasize the reality that when people move, identities, perspectives, and definitions change. If the category "Indian" *seemed* secure, positive, and affirmative within India, the same term takes on a reactive, strategic character when it is pried loose from its nativity. The issue then is not just "being Indian" in some natural and self-evident way ("being Indian" naturally is itself a highly questionable premise given the debacle of nationalism, but that is not my present concern), but "cultivating Indian-ness" self-consciously for certain reasons; for example, the reason could be that one does not want to lose one's past or does not want to be homoge-nized namelessly, or one could desire to combat mainstream racism with a politicized deployment of one's own "difference." To put it simply, one's very being becomes polemical. Is there a true and authentic identity, more lasting than mere polemics and deeper than strategies?

Before I get into an analysis of this problem, I wish to sketch briefly a few responses to the home country that I consider wrong and quite dangerous. First, from the point of view of the assimilated generation, it is all too easy to want to forget the past and forfeit community in the name of the "free individual," a path open to first-generation citizens. As Malcolm X, Du Bois, and others have argued, it is in the nature of a racist, capital-ist society to isolate and privatize the individual and to foster the myth of the equal and free individual unencumbered by either a sense of commu-nity or a critical sense of the past. As the Clarence Thomas nomination has amply demonstrated, the theme of "individual success" is a poisoned candy manufactured by capitalist greed in active complicity with a racist disregard for history. We cannot afford to forget that we live in a society that is profoundly anti-historical, and that leaders represent us who believe that we have buried the memories of Vietnam in the sands of the Gulf War, which itself is remembered primarily as a high-tech game intended for visual pleasure. We must not underestimate the capacity of capitalism, superbly assisted by technology, to produce a phenomenology of the present so alluring in its immediacy as to seduce the consumer to forget the past and bracket the future.

The second path is the way of the film *Mississippi Masala*, reveling un-critically in the commodification of hybridity. The two young lovers walk away into the rain in a Hollywood resolution of the agonies of history. Having found each other as "hybrids" in the here and now of the United States, the two young adults just walk out of their "prehistories" into the innocence of physical, heterosexual love. The past *sucks*, parents *suck*, Mississippi *sucks*, as do India and Uganda, and the only thing that matters is the bonding between two bodies that step off the pages of history, secure in their "sanctioned ignorance," to use Gayatri Chakravorty Spivak's ringing phrase. What is disturbing about the "masala" resolution is that it seems to take on the question of history, but it actually trivializes histories (there is more than one implicated here) and celebrates a causeless rebel-lion in the epiphany of the present. Just think of the racism awaiting the two lovers. In invoking the term "masala" superficially, the movie begs us to consume it as exotica and make light of the historical ingredients that go into making "masala." My point here is that individualized escapes (and correspondingly, the notion of the "history of the present" as a total break from the messy past) may serve an emotional need, but they do not provide an understanding of the histories of India, Uganda, or the racialized South.

What about the options open to the generation emotionally committed to India? First, it is important to make a distinction between *information about and knowledge of India* and an *emotional investment in India*. What can be shared cognitively between the two generations is the former. It would be foolish of me to expect that India will move my son the same way it moves me. It would be equally outrageous of me to claim that somehow my India is more real than his; my India is as much an invention or production as his. There is more than enough room for multiple versions of the same reality. But here again, our inventions and interpretations are themselves products of history and not subjective substitutes for history. The discovery of an "authentic" India cannot rule over the reality of multiple perspectives, and, moreover, we cannot legislate or hand down authenticity from a position of untested moral or political high ground.

Second, my generation has to actively learn to find "Indianness" within and in conjunction with the minority-ethnic continuum in the United States. To go back to my conversations with the younger generation, it is important to understand that many of them confess to finding their "ethnic Indian" identity (as distinct from the "Indian" identity experienced at home) not in isolation but in a coalition with other minorities. It is heartening to see that a number of students identify themselves under the third world umbrella and have gone so far as to relate the "third world out there" and "the third world within." (I am aware that the term "third world" is deeply problematic and often promotes an insensitive dedifferentiation of the many histories that comprise the third world, but this term when used by the groups that constitute it has the potential to resist the dominant groups' divide-and-rule strategies.)

My generation is prone, as it ages, to take recourse to some mythic India as a way of dealing with the contemporary crises of fragmentation and racialization in the United States. Instead, we could learn from first-generation Indians who have developed solidarity and community by joining together in political struggle. The crucial issue for the older generation here is to think through the politics of why we are here and to deliberate carefully about which America they want to identify with: the white, male, corporate America or the America of the Rainbow Coalition. In cases where economic betterment is the primary motivation for immigration into the United States, and especially when these cases are successful, it is easy to deny the reality of our racially and *colorfully* marked American citizenship. Even as I write, communities are targeting schoolteachers with "foreign" accents for dismissal.

Third, it is disingenuous of my generation to behave as though one India exists "out there" and our *interpretation of India* is it. This is a generation both of and distant from India, therefore the politics of proximity has to negotiate dialectically and critically with the politics of distance. We may not like this, but it is our responsibility to take our daughters and sons seriously when they ask us, Why then did you leave India? I believe with Amitav Ghosh (I refer here to his novel *The Shadow Lines*) that places are both real and imagined, that we can know places that are distant as much as we can mis-understand and misrepresent places we inhabit. As Arjun Appadurai, among others, has argued, neither distance nor proximity guarantees truth or alien-ation. One could live within India and not care to discover India or live "abroad" and acquire a nuanced historical appreciation of the home country, and vice versa. During times when the demographic flows of peoples across territorial boundaries have become more the norm than the exception, it is counterproductive to maintain that one can only understand a place when one is in it. It is quite customary for citizens who have emigrated to expe-rience distance as a form of critical enlightenment or a healthy "estrange-ment" from their birthland, and to experience another culture or location as a reprieve from the orthodoxies of their own "given" cultures. It is also quite normal for the same people, who now have lived a number of years in their adopted country, to return through critical negotiation to aspects of their culture that they had not really studied before and to develop criticisms of their chosen world. Each place or culture gains when we open it to new standards.

In saying this I am not conceding to individuals the right to rewrite col-lective histories that determine individual histories in the first place, nor am I invoking diasporan cultural politics as a facile answer to the structural problem of asymmetry and inequality between "developed" and "underde-veloped" nations. My point is that the diaspora has created rich possibilities of understanding different histories. And these histories have taught us that identities, selves, traditions, and natures do change with travel (and there is nothing decadent or deplorable about mutability) and that we can achieve such changes in identity intentionally. In other words, we need to make substantive distinctions between "change as default or as the path of least resistance" and "change as conscious and directed self-fashioning."

Among these mutable, changing traditions and natures, who are we to ourselves? Is the identity question so hopelessly politicized that it cannot step beyond the history of strategies and counter-strategies? Do I know in some abstract, ontological, transhistorical way what "being Indian" is all about and on that basis devise strategies to hold on to that ideal identity, or do I – when faced by the circumstances of history – strategically practice Indian identity to maintain my uniqueness and resist anonymity through homogenization? For that matter, why can't I be "Indian" without having to be "authentically Indian"? What is the difference and how does it matter? In the diasporan context in the United States, ethnicity is often forced to take on the discourse of authenticity just to protect and maintain its space and history. Would "black" have to be authentic if it were not pressured into a reactive mode by the dominance of "white"? It becomes difficult to determine if the drive toward authenticity comes from within the group as a spontaneous self-affirming act, or if authenticity is nothing but a paranoid reaction to the "naturalness" of dominant groups. Why should "black" be authentic when "white" is hardly even seen as a color, let alone pressured to demonstrate its authenticity?

Let us ask the following question: If a minority group were left in peace with itself and not dominated or forced into a relationship with the dominant world or national order, would the group still find the term "authentic" meaningful or necessary? The group would continue being what it is without having to authenticate itself. My point is simply this: When we say "authenticate," we also have to ask, "Authenticate to whom and for what purpose?" Who and by what authority is checking our credentials? Is "authenticity" a home we build for ourselves or a ghetto we inhabit to satisfy the dominant world?

I do understand and appreciate the need for authenticity, especially in first world advanced capitalism, where the marketplace and commodities are the norm. But the rhetoric of authenticity tends to degenerate into essentialism. I would much rather situate the problem of authenticity alongside the phenomenon of relationality and the politics of representation. How does authenticity speak for itself: as one voice or as many related voices, as monolithic identity or as identity hyphenated by difference? When someone speaks as an Asian-American, who exactly is speaking? If we dwell in the hyphen, who represents the hyphen: the Asian or the American, or can the hyphen speak for itself without creating an imbalance between the Asian and the American components? What is the appropriate narrative to represent relationality?

Back to my son's question again: True, both components have status, but which has the power and the potential to read and interpret the other on its terms? If the Asian is to be Americanized, will the American submit to Asianization? Will there be a reciprocity of influence whereby American identity itself will be seen as a form of openness to the many ingredients that constitute it, or will "Americanness" function merely as a category of marketplace pluralism?

Very often it is when we feel deeply dissatisfied with marketplace plural-ism and its unwillingness to confront and correct the injustices of dominant racism that we turn our diasporan gaze back to the home country. Often, the gaze is uncritical and nostalgic. Often, we cultivate the home country with a vengeance. Several dangers exist here. We can cultivate India in total diasporan ignorance of the realities of the home country. By this token, anything and everything is India according to our parched imagination: half-truths, stereotypes, so-called traditions, rituals, and so forth. Or we can cultivate an idealized India that has nothing to do with contemporary history. Then again, we can visualize the India we remember as an antidote to the maladies both here and there and pretend that India hasn't changed since we left its shores. These options are harmful projections of individual psychological needs that have little to do with history. As diasporan citizens doing double duty (with accountability both here and there), we need to understand as rigorously as we can the political crises in India, both because they concern us and also because we have a duty to represent India to our-selves and to the United States as truthfully as we can.

Our ability to speak for India is a direct function of our knowledge about India. The crisis of secular nationalism in India, the ascendancy of Hindu fundamentalism and violence, the systematic persecution of Muslims, the incapacity of the Indian national government to speak on behalf of the entire nation, the opportunistic playing up of the opposition between secularism and religious identity both by the government and the opposition, the lack of success of a number of progressive local grassroots movements to in-fluence electoral politics – these and many other such issues we need to study with great care and attention. Similarly, we need to make distinctions between left-wing movements in India that are engaged in critiquing secu-larism responsibly with the intention of opening up a range of indigenous alternatives, and right-wing groups whose only intention is to kindle a politics of hatred. Diasporan Indians should not use distance as an excuse for ignoring happenings in India. It is heartening to know that an alliance for a secular and democratic South Asia has recently been established in Cambridge, Massachusetts.

The diasporan hunger for knowledge about and intimacy with the home country should not turn into a transhistorical and mystic quest for origins. It is precisely this obsession with the sacredness of one's origins that leads peoples to disrespect the history of other people and to exalt one's own. Feeling deracinated in the diaspora can be painful, but the politics of origins cannot be the remedy.

Time now for one final episode. Watching Peter Brook's production of the Hindu epic *Mahabharatha* with a mixed audience, I was quite surprised by the different reactions. We were viewing this film after we had all seen the homegrown TV serials *The Ramayana* and the *Mahabharatha*. By and large, initially my son's generation was disturbed by the international cast that seemed to falsify the Hindu/the Indian (again, a dangerous conflation) epic. How could an Ethiopian play the role of Bheeshma and a white European (I think Dutch) represent Lord Krishna? And all this so soon after they had been subjected to the "authentic version" from India? But soon they began enjoying the film for what it was. Still, it deeply upset a number of adults of my generation. To many of them, this was not the real thing, this could not have been the real Krishna. My own response was divided. I appreciated and enjoyed humanizing and demystifying Krishna, endorsed *in principle* globalizing a specific cultural product, and approved the production for not attempting to be an extravaganza. On the other hand, I was critical of some of its modernist irony and cerebral posturing, its shallow United Nations-style internationalism, its casting of an African male in a manner that endorsed certain black male stereotypes, and finally a certain Western, Eurocentric arrogance that commodifies the work of a different culture and decontextualizes it in the name of a highly skewed and uneven globalism.

Which is the true version? What did my friend mean when he said that this was not the real thing? Does he have some sacred and unmediated access to the real thing? Is his image any less an ideological fabrication (or the result of Hindu-Brahmanical canonization) than that of Peter Brook? Did his chagrin have to do with the fact that a great epic had been produced critically, or with the fact that the producer was an outsider? What if an Indian feminist group had produced a revisionist version? Isn't the insider's truth as much an invention and an interpretation as that of the outsider? How do we distinguish an insider's critique from that of the outsider? If a Hindu director had undertaken globalizing the Hindu epic, would the project have been different or more acceptable or more responsive to the work's origins? But on the other hand, would a Western audience tolerate the Indianization of Homer, Virgil, or Shakespeare? Questions, more questions. I would rather proliferate questions than seek ready-made and ideologically overdetermined answers. And in a way, the diaspora is an excellent opportunity to think through some of these vexed questions: solidarity and criticism, belonging and distance, insider spaces and outsider spaces, identity as invention and identity as natural, location–subject positionality and the politics of representation, rootedness and rootlessness.

When my son wonders who he *is*, he is also asking a question about the future. For my part, I hope that his future and that of his generation will have many roots and many pasts. I hope, especially, that it will be a future where his identity will be a matter of rich and complex negotiation and not the result of some blind and official decree.

References

Ahmad, Aijaz. *In Theory*. London: Verso, 1992.
Amin, Samir. *Eurocentrism*. New York: Monthly Review Press, 1989.
Anderson, Benedict. *Imagined Communities: Reflections on the Origin and Spread of Nationalism*. London: Verso, 1983.
Anzaldúa, Gloria. *Borderlands/La Frontera*. San Francisco: Aunt Lute Books, 1987.
Appadurai, Arjun. "Disjuncture and Difference in the Global Cultural Economy." *Public Culture* 2.2 (1990): 1–24.
Bhabha, Homi K., ed. *Nation and Narration*. New York: Routledge, 1990.
Chatterjee, Partha. *Nationalist Thought and the Colonial World: A Derivative Discourse*. Delhi: Oxford Univeristy Press, 1986.
Chow, Rey. *Woman and Chinese Modernity: The Politics of Reading between West and East*. Minneapolis: University of Minnesota Press, 1991.
Dasgupta, Sayantini. "Glass Shawls and Long Hair: South Asian Women Talk Sexual Politics." *Ms.* 3.5 (March–April 1993): 76–7.
Dhareshwar, Vivek and James Clifford, eds. *Inscriptions* 5 (1989).
Ghosh, Amitav. *The Shadow Lines*. London: Bloomsbury, 1988.
hooks, bell. *Black Looks: Race and Representation*. Boston, MA: South End Press, 1992.
Jayawardena, Kumari. *Feminism and Nationalism in the Third World*. New Delhi: Kali for Women, 1986.
Kingston, Maxine Hong. *The Woman Warrior*. New York: Knopf, 1976.
Kishwar, Madhu. "Why I Do Not Call Myself a Feminist." *Manushi* 62 (1990): 2–8.
Lloyd, David and Abdul JanMohamed, eds. *The Nature and Context of Minority Discourse*. New York: Oxford University Press, 1990.
Manushi 74–5 (double issues, January/February, March/April, 1993).
Mohanty, Chandra Talpade. "On Race and Voice: Challenges for Liberal Education in the 1990s." *Cultural Critique* 14 (winter 1989–90): 179–208.
—— ed. *Third World Women and the Politics of Feminism*. Bloomington: Indiana University Press, 1992.
Morrison, Toni, ed. *Race-ing, Justice, En-gendering Power*. New York: Pantheon, 1992.
Mufti, Aamir and John McClure, eds. Special issue on postcoloniality. *Social Text* 31/32.
Mutman, Mahmut and Meyda Yegenoglu, eds. *Inscriptions* 6: "Orientalism and Cultural Differences."
Nandy, Ashis, ed. *Science, Hegemony and Violence: A Requiem for Modernity*. Oxford: Oxford University Press, 1988.
Radhakrishnan, R. "Culture as Common Ground: Ethnicity and Beyond." *MELUS*, 14.2 (summer 1987): 5–19.
—— "Postcoloniality and the Boundaries of Identity." *Callaloo* 16.4 (fall 1993): 750–71.
Rosaldo, Renato. *Culture and Truth: The Remaking of Social Analysis*. Boston, MA: Beacon Press, 1989.

Rushdie, Salman. *Imaginary Homelands.* New York: Penguin Books, 1992.

Said, Edward W. *Orientalism.* New York: Vintage Books, 1978.

—— *Culture and Imperialism.* New York: Knopf, 1993.

Sangari, Kumkum and Sudesh Vaid, eds. *Recasting Women: Essays in Indian Colonial History.* New Brunswick, NJ: Rutgers University Press, 1990.

Shiva, Vandana. *Staying Alive: Women, Ecology and Survival in India.* Delhi: Kali for Women, 1988.

Sunder Rajan, Rajeswari, ed. *The Lie of the Land: English Literary Studies in India.* Oxford: Oxford University Press, 1992.

5

Heterogeneity, Hybridity, Multiplicity: Marking Asian-American Differences

Lisa Lowe

Lisa Lowe's landmark essay in the field of Asian American Studies offers a useful way to conceptualize immigrant and minority cultures in the United States. Discussing a range of canonical and emergent Asian-American cultural works and drawing on important Marxist cultural theory, the essay argues against the tendency to see "Asian-American" as a construction that is hierarchical and familial. Lowe suggests that to think of Asian-American cultural politics as a struggle between first and second generations within a familial framework overlooks the multiple ways in which histories of exclusion and differentiation have traditionally placed Asians apart from America. Instead of thinking of culture as something that is unchanging and transmitted "vertically" from one generation to another, she argues that culture is also worked out "horizontally" between communities and across lines of gender, race, and national origin.

Arguing against the logic that would see Asian Americans as an amorphous indistinct mass, she evokes the terms heterogeneity, hybridity, and multiplicity to suggest that even though there are compelling reasons to think of Asian Americans as a collective bloc, it is also important to introduce a critical vocabulary to explore how Asian Americans are materially – socially, culturally, and economically – distinct. The essay also suggests that a definition of Asian America must be cognizant of both the differences between various Asian groups and the ways in which Asian Americans have fought to establish unity among themselves. Lowe argues that if hegemony and the processes by which majorities and minorities are formed are to be transformed, it is crucial to remember that alliances can and must be formed across lines of race, ethnicity, national origin, class, gender, and sexuality.

This is an edited version of Lowe's essay: [. . .] indicates where text has been omitted.

In a poem by Janice Mirikitani, a Japanese-American nisei woman describes her sansei daughter's rebellion. The daughter's denial of Japanese-American culture and its particular notions of femininity reminds the nisei speaker that she, too, has denied her antecedents, rebelling against her own more traditional issei mother:[1]

> I want to break tradition – unlock this room
>   where women dress in the dark.
>   Discover the lies my mother told me.
>   The lies that we are small and powerless
>   that our possibilities must be compressed
>   to the size of pearls, displayed only as
>   passive chokers, charms around our neck.
> Break Tradition.
>   I want to tell my daughter of this room
>   of myself
>   filled with tears of shakuhatchi,
>   . . .
>   poems about madness,
>   sounds shaken from barbed wire and
>   goodbyes and miracles of survival.
>   This room of open window where daring ones escape.
> My daughter denies she is like me . . .
>   her pouting ruby lips, her skirts
>   swaying to salsa, teena marie and the stones,
>   her thighs displayed in carnivals of color.
>   I do not know the contents of her room.
> She mirrors my aging.
> She is breaking tradition.[2]

The nisei speaker repudiates the repressive confinements of her issei mother: the disciplining of the female body, the tedious practice of diminution, the silences of obedience. In turn, the crises that have shaped the nisei speaker – internment camps, sounds of threatening madness – are unknown to and unheard by her sansei teenage daughter. The three generations of women of Japanese descent in this poem are separated by their different histories and by different conceptions of what it means to be female and Japanese. The poet who writes "I do not know the contents of her room" registers these separations as "breaking tradition."

In another poem, by Lydia Lowe, Chinese women workers are also divided by generation but, even more powerfully, by class and language. The

speaker is a young Chinese American who supervises an older Chinese
woman in a textile factory.

> The long bell blared,
> and then the *lo-ban*
> made me search all your bags
> before you could leave.
>
> Inside he sighed
> about slow work, fast hands,
> missing spools of thread –
> and I said nothing.
>
> I remember that day
> you came in to show me
> I added your tickets six zippers short.
> It was just a mistake.
>
> You squinted down
> at the check in your hands
> like an old village woman peers
> at some magician's trick.
>
> That afternoon
> when you thrust me your bags
> I couldn't look or raise my face.
> *Doi m-jyu.*
>
> Eyes on the ground,
> I could only see
> one shoe kicking against the other.[3]

This poem, too, invokes the breaking of tradition, although it thematizes
another sort of stratification among Asian women: the structure of the
factory places the English-speaking younger woman above the Cantonese-
speaking older one. Economic relations in capitalist society force the young
supervisor to discipline her elders, and she is acutely ashamed that her
required behavior does not demonstrate the respect traditionally owed to
parents and elders. Thus, both poems foreground commonly thematized
topoi of immigrant cultures: the disruption and distortion of traditional
cultural practices – like the practice of parental sacrifice and filial duty or the
practice of respecting hierarchies of age – not only as a consequence of displacement to the United States but also as a part of entering a society with
different class stratifications and different constructions of gender roles.
Some Asian-American discussions cast the disruption of tradition as loss,
representing the loss in terms of regret and shame, as in the latter poem.
Alternatively, the traditional practices of family continuity and hierarchy may
be figured as oppressively confining, as in Mirikitani's poem, in which the
two generations of daughters contest the more restrictive female roles of the

former generations. In either case, many Asian-American discussions portray immigration and relocation to the United States in terms of a loss of the "original" culture in exchange for the new "American" culture.

In many Asian-American novels the question of the loss or transmission of the "original" culture is frequently represented in a family narrative, figured as generational conflict between the Chinese-born first generation and the American-born second generation.[4] Louis Chu's 1961 novel *Eat a Bowl of Tea*, for example, allegorizes the differences between "native" Chinese values and the new "westernized" culture of Chinese Americans in the conflicted relationship between father and son. Other novels have taken up this generational theme; one way to read the popular texts Maxine Hong Kingston's *The Woman Warrior* (1975) or Amy Tan's *The Joy Luck Club* (1989) would be to understand them as versions of this generational model of culture, refigured in feminine terms, between mothers and daughters. In this essay, however, I argue that interpreting Asian-American culture exclusively in terms of the master narratives of generational conflict and filial relation essentializes Asian-American culture, obscuring the particularities and incommensurabilities of class, gender, and national diversities among Asians. The reduction of the cultural politics of racialized ethnic groups, like Asian Americans, to first-generation/second-generation struggles displaces social differences into a privatized familial opposition. Such reductions contribute to the aestheticizing commodification of Asian-American *cultural* differences, while denying the immigrant histories of material exclusion and differentiation . . .

To avoid this homogenizing of Asian Americans as exclusively hierarchical and familial, I would contextualize the "vertical" generational model of culture with the more "horizontal" relationship represented in Diana Chang's "The Oriental Contingent."[5] In Chang's short story two young women avoid the discussion of their Chinese backgrounds because each desperately fears that the other is "more Chinese," more "authentically" tied to the original culture. The narrator, Connie, is certain that her friend Lisa "never referred to her own background because it was more Chinese than Connie's, and therefore of a higher order. She was tact incarnate. All along, she had been going out of her way not to embarrass Connie. Yes, yes. Her assurance was definitely uppercrust (perhaps her father had been in the diplomatic service), and her offhand didacticness, her lack of self-doubt, was indeed characteristically Chinese-Chinese" (p. 173). Connie feels ashamed because she assumes herself to be "a failed Chinese"; she fantasizes that Lisa was born in China, visits there frequently, and privately disdains Chinese Americans. Her assumptions about Lisa prove to be quite wrong, however; Lisa is even more critical of herself for "not being genuine." For Lisa, as Connie eventually discovers, was born in Buffalo and was adopted by American parents; lacking an immediate connection to Chinese culture, Lisa

projects on all Chinese the authority of being "more Chinese." Lisa con-
fesses to Connie at the end of the story: "The only time I feel Chinese is
when I'm embarrassed I'm not more Chinese – which is a totally Chinese
reflex I'd give anything to be rid of!" (p. 176). Chang's story portrays two
women polarized by the degree to which they have each internalized a cultural definition of "Chineseness" as pure and fixed, in which any deviation
is constructed as less, lower, and shameful. Rather than confirming a traditional anthropological model of "culture" in which "ethnicity" is passed from
generation to generation, Chang's story explores the relationship between
women of the same generation. Lisa and Connie are ultimately able to reduce
each other's guilt at not being "Chinese enough"; in each other they are
able to find a common frame of reference. The story suggests that the making
of Chinese-American culture – the ways in which it is imagined, practiced,
and continued – is worked out as much "horizontally" among communities
as it is transmitted "vertically" in unchanging forms from one generation
to the next. Rather than considering "Asian-American identity" as a fixed,
established "given," perhaps we can consider instead "Asian-American
cultural practices" that produce identity; the processes that produce such
identity are never complete and are always constituted in relation to historical and material differences. Stuart Hall has written that cultural identity "is
a matter of 'becoming' as well as of 'being.' It belongs to the future as much
as to the past. It is not something which already exists, transcending place,
time, history and culture. Cultural identities come from somewhere, have
histories. But, like everything which is historical, they undergo constant
transformation. Far from being eternally fixed in some essentialized past, they
are subject to the continuous 'play' of history, culture and power."[6]

Asian-American discussions of ethnic culture and racial group formation
are far from uniform or consistent. Rather, these discussions contain a spectrum of positions that includes, at one end, the desire for a cultural identity
represented by a fixed profile of traits and, at the other, challenges to the
notion of singularity and conceptions of *race* as the material *locus* of differences, intersections, and incommensurabilities. These latter efforts attempt
to define Asian-American identity in a manner that not only accounts for the
critical inheritance of cultural definitions and traditions but also accounts for
the *racial formation* that is produced in the negotiations between the state's
regulation of racial groups and those groups' active contestation and construction of racial meanings.[7] In other words, these latter efforts suggest that
the making of Asian-American culture may be a much less stable process than
unmediated vertical transmission of culture from one generation to another.
The making of Asian-American culture includes practices that are partly
inherited, partly modified, as well as partly invented; Asian-American culture
also includes the practices that emerge in relation to the dominant repre-

sentations that deny or subordinate Asian and Asian-American cultures as "other."[8] As the narrator of *The Woman Warrior* suggests, perhaps one of the more important stories of Asian-American experience is about the process of critically receiving and rearticulating cultural traditions in the face of a dominant national culture that exoticizes and "orientalizes" Asians. She asks: "Chinese-Americans, when you try to understand what things in you are Chinese, how do you separate what is peculiar to childhood, to poverty, insanities, one family, your mother who marked your growing with stories, from what is Chinese? What is Chinese tradition and what is the movies?"[9] Or the dilemma of cultural syncretism might be posed in an interrogative version of the uncle's impromptu proverb in Wayne Wang's film *Dim Sum:* "You can take the girl out of Chinatown, but can you take the Chinatown out of the girl?"[10] For rather than representing a fixed, discrete culture, "Chinatown" is itself the very emblem of shifting demographics, languages, and populations. The residents of the urban "bachelor society" Chinatowns of New York and San Francisco from the mid-nineteenth century to the 1950s, for example, were mostly male laborers – laundrymen, seamen, restaurant workers – from southern China, whereas today, immigrants from Taiwan, mainland China, and Hong Kong have dramatically reconfigured contemporary suburban Chinese settlements such as the one in Monterey Park, California.[11]

I begin with these particular examples drawn from Asian-American cultural texts in order to observe that what is referred to as "Asian-America" is clearly a heterogeneous entity ... [I]n relation to the state and the American national culture implied by that state, Asian Americans have certainly been constructed as different, and as other than, white Americans of European origin. But from the perspectives of Asian Americans, we are extremely different and diverse among ourselves: as men and women at different distances and generations from our "original" Asian cultures–cultures as different as Chinese, Japanese, Korean, Filipino, Indian, Vietnamese, Thai, or Cambodian – Asian Americans are born in the United States and born in Asia, of exclusively Asian parents and of mixed race, urban and rural, refugee and non-refugee, fluent in English and non-English-speaking, professionally trained and working class. As with other immigrant groups in the United States, the Asian-origin collectivity is unstable and changeable, with its cohesion complicated by intergenerationality, by various degrees of identification with and relation to a "homeland," and by different extents of assimilation to and distinction from "majority culture" in the United States. Further, the historical contexts of particular waves of immigration within single groups contrast one another; Japanese Americans who were interned during World War II encountered social and economic barriers quite different from those faced by individuals who arrive from Japan to southern California today. And the composition of different waves of immigrants varies in gender, class, and region. For example, in the case of the Chinese, the first groups of immigrants to the United States in the 1850s were from Canton Province, male by a ratio of ten to one, and largely of peasant backgrounds, whereas the more recent Chinese immigrants are from Hong Kong, Taiwan, or the People's Republic (themselves quite heterogeneous and of discontinuous "origins") or from the Chinese diaspora in other parts of Asia, such as Malaysia or Singapore, and they have a heterogeneous profile that includes male and female assembly and service-sector workers as well as "middle-class" professionals and business elites.[12] Further, once arriving in the United States, very few Asian immigrant cultures remain discrete, impenetrable communities; the more recent groups mix, in varying degrees, with segments of the existing groups; Asian Americans may intermarry with other racialized ethnic groups, live in neighborhoods adjacent to them, or work in the same businesses and on the same factory assembly lines. The boundaries and definitions of Asian-American culture are continually shifting and being contested from pressures both "inside" and "outside" the Asian-origin community.

I stress heterogeneity, hybridity, and multiplicity in the characterization of Asian-American culture as part of a twofold argument about cultural politics, the ultimate aim of which is to disrupt the current hegemonic relationship between "dominant" and "minority" positions. Heterogeneity, hybridity, and multiplicity are not used here as rhetorical or literary terms but are attempts at naming the material contradictions that characterize Asian-American groups. Although these concepts appear to be synonymous in their relationship to that of "identity," they can be precisely distinguished. By "heterogeneity" I mean to indicate the existence of differences and differential relationships within a bounded category – that is, among Asian Americans, there are differences of Asian national origin, of generational relation to immigrant exclusion laws, of class backgrounds in Asia and economic conditions within the United States, and of gender. By "hybridity" I refer to the formation of cultural objects and practices that are produced by the histories of uneven and unsynthetic power relations; for example, the racial and linguistic mixings in the Philippines and among Filipinos in the United States are the material trace of the history of Spanish colonialism, US colonization, and US neocolonialism. Hybridity, in this sense, does not suggest the assimilation of Asian or immigrant practices to dominant forms but instead marks the history of survival within relationships of unequal power and domination. Finally, we might understand "multiplicity" as designating the ways in which subjects located within social relations are determined by several different axes of power, are multiply determined by the contradictions of capitalism, patriarchy, and race relations, with, as Hall explains, particular contradictions surfacing in relation to the material conditions of a specific historical moment.[13] Thus, heterogeneity, hybridity, and multiplicity are concepts that assist us in critically understanding the material conditions of Asians in the United States, conditions in excess of the dominant, "orientalist" construction of Asian Americans. Although orientalism seeks to consolidate the coherence of the West as subject precisely through the representation of "oriental" objects as homogenous, fixed, and stable, contradictions in the production of Asians and in the non-correspondence between the orientalist object and the Asian-American subject ultimately express the limits of such fictions.

On the one hand, the observation that Asian Americans are heterogenous is part of a strategy to destabilize the dominant discursive construction and determination of Asian Americans as a homogeneous group . . . [T]hroughout the late nineteenth and early twentieth centuries, Asian populations in the United States were managed by exclusion acts, bars from citizenship, quotas, and internment, all of which made use of racialist constructions of Asian-origin groups as homogeneous. The "model minority" myth that constructs Asians as the most successfully assimilated minority group is a contemporary version of this homogenization of Asians. On the other hand, it is equally important to underscore Asian-American heterogeneities – particularly class, gender, and national differences among Asians – to contribute to a dialogue within Asian-American discourse, to point to the limitations inherent in a politics based on cultural, racial, or ethnic identity. In this sense, I argue for the Asian-American necessity to organize, resist, and theorize *as* Asian Americans, but at the same time I inscribe this necessity within a discussion of the risks of a cultural politics that relies on the construction of sameness and the exclusion of differences.

The first reason to emphasize the dynamic fluctuation and heterogeneity of Asian-American culture is to release our understandings of either the "dominant" or the emergent "minority" cultures as discrete, fixed, or homogeneous and to arrive at a different conception of the terrain of culture. In California, for example, it has become commonplace for residents to consider themselves as part of a "multicultural" state, as embodying a new phenomenon of cultural adjacency and admixture; this "multiculturalism" is at once an index of the changing demographics and differences of community in California and a pluralist attempt at containment of those differences.[14] For if racialized minority immigrant cultures are perpetually changing – in their composition, configuration, and signifying practices, as well as in their relations to one another – it follows that the "majority" or "dominant" culture, with which minority cultures are in continual relation, is also unstable and unclosed. The understanding that the general cultural terrain is one social site in which "hegemony" is continually being both established and contested permits us to theorize about the roles that racialized immigrant groups play in the making and unmaking of culture and to explore the ways that cross-race and cross-national projects may work to change the existing structure of power, the current hegemony. We remember that Antonio Gramsci writes about hegemony as not simply political or economic forms of rule but as the entire process of dissent and compromise through which a particular group is able to determine the political, cultural, and ideological character of a state.[15] Hegemony does not refer exclusively to the process by which a dominant group exercises its influence but refers equally to the process through which emergent groups organize and contest any specific hegemony.[16] The reality of any specific hegemony is that, although it may be for the moment dominant, it is never absolute or conclusive. Hegemony, in Gramsci's thought, is a concept that describes both the social processes through which a particular dominance is maintained, as well as the processes through which that dominance is challenged and new forces are articulated. When a hegemony representing the interests of a dominant group exists, it is always within the context of resistances from emerging groups.[17] We might say that hegemony is not only the political process by which a particular group constitutes itself as "the one" or "the majority" in relation to which "minorities" are defined and know themselves to be "other," but is equally the process by which various and incommensurable positions of otherness may ally and constitute a new majority, a "counter-hegemony."[18]

Gramsci writes of "subaltern," prehegemonic, not unified groups "un-realized" by the state, whose histories are fragmented, episodic, and identifiable only from a point of historical hindsight. They may go through different phases when they are subject to the activity of ruling groups, may articulate their demands through existing parties, and then may themselves produce new parties. In "History of the Subaltern Classes" in *The Prison Notebooks*, Gramsci describes a final phase at which the "formations [of the subaltern classes] assert integral autonomy" (p. 52). The definition of the subaltern groups includes some noteworthy observations for our understanding of the roles of racialized immigrant groups in the United States who have the histories of being "aliens ineligible to citizenship." The assertion that the significant practices of the subaltern groups may not be understood as hegemonic until they are viewed with historical hindsight is interesting, for it suggests that some of the most powerful practices may not always be the explicitly oppositional ones, may not be understood by contemporaries, and may be less overt and recognizable than others. That the subaltern classes are by definition "not unified" is provocative, too – that is, these groups are not a fixed, unified force of a single character. Rather, the assertion of "integral autonomy" by "not unified" classes suggests a coordination of distinct, yet allied, positions, practices, and movements – class-identified and not class-identified, in parties and not, race-based and gender-based – each in its own, not necessarily equivalent manner transforming, disrupting, and destructuring the apparatuses of a specific hegemony. The independent forms and locations of challenge – cultural, as well as economic and political – constitute what Gramsci calls a "new historical bloc," a new set of relationships that together embody a different hegemony and a different balance of power. In this sense, we have in the instance of the growing and shifting racialized immigrant populations in California an active example of this new historical bloc described by Gramsci; and in the negotiations between these groups and the existing "majority" over what interests constitute the "majority," we have an illustration of the concept of hegemony, not in the more commonly accepted sense of "hegemony maintenance," but in the often ignored sense of "hegemony creation."[19] The observation that the Asian-American community and other racialized and immigrant communities are both incommensurate and heterogeneous lays the foundation for several political operations. First, by reconceiving "the social" so as to centralize the emergent racialized and immigrant groups who are constantly redefining social relations in ways that move beyond static oppositions such as "majority" and "minority," or the binary axis "black" and "white," we recast cultural politics so as to account for a multiplicity of various, non-equivalent racialized groups, one of which is Asian Americans. Second, the conception of racialized group formation as heterogeneous provides a position for Asian Americans that is both historically specific and yet simultaneously uneven and unclosed. Asian Americans can articulate distinct challenges and demands based on particular histories of exclusion and racialization, but the redefined lack of closure – which reveals rather than conceals differences – opens political lines of affiliation with other groups in the challenge to specific forms of domination insofar as they share common features.

The articulation of an "Asian-American identity" as an organizing tool has provided a concept of political unity that enables diverse Asian groups to understand unequal circumstances and histories as being related. The building of "Asian-American culture" is crucial to this effort, for it articulates and empowers the diverse Asian-origin community *vis-à-vis* the institutions and apparatuses that exclude and marginalize it. Yet to the extent that Asian-American culture fixes Asian-American identity and suppresses differences – of national origin, generation, gender, sexuality, class – it risks particular dangers: not only does it underestimate the differences and hybridities among Asians, but it may also inadvertently support the racist discourse that constructs Asians as a homogeneous group, that implies Asians are "all alike" and conform to "types." To the extent that Asian-American culture dynamically expands to include both internal critical dialogues about difference and the interrogation of dominant interpellations, however, Asian-American culture can likewise be a site in which the "horizontal" affiliations with other groups can be imagined and realized. In this respect, a politics based exclusively on racial or ethnic identity willingly accepts the terms of the dominant logic that organizes the heterogeneous picture of differences into a binary schema of "the one" and "the other." The essentializing of Asian-American identity also reproduces oppositions that subsume other non-dominant groups in the same way that Asians and other groups are marginalized by the dominant culture: to the degree that the discourse generalizes Asian-American identity as male, women are rendered invisible; or to the extent that the Chinese are presumed to be exemplary of all Asians, the importance of other Asian groups is ignored. In this sense, a politics based on racial, cultural, or ethnic identity facilitates the displacement of intercommunity differences – between men and women or between workers and managers – into a false opposition of "nationalism" and "assimilation." We have an example of this in recent debates where Asian-American feminists who challenge Asian-American sexism are cast as "assimilationist," as betraying Asian-American "nationalism."

To the extent that Asian-American discourse articulates an identity in reaction to the dominant culture's stereotype, even if to refute it, the discourse may remain bound to and overly determined by the logic of the dominant culture. In accepting the binary terms ("white" and "non-white" or "majority" and "minority") that structure institutional policies about race, we forget that these binary schemas are not neutral descriptions. Binary constructions of difference utilize a logic that prioritizes the first term and subordinates the second; whether the pair "difference" and "sameness" is figured as a binary synthesis that considers "difference" as always contained within the "same" or that conceives of the pair as an opposition in which "difference" structurally implies "sameness" as its complement, it is important to see each of these figurations as versions of the same binary logic. The materialist argument for heterogeneity seeks to challenge the conception of difference as exclusively structured by a binary opposition between two terms, by proposing instead another notion of "difference" that takes seriously the historically produced conditions of heterogeneity, multiplicity, and non-equivalence. The most exclusive construction of Asian-American identity – one that presumes masculinity, American birth, and the speaking of English – is at odds with the formation of important political alliances and affiliations with other groups across racial and ethnic, gender, sexuality, and class lines. An exclusive "cultural identity" is an obstacle to Asian-American women allying with other women of color, and it can discourage laboring Asian Americans from joining with workers of other colors . . . It can short-circuit potential alliances against the dominant structures of power in the name of subordinating "divisive" issues to *the* national question.

Some of the limits of "identity politics" are discussed most pointedly by Frantz Fanon in his books about the Algerian resistance to French colonialism. Before turning to some Asian-American cultural texts to trace the ways in which the dialogues about identity and difference are represented within the discourse, I would like to consider one of Fanon's most important texts, *The Wretched of the Earth* (*Les Damnés de la terre*, 1961). Although Fanon's treatise was cited in the 1960s as the manifesto for a nationalist politics of identity, rereading it in the 1990s we ironically find his text to be the source of a serious critique of nationalism. Fanon argues that the challenge facing any movement that is dismantling colonialism (or a system in which one culture dominates another) is to provide for a new order that does not reproduce the social structure of the old system. This new order must avoid, he argues, the simple assimilation to the dominant culture's roles and positions by the emergent group, which would merely caricature the old colonialism, and it should be equally suspicious of an uncritical nativism or racialism that would appeal to essentialized notions of precolonial identity. Fanon suggests that another alternative is necessary, a new order, neither assimilationist nor nativist inversion, that breaks with the structures and practices of cultural domination, that continually and collectively criticizes the institutions of rule. One of the more remarkable turns in Fanon's argument occurs when he identifies both bourgeois assimilation and bourgeois nationalism as conforming to the same logic, as being responses to colonialism and reproducing the same structure of domination. It is in this sense that Fanon warns against the nationalism practiced by bourgeois postcolonial governments: the national bourgeoisie replaces the colonizer, yet the social and economic structure remains the same. Ironically, he points out, these separatisms, or "micronationalisms," are themselves legacies of colonialism: "By its very structure, colonialism is regionalist and separatist. Colonialism does not simply state the existence of tribes; it also reinforces and separates them."[20] That is, a politics of bourgeois cultural nationalism may be congruent with the divide-and-conquer logics of colonial domination. Fanon links the practices of the national bourgeoisie that has "assimilated" colonialist thought and practice with "nativist" practices that privilege one group or ethnicity over others; for Fanon, nativism and assimilationism are not opposites – they are similar logics that both enunciate the old order.

Fanon's analysis implies that an essentialized bourgeois construction of "nation" is a classification that excludes subaltern groups that could bring about substantive change in the social and economic relations, particularly those whose social marginalities are due to class: peasants, immigrant workers, transient populations. We can add to Fanon's criticism of nationalism that the category of "nation" often erases a consideration of women: the fact of difference between men and women and the conditions under which they live and work in situations of economic domination. This is why the concentration of women of color in domestic service or reproductive labor (child care, home care, nursing) in the contemporary United States is not adequately explained by a nation-based model of analysis.[21] It is also why the position of Asian and Latina immigrant female workers in the current global economy . . . exceeds the terms offered by racial or national analyses. We can make more explicit – in light of feminist theory that has gone perhaps the furthest in theorizing multiple determinations and the importance of posi-tionalities – that it may be difficult to act exclusively in terms of a single valence or political interest – such as race, ethnicity, or nation – because social subjects are the sites of a variety of differences. Trinh T. Minh-ha, Chela Sandoval, Angela Davis, and others have described the subject positions of women of color as constructed across a multiplicity of social relations. Trinh writes:

> Many women of color feel obliged [to choose] between ethnicity and womanhood: how can they? You never have/are one without the other. The idea of two illusorily separated identities, one ethnic, the other woman (or more precisely female), partakes in the Euro-American system of dualistic rea-soning and its age-old divide-and-conquer tactics . . . The pitting of anti-racist and anti-sexist struggles against one another allows some vocal fighters to dismiss blatantly the existence of either racism or sexism within their lines of action, as if oppression only comes in separate, monolithic forms.[22]

In other words, the conceptualization of racism and sexism as if they were distinctly opposed discourses is a construction that serves the dominant formations; we cannot isolate "race" from "gender" without reproducing the logic of domination. To appreciate this interconnection of different, non-equivalent discourses of social stratification is not to argue against the strategic importance of Asian-American identity or against the building of Asian-American culture. Rather, it is to suggest that acknowledging class and gender differences among Asian Americans does not weaken the group. To the contrary, these differences represent greater opportunity to affiliate with other groups whose cohesions may be based on other valences of oppression rather than "identity." Angela Davis argues, for example, that we might conceive of "US women of color" not as a "coalition" made up of separate groups organized around racial identities but as a *political formation* that decides to work together on a particular issue or agenda. She states: "A woman of color formation might decide to work around immigration issues. This political commitment is not based on the specific histories of racialized communities or its constituent members, but rather constructs an agenda agreed upon by all who are a part of it. In my opinion, the most exciting potential of women of color formations resides in the possibility of politi-cizing this identity – basing the identity on politics rather than the politics on identity."[23]

As we have already seen, within Asian-American discourse there is a varied spectrum of discussion about the concepts of racialized group identity and culture. At one end are discussions in which cultural identity is essentialized as the cornerstone of a cultural nationalist politics. In these discussions the positions of "cultural nationalism" and of assimilation are represented in polar opposition: cultural nationalism's affirmation of the separate purity of its culture opposes assimilation of the standards of dominant society. Stories about the loss of a "native" Asian culture tend to express some form of this opposition. At the same time, there are criticisms of this cultural nationalist position, most often articulated by feminists who charge that Asian-American nationalism prioritizes masculinity and does not account for women. Finally, at the other end, interventions exist that refuse static or binary conceptions of culture, replacing notions of "identity" with multiplicity and shifting the emphasis from cultural "essence" to material hybridity. Settling for neither nativism nor assimilation, these interventions expose the apparent opposition between the two as a constructed figure (as Fanon does when he observes that bourgeois assimilation and bourgeois nationalism often conform to the same colonialist logic). In tracing these different types of discussions about identity through Asian-American cultural debates, literature, and film, I have chosen several texts because they are accessible, "popular," and commonly held. But I do not intend to limit "discourse" to only these particular forms. By "discourse" I intend a rather extended meaning – a network that includes not only texts and cultural documents but also social practices, formal and informal laws, policies of inclusion and exclusion, institutional forms of organization, and so forth, all of which constitute and regulate knowledge about its object, Asian America.

The terms of the debate about "nationalism" and "assimilation" become clearer if we look first at the discussion of Asian-American identity in certain debates about the representation of culture. Readers of Asian-American literature will be familiar with the attacks by Frank Chin, Ben Tong, and others on author Maxine Hong Kingston, attacks that have been cast as nationalist criticisms of Kingston's "assimilationist" works. Her novel/autobiography *The Woman Warrior* is the target of such criticism because it was virtually the first "canonized" piece of Asian-American literature. In this sense, a critique of how and why this text became fetishized as the exemplary representation of Asian-American culture is necessary and important. But Chin's critique reveals other kinds of notable tensions in Asian-American culture: he does more than accuse Kingston of having exoticized Chinese-American culture, arguing that she has "feminized" Asian-American literature and undermined the power of Asian-American men to combat the racist stereotypes of the dominant white culture. Kingston and other women novelists such as Amy Tan, Chin charges, misrepresent Chinese history to exaggerate its patriarchal structure; as a result, Chinese society is portrayed as being even more misogynistic than European society. While Chin and others have cast this conflict in terms of nationalism and assimilationism, perhaps it may be more productive to see this debate, as Elaine Kim does, as a symptom of the tensions between nationalist and feminist concerns in Asian-American discourse.[24] I would add to Kim's analysis that the dialogue between nationalist and feminist concerns animates a debate about identity and difference, or identity and heterogeneity, rather than between nationalism and assimilationism. It is a debate in which Chin and others insist on a fixed masculinist identity, whereas Kingston, Tan, or such feminist literary critics as Shirley Lim or Amy Ling, with their representations of female differences and their critiques of sexism in Chinese culture, throw this notion of identity repeatedly into question. Just as Fanon points out that some forms of nationalism can obscure class, Asian-American feminists point out that Asian-American cultural nationalism – or the construction of a fixed, "native" Asian-American subject – obscures gender. In other words, the struggle that is framed as a conflict between the apparent opposites of nativism and assimilation can mask what is more properly characterized as a struggle between the desire to essentialize ethnic identity and the condition of heterogeneous differences against which such a desire is spoken. The trope that opposes nativism and assimilationism can be itself a "colonialist" figure used to displace the challenges of heterogeneity, or subalternity, by casting them as assimilationist or anti-cultural nationalist.

The trope that opposes nativism and assimilation does not only organize the cultural debates of Asian-American discourse but figures *in* Asian-American literature as well. More often than not, however, this symbolic conflict between nativism and assimilation is figured in the topos with which I began, that of generational conflict. There are many versions of this topos; I will mention only a few so as to elucidate some of the most relevant cultural tensions. In one model, a conflict between generations is cast in strictly masculinist terms, between father and son; in this model, mothers are absent or unimportant, and female figures exist merely as peripheral objects to the side of the central drama of male conflict. Louis Chu's *Eat a Bowl of Tea* exemplifies this masculinist generational symbolism, in which a conflict between nativism and assimilation is allegorized in the relationship between the father Wah Gay and the son Ben Loy in the period when the predominantly Cantonese New York Chinatown community changes from a "bachelor society" to a "family society."[25] Wah Gay wishes Ben Loy to follow "Chinese" tradition and to submit to the father's authority, whereas the son balks at his father's "old ways" and wants to make his own choices. When

Wah Gay arranges a marriage for Ben Loy, the son is forced to obey. Although the son had had no trouble leading an active sexual life before his marriage, once married, he finds himself to be impotent. In other words, Chu's novel figures the conflict of nativism and assimilation in terms of Ben Loy's sexuality: submitting to the father's authority, marrying the "nice Chinese girl" Mei Oi and having sons, is the so-called traditional Chinese male behavior; this path represents the nativist option. By contrast, Ben Loy's former behaviors – carrying on with American prostitutes, gambling, and the like – are coded as the American path of assimilation. At the "nativist" Chinese extreme, Ben Loy is impotent and is denied access to erotic pleasure, and at the "assimilationist" American extreme, he has great access and sexual freedom. Rather than naming the US state as the "father," whose immigration laws determined the restricted conditions of the "bachelor" society for the first Chinese immigrants, and the repeal of which permitted the gradual establishment of a "family" society for the later generations, Chu's novel allegorizes Ben Loy's cultural options in the "oedipal" story of the son's sexuality. The novel suggests that a third "Chinese-American" alternative becomes available, in which Ben Loy is able to experience erotic pleasure with his Chinese wife, when the couple moves away to another state, away from his father Wah Gay; Ben Loy's relocation to San Francisco Chinatown and the priority of pleasure with Mei Oi over the begetting of a son (which they ultimately do have) both imply important breaks from his father's authority and the father's representation of "Chinese" tradition. Following Fanon's observations about the affinities between nativism and assimilation, we can consider Chu's 1961 novel as an early masculinist rendering of culture as conflict between the apparent opposites of nativism and assimilation, with an oedipal resolution in a Chinese-American male "identity." Only with hindsight can we propose that the opposition may itself be a construction that allegorizes the dialectic between an articulation of a fixed symbolic cultural identity and the context of heterogeneous differences.

Amy Tan's more recent *Joy Luck Club* refigures this topos of generational conflict in a different social context, among first- and second-generation Mandarin Chinese in San Francisco. Tan's book rearticulates the generational themes of *Eat a Bowl of Tea* but deviates from the figuration of Asian-American identity in a masculine oedipal dilemma by refiguring it in terms of mothers and daughters. This shift to the relationship between women alludes to the important changes after the repeal acts of 1943–52, which permitted Chinese women to immigrate to the United States and eventually shifted the "bachelor" society depicted in Chu's novel to a "family" society. Yet to an even greater degree than *Eat a Bowl of Tea, Joy Luck Club* risks being appropriated as a text that privatizes social conflicts and contradictions, precisely by confining them to the "feminized" domestic sphere of family relations. In *Joy Luck Club* both privatized generational conflict and the "feminized" relations between mothers and daughters are made to figure the broader social shifts of Chinese immigrant formation.[26]

Joy Luck Club represents the first-person narratives of four sets of Chinese-born mothers and their American-born daughters; the daughters attempt to come to terms with their mothers' demands, while the mothers try to interpret their daughters' deeds, the novel thus expressing a tension between the "Chinese" expectation of filial respect and the "American" inability to fulfill that expectation. Although it was heralded and marketed as a novel about mother–daughter relations in the Chinese-American family (one cover review characterized it as a "story that shows us China, Chinese-American women and their families, and the mystery of the mother–daughter bond in ways that we have not experienced before"), *Joy Luck Club* also betrays antagonisms that are not exclusively generational but due as well to different conceptions of class and gender among Chinese Americans. Toward the end of the novel, for example, Lindo and Waverly Jong reach a climax of misunderstanding, in a scene that takes place in a central site for the production of American femininity: the beauty parlor. After telling the stylist to give her mother a "soft wave," Waverly asks her mother, Lindo, if she is in agreement. The mother narrates: "I smile. I use my American face. That's the face Americans think is Chinese, the one they cannot understand. But inside I am becoming ashamed. I am ashamed she is ashamed. Because she is my daughter and I am proud of her, and I am her mother but she is not proud of me."[27] The American-born daughter believes she is treating her mother, rather magnanimously, to a day of pampering at a chic salon; the Chinese-born mother receives this gesture as an insult, clear evidence of a daughter ashamed of her mother's looks. The scene not only marks the separation of mother and daughter by generation but, perhaps more important, their separation by class and cultural differences that lead to divergent interpretations of how "femininity" is understood and signified. On the one hand, the Chinese-born Lindo and American-born Waverly have different class values and opportunities; the daughter's belief in the pleasure of a visit to an expensive San Francisco beauty parlor seems senselessly extravagant to the mother whose rural family had escaped poverty only by marrying her to the son of a less humble family in their village. On the other hand, the mother and daughter also conflict over definitions of proper female behavior. Lindo assumes female identity is constituted in the practice of a daughter's deference to her elders, whereas for Waverly, this identity is determined by a woman's financial independence from her parents and her financial equality with men, by her ability to speak her desires, and is cultivated and signified in the styles and shapes that represent middle-class feminine beauty. In this sense, it is possible to read *Joy Luck Club* not as a novel that exclusively depicts "the mystery of the mother–daughter bond" among generations of Chinese-American women, but rather as a text that thematizes how the trope of the mother–daughter relationship comes to symbolize Asian-American culture. That is, we can read the novel as commenting on the national public's aestheticizing of mother–daughter relationships in its discourse about Asian Americans, by placing this construction within the context of the differences – of class and culturally specific definitions of gender – that are rendered invisible by the privileging of this trope.

Before concluding, I turn to a final text that not only restates the narrative that opposes nativism and assimilation but also articulates a critique of that narrative, calling the nativist/assimilationist dyad into question. If *Joy Luck Club* can be said to pose the dichotomy of nativism and assimilation by multiplying the figure of generational conflict and thematizing the privatized trope of the mother–daughter relationship, then Peter Wang's film *A Great Wall* (1985) – both in its emplotment and in its medium of representation – offers yet another alternative.[28] Wang's film unsettles both poles of the antinomy of nativist essentialism and assimilation by performing a continual geographical juxtaposition and exchange between the national spaces of the People's Republic of China and the United States. *A Great Wall* portrays the visit of Leo Fang's Chinese-American family to China and their month-long stay with Leo's sister's family, the Chaos, in Beijing. The film concentrates on the primary contrast between the habits, customs, and assumptions of the Chinese in China and the Chinese Americans in California by going back and forth between shots of Beijing and northern California, in a type of continual filmic "migration" between the two, as if to thematize in its very form the travel between cultural spaces. From the first scene, however, in the opposition between "native" and "assimilated" spaces, the film foregrounds that neither space begins as a pure, uncontaminated site or origin; and as the camera eye shuttles back and forth, both poles of the constructed opposition shift and are altered. (Indeed, the Great Wall of China, from which the film takes its title, is a monument to the historical condition that not even ancient China was "pure" but coexisted with "foreign barbarians" against which the Middle Kingdom erected such barriers.) In this regard, the film contains a number of emblematic images that call attention to the syncretic, composite quality of many cultural spaces, particularly in the era of transnational capital: the young Chinese Liu is given a Coca-Cola by his scholar-father when he finishes the college entrance exam; children crowd around the single village television to watch a Chinese opera singer imitate Pavarotti singing Italian opera; the Chinese student learning English recites the Gettysburg Address.

Although the film concentrates on both illustrating and dissolving the apparent opposition between Chinese Chinese and American Chinese, a number of other contrasts are likewise explored: the differences between generations within both the Chao and the Fang families; differences between men and women (accentuated by two scenes, one in which Grace Fang and Mrs. Chao talk about their husbands and children, the other in which Chao and Leo get drunk together); and finally, the differences between capitalist and communist societies (highlighted in a scene in which the Chaos and Fangs talk about their different attitudes toward "work"). The representations of these other contrasts complicate and diversify the ostensible focus on cultural differences between Chinese and Chinese Americans, as if to testify to the condition that there is never only one exclusive valence of difference but rather that cultural difference is always simultaneously bound up with gender, economics, age, and other distinctions. In other words, when Leo says to his wife that the Great Wall makes the city "just as difficult to leave as to get in," the wall at once signifies the construction of a variety of barriers – not only between Chinese and Americans but also between generations, men and women, capitalism and communism – as well as the impossibility of ever remaining bounded and impenetrable, of resisting change, recomposition, and reinvention.

The film continues with a series of contrasts: the differences in their bodily comportments when the Chinese-American Paul and the Chinese Liu play table tennis, between Leo's jogging and Mr. Chao's tai chi, between Grace Fang's and Mrs. Chao's ideas of what is fitting and fashionable for the female body. The two families have different senses of space and of the relation between family members. Ultimately, just as the Chaos are marked by the visit from their American relatives, by the time the Fang family returns home to California, each brings back a memento or practice from their Chinese trip, and they, too, are altered. In other words, rather than privileging either a nativist or assimilationist view or even espousing a "Chinese-American" resolution of differences, A Great Wall performs a filmic "migration" by shuttling between the two national cultural spaces. We are left, by the end of the film, with the sense of culture as dynamic and open material site.

In keeping with the example of A Great Wall, we might consider as a possible model for the ongoing construction of "identity" the migratory process suggested by Wang's filmic technique and emplotment, conceiving of the making and practice of Asian-American culture as contested and unsettled, as taking place in the movement between sites and in the strategic occupation of heterogeneous and conflicting positions. This is not to suggest that "hybrid" cultural identities are occasioned only by voluntary mobility and literally by the privileges that guarantee such mobility; as Sau-ling Cynthia

Wong has pointed out in *Reading Asian-American Literature*, the American nation is founded on myths of mobility that disavow the histories of both the immobility of ghettoization and the forced dislocations of Asian Americans.[29] Rather, the materialist concept of hybridity conveys that the histories of forced labor migrations, racial segregation, economic displacement, and internment are left in the material traces of "hybrid" cultural identities; these hybridities are always in the process of, on the one hand, being appropriated and commodified by commercial culture and, on the other, of being rearticulated for the creation of oppositional "resistance cultures." Hybridization is not the "free" oscillation between or among chosen identities. It is the uneven process through which immigrant communities encounter the violences of the US state, and the capital imperatives served by the United States and by the Asian states from which they come, and the process through which they survive those violences by living, inventing, and reproducing different cultural alternatives.

The grouping "Asian American" is not a natural or static category; it is a socially constructed unity, a situationally specific position, assumed for political reasons. It is "strategic" in Gayatri Chakravorty Spivak's sense of a "strategic use of a positive essentialism in a scrupulously visible political interest."[30] The concept of "strategic essentialism" suggests that it is possible to utilize specific signifiers of racialized ethnic identity, such as "Asian American," for the purpose of contesting and disrupting the discourses that exclude Asian Americans, while simultaneously revealing the internal contradictions and slippages of "Asian American" so as to insure that such essentialisms will not be reproduced and proliferated by the very apparatuses we seek to disempower. This is not to suggest that we can or should do away with the notion of Asian-American identity, for to stress only differences would jeopardize the hard-earned unity that has been achieved in the last thirty years of Asian-American politics. Just as the articulation of identity depends on the existence of a horizon of differences, the articulation of differences dialectically depends on a socially constructed and practiced notion of identity. As Stuart Hall suggests, cultural identity is "not an essence but a *positioning*. Hence, there is always a politics of identity, a politics of position, which has no absolute guarantee in an unproblematic, transcendental 'law of origin.'"[31] In the 1990s we can afford to rethink the notion of racialized ethnic identity in terms of differences of national origin, class, gender, and sexuality rather than presuming similarities and making the erasure of particularity the basis of unity. In the 1990s we can diversify our practices to include a more heterogeneous group and to enable crucial alliances – with other groups of color, class-based struggles, feminist coalitions, and sexuality-based efforts – in the ongoing work of transforming hegemony.

Notes

1   *Issei, nisei,* and *sansei* are Japanese terms meaning first-generation, second-generation, and third-generation Japanese Americans.
2   Janice Mirikitani, "Breaking Tradition," *Ikon* 9, *Without Ceremony: A Special Issue by Asian Women United* (1988): 9.
3   Lydia Lowe, "Quitting Time," *Ikon* 9, *Without Ceremony: A Special Issue by Asian Women United* (1988): 29.
4   See Elaine Kim, *Asian American Literature: An Introduction to the Writings and Their Social Context* (Philadelphia, PA: Temple University Press, 1982).
5   Diana Chang, "The Oriental Contingent," in *The Forbidden Stitch,* ed. Shirley Geok-lin Lim, Mayumi Tsutakawa, and Margarita Donnelly (Corvallis, OR: Calyx, 1989), 171–7.
6   Stuart Hall, "Cultural Identity and Diaspora," in *Identity: Community, Culture, Difference,* ed. Jonathan Rutherford (London: Lawrence and Wishart, 1990), p. 225.
7   See the discussion of Michael Omi and Howard Winant in chapter 1 of this volume. [*Editors' note:* Lowe refers to chapter 1 of her book *Immigrant Acts.*]
8   Recent anthropological discussions of cultures as syncretic systems echo some of these concerns of Asian-American writers. See, for example, Michael M. J. Fischer, "Ethnicity and the Post-Modern Arts of Memory," in *Writing Culture,* ed. James Clifford and George Marcus (Berkeley: University of California Press, 1986); and James Clifford, *The Predicament of Culture: Twentieth-Century Ethnography, Literature, and Art* (Cambridge, MA: Harvard University Press, 1988). For an anthropological study of Japanese-American culture that troubles the paradigmatic construction of kinship and filial relations as the central figure in culture, see Sylvia Yanagisako's *Transforming the Past: Kinship and Tradition among Japanese Americans* (Stanford, CA: Stanford University Press, 1985).
9   Maxine Hong Kingston, *The Woman Warrior* (New York: Random, 1975), p. 6.
10 Wayne Wang, *Dim Sum* (1984).
11 See Peter Kwong, *Chinatown, NY: Labor and Politics,* 1930–1950 (New York: Monthly Review Press, 1979); and Victor G. Nee and Brett de Bary Nee, *Longtime Californ': A Documentary Study of an American Chinatown* (New York: Pantheon, 1972). Since the 1970s the former Los Angeles "Chinatown" has been superseded demographically and economically by Monterey Park, the home of many Chinese Americans, as well as newly arrived Chinese from Hong Kong and Taiwan. On the social and political consequences of these changing demographics, see Timothy Fong, *The First Suburban Chinatown: The Remaking of Monterey Park, CA* (Philadelphia, PA: Temple University Press, 1993); and Leland Saito, "Contrasting Patterns of Adaptation: Japanese Americans and Chinese Immigrants in Monterey Park," in *Bearing Dreams, Shaping Visions,* ed. Linda Revilla, Gail Nomura, Shawn Wong, and Shirley Hune (Pullman: Washington State University Press, 1993).

12   Sucheng Chan, *This Bittersweet Soil: The Chinese in California Agriculture, 1860–1910* (Berkeley: University of California Press, 1986); Paul Ong, Edna Bonacich, and Lucie Cheng, eds. *The New Asian Immigration in Los Angeles and Global Restructuring* (Philadelphia, PA: Temple University Press, 1994).

13   See Stuart Hall, "Signification, Representation, Ideology: Althusser and the Post-Structuralist Debates," *Critical Studies in Mass Communication* 2.2 (June 1985): 91–4.

14   While California's "multiculturalism" is often employed to further an ideological assertion of equal opportunity for California's different immigrant groups, I am here pursuing the ignored implications of this characterization: that is, despite the rhetoric about increasing numbers of racialized immigrants racing to enjoy California's opportunities, for racialized immigrants, there is not equality but uneven opportunity, regulation, and stratification.

15   See Antonio Gramsci, *Selections from the Prison Notebooks,* ed. and trans. Quinton Hoare and Geoffrey Nowell Smith (New York: International Publishers, 1971).

16   The notion of "the dominant" – defined by Raymond Williams in a chapter discussing the "dominant, residual, and emergent" as "a cultural process . . . seized as a cultural system, with determinate dominant features: feudal culture or bourgeois culture or a transition from one to the other" – is often conflated in recent cultural theory with Gramsci's concept of "hegemony." Indeed, Williams writes in *Marxism and Literature* (Oxford: Oxford University Press, 1977), "We have certainly still to speak of the 'dominant' and the 'effective,' and in these senses of the hegemonic" (p. 121), as if the "dominant" and the "hegemonic" are synonymous.

It is important to note, however, that in Gramsci's thought, "hegemony" refers equally to a specific hegemony (for example, bourgeois class hegemony), as it does to the process through which "emergent" groups challenging that specific hegemony assemble and contest the specific ruling hegemony.

17   See Antonio Gramsci, "History of the Subaltern Classes: Methodological Criteria," in *Prison Notebooks,* pp. 52–60. Gramsci describes "subaltern" groups as by definition not unified, emergent, and always in relation to the dominant groups: "The history of subaltern social groups is necessarily fragmented and episodic. There undoubtedly does exist a tendency to (at least provisional stages of) unification in the historical activity of these groups, but this tendency is continually interrupted by the activity of the ruling groups; it therefore can only be demonstrated when an historical cycle is completed and this cycle culminates in a success. Subaltern groups are always subject to the activity of ruling groups, even when they rebel and rise up: only 'permanent' victory breaks their subordination, and that not immediately" (p. 54).

18   "Hegemony" still remains a suggestive construct in Gramsci, however, rather than an explicitly interpreted set of relations. Within the current globalized political economy, it is even more important to specify which particular forms of challenge to an existing hegemony are significantly transformative and which forms may be neutralized or appropriated by that hegemony. We must go beyond Gramsci's notion of hegemony to observe that, in the present con-

junction in which "modern" state forms intersect with "postmodern" movements of capital and labor, the social field is not a totality consisting exclusively
of the dominant and the counter-dominant but rather "the social" is an open
and uneven terrain of contesting antagonisms and signifying practices, some of
which are neutralized, others of which can be linked together to build pressures
against an existing hegemony. See chapter 1, note 19. [*Editors' note*: Lowe refers
to chapter 1 of her book *Immigrant Acts.*]

19   Walter Adamson, *Hegemony and Revolution: A Study of Antonio Gramsci's Political and Cultural Theory* (Berkeley: University of California Press, 1980). Anne
Showstack Sassoon, "Hegemony, War of Position, and Political Intervention,"
in *Approaches to Gramsci*, ed. Anne Showstack Sassoon (London: Writers and
Readers, 1982). See Stuart Hall's reading of Gramsci, "Gramsci's Relevance for
the Study of Race and Ethnicity," *Journal of Communication Inquiry* 10
(summer 1986).

20   Frantz Fanon, *The Wretched of the Earth*, trans. Constance Farrington (New
York: Grove, 1968), p. 94.

21   The work of Evelyn Nakano Glenn is outstanding in this regard; see especially
"Occupational Ghettoization: Japanese-American Women and Domestic
Service, 1905–1970," *Ethnicity* 8.4 (December 1981): 352–86, a study of the
entrance into and continued specialization of Japanese-American women in
domestic service and the role of domestic service in the "processing" of immigrant women into the urban economy.

22   See Trinh T. Minh-ha, *Woman, Native, Other: Writing Postcoloniality and Feminism* (Bloomington: Indiana University Press, 1989), p. 105.

23   Angela Davis, "Interview," in *The Politics of Culture in the Shadow of Capital*,
ed. Lisa Lowe and David Lloyd (Durham, NC: Duke University Press, 1997).

24   See Elaine Kim, "'Such Opposite Creatures': Men and Women in Asian
American Literature," *Michigan Quarterly Review* (winter 1990): 68–93, for a
comprehensive analysis of this debate between nationalism and feminism in
Asian-American discourse.

25   For an analysis of generational conflict in Chu's novel, see Ted Gong,
"Approaching Cultural Change through Literature: From Chinese to Chinese
American," *Amerasia* 7.1 (1980): 73–86. Gong asserts that "the father/son
relationship represents the most critical juncture in the erosion of a traditional
Chinese value system and the emergence of a Chinese American character.
Change from Chinese to Chinese American begins here" (pp. 74–5).

26   Wayne Wang's film production of *The Joy Luck Club* has taken liberties with
Tan's novel, the novel already being a text that is somewhat dehistoricized and
fanciful. See, for example, Sau-ling Cynthia Wong, "Sugar Sisterhood: Situating
the Amy Tan Phenomenon," in *The Ethnic Canon: Histories, Institutions, and
Interventions*, ed. David Palumbo-Liu (Minneapolis: University of Minnesota
Press, 1995). Unfortunately, Wang's film moves in this direction and tends to
exemplify, rather than criticize, the privatization and aestheticizing of the
Chinese mother–daughter relationship.

27   Amy Tan, *The Joy Luck Club* (New York: Putnam, 1989). The cover review cited
is by Alice Walker.

28   Peter Wang, *A Great Wall* (1985).
29   Sau-ling Cynthia Wong, *Reading Asian American Literature: From Necessity to Extravagance* (Princeton, NJ: Princeton University Press, 1993); see chapter 3, "The Politics of Mobility."
30   Gayatri Chakravorty Spivak, "Subaltern Studies: Deconstructing Historiography," in *In Other Worlds* (New York: Routledge, 1988), p. 205.
31   Hall, "Cultural Identity and Diaspora," p. 226.

Additional Readings on Ethnicity, Identity, and Diaspora

Ang, Ien. "To Be or Not to Be Chinese: Diaspora, Culture and Postmodern Ethnicity." *Southeast Asian Journal of Social Science* 21.1 (1993): 1–17.

Anthias, Flora. "Evaluating 'Diaspora': Beyond Ethnicity?" *Sociology* 32.3 (1998): 557–80.

Blakely, Allison. *Blacks in the Dutch World: The Evolution of Racial Imagery in a Modern Society*. Bloomington: Indiana University Press, 1993.

Chomsky, Aviva. "'Barbados or Canada?' Race, Immigration and Nation in Early Twentieth Century Cuba." *Hispanic American Historical Review* 80.3 (2000): 415–62.

Dabydeen, David and Brinsley Samaroo, eds. *Across the Dark Waters: Ethnicity and Indian Identity in the Caribbean*. Basingstoke: Macmillan, 1996.

England, Sarah. "Negotiating Race and Place in the Garifuna Diaspora: Identity Formation and Transnational Grassroots Politics in New York City and Honduras." *Identities: Global Studies in Culture and Power* 6.1 (1999): 5–53.

Eriksen, Thomas Hylland. *Us and Them in Modern Societies. Ethnicity and Nationalism in Mauritius, Trinidad and Beyond*. Stockholm: Scandinavian University Press, 1992.

Garvey, Johanna X. K. "Passages to Identity: Re-Membering the Diaspora." *Black Imagination and the Middle Passage*. Ed. Henry Louis Gates Jr., Maria Diedrich and Carl Pedersen. Oxford: Oxford University Press, 1999. 255–70.

George, Rosemary Marangoly. "'From Expatriate Immigrant to Immigrant Nobody': South Asian Racial Strategies in the Southern Californian Context." *Diaspora* 6.1 (1997): 31–60.

Gilman, Sander L. and Milton Shain. *Jewries at the Frontier: Accommodation, Identity, Conflict*. Bloomington: Indiana University Press, 1999.

Glick-Schiller, Nina Fouron, and Georges Fouron. "Transnational Lives and National Identities: The Identity Politics of Haitian Immigrants." *Comparative Urban and Community Research* 6 (1998): 130–61.

Gordon, Edmund Taylor. *Disparate Diasporas: Identity and Politics in an African Nicaraguan Community*. Austin: University of Texas Press, Institute of Latin American Studies, 1998.

Grosfoguel, R. and Chloe S. Georas. "'Coloniality of Power' and Racial Dynamics: Notes toward a Reinterpretation of Latino Caribbeans in New York City." *Identities: Global Studies in Culture and Power* 7.1 (2000): 85–125.

Hanchard, Michael. "Racial Consciousness and Afro-Diasporic Experiences. Antonio Gramsci Reconsidered." *Socialism and Democracy* 3 (1991): 83–106.

Hargreaves, Alex G. *Immigration, Race and Ethnicity in Contemporary France.* London: Routledge, 1995.

Harney, Stefano. *Nationalism and Identity: Culture and the Imagination in a Caribbean Diaspora.* Atlantic Highlands, NJ: Zed Books, 1996.

Harper, Philip Brian. "Take Me Home: Location, Identity, Transnational Exchange." *Callaloo* 23.1 (2000): 461–78.

Henry, Frances. *The Caribbean Diaspora in Toronto: Learning to Live With Racism.* Toronto: University of Toronto Press, 1994.

Ifekuwingwe, Jayne O. "Diaspora's Daughters, Africa's Orphans?: On Lineage, Authenticity and 'Mixed Race' Identity." *Black British Feminism.* Ed. Heidi Safia Mirza. London: Routledge, 1997. 127–52.

——*Scattered Belongings: Cultural Paradoxes of "Race", Nation and Gender.* London: Routledge, 1999.

Jules-Rosette, Benneta. "Identity Discourses and Diasporic Aesthetic in Black Paris: Community Formation and the Translation of Culture." *Diaspora* 9.1 (2000): 39–48.

Kasinitz, Philip. *Caribbean New York: Black Immigrants and the Politics of Race.* Ithaca, NY: Cornell University Press, 1992.

Kitson, Thomas J. "Tempering Race and Nation: Recent Debates in Diaspora Identity." *Research in African Literatures* 30.2 (1999): 88–95.

Kolsto, Pal. "The New Russian Diaspora: An Identity of Its Own? Possible Identity Trajectories for Russians in the Former Soviet Republic." *Ethnic and Racial Studies* 19.3 (1996): 609–39.

Kondo, Dorinne. *About Face: Performing Race in Fashion and Theater.* London: Routledge, 1997.

Korom, Frank J. "Memory, Innovation and Emergent Ethnicity: The Creolization of an Indo-Trinidadian Performance." *Diaspora* 3.2 (1994): 135–55.

Lavie, Smadar and Ted Swedenburg, eds. *Displacement, Diaspora and Geographies of Identity.* Durham, NC: Duke University Press, 1996.

Lynn, Martin. "Technology, Trade and 'A Race of Native Capitalists': The Krio Diaspora of West Africa and the Steamship, 1852–95." *Journal of African History* 33.3 (1992): 421–40.

Madan, Manu. " 'It's Not Just Cricket!' World Series Cricket: Race, Nation, and Diasporic Indian Identity." *Journal of Sport and Social Issues* 24.1 (2000): 24–35.

Markowitz, Fran. "Criss-Crossing Identities: The Russian Jewish Diaspora and the Jewish Diaspora in Russia." *Diaspora* 4.2 (1995): 201–10.

Page, Helan Enoch. "No Black Public Sphere in White Public Space: Racialized Information and Hi-Tech Diffusion in the Global African Diaspora." *Transforming Anthropology* 8.1–2 (1999): 111–28.

Panossian, Razmik. "Ambivalence and Intrusion: Politics and Identity in Armenia–Diaspora Relations." *Diaspora* 7.2 (1998): 149–96.

Patton, Adell. *Physicians, Colonial Racism and Diaspora in West Africa*. Gainesville: University of Florida Press, 1996.

Pease, Donald. "National Identity, Postmodern Artifacts and Postnational Narratives." *Boundary 2* 19.1 (1992): 1–13.

Qureshi, Karen and Shaun Moores. "Identity Remix: Tradition and Translation in the Lives of Young Pakistani Scots." *European Journal of Cultural Studies* 2.3 (1999): 311–30.

Ribenmayor, R. and A. Skotes, eds. *Migration and Identity*. Oxford: Oxford University Press, 1994.

Roy, Anindyo. "Postcoloniality and the Politics of Identity in the Diaspora: Figuring 'Home,' Locating Histories." *Postcolonial Discourse and Changing Cultural Contexts: Theory and Criticism*. Ed. Gita Rajan and Radhika Mohanram. Westport, CT: Greenwood Press, 1995.

Roy-Fequiere, Magali. "Contested Territory: Puerto Rican Women, Creole Identity and Intellectual Life in the Early Twentieth Century." *Callaloo* 17.3 (1994): 916–24.

Ryang, Sonia. "Nationalist Inclusion or Emancipatory Identity? North Korean Women in Japan." *Women's Studies International Forum* 21.6 (1998): 581–97.

Schiller, Nina Glick, Linda Basch, and Cristina Blanc-Szanton, eds. *Towards a Transnational Perspective on Migration: Race, Class, Ethnicity and Nationalism Reconsidered*. New York: New York Academy of Sciences, 1992.

Shami, Seteney. "Transnationalism and Refugee Studies: Rethinking Forced Migration and Identity in the Middle East." *Journal of Refugee Studies* 9.1 (1996): 3–26.

Sharpe, Jenny. "Is the United States Postcolonial? Transnationalism, Immigration and Race." *Diaspora* 4.2 (1995): 181–99.

Shokeid, Moshe. "My Poly-Ethnic Park: Some Thoughts on Israeli-Jewish Ethnicity." *Diaspora* 7.2 (1998): 225–46.

Smith-Hefner, Nancy Joan. *Khmer American: Identity and Moral Education in a Diasporic Community*. Berkeley: University of California Press, 1999.

Sollors, Werner, ed. *Multilingual America: Transnationalism, Ethnicity, and the Languages of American Literature*. New York: New York University Press, 1998.

Sorenson, John. "Essence and Contingency in the Construction of Nationhood: Transformations of Identity in Ethiopia and Its Diasporas." *Diaspora* 2.2 (1992): 201–28.

Soysal, Yasemin Nuhoglu. "Citizenship and Identity: Living in Diasporas in Post-War Europe?" *Ethnic and Racial Studies* 23.1 (2000): 1–15.

Takenaka, Ayumi. "Transnational Community and Its Ethnic Consequences: The Return Migration and the Transformation of Ethnicity of Japanese Peruvians." *American Behavioral Scientist* 42.9 (1999): 1459–74.

Thomas, Mandy. *Place, Memory and Identity in the Vietnamese Diaspora*. New York: Allen and Unwin, 1998.

Torres, Maria de los Angeles. "*Encuentros y Encontronazos*: Homeland in the Politics and Identity of the Cuban Diaspora." *Diaspora* 4.2 (1995): 211–38.

Torres-Saillant, Silvio. "Diaspora and National Identity: Dominican Migration in the Postmodern Society." *Migration World Magazine* 25.3 (1997): 18–22.

Wellmeier, Nancy J. *Ritual, Identity and the Mayan Diaspora*. New York: Garland, 1998.

Wieviorka, Michel. "Racism and Diasporas." *Thesis Eleven* 52–5 (1998): 69–81.

Young, Robert J. C. *Colonial Desire: Hybridity in Theory, Culture and Race*. London: Routledge, 1995.

Yue, Ming Bao. "On Not Looking German: Ethnicity, Diaspora and the Politics of Vision." *European Journal of Cultural Studies* 3.2 (2000): 173–94.

Part III

Sexuality, Gender, and Diaspora

6

Against the Lures of Diaspora: Minority Discourse, Chinese Women, and Intellectual Hegemony

Rey Chow

As suggested by both its title and subtitle, Rey Chow's important essay is an incisive critique of knowledge production in the North American academy. Focusing on the example of Chinese studies – in particular, the place of women in this field – Chow inquires into the place of Chinese intellectuals as "knowledge brokers" in the diaspora. Primarily occupying positions within institutions of higher learning in the United States, many Chinese intellectuals concern themselves with studying and researching literatures and cultures of China. Chow asks what it means that many Chinese intellectuals' "object of study" are people who are located in spaces and cultures to which these intellectuals will probably never return. How, Chow asks, is the interest in studying the place of minorities "back home" analogous to the colonizer/colonized relation that is characteristic of postcolonial diasporic spaces?

Noting that intellectuals in diaspora are rewarded and praised for their work on minority cultures and that they have also been important in disrupting the nature of knowledge production in the "West" about the "East," Chow also reminds us that the voices of the oppressed remain unheard and persecution continues. Chow carefully notes that this concern is not about who is more "authentic," but rather it is a way to clarify what is at stake in the research agendas of intellectuals in diaspora. Grappling with the notion that the knowledge produced by diasporic intellectuals is hegemonic over that of scholars "at home," she suggests that scholarship centered around the place of "women" and "minorities" in the "third world" needs to be aware of the historical conditions that make it possible for this type of work to emerge and that privilege diaspora intellectuals over those at home. Ultimately, she suggests that one must be wary of the idea that the privileged space of intellectual discourse is helping to save "oppressed victims" back in the "third world."

Modern Chinese Literature as "Minority Discourse"

The questions I would like to address in this chapter can be stated very simply: Why is it so difficult to bring up the topic of women in the field of Chinese studies? What can the critical spotlight received by "Chinese women" tell us about the discursive politics in play? These questions are not only questions about women and Chinese studies. They have to do with the problematic of the postcolonial discursive space in which many "third world" intellectuals who choose to live in the "first world" function. Within that space, these intellectuals are not only "natives" but spokespersons for "natives" in the "third world." Currently, the prosperity of that space is closely tied up with the vast changes taking place in Western academic institutions, notably in North America, where many intellectuals "of color" are serving as providers of knowledge about their nations and cultures. The way these intellectuals function is therefore inseparable from their status as cultural workers/brokers: in diaspora, which may be a result of graduate studies, research visiting or permanent appointments, immigration, and, in some cases, exile or political asylum. In this chapter I want to use the increasing interest in "women" in the field of Chinese studies as a way to focus the problems of the "third world" intellectual in diaspora. The implications of these problems go far beyond narrow institutional designators such as "women's studies" and "area studies" in which the study of "third world women" is most commonly lodged.

Superficial developments in the humanities across the US indicate the opposite of the first of my opening questions. Following the legitimation of feminist interests in the West, receptivity to women's issues in other parts of the world seems unprecedentedly great at present. In the Asian field, it is not difficult to find research projects, dissertations, books, and conferences devoted to women. For the first time in Asian history, perhaps, we can identify a visible group of scholars, largely women, whose work centers on women. And yet the spotlight on "women" in our field seems also to make the shape and sound of the enemy more pronounced than ever.

I use "enemy" to refer not to an individual but to the attitude that "women" is still not a legitimate scholarly concern. Depending on the occasion, this enemy uses a number of different but related tactics. The first tactic may be described as habitual myopia: "You don't exist because I don't see you." The second is conscience-clearing genitalism:[1] "Women? Well, of

course! . . . But I am not a woman myself, so I will keep my mouth shut."
The third is scholarly dismissal: "Yes, women's issues are interesting, but they
are separate and the feminist approach is too narrow to merit serious study."
The fourth is strategic ghettoization: since "women" are all talking about
the same thing over and over again, give them a place in every conference
all in one corner, let them have their say, and let's get on with our business.
These tactics of the enemy – and it is important for us to think of the enemy
in terms of a dominant symbolic rather than in terms of individuals, that is,
a corpus of attitudes, expressions, discourses, and the *value* espoused in them
– are not limited to the China field. They are descriptive of the problems
characteristic of the study of non-hegemonic subjects in general.

Leaving aside the issue of women for the time being, I would like to argue
that the notion of modern Chinese literature as we know it today depends,
implicitly, on the notion of a "minority discourse" in the postcolonial era.
As two critics define it, "minority discourse is, in the first instance, the
product of damage, of damage more or less systematically inflicted on cultures produced as minorities by the dominant culture."[2] Modern Chinese
literature is, in this respect, not different from other postcolonial national
literatures; its problems are symptomatic of the histories of non-Western cultures' struggles for cultural as well as national autonomy in the aftermath of
Western imperialism. Because postcolonial literatures are linked to the hegemonic discourse of the West as such, they are, in spite of the typical nativist
argument for their continuity with the indigenous traditions,[3] always effectively viewed as a kind of minority discourse whose existence has been victimized and whose articulation has been suppressed.

While the "world" significance of modern Chinese literature derives from
its status as minority discourse, it is precisely this minority status that makes
it so difficult for modern Chinese literature to be legitimized as "world"
literature, while other *national* literatures, notably English, French, and
Russian, have had much wider claims to an international modernity in spite
of their historical and geographical specificity. In spite – and because – of the
current clamor for "minority discourses," there is no lack of voices supporting the opposite viewpoint. The debates in the US on the issue of canon-
icity, for instance, are driven by the urge to perpetuate what has been
established as the "universals" of "cultural literacy." In fact, the more frequently "minor" voices are heard, the greater is the need expressed by the
likes of Allan Bloom and E. D. Hirsch, Jr. for maintaining a canon, so that
a Western notion of humanity can remain as the norm.[4] We understand from
the Gulf War that it is by resorting to the rhetoric of preserving universals
– love, knowledge, justice, tradition, civilization, and so forth, argued both
in George Bush's "new world order" and Saddam Hussein's pan-Arabism –
that political power sustains its ideological hold on the populace. The

rhetoric of universals, in other words, is what ensures the ghettoized existence of the other, be it in the form of a different culture, religion, race, or sex. As all of us know, the battle against the ideology embedded in the rhetoric of universals is also one faced by those working on "women" in the China field.

The proposal I want to make, however, is that, for the investigators of "Chinese women," this battle *cannot* simply be fought by a recourse to "minority discourse," or to Chinese women as the suppressed and victimized other. I will explain by discussing the precarious relation between "minority discourse" and "women" in the China field, with special emphasis on the difficult and challenging role of Chinese women intellectuals today.

Consider one of the primary tasks faced by Chinese intellectuals in the twentieth century – that of establishing, in the throes of imperialism, a national literature. If the desire to establish a national literature is a desire for a kind of universal justice – a justice in the eyes of which Chinese literature and culture would become legitimate internationally rather than simply "Chinese" – how is this desire pursued? While there are many efforts to demonstrate modern Chinese literature's continuity with past literary achievements, what distinguishes modern Chinese writings is an investment in suffering, an investment that aims at exposing social injustice. This investment in – or cathexis to – suffering runs through Chinese cultural production from the beginning of the twentieth century to the present – from the upsurge of interest in romantic love in popular Mandarin Duck and Butterfly stories of the 1910s, to the pro-science and pro-democracy attempts at national self-strengthening in May Fourth writings, to the focuses on class struggle in the literature of the 1930s and 1940s, to the official communist practice of "speaking bitterness" (*suku*), by which peasants were encouraged by cadres of the liberation forces to voice their sufferings at mass meetings in the 1950s and 1960s, and to the outcries of pain and betrayal in the "literature of the wounded" (*shanghen wenxue*) of the post-Cultural Revolution period. In other words, the attempt to establish a *national* literature in the postcolonial era requires a critical edge other than the belief in a magnificent past. For twentieth-century Chinese intellectuals, this critical edge has been *class consciousness*. In orthodox Marxist terms, "class" is that contradiction between the surplus of capital on the one hand and labor on the other. The surplus of capital leads to a situation in which those who do the least work enjoy the most privilege, while those who work continue to have the products of their labor taken or "alienated" from them. The category of "class" thus supplies a means of analyzing social injustice in economic terms, as the unequal distribution of wealth between the rich and the poor.[5] In the Chinese context, in which intellectual work was formerly part of the hegemony of the state, "class consciousness" is inseparable from *cultural* revolution, a revolution that seeks to overthrow not only the economic but specifically the ideological dominance of the ruling classes. Thus even in the crudest usage by the Chinese communists, "alienated labor" carries ideological as well as economic implications.

The historian Arif Dirlik refers to the use of class for nation-building as the practice of the "proletarian nation." Commenting on a passage from *The Crisis of the Arab Intellectual* by Abdallah Laroui (who derived much of his historicism from Joseph Levenson's work on China), Dirlik writes:

> [The new China is] the "proletarian" nation of revolutionary intellectuals (Li Dazhao, Sun Yat-sen, Mao Zedong come to mind immediately). If it does not bring the proletariat (or the oppressed classes) into the forefront of history, it at least makes them into a central component of the national struggle – as a referent against which the fate of ideas and values must be judged.[6]

We cannot understand modern Chinese literature without understanding the ways in which nationhood and class are intertwined in literary discourse. The use of "class consciousness" as a way to build a national culture is one of the most important signs of Chinese literature's modernity, a modernity that is, as May Fourth and subsequent writings show, self-consciously revolutionary. If modern Chinese literature emerges as an "other," a "minor" literature in the global scene, it also emerges by putting the spotlight on its oppressed classes, among which women occupy one but not the only place.

In its investment in suffering, in social oppression, and in the victimization and silencing of the unprivileged, modern Chinese literature partakes of the many issues of "minority discourse" that surface with urgency in the field of cultural studies/cultural criticism in North America today. Central to such issues is the question "can the subaltern speak?" as we find it in Gayatri Spivak's essay of the same title.[7] In this regard, the history of modern Chinese literature can be seen as a paradigm for contemporary cultural studies, simply because the most "written" figure in this history is none other than the subaltern, whose "speech" has been coming to us through fiction, poetry, political debates, historical writings, journalistic representations, as well as radio plays, films, operas, and regional cultural practices. In a fashion paralleling the theorizations of "minority discourse" that emphasize the production of postcolonial subjects whose speeches and/or writings disrupt the hegemonic discourse of the imperialist, modern Chinese literature specializes, one might argue, in producing figures of minority whose overall effect has been an ongoing protest against the cultural violence they experience at physical, familial, institutional, and national levels. At the same time, the conscious representation of the "minor" as such also leads to a situation in which it is locked in opposition to the "hegemonic" in a permanent bind. The "minor" cannot rid itself of its "minority" status because it is that status that gives it its only legitimacy;[8] support for the "minor," however sincere, always becomes support for the center. In communist China one could go as far as saying that "class consciousness," as it becomes an ideological weapon of the state, offers a "critical edge" only insofar as it permanently regenerates the reality of social injustice rather than its dissolution.

How is this so? Let me explain by relating "class consciousness" to the conceptualization of social change *through language*. Among Marxist critics working in the West, the advocacy of "class consciousness" is often closely related to a specific theory of language. For instance, speaking of the "subaltern," Gayatri Spivak says:

> The subaltern is all that is not elite, but the trouble with those kinds of names is that if you have any kind of political interest you name it in the hope that the name will disappear. That's what class consciousness is in the interest of: the class disappearing. What politically we want to see is that the name would not be possible.[9]

The theory of language offered here is that the act of articulating something moves and changes it, and therefore may cause it to disappear. In China, however, the relation between language and reality has been very differently conceived because of the lingering force of Confucius's concept of *zheng-ming* – the rectification of names. The Confucian attitude toward language is expressed in a well-known passage in *Lunyü* (*The Analects*):

> If names be not correct, language is not in accordance with the truth of things. If language be not in accordance with the truth of things, affairs cannot be carried on to success . . .
> Therefore a superior man considers it necessary that the names he uses may be spoken *appropriately*, and also that what he speaks may be carried out *appropriately*. What the superior man requires is just that in his words there may be nothing incorrect.[10]

For Confucius, as for the majority of Chinese people, naming is the opposite of what Spivak suggests. Instead of causing the reality to disappear, naming is the way to make a certain reality "proper," that is, to make it real. That is why it is so important to have the right name and the right language.

To use the words of Slavoj Žižek, we may say that Confucius understood "the radical contingency of naming, the fact that naming itself retroactively constitutes its reference." It is "the name itself, the signifier, which supports the identity of the object."[11] "In other words," Žižek writes, "the only possible definition of an object in its identity is that this is the object which is always designated by the same signifier – tied to the same signifier. It is the signifier which constitutes the kernel of the object's 'identity.'"[12] Strictly speaking, there is nothing false or misleading about Confucius's theory of language. As a process, *zhengming* demonstrates the practical politics involved in any claim to visibility and existence – namely, that such a claim must be at the same time a claim to/in language. Hence, even though – in fact, precisely because – it is no more *than a claim*, language is the absolutely essential means of access to power. In their struggles to be seen and heard, minority groups all prove the truth of Confucius's theory: before "dismantling" and "decentering" power in the way taught by deconstructionists, they argue, they must first "have" power and be named, that is, recognized, so.

The act of naming, then, is not intrinsically essentialist or hierarchical. It is the social relationships in which names are inserted that may lead to essentialist, hierarchical, and thus detrimental consequences.[13] Historically, the problem with Confucius's teaching was that it was used to address civil servants in their service to the state. A very astute understanding of language was thus instrumentalized in organizing political hierarchy and consolidating centralized state power, with all the reactionary implications that followed. *Zhengming* became a weapon that ensured the immovability of an already established political hegemony and in that sense a paradigmatic case, in Derrida's terms, of *logocentric* governance.

By extension, we understand why, in their mobilization of "class consciousness," the Chinese communists have actually been following the Confucian model of language as it is inherited in Chinese politics in spite of their overt "ideological" contempt for the Master. The raising of "class consciousness" as official "reeducational" policy during the two decades following 1949 did not so much lead to the disappearance of class as it did to a reification/rectification of the name "class" as the absolute reality to which every citizen had to submit in order to clear their "conscience." Hence, in pursuit of the ideal of the "proletarian nation," strengthening national culture became equal to hounding down the class enemy, even though "class enemy" was *simply a name*. In a discussion of the contemporary Chinese political situation by way of Jacques Lacan's notion of *jouissance*, Kwai-cheung Lo writes:

> The "class enemy" in the Chinese Cultural Revolution is, in a sense, a fetish structuring the jouissance. The whole country is summoned to ferret out the class enemy, to uncover the hidden counterrevolutionaries. The class enemy is everywhere, in every nook and corner of our social life, but it is also nowhere, invisible and arcane. It is clear that the class enemy is jouissance, which is an impossibility but can produce traumatic effects. It is also the *objet petit a*, a pure void which keeps symbolic order working and sets the Cultural Revolution in motion. The paradoxical character of the class enemy is that it always returns to the same place, exerts effects on the reality of the subject, and it is

itself a nothing, a negativity. Thus, in the end, when we have looked in every corner to ferret out the class enemy, we then have to uncover the enemy in our heart. The Cultural Revolution turns out to be a Stalinist trial. Everyone must examine their whole life, their entire past, down to the smallest detail, to search for the hidden fault and, finally, confess themselves as sinners . . .

When the people are asked to confess, to "open their hearts to" [*jiaoxin*] the party, and they look deep into their hearts, what they find is not a subject who is unable to express the signified, but a void, a lack which has to be filled out by the object, the sin, the incarnation of impossible enjoyment, jouissance.[14]

In their obsession with the name "class enemy," the "rectification" of which led to the madness of the Cultural Revolution, the Chinese communists thus proved themselves to be loyal disciples of Confucius's teaching about state control.

Perhaps the greatest and most useful lesson modern Chinese culture has to offer the world is the pitfall of building a nation – "the People's Republic of China" – on a theory of social change – "class consciousness" – in the illusion that the hope offered by that theory – the disappearance of class itself – can actually materialize in human society. Chinese communism was the dream of materializing that theory by officializing a concept of language and literature in which the minorities, the oppressed, and the exploited are to be vindicated. But when the force of "class consciousness" is elevated to official ideology rather than kept strictly as an analytical instrument (as it was in the texts of Marx), it also becomes mechanical and indistinguishable from other ideological strongholds of governmental power.[15] To date, the mainland government is still trying to keep this rhetoric of "class consciousness" alive after its latest abuse of the peaceful seekers of democratic reforms. When a government that was originally founded on the ideal of social justice dwindles to the level of open injustice and continual deception of its people, as the Chinese government does today, we must seek strategies that are alternative to a continual investment in minority, in suffering, and in victimization.

Masculinist Positions in the China Field: Women to the West, Fathers to Chinese Women

The clarified relation between "nation" and "class" in twentieth-century China allows one to ask: How do women intervene? How can we articulate women's *difference* without having that difference turned into a cultural ghettoization of women while the enemy remains intact? How can women "speak"?

Current trends in contemporary cultural studies, while being always supportive of categories of difference, also tend to reinscribe those categories in
the form of fixed identities. As in *zhengming*, categories such as "race,"
"class," and "gender" were originally named in order to point out what has
been left out of mainstream categorizations and thus what still remains to
be named, seen, and heard. "Names" of "difference" as such are meant as
ways for the marginalized to have some access to the center. And yet one
feels that these categories of difference are often used in such a way as to
stabilize, rather than challenge, a preestablished method of examining "cultural diversity," whereby "difference" becomes a sheer matter of adding new
names in an ever-expanding pluralistic horizon. If categories such as "race,"
"class," and "gender" are to remain useful means of critical intervention,
they must not be lined up with one another in a predictable refrain and
attached to all investigations alike as packaging. Instead, as terms of intervention, they must he used to analyze, decode, and criticize one another, so
that, for instance, "gender" is not only "gender" but what has been muted
in orthodox discussions of class, while "class" is often what notions such as
"woman" or even "sexual difference" tend to downplay in order to forge a
gendered politics. How do we conceive of gender within class and distinguish class within gender? How is it that scholars, including Asianists, seem
more ready to accept "gender" when it is spoken of *generally* across the disciplines, while to bring it up in the interpretation of specific texts within a
particular field such as Chinese studies, one still runs the risk of being considered unscholarly and non-objective?

A valid point made by Dirlik is that in order to destroy culturalist hegemony, it is not enough to concentrate on unequal relations between nations
(such as those between the "first" and the "third" worlds). What is of similar
importance is an investigation of the unequal relations *within* societies. In
the context of China, the narrative of "class" as a way to address the unequal
relations within society has proved itself inadequate because of its official
abuse, an abuse which takes the form of an armed appropriation – a turning
into property and propriety – of a particular language, the language of the
oppressed or what we have been calling "minority discourse." That is to say,
if the past forty years of Chinese political history has been a failed revolution, it is in part because the revolution has been a secret cohabitation
between Confucius and the communists, between *zhengming* and a theory
of language in which "naming" is, ideally, the first step to changing social
reality. In this cohabitation, Confucius, saturated with practices of bureau-
cratic hierarchy, remains on top.

After June 4, 1989, it is unlikely that the Chinese intellectuals who have
begun careers in the West will "return" to China. In their diaspora, Chinese
intellectuals will emerge as a group whose distinction from the "objects"

they use for their research will be more and more pronounced. Geographic, linguistic, and political differences are going to turn internationalized Chinese women intellectuals, for instance, into a privileged class *vis-à-vis* the women in China. As we continue to use Chinese women's writings and lives as the "raw material" for our research in the West, the relationship between us as intellectuals overseas and them "at home" will increasingly take on the coloration of a kind of "master discourse/native informant" relationship. The inequality of this relationship should now be emphasized as that inequality *within* a social group that Dirlik mentions. While intellectuals are rewarded for their work in the West, voices of the oppressed continue to be unheard and intellectual work continues to be persecuted in China. There is very little we can do overseas to change the political situation "back there." The attention bestowed upon Chinese events by the world media is arbitrary. In early 1991, for instance, as global attention was directed toward the Gulf War, the Chinese government's trial and sentencing of the June 4 protesters went largely unnoticed. Whether we like it or not, our position with regard to China is one of waiting and hoping.

As "minority discourse" becomes a hot topic in cultural studies in the West, some overseas Chinese intellectuals are now choosing to speak and write from a "minor" position. While enjoying the privilege of living in the West, they cling, in their discourse, to the status of the neglected "other." While this espousal of minority status may not be stated as such, it is most often detected in discourses which moralistically criticize "the West" in the name of "real" "Chinese" difference or otherness. Depending on the political interest of the person, "Chinese difference" (by which is usually meant Chinese identity) may take the form of a reactionary confirmation of traditional, humanistic attitudes toward "culture" and "knowledge," or it may assume a liberalist guise by reading Chinese culture in terms of the Bakhtinian "dialogic" and "carnivalesque." In some cases, while being fashionably skeptical of "Western theory," these intellectuals nonetheless revere Fredric Jameson's ethnocentric notion that all "third world" texts are necessarily to be read as "national allegories"[16] and proceed to read Chinese culture accordingly. However, to "nationalize" "third world" cultural productions "allegorically" this way is also to "other" them uniformly with a logic of production that originates in the West. What is being forgotten here is how "first world" production comprises not only the production of tangible goods but also intangible value. The latter, as I will argue in the following pages, is exported as ideological exploitation, which plays a far more crucial role in structuring the lives of peoples in the non-West. Without a discussion of "value" as such, the notion that all "third world" peoples are necessarily engaged in national struggles and that all "third world" texts are "national allegories" is quite preposterous.[17] In Jameson's model, "third world" intellectuals are, regardless of their class and gender, made to speak uniformly as minors and women to the West. Following Jameson, many contemporary Chinese intellectuals' desire to play the role of the other confirms what Nancy Armstrong, writing about the historicization of sexuality in the British novel, says: "the modern individual was first and foremost a woman."[18]

Vis-à-vis the "insiders" of the China field, on the other hand, these intellectuals' strategy is decidedly different. There, faced with new types of research and new interests such as women's issues, their attitude becomes, once again, patriarchal and mainstream; women's issues do not interest them the way *their own minority* in relation to "the West" does. Faced with women, their attitude resembles that of right-wingers in the American academy. They defend tradition, sinocentrism, and heritage, and denounce feminist scholarship as unscholarly. It is as if, dealing with the "insiders," they no longer remember the political significance of the "minority discourse" which they speak only when it is opportune for them to do so. They are minors and women when faced with "foreigners"; they are fathers when faced with "insiders," especially women.

To return, then, to the question of why it is so difficult to bring up the topic of women in the field of Chinese studies. It is difficult not because women's issues are insignificant – there has been interest in "woman" and "the new woman" in Chinese writings since before the 1910s. Quite to the contrary, it is because "woman," like the "minor," offers such an indispensable position *in discourse*, traditional and modern, that feminists have difficulty claiming "her." One question that traditionalists in the field often ask feminists is: "But there is no lack of femininity in classical Chinese literature! Why are you saying that the feminine has been suppressed?" A look at Chinese literary history would suggest that these traditionalists are, literally, right: *Chinese literary history has been a history of men who want to become women.* In the past, male authors adopted women's voices and wrote in "feminine" styles; in the modern period, male authors are fascinated by women as a new kind of literary as well as social "content." We may therefore argue that it is in the sense of men preempting women's place as the minor (*vis-à-vis* both tradition and the West) and claiming that place for themselves that "the Chinese woman," to use Mao Zedong's words to André Malraux, "doesn't yet exist."[19] Chinese women are, in terms of the structure of discourse, a kind of minor of the minor, the other to the woman that is Chinese man.

Throughout the twentieth century, it is the continual creation of alternative *official minor positions* that continually puts off a direct attack on the subjugation of women. To defend the "Chinese culture," pairs of oppositions are always set up: tradition and modernity, China and the West, China and Japan, the communists and the nationalists, the feudal landlords and the people, the rich and the poor, and so forth. The place of a minor discourse – as that which must struggle to speak – is therefore always already filled as long as there is always a new political target to fight against. The common view that women's issues always seem to be subsumed under the "larger" historical issues of the nation, the people, and so forth is therefore true but also a reversal of what happens in the process of discourse construction. For in order for us to construct a "large" historical issue, a position of the victim/minor must always already be present. In terms of language, this means that for a (new) signifier to emerge as a positive presence, there must always be a lack/negative supporting it. The producer of the new signifier, however, always occupies (or "identifies with") the space of the lack/negative (since it is empty) in order to articulate. This goes to show why, for instance, among all the "Chinese people," it is the peasants, the ones who are most illiterate, most removed from the intellectuals, and therefore most "lacking" in terms of the dominant symbolic, who most compel progressive Chinese intellectuals' fantasy.[20] Chinese women, on the other hand, are always said to be as powerful as Chinese men: we keep hearing that they "hold up half the sky." If minority discourse is, like all discourse, not simply a fight for the content of oppression it is ostensibly about, but also a fight for the ownership – the propriety, the property – of speaking (that is, for *zhengming*), then Chinese women are precluded from that ownership because it has always been assumed by others in the name of the people, the oppressed classes, and the nation.

Precisely because the truly minor is the voiceless, it can be seized upon and spoken for. As Spivak says, "If the subaltern can speak . . . the subaltern is not a subaltern any more."[21] The Chinese communist government serves as a good example of an agency speaking for "minorities" in order to mobilize an entire nation. As such, its governance is in accordance with a notion of marginality "which implicitly valorizes the center."[22] For intellectuals working on "women" in the China field, therefore, the first critical task is to break alliance with this kind of official sponsorship of "minority discourse." Instead, they need to use their work on Chinese women to deconstruct the paternalistic social consequences resulting from a hegemonic practice of *zhengming* itself.

The Dissolute Woman and the Female Saint

In a recent interview with the press in Hong Kong, the Taiwanese feminist Xü Xiaodan, well known for her use of nudity in political campaigns, described her ambition in the following way: "I will enter Congress in the image of a dissolute woman; I will love the people with the soul of a female saint."[23] What is remarkable about Xü Xiaodan's statements is the introduction of a feminist practice that refuses conformity with the Chinese "elite." The meaning of the term "elite" varies from society to society,[24] and I use it here to designate those among the Chinese who have had the privilege of being highly educated and whose views of female sexuality remain in accordance with the Confucian and neo-Confucian notions of female chastity. The point, however, is not for Chinese intellectuals to exclude/excuse themselves from the "elite," but rather to break up the traditional alliance between education and Confucian standards of female sexuality.

While being well educated herself, Xü Xiaodan challenges the traditional morality that demands Chinese women to be chaste, self-sacrificing, and thus virtuous. Her politics is different from the sentimental sponsorship of "the oppressed" that we often encounter in "minority discourse." For if traditional morality organizes female sexuality by upholding the female saint and condemning the dissolute woman, Xü Xiaodan does not simply criticize that morality by speaking up as the "minor" – the dissolute woman – only. Instead she shows that it is by straddling the positive and the negative, the clear distinction between which is absolutely essential for traditional morality's functioning, that she speaks and acts as a feminist. Instead of speaking from the position of "minority," then, she offers a model which by its very impure nature defies the epistemic violence underlying the perpetual dependence of the "minor" on the center. Women's sexuality, hitherto strictly organized according to the difference between the female saint and the dissolute woman, returns to a freedom which is not an arbitrary freedom to act as one wishes, but rather a freedom *from* the mutual reinforcement between education and morality, which are welded together by stratifying female sexuality.

Where the notion of "class" allows us the negative capacity to criticize "privilege" but never identify with it, the notion of gender can operate both from and against privilege, allowing us the possibility of both identification and opposition. This means that we can, as we must, attack social injustice without losing sight of the fact that even as "women" speaking for other "women" within the same gender, for instance, we speak from a privileged position. While an orthodox "class consciousness" would have us repress the self-reflexive knowledge of the speaking intellectual's social position as such (since to reflect on one's own privileged voice would be to destroy the illusion that one is speaking purely for universal justice), gender, insofar as it shows the organization of female sexuality in ways that are related but not restricted to class, makes it easier (though not necessary) to reflect on the difference between the speaking subject and the spoken object. This is because that difference (between the privileged and unprivileged) has not been prescribed as the definitive object of attack as it is in "class consciousness." Paradoxically, therefore, it is because "class consciousness" has chosen "social injustice" as its target and its content that it cannot reflect on the form of its own possibly privileged, unjust utterances. Self-reflection of this kind leads only to paralysis, as we see in many examples of May Fourth literature.

Lu Xun's literary texts, I think, best illustrate this point. The question that his stories often imply is: How can intellectuals pretend to be speaking for the oppressed classes since, precisely, we have a voice while they don't? Don't speaking and writing already mark our social privilege and permanently separate us from them? If it is true that "our" speech takes its "raw materials" from the suffering of the oppressed, it is also true that it takes its capital from the scholarly tradition, from the machineries of literacy and education, which are affordable only to a privileged few.

On the other hand, because its target and content is the inequality between the sexes, an issue which is not limited to a narrow definition of class difference (in which having privilege equals "bad" and not having privilege equals "good"), "gender" has room for enabling reflection on the inequality inherent in the construction of discourse, i.e., the difference that separates those who speak and those who are spoken of/for. Precisely because its content is not necessarily economic (in the narrow sense described above), the discourse of gender *can* know its own economic privilege. Knowing its own form as such does not, unlike in the case of a practice of "class consciousness" that must remain blind to itself, annul its project.

In the field of China studies, gender and women's issues are likely to emerge as the predominant critical paradigm in the years to come. This will be so *not only* because of Chinese women's traditionally "minor" status. Rather, it will be because, even while they may choose, from time to time, to forsake the claims of their "femininity," *intellectual* Chinese women who speak of "Chinese women" will, I hope, not forget their own social position. While they do not lose sight of the oppression of women, these intellectuals should admit rather than repress the inequality inherent in discourse and the difference between them and their "objects." They should articulate women's issues both as "dissolute women" and as "female saints," but never as either one only. If the relative freedom in intellectual work that the Chinese living in the liberal West enjoy is a privilege, Chinese intellectuals must use this privilege as truthfully and as tactically as they can – not merely to speak as exotic minors, but to fight the crippling effects of Western imperialism and Chinese paternalism at once.

Postscript: The Lures of Diaspora

At the two conferences where the bulk of this chapter was presented,[25] there were questions as to whether what I am doing is not a kind of essentialist "identity politics" in which, once again, the "authenticity" of a particular group is privileged. These questions demand a detailed response.

If we describe the postcolonial space in Hegelian terms, we can say that it is a space in which the object (women, minorities, other peoples) encounters its Notion (criterion for testing object), or in which the "being-in-itself" encounters the "being-for-an-other." In this encounter, "consciousness" undergoes a transformation, so that it is no longer only consciousness of the object but also consciousness of itself, of its own knowledge. What consciousness previously took to be the object *in-itself*, Hegel writes, is not an *in-itself* but an in-itself (an object) *for consciousness*. Hence "consciousness" has, in truth, *two* objects – object and knowledge of object – which do not mutually correspond but which are related in a movement Hegel calls experience:

> Since consciousness thus finds that its knowledge does not correspond to its object, the object itself does not stand the test; in other words, the criterion for testing is altered when that for which it was to have been the criterion fails to pass the test; and the testing is not only a testing of what we know, but also a testing of the criterion of what knowing is.
> ... *In as much as the new true object issues from it*, this *dialectical* movement which consciousness exercises on itself and which affects both its knowledge and its object, is precisely what is called *experience* [*Erfahrung*].[26]

Supplementing Hegel, we may say that this *dialectics of experience* finds one of its most compelling personifications in the "third world" intellectual in diaspora. While their cultures once existed for Western historians and anthropologists as objects of inquiry within well-defined geographical domains, the growing presence of these intellectuals in "first world" intellectual circles fundamentally disrupts the production of knowledge – what Edward Said calls Orientalism – that has hitherto proceeded by hiding the agenda of the inquirers and naturalizing the "objects" as givens. To paraphrase Hegel, "first world" inquirers must now cope with the fact that their "objects" no longer correspond to their "consciousness." "Third world" intellectuals, on their part, acquire and affirm their own "consciousness" only to find, continually, that it is a "consciousness" laden with the history of their objecthood. This history confronts them all the more acutely once they live in the "first world," where they discover that, regardless of personal circumstances, they are beheld as "the other."

The explosive nature of this dialectics of experience deals the death blow to older forms of protest that were bound to native territorial and cultural propriety. *For "third world" intellectuals especially,* this means that the recourse to alterity – the other culture, nation, sex, or body in another historical time and geographical space – no longer suffices as a means of intervention simply because alterity as such is still the old pure "object" (the being-in-itself) that has not been dialectically grasped. Such recourse to alterity is repeatedly trapped within the lures of a "self"-image – a nativism – that is, precisely, imperialism's other.

In naming "Chinese women intellectuals," thus, my intention is not to establish them as a more authentic group of investigators whose claim to "women" in the Chinese field would exclude that of other investigators. Naming here is, first and foremost, a way to avoid repeating the well-worn discursive paradigm of Orientalism, in which the peoples of the non-West are taken factographically as "objects" without consciousness while the historical privileges of speaking subjects – in particular the privilege of "having" consciousness – remain unarticulated.

Second, naming is also a way of *not giving* in to the charms of an alterity in which so many of the West's "others" are now called upon to speak. Naming is not so much an act of consolidating power as it is an act of making explicit the historical predicament of investigating "China" and "Chinese women," especially as it pertains to those who are ethnically Chinese and/or sexually women.

Third, it follows that naming the investigators amid the current "multicultural" interest in "women" in non-Western fields is also a means of accentuating the otherwise *muted* fact of intellectual women's privilege as intellectuals and thus (particularly in the Chinese context) as members of the elite. While this privilege is, at this point, hardly acknowledged in the masculinist explorations of modernity, nationhood, and literature, because masculinist explorations are themselves preoccupied with their own minority and womanhood *vis-à-vis* the West, it is peremptory that women investigators, especially Chinese women investigators investigating the history of Chinese women's social subordination, handle the mode of their speech – which historically straddles the elite and the subaltern – with deliberate care. In naming them as such, therefore, my point is to place on them the burden of a kind of critical awareness that has yet to be articulated in their field. The weight of each of the terms under which they work – Chinese, women, intellectual – means that their alliances with other discursive groups, as well as their self-reflection on their own positions, must always be astute. Both practices, allying with others and reflecting on oneself, are by necessity more demanding than a blanket dismissal of names and identities as "essential-ist."[27] Such a dismissal is often the result of an ahistorical espousal of "dif-ference" and "femininity" as is found in some influential theories which, by equating the feminine with the negative and the unrepresentable, dismiss all processes of identification as positivistic. (A good case in point is the work of Julia Kristeva, which is popular with many feminist critics despite Kristeva's unwillingness to name "woman"[28] and to name herself "feminist.") The question on which to insist, however, is not "to name or not to name" but: What is to be gained or lost in naming what and whom, and by whom?

What I am arguing can also be stated in a different way: What are we doing talking about modern Chinese literature and Chinese women in the North American academy in the 1990s? As such activities of speaking and writing are tied less to the oppressed women in Chinese communities "back home" than to our own intellectual careers in the West, we need to unmask ourselves through a scrupulous declaration of self-interest. Such declaration does not clean our hands, but it prevents the continuance of a tendency, rather strong among "third world" intellectuals in diaspora as well as researchers of non-Western cultures in "first world" nations, to sentimen-talize precisely those day-to-day realities from which they are distanced.

The diasporic postcolonial space is, as I already indicate, neither the space of the native intellectual protesting against the intrusive presence of foreign imperialists in the indigenous territory, nor the space of the postcolonial critic working against the lasting effects of cultural domination in the home country (now an independent "nation") after the phase of territorial impe-rialism. In the case of China it is necessary to remember that "Chinese" ter-ritory, with the exceptions of Taiwan from 1895 to 1945, Hong Kong from 1842 to 1997, and Macau (occupied by the Portuguese since the mid-sixteenth century) from 1887 to 1997, was never completely "colonized" over a long period by any one foreign power, even though the cultural effects of imperialism are as strong as in other formerly colonized countries in Asia, Africa, and Latin America. One could perhaps say that such cultural effects of foreign dominance are, in fact, *stronger*: they are most explicit, paradox-ically, when one sees how the mainland Chinese can hold on to the illusion – born of modern Western imperialism but itself no less imperialistic – of a "native land," a *zuguo*, that was never entirely captured and that therefore remains glorious to this day.

The space of "third world" intellectuals in diaspora is a space that is removed from the "ground" of earlier struggles that were still tied to the "native land." Physical alienation, however, can mean precisely the intensi-fication and aestheticization of the values of "minority" positions that had developed in the earlier struggles and that have now, in "third world" intellectuals' actual circumstances in the West, become defunct. The unselfreflexive sponsorship of "third world" culture, including "third world" women's culture, becomes a mask that conceals the hegemony of these intellectuals over those who are stuck at home.

For "third world" intellectuals, the lures of diaspora consist in this masked hegemony. As in the case of what I call masculinist positions in the China field, their resort to "minority discourse," including the discourse of class and gender struggles, veils their own fatherhood over the "ethnics" at home even while it continues to legitimize them as "ethnics" and "minorities" in the West. In their hands, minority discourse and class struggle, especially when they take the name of another nation, another culture, another sex, or another body, turn into signifiers whose major function is that of discursive exchange for the intellectuals' self-profit. Like "the people," "real people," "the populace," "the peasants," "the poor," "the homeless," and all such names, these signifiers *work* insofar as they gesture toward another place (the lack in discourse-construction) that is "authentic" but that cannot be admitted into the circuit of exchange.

What happens eventually is that this "third world" that is produced, circulated, and purchased by "third world" intellectuals in the cosmopolitan diasporic space will be exported "back home" in the form of values – intangible goods – in such a way as to obstruct the development of the native industry. To be sure, one can perhaps no longer even speak of a "native industry" as such in the multinational corporate postmodernity, but it remains for these intellectuals to face up to their truthful relation to those "objects of study" behind which they can easily hide – as voyeurs, as "fellow victims," and as self-appointed custodians.

Hence the necessity to read and write against the lures of diaspora: any attempt to deal with "women" or the "oppressed classes" in the "third world" that does not at the same time come to terms with the historical conditions of its own articulation is bound to repeat the exploitativeness that used to and still characterizes most "exchanges" between "West" and "East." Such attempts will also be expediently assimilated within the plenitude of the hegemonic establishment, with all the rewards that that entails. No one can do without some such rewards. What one can do without is the illusion that, through privileged speech, one is helping to save the wretched of the earth.[29]

Notes

1   "Genitalism," per Gayatri Spivak, is the attitude that "depending on what kind of genitals you have, you can or cannot speak in certain situations." See "Questions of Multi-culturalism," *The Post-Colonial Critic: Interviews, Strategies, Dialogues*, ed. Sarah Harasym (London: Routledge, 1990), p. 62.

2   Abdul R. JanMohamed and David Lloyd, "Introduction: Minority Discourse – What Is to Be Done?" *Cultural Critique* 7 (fall 1981): 7.
3   Nativism is not necessarily an attitude held by "natives." Scholars who study a particular culture can espouse nativism as a way to fence off disciplinary territories, and this often happens in non-Western fields such as Asian studies. For an extended argument on this point, see the next chapter. [*Editors' note*: this refers to *Writing Diaspora: Tactics of Intervention* (Bloomington: Indiana University Press, 1993)].
4   I have in mind Allan Bloom, *The Closing of the American Mind* (New York: Simon & Schuster, 1981), and E. D. Hirsch, Jr., *Cultural Literacy* (Boston, MA: Houghton Mifflin, 1981).
5   In his study of the history of Chinese communism, Arif Dirlik shows that, beginning in the earliest period of their acquaintance with the ideas of Marx, the Chinese communists have tended to be most fascinated with what is arguably Marx's most problematic area – his economism. See Dirlik, *The Origins of Chinese Communism* (Oxford: Oxford University Press, 1989), especially chapters 2 through 6.
6   Arif Dirlik, "Culturalism as Hegemonic Ideology and Liberating Practice," *Cultural Critique* 6 (spring 1981): 37.
7   Gayatri Spivak, "Can the Subaltern Speak?" in Cary Nelson and Lawrence Grossberg, eds., *Marxism and the Interpretation of Culture* (Urbana: University of Illinois Press, 1988), pp. 271–313.
8   For an argument of this predicament characterizing minority discourse, see Abdul R. JanMohamed, *Manichean Aesthetics: The Politics of Literature in Colonial Africa* (Amherst: University of Massachusetts Press, 1983).
9   Gayatri Spivak, "The New Historicism: Political Commitment and the Postmodern Critic," *The Post-Colonial Critic*, p. 158.
10   Confucian Analects, chapter III, 5, 7; The Four Books: The Great Learning, The Doctrine of the Mean, Confucian Analects, and The Works of Mencius, with English translation and notes by James Legge (Taipei: Culture Book Co., 1973), p. 298; emphases in the translation.
11   Slavoj Žižek, *The Sublime Object of Ideology* (London: Verso, 1989), p. 95.
12   Žižek, *Sublime Object*, p. 98.
13   As I am writing this in April 1991, a controversy over the ethics of naming rape victims has just broken out across the US media. The immediate cause is the naming by several news institutions (*The Globe*, NBC, and *The New York Times*) of the female victim in an alleged case of rape by a member of the Kennedy family. The pros and cons of whether the victim should be named touch on individual rights to privacy, media consumer needs, the dissemination of news for financial profit, abuses suffered by rape victims at legal proceedings, and more, all of which have to do with social relationships rather than with the pure act of naming itself.
14   Kwai-cheung Lo, "The Real in Lacan: Some Reflections on 'Chinese Symptoms,'" *Polygraph* 4 (1990–1): 86–7.
15   "With great trepidation I would say that Marxism in fact is a critical philosophy. Its transformation into a substantive philosophy, a utopian philosophy that

can be adequately represented by revolution and social reform has been in fact a centrist mistake." Spivak, "The *Intervention* Interview," *The Post-Colonial Critic*, p. 131.

16   Fredric Jameson, "Third-World Literature in the Era of Multinational Capital," *Social Text* 15 (fall 1986): 69.

17   See Spivak's discussion of this point in "The New Historicism," pp. 161–2.

18   Nancy Armstrong, *Desire and Domestic Fiction: A Political History of the Novel* (Oxford: Oxford University Press, 1987), p. 8.

19   Quoted in Juliet Mitchell, *Psychoanalysis and Feminism* (New York: Vintage Books, 1975), p. 416.

20   Kwai-cheung Lo, "The Real in Lacan," p. 89.

21   Spivak, "The New Historicism," p. 158.

22   Spivak, "The New Historicism," p. 156.

23   *Xin Bao/Overseas Chinese Economic Journal* (the US edition of *The Hong Kong Economic Journal*), January 1991.

24   Writing about colonial India, Ranajit Guha uses the term "elite" to describe the dominant social groups, made up of "mainly British officials of the colonial state and foreign industrialists, merchants, financiers, planters, landlords and missionaries," on the one hand, and of powerful indigenous elements at the "all-India" and the "regional and local" levels, on the other. See "On Some Aspects of the Historiography of Colonial India," *Subaltern Studies I: Writings on South Asian History and Society*, ed. Ranajit Guha (Delhi: Oxford University Press, 1986), p. 8. Spivak, while defining the "subaltern" as "all that is not elite" ("The New Historicism," p. 158), points also to the "gendered subaltern" as being paradigmatic of the subaltern subject ("Practical Politics of the Open End," *The Post-Colonial Critic*, p. 103). Because education traditionally plays such an important role in determining class difference in Chinese society, I think the relation between the "elite" and the "subaltern" in China needs to be formulated *primarily* in terms of the way education and gender work together.

25   The conference "Sexuality and Gender in Twentieth-Century Chinese Literature and Society" at the University of Iowa, March 1991, and the panel "Gender, Class, and Twentieth-Century Chinese Fiction" at the Annual Meeting of the Association for Asian Studies, New Orleans, April 1991.

26   *Hegel's Phenomenology of Spirit*, trans. A. V. Miller, with analysis of the text and foreword by J. N. Findlay (New York: Oxford University Press, 1977), pp. 54–5; emphases in the original.

27   The extensiveness of the philosophical, political, and feminist arguments about "essentialism" is such that I can merely point to it here. Two recent publications readers can consult are Diana Fuss, *Essentially Speaking* (New York: Routledge, 1989), and *differences* 1.2 (summer 1989), a special issue on essentialism.

28   "In 'woman' I see something that cannot be represented, something that is not said, something above and beyond nomenclatures and ideologies." Kristeva, "Woman Can Never Be Defined," trans. Marilyn A. August, in Elaine Marks and Isabelle de Courtivron, eds., *New French Feminisms* (New York: Schocken Books, 1981), p. 137.

29   I want to acknowledge those who have contributed to the final version of this chapter. I have benefited from comments made by Wendy Larson and Lydia Liu at the conferences at Iowa and in New Orleans. Continual discussions with Kwai-cheung Lo, Tonglin Lu, and Ming-bao Yue about this chapter and other related issues give me the support of a strong critical community. Most of all, I am indebted to Yu-shih Chen for a forceful and enabling critique, which made me restate my concerns with a clarity that had been previously missing.

7

Returning(s): Relocating the Critical Feminist Auto-Ethnographer[1]

Jayne O. Ifekwunigwe

In this essay Jayne O. Ifekwunigwe adopts feminist critique and auto-ethnography as methodologies through which to examine the lived experiences of diaspora for women, including herself, who have family members of more than one nationality and who have lived in more than one national location. Auto-ethnography, first introduced by anthropologists and later adapted by literary scholars such as Françoise Lionnet, Mary Louis Pratt, Julia Watson, and others is a hybrid methodology that is informed by ethnography, anthropology, and autobiography studies; as a hybrid form it emphasizes the writing of the self in relation to and as a writing of the *ethnos*, group. Ifekwunigwe deploys these "mixed" methodologies to examine the "mixed" diasporic belongings of identity for those who have lived in diaspora and for those who are frequently multiracial as well as multi- or transnational.

This is an edited version of Ifekwunigwe's essay: [. . .] indicates where text has been omitted.

In this world through which I travel. I am endlessly creating myself.

Frantz Fanon

It is out of chaos that new worlds are born.

Audre Lorde

This chapter unfolds as a kaleidoscopic series of narratives, which I place under the subheadings of "Turning(s)." Some of the narratives will be photopoetic chronicles of my childhood. Others will be my retelling of pivotal moments that have shaped my complex subjectivity. The rest will be frozen snapshots of experiences reconfigured as anecdotes. Although by no means definitive, collectively these texts capture my particular complex evolving everyday lived realities as a *métisse* woman. [. . .] Ultimately, these narratives of self contextualize my specific feminist "standpoint" as auto-ethnographer:

> The notion of traveling through space is integral to the unfolding of history and the development of the individual's consciousness with regard to the past. The voyage over geographic space is an expanded metaphor for the process of one person's coming to know who she is. (Willis 1985: 220)

Turning(s)

Sparkling grape juice, jacket potato baked to perfection – crunchy on the outside, soft on the inside, courgettes (zucchini) with tomato and onion sauce, green salad with lettuce, tomatoes, cucumbers, apples, avocados, and tossed with a honey mustard dressing, corn on the cob, hot relish, chutney, melon, strawberries and cream.

It is late 1991, I am sitting in the sunny front room of Bisi's home in central Bristol. We have just finished eating one of Bisi's famous eclectic lunches. Bisi is my sister-friend as well as one of the six newfangled *métisse griottes* featured in this text. She has the uncanny and consistent ability to prepare the most creative and the most sumptuous meals from bits and pieces found in her kitchen. These are the fruits of labor of a mother of four and an accomplished visual artist.

This gathering is one of the last times I will spend with Bisi and the other regulars – her sister Yemi, Sarah, Angustia, Aduah – before returning to the United States to write my Ph.D. dissertation. Bisi is working on another animation piece and asks us if we will share some of our experiences on camera. The challenge is to recall a turning point in our lives, or rather a choice/decision we made (or that was made for us) which changed our lives. Bisi said it was going to Greece, where she met her husband. That question was easy for me: the countless times I have been uprooted, transported and transplanted, initially as part of my parents' belongings and then subsequently as an adult in pursuit of education and (self-)knowledge. As I write, I am still returning.

Turning(s)

There is a naming tradition in Igbo families wherein one names children on the basis of the events that are transpiring at the time the mother is pregnant or at the moment the child is born. Through my Igbo name as well as those of my siblings, one can chronicle our early family history spent in England and Nigeria:

For my lineages
*What is in a Name? or What is in a Name. or We Need to Re-Member
   so That*
Others Will not Forget

Number One
24 December, 1959
Muriel St. Clair Freeman
Daughter of Mary Freeman of South Shields, England and Lionel
Freeman of Le Guan, Guyana
and Aaron Ezebuilo (a king will have many enemies) Ifekwunigwe, son
of
Chief Aaron Nsiegbuna (may poison not kill) Ifekwunigwe and
   Florence
Ugoye (pride of the Oye Market) Ifekwunigwe of Nando, Onitsha
Nigeria
are married by Archbishop Patterson in Onitsha Cathedral, Nigeria
They return to England
Daddy finishes medical school and starts rotations
Money is scarce
Life is uncertain
Mum is carrying her first child

28 February, 1961
My older brother Christopher is born
in Sorrento Hospital in Birmingham, England
Chukwuma
Only that greater force knows what the future will bring

Number Two
Daddy finishes rotations
Our family moves back to London
Mum is carrying her second child

2 July, 1963
Jayne is born in Hammersmith Hospital, London, England
Daddy is offered and accepts a position heading the teaching hospital
   at
the University of Ibadan in Nigeria
Obiageli
Someone who came into the world to enjoy life – the privileged one

Number Three
Our family settles in to life in Nigeria
Daddy goes off to Uganda on business
Mum is carrying her third child

Daddy and a Swedish doctor are in an automobile accident
Swedish doctor is killed instantly
National news confuses facts
Daddy is presumed dead

Friends flock to family home to console Mum
To offer assistance with funeral arrangements
Daddy has already phoned Mum from emergency room in Uganda
He is very much alive
5 June 1965
David is born in Ibadan Hospital, Nigeria
Chukwumeka
That greater force has done a very good thing

Number Four
1960 – Nigeria gains independence from Britain
The country is carved up into three regions
North/East/West
Hausa/Igbo/Yoruba
January, 1966
Igbos, Easterners, our people, kill Prime Minister Sir Abubakar Tafawa
and the Premiers of the Northern and Western Regions
Our family is living in Ibadan – the West – Yoruba land
Northern and Western soldiers are going door to door
Killing any and all Igbos
Mum is carrying her last child

Our family flees in the middle of the night to the East to Igbo land to
Nando, Onitsha, to my Grandparents Papa and Mama
Papa is the Chief there

Mum requires a Caesarean section
She has us all that way
14 December, 1966
She gives birth to her last child
A girl – Ann Mary in Enugu, Nigeria
In a civilian hospital converted into army barracks
There are wounded soldiers on either side of her
Nkiruka
Hope for the future
The future will be brighter

Ifekwunigwe
The meaning of my Igbo surname?
It means

People in a multitude stand together
Strength in unity
United we are strong
18 February, 1991
Bristol, England

Turning(s)

I was about four. We were living in Nigeria during the Biafran War.[2] For obvious reasons, it was no longer safe for our family to be living there. So it was agreed that my mum, my siblings, and I would return to England. However, my father, a Biafran physician, decided to stay behind to provide medical relief.[3]

At Port Harcourt we boarded a mercenary plane without seats and were strapped to the floor, wherein we began a days-long journey ending with a crash-landing in Lisbon, Portugal. My only memory of that journey is stepping out onto the steps of the aircraft to depart and just vomiting.[4] Mum contacted the British Embassy and my maternal grandparents, who were by then divorced. We eventually made our way to semi-rural Nelson, Lancashire, the post-industrial North,[5] where my Guyanese grandad was living with his second wife, whom we would later refer to as Auntie Dan.

Turning(s)

My father, a stranger of sorts, returned from Biafra.[6] As a result of his wartime research on pediatric malnutrition, for a year, he was granted a fellowship at Harvard University's School of Public Health in Cambridge, Massachusetts, United States of America. During that time, we all lived in Harvard's International House, which was a safe, exciting, multicultural haven from the seeming brutality that can characterize East Coast living. Our first New England educational moments coincided with the period of forced desegregation of the city of Boston's public schools.

Turning(s)

We survived Cambridge, Massachusetts, returned to England, only to learn that we were moving again – to California, back to the United States. Daddy had been offered an academic medicine position at the University of California, Los Angeles. In preparation for our departure, my English gran would sing "California here I come, right back where I started from, open up those golden gates, California here I come . . ."

I was about ten years old when we left rural Nelson, Lancashire, England, where I was obliviously happy. Oblivious in the sense that I do not recall any overt experiences of racism. Retrospectively, however, I do recall my first years at the Anglican school, which my older brother and I attended, wherein as the youngest member of the school, I was treated like a little fuzzy-haired, sun-kissed, school mascot of sorts. Older pupils took turns giving me piggy back rides around the tarmac playground. Under quite stressful circumstances, mum tried to give me and my three siblings as normal an upbringing as was materially possible. For my older brother Christopher and me, this included horseriding lessons and old-time dancing. In fact, at the time that our family was to emigrate to the United States, having just secured a silver medal, my brother Christopher and I were among the old-time dancing stars of Nelson. I am convinced we were on our way to garnering the gold medal, had the move not interrupted our practice sessions. Needless to say, I was not enthusiastic about yet another migration. At that time, England was my home.

I was then dropped into the middle of pulsating urban West Los Angeles where American school children of many hues deemed me and my siblings simply inappropriate in every way. Wrong hairstyle, funny clothes, and "Why do you talk like that?" I distinctly remember one cheeky classmate of mine named Peter, who derived great pleasure from hearing me say his name – with my "hybrid" English accent, of course! I was a chubby school girl and I used to wear plaits in my hair and silky ribbons to match my unfashionable (by urban Westside LA standards) English ensembles – cardigans, plaid pinafore dresses, knee-high white socks, and sandals – with the toes left in. At recess, Peter's assignment was to yank one of my silky ribbons from my head, dangle it in front of my face and then begin running around the playground. Not to be outdone, I ran after him all the while shouting, "Peetah, Peetah, give me back my ribbon." As per usual, a small crowd of our peers assembled at the edge of the playground quite amused by the spectacle. Years later, I realized Peter fancied me more than the attention he received from his classmates.

There is something to be said for Labov's theories on codeswitching (Trudgill 1974). My siblings and I had it down to a fine art. I had learned that the only way I was going to survive on the playgrounds of West Los Angeles was by mutating my vowels and consonants to more approximate an American accent. I learned that my brothers and my sister had taken the linguistic plunge as well. It became our secret, we would speak "American" at school and resort to the "Queen's English" at home under the watchful eye of our quasi-ex-colonial Nigerian father. The worst crime was to be caught "speaking American" at home. We all knew it and we would monitor each other's speech, eavesdrop on telephone conversations, anxious for a slip-up, and the opportunity to turn the culprit in to the man who revered *The Oxford English Dictionary* as much, if not more, than the Bible. Mum was a bit more relaxed. In fact, I noticed her speech patterns slowly shifting under the weight of American assimilation.

Turning(s)

As I have already mentioned, at the age of ten, I terminated full-time child-hood residency in England. Although, while gradually becoming American-ized, almost every summer, my family and I still returned to England, where we divided our time equally between my gran in Birmingham and my grandad in Nelson. However, in 1989 I embarked on an exploratory anthro-pological journey that would lead to my two-year ethnographic and auto-biographical sojourn in Bristol. In 1995 I returned again to Bristol. In 1996 I found my way back to London, the city of my birth, which is where I live at the moment. Being Nigerian – Irish/English – Guyanese and having lived in England, Nigeria and the United States, I am the quintessential product of the "Triangular Trade." I view the world through a kaleidoscope of cultures. Like so many daughters (and sons) of the diaspora(s), I have a historical sense of myself that is rooted in Africa, Europe, the Caribbean and, most recently, North America.

My mother was raised by a White English Geordie mother and a Black Guyanese anglicized father. My Igbo Nigerian father was born and raised an African, which by definition also means partial psychic infiltration by both Mother England during colonialism and Christianity during the reign of the missionaries. Hence, in no particular order, my upbringing was an interest-ing *mélange* of Victorian English, South Shields Geordie, Onitsha Igbo, Le Guan Guyanese, Anglican Christian, and assimilating Southern California (upper-middle-class Jewish West Los Angeles) cultural traditions. Moreover, despite the lure of acculturation and/or assimilation in Los Angeles, I can recall many examples of the ways in which Britannia ruled our roost. For one, the aforementioned codeswitching. Another was the strictly enforced eating with knife and fork at the dinner table.

Turning(s)

Our family had lost all our belongings in the Biafran War. We began the slow recoupment process in England. Through the resilience of my parents, we eventually found our feet again in Southern California. At the moment, my parents live in a verdant, upper-middle-class community in the hills of West Los Angeles, which was predominantly Jewish when I lived there during my formative pre-adolescent and adolescent years. Today, in part, due to the exorbitant real estate prices and unstable economy, there are fewer families with children and more couples without children living in this area. Both my parents are professionals, so one could say that in this country and perhaps in Nigeria, I grew up in an upper-middle-class background. However, with the class system or rather the caste system in England, we would probably be considered middle class. Unlike the Horatio Alger myth of economic mobility and success which operates in the United States, in England if one is born into a working-class family, moving out of those ranks is extremely difficult. Being what British society would classify as "Black" compounds the problem. Moreover, in England, despite the existence of the post-Thatcherite *nouveaux riches* and current newfound Blair/Labour-induced economic optimism, rank, particularly in the upper echelons, is still determined by pedigree. On the other hand, in the United States, the class system is supposedly structured exclusively on the basis of color-blind accumulated capital.

In Bristol, by virtue of my schooling and the way I spoke, most continental African, African Caribbean, South Asian and *métis(se)* people I encountered referred to me as middle class. I was differentially received in White English communities. In middle- and upper-class White English circles my acceptance was contingent upon my being introduced via mutual White English buffer-friends or acquaintances. Unless I spoke and depending on my manner of dress, at times, working-class White English individuals presumed bi-racialized same-class status. In general, I am conscious of the ways in which my multicultural, transnational upbringings have provided me with access to education, travel, and other forms of privilege. While living and working in Bristol, these attributes were an invaluable form of "cultural capital" and facilitated daily travel and negotiations within geographically close but socially and economically segregated communities (Bourdieu 1984).

Turning(s)

While growing up in a predominantly White upper-middle-class Jewish sub-urban Los Angeles environment, how easy it was for me (and my siblings) to privilege and celebrate my (our) "White English bits" at the expense of my (our) Brown Guyanese and Black Nigerian identities. I regret that until my adult years, save cuisine and the occasional wedding or christening, much of my Nigerian heritage had been submerged or maybe subverted. While

Bisi's and Yemi's [. . .] father's code telephone language was Yoruba, my father's was Igbo. Like the two of them and the rest of my family, I too was able to decipher the gist of the conversation by stringing together the English words that did not have Yoruba, or in our case Igbo, equivalents. Unfortunately, my father's schedule did not permit Igbo instruction, so until very recently, I have remained mute in my native tongue.

Turning(s)

In 1978 I made a momentous journey with mum to Guyana to meet the Caribbean branch of our polychromatic family tree. Because my Guyanese grandfather had internalized "the British" in British Guyanese, my close relationship with him ensured that I had much to learn about what it means to be Guyanese in the African Caribbean sense of the term. Hence, the plight, or rather the challenge – some may say the advantage – of being *métisse* and a child of so many diaspora(s).

Turning(s)

I was born in 1963, in Hammersmith, London, England, the first daughter of an Irish – English – Guyanese mother and a Nigerian (Igbo/Biafran) father. As I have been researching ideologies and ambiguities associated with British/English social, cultural, and pseudoscientific constructions of "race" and their impact on the lived realities of multiple generations of *métis(se)* people, I have learned a great deal about my own multi-generational, transnational, and multi-ethnic family. I have an older brother, Christopher, a younger brother, David, and a younger sister, Ann. Each one of us has different emotional and experiential ties to England, not to mention Nigeria, Guyana, and the United States. By virtue of genotypic inheritances, each of us also has a different relationship to the phenotypic skins we inhabit. My younger brother David and I are relatively speaking the "darker" members of our family and we have our mum's facial features. On the other hand, my older brother Christopher and my younger sister Ann are "fairer" than we are and have our father's African features.

I am painfully aware of the legacy of pseudoscientific and bi-racialized nineteenth-century rhetoric and the ways in which these hierarchical and oppositional discourses of perceived differences permeate the everyday binary language of Black and *métis(se)* families. We are constantly discussing so and so's "good" and "bad" hair textures, "fair" and "dark" skin complexions, "thin" and "thick" lips, "broad" or "pointy" noses, "African" or "European" bums – the list of qualitative descriptions is endless [. . .]

I grew up in two bi-racialized "one drop" societies – the United Kingdom and the United States – as well as in Nigeria. In all three social millieux, Black women (and men) still purchase skin bleach to lighten their skin and women (and men) still chemically relax or weave synthetic or human hair into their beautiful African locks in order to create that "pseudo-European look." I am aware of how easily these insidious concepts seep into people's consciousness and destroy a fundamental love of self.

"What am I going to do with my hair?" I would say. "What have you done to your hair?" my mum would exclaim. Up until this past year when I decided to reclaim my naturally "kinky" hair, I, too, was enslaved by my locks. In Europe, North America, the Caribbean, and even South Africa, I have spent many hours in numerous Black hair salons attempting to tame what I was conditioned to believe were "nappy" and unattractive tresses. In fact, those who have known me over the years can trace the emergence, the lapses, and the resurgence of my political consciousness by the particular hairstyles I have sported: relaxed, curly perm, short and natural, braids with extensions and the ultimate – almost bald. Today, under the loving and gentle care of Ms Margaret Inniss, hair stylist/braider and *confidante extraordinaire*, I have been slowly coaxing my locks back into either tight Senegalese twists or tiny braids.

Turning(s)

Genealogical and folkloric information about the maternal side of my family I acquired over many cups of tea with my Geordie gran in Birmingham, while she was still alive. However, even before my discussions with gran, that 1978 trip to LeGuan, Guyana with my mum, the year after the Jonestown massacre, convinced me that "racial" and ethnic intermingling had taken place for multiple generations on my grandad's side. I met aunts, uncles, cousins, and other relations who ranged in appearance from cinnamon-colored Amerindian to pink-skinned, blonde-haired blue-eyed Dutch. As it happens, my Guyanese grandad who married my English gran was allegedly himself *métis*. Although I never met him, according to my gran, my great-grandfather was Scottish. On that journey, I did meet my great-grandmother and my namesake, who, although I did not know it at the time, was supposedly Amerindian, transplanted LeGuan African, and East Indian.

Turning(s)

Piecing together the paternal Nigerian side is less straightforward, since it is partially based on conjecture – phenotypic evidence and informal family historical sleuthing. My paternal papa was an Igbo chief; my paternal mama was also Igbo. I continue to investigate my father's side of the family in an attempt to discern whether his very fair *oyingbo* complexion,[7] red hair and brown eyes, and that of three out of four of his siblings are a result of what some people would refer to as natural variation. Contrary to what many people may believe, he is not an albino. Whenever European men and continental African women, as one example of many, come into contact with each other there are likely to be voluntary or involuntary sexual interactions. In the case of my father and his siblings, I have reason to believe that two generations or more before my father's birth, a missionary encounter on either papa's or mama's side added a bit of cream to the coffee, and resulted in my father's pink skin, reddish hair, and light-brown eyes. Or, as my brother Chris says, "Somebody hopped the fence." The fact that papa was a chief means that his family would have had more contact with British missionaries. As already mentioned, enhanced by the Scottish, Irish, and the English on my mum's side, both my brother Chris and my sister Ann have also reproduced daddy's coloring.

Turning(s)

While still living in Bristol, I remember a conversation I had with some of what Bristol-based sociologist Steve Fenton refers to as the "YBI" (Young Black Intelligentsia). I had just seen John Akomfrah's 1992 film *A Touch of the Tar Brush,* which interrogates taken-for-granted notions of Englishness and presumptions that being English is synonymous with being White. My sister-in-law Shauna was pregnant with my nephew, David Aaron, Jr. I described the baby's pedigree for the group – Tanzanian, German, African American, Cherokee, Nigerian, Irish, English, and Guyanese. Beyond the designated conventional one-drop category Black, we speculated about how to name and locate this prospective multinational and mult-iethnic child. Without missing a beat, Devon said, "Why, he/she will be English of course!"

Turning(s)

When I reflect on my studies at the University of California, Berkeley, one aspect of my postgraduate student life I thoroughly enjoyed was attending talks by various visiting professors. Not long after returning from Bristol, at the School of Education, I attended a lecture by English sociologist Paul Willis. Afterwards, using a mutual friend as an entrée, I introduced myself. While I was talking with him, I noticed that there was a rather puzzled expression on his face. I suddenly realized that, like so many other transatlantic linguistic monitors, he was trying "to place my accent" – by now among other influences an odd mixture of Bristolian English and Berkeley Californian. Eventually he exclaimed, "I cannot figure out if you are American or English!" "Well," I replied, "to be precise I am Americanized Nigerian – Irish – English – Guyanese." At which point, he said, "Today, that means English."

Turning(s)

In Berkeley, California, while writing up my Ph.D. dissertation, I made my usual nocturnal run to the local 7–11 convenience shop for a fix of a vice I had acquired while writing – 44 ounces of a healthy cocktail of aspartame-laced diet sodas – caffeine-free Diet Coke, Diet Coke, and Diet Pepsi – also known as "the Big Gulp" and at the time it cost precisely 96 cents. Anyway, before leaving the shop, I completed my second ritual, which entailed perusing the newsstand for any relevant headlines. Staring back at me was a special issue of *Time* magazine.[8] It had a red cover with a picture of a very attractive woman on it. By the woman's face, the copy read: "Take a good look at this woman. She was created by a computer from a mix of several races. What you see is a remarkable preview of . . ." And underneath her face and the title of the special issue were the words: "The New Face of America: How Immigrants are Shaping the World's First Multicultural Society."

This special edition of *Time* is yet another example of the dangerous ways in which confused media such as the active imaginations of Madison Avenue advertising executives induce fantasies about a future replete with interracial cyborgs. Yet, [. . .] the notion of biological "hybridity" is itself problematic. The presumption here is that the "races" that are being mixed are themselves discrete and pure. Moreover, as to be expected, there is a conflation of constructs of "race," nationality, ethnicity, and culture and, of course, the image of immigrant as interloper is propagated. One need only stroll down the streets of Berkeley, California or Bristol, England to be reminded of the obvious: these heralded acts of so-called transracial transgression actually transpired long before they were reinvented by the American (and British) media.[9] And this "old story" continues . . .

Locating the Critical Feminist Auto-Ethnographer

We cannot escape our origins however hard we try, those origins which contain the key – could we but find it – to all that we later become. (Baldwin 1955: 27)

"Where are you from?"

On an empowered day, I describe myself as a diaspora(s) daughter with multiple migratory and ancestral reference points in Nigeria, Ireland, England, Guyana, and the United States. On a disempowered day, I am a nationless nomad who wanders from destination to destination in search of a singular site to name as home.

Writing home/no fixed address/reconfiguring the English–African Diaspora

An important and ongoing discussion among historians provides the theoretical backdrop for the second half of this chapter. That is, certain scholars refute the notion that it was the dispersal of continental Africans during the transatlantic slave trade that created the first and only significant African diasporic rupture. Although arguably the most socially and culturally disruptive, the forced migration of continental Africans for the purposes of labor exploitation was not the first African diaspora. Cheik Anta Diop (1991), Ivan Van Sertima (1976), and Runoko Rashidi (1992), among other revisionist scholars, have provided ample historical and archeological evidence that continental Africans circumnavigated the globe – the New World in general and the Americas in particular – many centuries before the celebrated journey of Christopher Columbus, among other explorers. These scholarly interventions pave the way for reconceptualizations of contemporary (pre- and post-Columbus) African diasporas. In turn, these periodized reformulations of African diaspora(s) carve out cogent spaces for contemporary discourses on the English – African diaspora. In particular, as I have defined it, the English – African diaspora conventionally comprises African postcolonial constituents from the Caribbean, North and Latin America, and continental Africa who find themselves in England for labor, schooling, political asylum, and frequently, by birth.

In the English – African diaspora the idea of "home" has particular layered, textured, and contradictory meanings for *métis(se)* individuals. In a travel essay chronicling his rediscovery of Britain, Black Nigerian and White English writer Adewale Maja-Pearce wages existential war with the meaning of "home" as it is experienced as competing and conflicting bi-racialized nationalisms:

> I had to learn as best I could to be at home, but even the word "home" had complex connotations. Where was home? Was it Nigeria, my father's country? Or was it Britain, my mother's country? And how far did allegiance to the one involve a betrayal of the other? My inability to see was inseparable from the sense of betrayal.

If I didn't look, if I didn't admit the reality of the particular corner of the world in which I happened to be, in this case Britain – "The blessed plot, this earth, this realm, this England" – then I couldn't properly live here. This in turn meant that I was released from the necessity of confronting the nature of my allegiance because to admit Britain, to say that I was British was to deny Nigeria. I was like a man married to one woman but trying to remain faithful to another. If I wasn't careful I would lose both, and in the end I would be the one to suffer for it: to live like this is to condemn oneself to a half-life, which is the predicament of the outsider. (Maja-Pearce 1990: 12–13)

In his personal exploration, Maja-Pearce (1990) laments "the half-life of the outsider" and in so doing he articulates the complex nature of belonging for other transnational *métis(se)* subjects. In addition, he conveys a broader collective African diasporic consciousness forged from the lived realities and the legacies of interwoven (post-)colonial histories characterized by racism, sexism, class discrimination, ethnocentrism, and other forms of oppression (Gilroy 1993). Somers and Gibson would refer to these individual/collective testimonials as "public narratives . . . those narratives attached to cultural and institutional formations larger than the single individual, to intersubjective networks or institutions, however local or grand, micro or macro" (Somers and Gibson 1994: 62). Locating *métis(se)* declarations in spatial, temporal, and indeed multiple African diasporic contexts, Boyce-Davies's conception of migratory subjectivity is also relevant: "as elsewhere denotes movement . . . asserts agency as it crosses the borders, journeys, migrates and so reclaims as it reasserts" (Boyce-Davies 1994: 37).

These transnational alliances are predicated on the profound paradoxes of citizenship (Gilroy 1996; Cohen 1994). Though daughters and sons of Africa's various diasporas are living in England, they must acknowledge the actual and significant impact of White English exclusionary practices on reconstructions of cultural and transnational local identities (Mercer 1994). Stuart Hall refers to this ongoing psychopolitical project as "Identity Politics One":

the first form of identity politics. It had to do with the constitution of some defensive collective identity against the practices of racist society. It had to do with the fact that people were being blocked out of and refused an identity and identification within the majority nation, having to find some other roots on which to stand. (Hall 1991)

The outcome of the prescribed specificity of White Englishness is that Black sons and daughters of the English–African diaspora are denied full citizenship (Hall 1996). The one-drop rule also means that *métis(se)* children with White English mothers or fathers are also denied access to an English identity that they can rightfully claim on the basis of parentage.

As we approach the twenty-first century, there are at least several ongoing and unresolved political debates. First, should English-born Black people, *métis(se)* or with both parents from either continental Africa or the Caribbean, demand to be included under the preexisting English umbrella? Alternatively, as children of a global African diaspora, should they carve out a separate space wherein they acknowledge links and foster social, cultural, and political allegiances with other diasporic constituents in the United States, Canada, Brazil, the Caribbean, among other points on the globe? From the vantage point of agency and not victimization, is there some way of reconciling their subjugated connections with former Empire, which will then enable them, whether *métis(se)* or not, to proudly wear the badge of belonging to/in England? Most importantly, are indigenous White English residents prepared to redefine what it means to be English in order to include on equal footing both *métis(se)* as well as English-born children of so-called immigrant parents, whose natal origins are South Asian, Caribbean, or continental African? As the year 2000 approaches, as a nation, England has yet to crack these conundrums.

As cultural critiques, the testimonies of the six *métisse* women tackle these transnationalist complex concerns. The women's stories also chart what Ang-Lygate refers to as "the spaces of (un)location where the shifting and contextual meanings of diaspora reside – caught somewhere between, and inclusive of the more familiar experiences of (re)location and (dis)location" (Ang-Lygate 1997: 170). However, as cumulative text, their individual evocations also illustrate the collective psychosocial problematics of a wider African diaspora(s)' angst in its specific geopolitical manifestations (Hesse 1993). In the conclusion to their edited collection *Place and the Politics of Identity,* Pile and Keith indirectly legitimate the (English – African diaspora) as a shifting political space where senses of place are (re)negotiated and identities are (re)constructed:

> spatiality needs to be seen as the modality through which contradictions are normalized, naturalized and neutralized. Politics is necessarily territorial but these territories are simultaneously real, imaginary and symbolic . . . spatiality should simultaneously express people's experiences of, for example, displacement (feeling out of place), dislocation (relating to alienation) and fragmentation (the jarring multiple identities). Spatialities represent both the spaces between multiple identities and the contradictions within identities. (Pile and Keith 1993: 224–5)

Despite, or perhaps because of, my own itinerant *métis(se)* African diasporic family background prior to 1989, my cultural perception of my birthplace and former home was, if not predominantly White, most definitely

English.[10] However, in the summer of 1989 I flew to England. This time I returned on my own and on my own terms. At the point of my arrival I did not realize that I would depart three years later with the beginnings of a critical auto-ethnography:

> critical ethnographies provide another genre wherein the represented culture is located within a larger historical, political, economic, social and symbolic context than is said to be recognized by cultural members . . . auto-ethnographies have emerged in which the culture of the writer's own group is textualized. Such writings often offer a passionate, emotional voice of a positioned and explicitly judgemental fieldworker and thus obliterate the customary and ordinarily, rather mannerly distinction between the researcher and the researched. (Van Maanen 1995: 9–10)

Nor could I anticipate the profound ways in which I would be forced "to step in and step out" (Powdermaker 1966: 15–16) of roles while simultaneously resisting the insider/outsider label of "inappropriate Other":

> The moment the insider steps out from the inside she's no longer a mere insider. She necessarily looks in from the outside while also looking out from the inside. Not quite the same, not quite the other, she stands in that undetermined threshold place where she constantly drifts in and out. Undercutting the inside/outside opposition, her intervention is necessarily that of both not quite an insider and not quite an outsider. She is, in other words, this inappropriate other or same who moves about with always at least two gestures: that of affirming "I am like you" while persisting in her difference and that of reminding "I am different" while unsettling every definition of otherness arrived at. (Minh-ha 1990: 374–5)

For the first time my plan was not to visit family, but rather to do exploratory research for my impending Ph.D. thesis, which, at that stage, would be examining the emergence of political consciousness among Black youth in England. This critical feminist ethnographic work would take me out of the primarily "lily-White" English working-class and middle-class communities, which reflected my early childhood, and into the more ethnically and so-called racially mixed but not necessarily more harmonious communities in Manchester, Birmingham, London, and Bristol:

> It is, however, clear that in specific contexts some forms of difference may be more important than others. It follows from this that the interrelations between the various forms of difference will always require specifications in given historical contexts. We cannot assume we know the significance of any particular set of intersections between class, race and gender prior to our analysis of these

intersections. The task for feminist anthropologists, as for scholars in other disciplines, is to find ways of theorizing these highly variable intersections between the various forms of difference. (Moore 1988: 197)

In short, according to Marcus and Fischer, what I was attempting was an anthropological "repatriation" with cultural critique as my motivation (Marcus and Fischer 1986: 111). It was then that I first experienced the English – African diaspora.

Points of entry/sites of convergences

In the United States I had conducted extensive ethnographic research on cultural constructions of adulthood for African-American young men and women. In their homes in the context of extended families, in schools, in community centers, or just "hangin' out," they told me what it was like to be a young African-American man or woman living in a legislated social context wherein the criteria for adult status differed remarkably from their own conceptions. I had worked most extensively with young African-American women, many of whom were young mothers. I also discovered that popular culture, in the form of then-burgeoning rap music, was another important way to understand African-American youth cultures. I was particularly interested in young women rappers' roles in this sociopolitical movement, and was already convinced that their songs offered both political commentary and cultural critique.

With the African diaspora as the framework, I planned to look comparatively at the lived experiences of African-American youth in the Bay Area in California, USA, which I had already done, and the lives of African-Caribbean young people in Bristol, England, my proposed research project. In spring 1990 I arrived in Bristol and began acquainting myself with the young people in Thatchapee, the community I had chosen to plant myself in. Most of the youth I encountered in these various contexts were very friendly and seemed interested in talking with someone who would leave America to come to this "Debi Debi" (naff, awful) place. However, over time, these same young people expressed no interest in officially participating in my project. In fact, in so many words they said, "Jayne, we enjoy talking with you, but we have no interest in your project." I could not hide my disappointment nor my frustration, though I was somewhat relieved since, despite the comradeship created by both my personality as well as my direct connection to the heralded "States," I still detected a certain amount of social distance between us – one that I sensed time would not bridge. This was brought on by the age difference, at times gender, culture, perceived power differential with my role as voluntary youth worker and social class:

> "Cultures" do not hold still for their portraits. Attempts to make them do so always involve simplification and exclusion, selection of a temporal focus, the construction of a particular self–other relationship, and the imposition or negotiation of a power relationship. (Clifford 1986: 10)

My favorite expression while living there and one that I still use today is: "As you see, so are you seen." I think this revelation is the most fascinating test aspect of doing ethnographic fieldwork. For me, it became the turning point of my research. When I returned to England I did not have a clear sense as to how I would refer to myself, whether I would identify as American or British. Until I got to know people, they decided for me. I was "that American gyal." Having said that, the injuries of race and color were omnipresent in Thatchapee. I was also referred to as "that red-skinned American gyal" or less frequently "that half-caste American gyal." These last two expressions were meant to mark my light skin and my presumed *métisse* status. Because of the bi-racialized politics of colonialism, residents of Thatchapee assumed, and usually rightly so, that any light-skinned person was *métis(se)*. Although this assumption was complicated by the fact that in a genealogical sense, most of the residents from the African Caribbean were themselves *métis(se)*.

Who is on the ethnographic fringes depends on who is defining the center:

> Ethnography is actively situated *between* powerful systems of meaning. It poses its questions at the boundaries of civilizations, cultures, classes, races and gender. Ethnography decodes and recodes, telling the grounds of collective order and diversity, inclusion and exclusion. It describes processes of innovation and structuration, and is itself part of these processes. (Clifford 1986: 2–3)

On my daily travels, in addition to the young people, I found myself meeting people from every segment of both Bristolian and Thatchapee societies. However, I found that I made the most profound connections with individuals who lived life at what Anzaldúa (1987) would refer to as "the borderlands." Deemed "marginal" people, those presumed to be on the edge, seemingly unbelonging, these men, women, and children were generally *métis(se)*. Some of them I never even actually spoke with. We communicated in our silences. I eventually decided to go with the proverbial flow and focus on the poetics and politics of what I was then calling "mixed race" identities, thereby producing a microethnography:

> Also known as focused or specific ethnography, microethnography zeroes in
> on particular settings (cultural events or "scenes") drawing on the ways that a
> cultural ethos is reflected in microcosm in selected aspects of everyday life but
> giving emphasis to particular behaviors in particular settings rather than
> attempting to portray a whole cultural system. (Wolcott 1995: 102)

After some thought, more than twenty-five *métis(se) griot(tes)* wanted to
testify. However, demands of daily life affected each person's ability to
commit to the project.

The primary twenty-five testimonies of redemption came from (a)
métis(se) people from diverse social worlds whom I had met along the first
year of my journey; (b) others from people I knew, such as social workers,
teachers, youth workers, artists who were not necessarily *métis(se)* but who
knew people who might want to participate; and (c) others still from other
métis(se) friends of participants. For at least two reasons, those I did speak
with convinced me of the importance of this undertaking. First, embarking
on such an endeavor would force a creative tension between the process of
doing "insider/outsider" anthropology and the product, an ethnography
that perpetuates the cultural anthropological remit: "interest in other peoples
and their ways of life and concern to explain them within a frame of reference that includes ourselves" (Hymes 1974: 11). Second, "getting the news
out" (Wolf 1992: 1) would bring to life the words of novelist Michelle Cliff:
"We are not exotic – or aromatic – or poignant. We are not aberrations. We
are ordinary. All this has happened before" (Cliff 1980: 7).

Project participants' local synthesized individual and collective voices
represent the significant part of a greater multigenerational whole com-
prising people in England with Black continental African or African-
Caribbean fathers *and* White British or continental European mothers.
More pointedly, in general, they map the specificities of the local, yet they
also problematize the parameters and boundaries delimiting the local and
the global:

> the local exists nowhere in a pure state . . . the local is only a fragmented set
> of possibilities that can be articulated into a momentary politics of time and
> place . . . this is to take the local not as the end point but as the start. This is
> not to idealize the local as the real, but to look at the ways in which injustices
> are naturalized in the name of the immediate. In conceiving of the local as a
> nodal point, we can begin to deconstruct its movements and its meanings.
> (Probyn 1990: 187)

In particular, the six *métisse* women's living stories meld the macrostructural
bi-racialized and gendered processes of diasporic and indigenous English
histories with the microstructural concerns of identity politics as they are

manifest, negotiated, and reinvented through the simultaneous prisms of gender, generation, "race," class, and ethnicity.

Notes

1 Mindful of the ongoing debates as to what constitute feminism(s), I have chosen Barbara Smith's definition of feminism as my working definition: "The political theory and practice that struggles to free all women: women of color, working-class women, poor women, disabled women, lesbians, old women, as well as white economically privileged heterosexual women." See Smith (1990): 25.

2 See Flora Nwapa (1980) *Wives at War*, Enugu: Tana Press; Sonia Bleeker (1969) *The Ibo of Biafra*, New York: William and Morrow; Chinua Achebe (1993) *The Trouble with Nigeria*, Oxford: Heinemann; C. Ojukwu (1969) *Biafra*, New York: Perennial; Arthur Nwankwo (1972) *Nigeria: The Challenge of Biafra*, London: Rex Collings; Elechi Amadi (1973) *Sunset in Biafra*, London: Heinemann; Rex Niven (1970) *The War of Nigerian Unity*, London: Evans Brothers; Dan Jacobs (1987) *The Brutality of Nations*, New York: Paragon; Chukwumeka Ike (1976) *Sunset at Dawn*, London: Fontana; Frederick Forsyth (1969) *The Making of an African Legend: The Biafra Story*, Harmondsworth: Penguin Books; Buchi Emecheta (1986) *Head Above Water: An Autobiography*, London: Fontana. For a compelling fictionalized account of the impact of the war on two families, see Anne Giwa-Amu (1996) *Sade*, London: Ace.

3 Dan Jacobs, author of *The Brutality of Nations* (see note 2) visited my father in Biafra and reported the results of a survey my father had conducted on famine-induced starvation:

> Ifekwunigwe found in March 1968 that, during this early period of starvation, 89 percent of those affected were children under five years of age, while the remaining 11 percent were children five to fifteen. This resulted from a shortage of protein foods, as small children need proportionately more protein for their growing bodies than do adults. Later, however, the elderly would be affected, and the following year, when carbohydrates would be in short supply as well, all age groups would suffer malnutrition and starvation. (Jacobs 1987: 313)

4 While reading an earlier version of this manuscript, my mum insisted that it was my older brother Christopher and not I who vomited on the steps. However, there are several versions to every story, and I did not let my mother deter me. The fact that I remembered and believed my retelling of the story to be the truth seemed most important.

5 In 1992, not long after leaving Bristol to return to Berkeley, I met someone from England and he informed me that Nelson, one of my many former home towns, has one of the highest suicide rates in Britain. This information nearly spoiled my sugar-coated memories of life there.

6   The precise date of his return is fuzzy to me. However, on my last visit to Los Angeles I acquired an old local (Nelson, Lancashire) newspaper clipping from my mother. Dated January 30, 1970, it discloses the contents of a letter from Lord Hunt, leader of the official British government fact-finding party in Biafra: "This is just to say that Aaron is well and doing a magnificent job caring for some 1,500 children in the hospital. He has faced grave danger and has remained at his post when other doctors fled."
7   (Also *oyigbo*) An Igbo colloquial expression which means "White person" or "European person." When we traveled back to Nigeria with our father, we were implicated as *oyingbos* as well.
8   Fall, 1993 *Time* Special Issue, "The New Face of America: How Immigrants Are Shaping the World's First Multicultural Society."
9   Gary Younge "Beige Britain," the *Guardian*, May 22, 1997.
10   Two of the major assumptions I intend to challenge in this book is that Whiteness is the normative and naturalized signifier by which deviations of Blackness are determined as well as the presumption that Englishness is synonymous with Whiteness. See chapter 10 for an extensive discussion of these problematics. [*Editors' note*: Ifekwunigwe refers to her book *Scattered Belongings: Cultural Paradoxes of "Race," Nation and Gender* (London: Routledge, 1999).]

References

Achebe, Chinua. *The Trouble with Nigeria*. Oxford: Heinemann, 1993.
Amadi, Elechi. *Sunset in Biafra*. London: Heinemann, 1973.
Ang-Lygate, Magdalene. "Charting the Spaces of (Un)location: On Theorizing Diaspora." *Black British Feminism*. Ed. Heidi Mirza. London: Routledge, 1997. 153–70.
Anzaldua, Gloria. *Borderlands/La Frontera: The New Mestiza*. San Francisco, CA: Aunt Lute Books, 1987.
Baldwin, James. *Notes of a Native Son*. Boston, MA: Beacon Press, 1955.
Bleeker, Sonia. *The Ibo of Biafra*. New York: William and Morrow, 1969.
Bourdieu, Pierre. *Distinction: A Social Critique of the Judgement of Taste*. Cambridge, MA: Harvard University Press, 1984.
Boyce-Davies, Carole. *Black Women, Writing and Identity*. London: Routledge, 1994.
Cliff, Michelle. *Claiming an Identity They Taught Me To Despise*. Watertown, MA: Persephone Press, 1980.
Clifford, James. "Partial Truths." *Writing Culture*. Ed. J. Clifford and M. George. Berkeley: University of California Press, 1986. 1–26.
Cohen, Robin. *Frontiers of Identity*. London: Longman, 1994.
Diop, Cheik Anta. *Civilization or Barbarism: An Authentic Anthropology*. New York: Lawrence Hill, 1991.
Emecheta, Buchi. *Head Above Water: An Autobiography*. London: Fontana, 1986.
Fanon, Frantz. *Black Skin, White Masks*. Translated by Charles Lam Markmann. New York: Grove Press, 1969.

Forsyth, Frederick. *The Making of an African Legend: The Biafra Story.* Harmondsworth: Penguin Books, 1969.

Gilroy, Paul. *The Black Atlantic.* London: Verso, 1993.

—— "Route Work: The Black Atlantic and the Politics of Exile." *The Post-Colonial Question.* Ed. I. Chambers and L. Curtis. London: Routledge, 1996. 17–29.

Giwa-Amu, Anne. *Sade.* London: Ace, 1996.

Hall, Stuart. "Old and New Identities, Old and New Ethnicities." *Culture, Globalization and the World System.* Ed. A. King. London: Macmillan, 1991. 41–68.

—— "The Formation of a Diasporic Intellectual." *Stuart Hall: Critical Dialogues in Cultural Studies.* Ed. D. Morley and K.-H. Chen. London: Routledge, 1996. 484–503.

Herskovits, Melville. *The Myth of the Negro Past.* Boston, MA: Beacon Press, 1958.

Hesse, Barnor. "Black to Front and Black Again: Racialization through Contested Times and Spaces." *Place and the Politics of Identity.* Ed. M. Keith and S. Pile. London: Routledge, 1993. 162–82.

Hymes, Dell. "The Use of Anthropology." *Reinventing Anthropology.* Ed. D. Hymes. New York: Vintage Books, 1974. 3–82.

Ike, Chukwumeka. *Sunset at Dawn.* London: Fontana, 1976.

Jacobs, Dan. *The Brutality of Nations.* New York: Paragon, 1987.

Lorde, Audre. *Zami, A New Spelling of My Name.* Watertown, MA: Persephone Press, 1982.

Maja-Pearce, Adewale. *How Many Miles to Babylon?* London: Heinemann, 1990.

Marcus, George and Fischer, Michael. *Anthropology as Cultural Critique.* Chicago, IL: University of Chicago Press, 1986.

Mercer, Kobena. *Welcome to the Jungle: New Positions in Black Cultural Studies.* London: Routledge, 1994.

Minh-ha, Trinh T. "Not you/Like you: Post-colonial Women and the Interlocking Questions of Identity and Difference." *Making Face, Making Soul.* Ed. G. Anzaldua. San Francisco, CA: Aunt Lute Press, 1990. 371–75.

Moore, Henrietta. *Feminism and Anthropology.* Cambridge: Polity Press, 1988.

"The New Face of America: How Immigrants Are Shaping the World's First Multicultural Society." *Time* Fall 1993.

Niven, Rex. *The War of Nigerian Unity.* London: Evans Brothers, 1970.

Nwankwo, Arthur. *Nigeria: The Challenge of Biafra.* London: Rex Collings, 1972.

Nwapa, Flora. *Wives at War.* Enugu: Tana Press, 1980.

Ojukwu, C. *Biafra.* New York: Perennial, 1969.

Pile, Steve and Keith, Michael, eds. *Place and the Politics of Identity.* London: Routledge, 1993.

Powdermaker, Hortense. *Stranger and a Friend.* New York: W. W. Norton, 1966.

Probyn, Elspeth. "Travels in the Postmodern: Making Sense of the Local." *Feminism and Postmodernism.* Ed. L. Nicholson. London: Routledge, 1990. 176–89.

Rashidi, Runoko. *Introduction to the Study of African Classical Civilization.* London: Karnak House, 1992.

Smith, Barbara. "Racism and Women's Studies." *Making Face, Making Soul.* Ed. G. Anzaldua. San Francisco, CA: Aunt Lute Press, 1990. 25.

Somers, Margaret and Gibson, Gloria. "Reclaiming the Epistemological Other: Narrative and the Social Constitution of Identity." *Social Theory and the Politics of Identity*. Ed. C. Calhoun. Oxford: Blackwell, 1994. 37–99.

Trudgill, Peter. *Sociolinguistics*. Harmondsworth: Penguin Books, 1974.

Van Maanen, John, ed. *Representation in Ethnography*. London: Sage, 1995.

Van Sertima, Ivan. *They Came Before Columbus*. New York: Random House, 1976.

Willis, Susan. "Black Women Writers Take a Critical Perspective." *Making a Difference: Feminist Literary Criticism*. Ed. G. Greene and C. Khan. New York: Methuen, 1985. 211–37.

Wolcott, Harry. "Making a Study More Ethnographic." *Representation in Ethnography*. Ed. J. Van Maanen. London: Sage, 1995. 79–111.

Wolf, Margery. *A Thrice Told Tale: Feminism, Postmodernism and Ethnographic Responsibility*. Stanford, CA: Stanford University Press, 1992.

Younge, Gary. "Beige Britain." *Guardian*, May 22, 1997.

8

In the Shadows of Stonewall: Examining Gay Transnational Politics and the Diasporic Dilemma

Martin F. Manalansan IV

This essay takes scholarship on diaspora and sexuality in a new direction. Manalansan argues against the prevailing notion that non-Western definitions and understandings of same-sex sexual practices are less modern or liberated than their Western counterparts, and suggests that gay practices need to be understood more broadly. As suggested by the title, the essay moves away from thinking of the Stonewall Riots as the defining moment in transnational gay and lesbian history. Instead, Manalansan asks how local practices and local histories might be as, if not more, important in shaping gay subjectivities in specific places. Juxtaposing texts about the international gay movement with narratives by Filipino gay men in New York City and the Philippines, the essay argues that national culture, history, religion, class, and region play an important role in determining gay cultural practices.

By focusing on same-sex sexual practices among Filipino men in the Philippines and Filipino American men in the US, Manalansan argues against the tendency to construct a globalizing definition of gayness that relegates the experiences of non-Western subjects to the margins. In the process of understanding how groups of men articulate same-sex sexual practices within specific political frameworks, Manalansan's essay offers us a way to think about how discourses of queerness and sexuality are affected by developments locally, nationally, and transnationally, thus moving away from a hierarchical logic that would position non-Western sexual practices as always inferior or behind those of the West.

In a world of collapsing borders, gay ideologies, practices, and images are tracing modernity's trajectories. Within this context the globalization of the gay "movement" has proven to be problematic. This essay was written on the heels of and in the "heat" of the celebration of the twenty-fifth anniversary in June 1994 of the Stonewall Rebellion. While this event is decisive in figuring certain globalizing ideas and practices, an increasingly globalized view of Stonewall and of the gay and lesbian political movement has been prevalent for the past two decades. Media and popular consciousness have long taken for granted that gay and lesbian culture and politics have spread worldwide. Consider the following events or representations from the Stonewall anniversary:

- The "official" Stonewall '25 march held on June 26, 1994, started not in Greenwich Village or more specifically in the bar where it all started, The Stonewall Bar, but at the United Nations building. Initially, the organizing committee proposed two starting points for the march, the Stonewall site or the UN building in midtown Manhattan. When the city government would only give a permit for one starting site, the committee chose the UN because of its "global symbolism."
- Souvenirs and artifacts being sold to commemorate the Stonewall festivities included T-shirts with the name Stonewall set against a globe and a pink pin with the words "Come Out UN."
- The brochure for the Stonewall march included a preamble similar to the Universal Declaration of Human Rights. In this document there is a call for the UN as an international governing body to promulgate the rights and well-being of gay, lesbian, and transgender peoples.

In this essay I examine the conditions for cultural production, circulation, and reception of the "international" gay and lesbian movement. I problematize this inquiry by juxtaposing descriptions, readings, and analyses of this "internationalism" against texts and narratives by Filipino "gay" men living in the Philippines and in New York City. I am interested in the movement and travel of bodies and ideas within a circuit of exchange as well as the crisscrossing chains of disjunctions and syncretic engagements that are experienced and transformed by Filipino gay men. I focus on the various configurations of "Stonewall" as a moment of universal gay and lesbian liberation and as a construction of "liberation" itself.

In the first section I examine the rhetoric of transnational[1] gay and lesbian politics by looking not only at the Stonewall march and its attendant cultural activities, but at the recent International Lesbian and Gay Association conference. A review of current scholarship on transnational processes and gay and lesbian studies suggests how contemporary "transnational" flows of gay and lesbian "culture" and politics raise the following questions:

- Who bestows legitimacy on the narration of Stonewall as the origin of gay and lesbian development? What does this narrative of origins engen-

der? What practices and locations are subordinated by a privileging of
Stonewall as origin?

- Does the search for "authentic" native or primordial "gay and lesbian"
  phenomena in the non-metropolitan periphery impose a Eurocentric universalism on the variety of sexual practices that exist worldwide?
- What political idioms and maneuvers are deployed to establish, execute,
  and justify international credos of egalitarianism?
- What strategies exist to resist such appropriations and subordinations?

My essay begins from the premise that the globalization of gay and lesbian
oppression obfuscates hierarchical relations between metropolitan centers
and suburban peripheries. By privileging Western definitions of same-sex
sexual practices, non-Western practices are marginalized and cast as "premodern" or unliberated. Practices that do not conform with Western narratives of the development of individual political subjects are dismissed as
unliberated or coded as "homophobic." I suggest, in contrast, that we must
conceive of "gay" practices as a broad category of analysis[2] and as multiply
determined by notions of culture, history, religion, class, and region, in and
across various cultural and political locations and even within a single group.
In this regard, Filipino gay men, whether immigrants to the United States
or residents of the Philippines, offer examples of practices that invoke and
strategically deploy multiple formations as they declare affinities and differences in response to global gay and lesbian agendas.

The second and third sections of the essay examine the configuration,
translation, affirmation, and negation of the rhetoric of gay and lesbian
oppression by Filipino gay men living in the Philippines and in New York
City. Drawing upon recent writings of Filipino gay writers and activists as
well as reflections on a two-year ethnographic study of Filipino gay men in
New York City, the second section specifically situates the notion of "gay liberation" within the existing cultural, political, and economic conditions of
the Philippines today. The third section consists of excerpts from interviews
with Filipino gay men living in New York City regarding Stonewall: the first
narrative is by a Filipino gay man who was present at the actual rebellion
and was arrested in the process; the second is taken from a conversation
between two informants after the 1994 Stonewall celebrations. The final
section is a reading of the themes and issues that have been presented.

Whose Rebellion? The Fable of Stonewall and the Rhetoric
of Global Oppression and Liberation of Gays and Lesbians

The official guide to the Stonewall festivities noted: "People will celebrate
the rebellion that transformed the existing Homophile Movement into our

contemporary, global, Lesbian, Gay and Transgender Rights Movement. Our goal is to mobilize the largest human rights march and rally the world has ever seen. We have victories to be proud of and injustices to protest. With pride, we celebrate our courage and accomplishments from around the world. We will hear how the struggle for human rights is being waged in different lands and cultures. We will recall/learn and teach our history. We see that we are fighting back and winning victories."[3] From this declaration we may observe that the discourse about Stonewall has changed from localized descriptions of a series of police raids in a downtown Manhattan gay bar in 1969 into a revolutionary moment that originates liberation for gays and lesbians everywhere. These transformations have repercussions for defining and shaping the category gay.

Gay within this view of Stonewall is defined within a temporalized understanding of both sexuality and society. That is, gay gains meaning according to a developmental narrative that begins with an unliberated, "prepolitical" homosexual practice and that culminates in a liberated, "out," politicized, "modern," "gay" subjectivity. Such temporalized narratives about gayness are widespread and accepted by many "queer" publications as well.[4] For example, in an anthology of international gay and lesbian writing, Stephen Likosky discusses gay writing after Stonewall and describes Stonewall as an event where "gays, many of them Third World transvestites, took to the streets of New York to battle the police, who had raided the Stonewall Inn, a neighborhood bar."[5] In marking the periods before and after Stonewall, Likosky employs Barry Adam's distinctions between anthropological or historical homosexuality and "modern" homosexuality.[6] Anthropological/historical homosexuality is "characteristic of societies where homosexuality is obligatory and universally practiced such as those where sexual relations between old and younger males are part of the socialization process into manhood (e.g. in Melanesia, central Africa, Amazonia and western Egypt)."[7] Modern homosexuality, on the other hand, is defined as follows:

- Homosexual relations have been able to escape the structure of the dominant heterosexual kinship system.
- Exclusive homosexuality, now possible for both partners, has become an alternative path to conventional family forms.
- Same-sex bonds have developed new forms without being structured around particular age or gender categories.
- People have come to discover each other and form large-scale social networks not only because of existing social relationships but also because of their homosexual interests.
- Homosexuality has come to be a social formation unto itself, characterized by self-awareness and group identity.

Gay in this instance, then, is meaningful within the context of the emergence of bourgeois civil society and the formation of the individual subject that really only occurs with capitalist and Western expansion. Categories of same-sex phenomena are placed within a Western-centered developmental teleology, with "gay" as its culminating stage. Other "non-gay" forms or categories are constructed metaleptically, rendered "anterior," and transformed into archeological artifacts that need only be reckoned with when excavating the roots of pan-cultural/pan-global homosexuality. In other words, the "internationalizing" transnational gay and lesbian movement does not as yet contain a critique of its own universalizing categories; without an interrogation of its Eurocentric and bourgeois assumptions, this globalizing discourse risks duplicating an imperial gaze in relation to non-Western non-metropolitan sexual practices and collectivities.

The Pink Book, a regular publication of the International Lesbian and Gay Association, contains many similar rhetorics and assumptions.[8] The ILGA, based in Belgium with strong chapters in the United States, was formed to provide the organizational and (sometimes) financial resources to monitor, react to, and understand the political and social conditions of gays and lesbians worldwide. *The Pink Book* is a kind of status report of the "global picture," with in-depth essays detailing the issues and problems of particular nations and an abbreviated survey of the social and legal positions of gays and lesbians "in various countries."

In the latest edition of this book, an essay by Tielman and Hammelburg "investigates" 202 countries, gathering data on 178 of them. In this survey the focus was on "(1) official attitudes and the law regarding homosexuality, (2) social attitudes to homosexuality, and (3) the gay and/or lesbian movements all over the world." Investigators found that the overall social and legal situations were "worst in Africa and best in Europe." The following entry on the Philippines is somewhat typical of many for other countries:

Philippines
Official Attitudes and the Law
Homosexual behavior between consenting adults is not mentioned in the law as being a criminal offense. Laws referring to "public morality" are used against gays and lesbians. The Philippines' immigration [authorities] has declared a "war against pedophiles," particularly in Manila. Foreigners are expected to be the first targets of the campaign. The government has banned the radical women's group "Gabriela" on November 7, 1988, as part of the government counterinsurgency program, "for having possible ties to some underground leftists."

Society
Closeted homosexuality is tolerated, but "sex tourism" has a negative impact on the social position of homosexual men. A minority of the population is in favor of gay and lesbian rights.

The Gay and/or Lesbian Movement
A group exists called the Movement for Social Equality and Recognition of
Homosexuals. In the AIDS Center, "The Library," many open gays are active.

The entries regularly employ words like *closet, homophobia, gay,* and *lesbian*
without interrogating the Western assumptions embedded in each term, as
if they were natural, given concepts that did not need to be contextualized
within specific national histories. Apart from the light and caricaturish
descriptions of social norms and attitudes, the survey boldly asserts a normative "gay" subject who is not dissimilar to the Euro-American modern
political subject. Like the "straight" modern political subject, the "gay"
subject moves from the "immature" in the "concealment" of his or her sexuality to the "mature" visibility of political participation in the public sphere.
The assumption that practices that are not organized around visibility are
"closeted" and the interpretation that lack of explicitly gay-identified people
in the public arena signifies that a "homophobic" attitude is prevalent in the
culture are not interrogated.

   While there is some perfunctory discussion of cultural diversity, the tendency to deploy monolithic and universalist constructions of gayness and gay
liberation in popular and scholarly literature is quite widespread and observ-
able. For example, at one of the ILGA preconference sessions held in
Manhattan after the Stonewall celebrations, where "people of color" issues
were to be discussed, potential participants were limited to "people of color
only." A number of delegates were puzzled about how they would categorize themselves. Although there may be some understanding among this
group that gender and sexuality are socially constructed, it seems a difficult
task to persuade the same people of the constructedness of race and nationality, and the imbrication of gender and sexuality within race and nationality. Efforts such as these to confront marginality within the "gay and lesbian
world community" by fixing and reifying racial difference have led ILGA to
create boundaries that actually promote more marginalization.

   The time and place of the ILGA conference in New York City provided
a kind of symbolic flag for the view that Stonewall is "ground zero" for all
gay and lesbian efforts. Holding the conference in the United States also
presented problems for potential participants, which the ILGA did not take
into account. A number of delegates (including some twenty from the
Philippines) were unable to attend because of financial or legal constraints;
conference registration cost $300, and Filipino delegates were denied visitor
visas by the US embassy in Manila.

   The ILGA, while attempting to host regional meetings in different parts
of the world, has at the same time insisted on a universalized vision of how
the politics and the future of all gay and lesbian political and cultural efforts

should look. In the introduction to *The Pink Book* the secretaries-general of ILGA write: "the increased visibility of lesbians, gay men and bisexuals, supported by a strong movement, has proved to be a successful *formula* for confronting and fighting homophobic tendencies in all types of society. Well organized groups in many countries have succeeded in at least partially improving our human rights."[9] The specular economy that measures political value in terms of visibility, profoundly rooted in epistemologies of revelation rooted in the European Enlightenment, is nowhere interrogated.

Within the context of transnational cultural, economic, and political challenges monolithic construction and prescriptions are, at the very least, doomed to failure. What do we really mean when we say *gay* in a world where hybridity and syncretism provide the grist for cultural production, distribution, and consumption? To what creative forms of engagement do people who live outside the gay-idyllic world of Europe resort in order to interrogate the discourses of "rights" and social acceptance? The next section is an attempt to respond to such questions by looking at the writings of three Filipino gay men living in the Philippines.

"Gay" Liberation: Philippine Style(s)

Homosexuality in the Philippines has long been seen by popular media and by many Filipinos to be a "non-issue." However, in recent years, with the ascendance of gay and lesbian studies in the West as well as the growth of the AIDS pandemic, cultural production around "gay" issues has increased tremendously in the Philippines. In this section I consider the works of three Filipino writers, Tony Perez, Jomar Fleras, and J. Neil C. Garcia. They are the most vibrant writers about gay political issues in the Philippines today, and they also present various modes of engagement with the issues of "gay" identity and politics (*qua* liberation). Before I analyze these three writers' works, it is necessary to contextualize their ideas within Filipino tradition around the *bakla*.

The bakla

Bakla is a Tagalog term used for particular types of men who engage in practices that encompass effeminacy, transvestism, and homosexuality. The *bakla* is conceptualized in terms of epicene characteristics.[10] On one hand, the *bakla* is stereotypically seen to exist in the vulgar public spaces of the carnival (*baklang karnabal*), the beauty parlor (*parlorista*), and the marketplace (*baklang palengke*). On the other, the *bakla* is also seen as the cross-dressing man with the female heart (*pusong babae*), searching for the real man and trying hard not to slip into vulgarity or dismal ugliness. These images form part of everyday discourse and sometimes find their way into the works of Filipino gay writers and activists.

Bakla as a form of selfhood is popularly seen as a lower-class phenomenon even among scholars. For example, Michael Tan equated *bakla* and "gay" with real class divisions. Creating a tripartite grouping of the subcultures of "men who have sex with men" or MSM,[11] he argues that the *parlorista* (signifying the stereotypical occupation of the male homosexual, which is that of a beautician or beauty parlor employee) or the stereotypical homosexual, is primarily found in low-income groups such as domestic servants, small market vendors, and waiters. The other two groups that compose this MSM constellation include the callboys or male sex workers (who are from the urban and rural poor), who oftentimes identify as "straight," and the "gays" who are from the higher-income groups.

Although Tan attempts to specify the *bakla* through terms like *parlorista*, it is unclear from his formulation how and if the complexity of practices that comprise the *bakla*, as selfhood, can exist across class lines. By lumping the *bakla* with the MSM population, he conflates the dynamics of self-fashioning not only in terms of sex object choice, but also with the act of same-sex physical encounters. While he recognizes the gender dimensions of the *bakla*, Tan's rigidly assigned class status to the *bakla* is itself a stereotypical view from a specific class position. I assume that he derives his categories from privileging the vantage point of educated, upper-class men who attended safe sex workshops in Manila.

In the next section it will be clear that I do not correlate directly or consistently the identification of either *bakla* or gay with specific class positions. Rather, my data suggest that class is inflected with race, immigration status, and a range of other factors. Furthermore, I suggest that the *bakla* is an extravagant and complicated figure whose practices go beyond the strictures of transvestism, same-sex encounters, gossip, and vanity. Fenella Cannell's ethnographic study of a small Filipino rural community provides illuminating views on this point.[12] She suggests that the *bakla* is a master of transformation and mimicry. Focusing on the performative aspects of identity and self-formation, Cannell emphasizes the mercurial aspects of the *bakla*. For example, the *bakla* from the rural poor is able to negotiate with "high-class" culture such as Hollywood icons and music through participation in beauty pageants and amateur shows, and may attempt to emulate the dress, visage, and manner of glamorous Tagalog and Hollywood female celebrities. In doing so, these men are able not only to negotiate with another culture or class, but, more importantly, they are able to make this culture – through successful imitation – their own. Significantly, Cannell asserts that the *bakla* is always careful not to slip into vulgarity. Therefore, class position and sexual and gender identities are more complicated than Michael Tan's static taxonomy of men who have sex with men.

Three Filipino gay writers

Tony Perez's collection of short stories and poetry, *Cubao 1980*, is subtitled *The First Cry of the Gay Liberation Movement in the Philippines* (my translation from Tagalog).[13] The ideas in the book are crystallized in one of its poems, "Manipesto" (Manifesto), which is an injunction to transform the *bakla* into the "gay" man. In the poem, Perez provides a kind of call-to-arms to eradicate the stereotype of the *bakla* as a gossip, an unambitious, bitchy, and effeminate queen. He declares that unless the "illusion" is destroyed and the "mistake" corrected, there can never be any attainment of rights. Writing from a self-conscious "gay liberationist" perspective, Perez views *bakla* salvation as conditional and contingent upon an unquestioned set of modern Western values and qualities that Nicanor Tiongson, a Filipino cultural historian, emphasizes in the book's foreword:
The *bakla* needs to accept:

1   That he was born biologically male and that he should stop feminizing his features or behavior.
2   That "gay" [men] are not some cheap impersonator(s) in some carnival but are honorable laborers, soldiers, priests, professors, businessmen, and athletes.
3   That the right partner for the *bakla* is another *bakla*, otherwise the relationship would be unequal.
4   That the gay relationship will never be the same as a heterosexual relationship that has the blessings of church and society.
5   That being *bakla* is not an illness that one can become cured of or that should be cured.[14]

Jomar Fleras's essay, "Reclaiming Our Historic Rights: Gays and Lesbians in the Philippines," extends Perez's argument into the "gay" history. Writing in the latest edition of the ILGA *Pink Book*, Fleras finds the rationale for gay and lesbian rights in male pre-Spanish religious shamans called *babaylan* who cross-dressed and reputedly indulged in same-sex practices. Significantly, *babaylan* occupied honored positions in the community. Fleras deploys the symbol of the once-dormant volcano, Mt. Pinatubo, figuring gay activism as an eruptive awakening from historical slumber and invisibility.

Fleras is not alone in this view (a gay group at the University of the Philippines is called Babaylan). While he links gays and the historically prior cross-dressing shamans in order to naturalize modern gay practice, Fleras also echoes Perez's views by disparaging the cross-dressing practices and transgender behavior of some Filipino gay men, and asserting that these practices and behaviors are historical remnants or residues of a former "premodern" past: "While the Stonewall riots gave birth to gay liberation in the US, in the Philippines, homosexual men and women were still perpetuating the feudal stereotypes. Gay men portrayed themselves in the media as 'screaming queens' who did nothing but gossip, act silly and lust after men . . . To legitimize their existence, homosexual men and women came out with the concept of gender dysporia [*sic*]: the gay man thought of himself as a woman trapped in a man's body while the lesbian envisioned herself with a trapped male soul that phallicized her."[15]

Fleras pathologizes the *bakla* and foretells the destruction of this "false" image. By asserting that gay liberation is gay men and lesbians "deconstructing and breaking away from the feudal stereotypes imposed upon them by society,"[16] he casts the *bakla* as "feudal," underdeveloped, and temporally prior to the "modern" gay. According to Fleras, with modernization, the future of the gay liberation movement in the Philippines is extremely bright. He notes, "Plans are even under way for a Gay Pride week, which will feature an international lesbian and gay film festival, a theater festival, mardi gras, and a symposium. Soon there will be a gay press. Gay men are now banding together to battle the spread of AIDS . . . Gay and lesbian activism [in the Philippines] is in practical terms just starting . . . Gay men and lesbian women will assert their personhood. They will fight and eventually win their historic rights as leaders and as healers."[17]

Fleras's nativist attempts to historicize the fight for gay and lesbian rights in the Philippines fall apart when he unconditionally takes the Western model of sexual object choice as characteristic of gay identity and repudiates the gender-based model of the *bakla*. Fleras falls into a kind of conceptual trap even as he tries to reveal the particularities of the Philippine experience of gays and lesbians. He does not interrogate the notion of visibility/invisibility and instead portrays the fight for rights in terms of public cultural practices such as parades, films, and books. He constructs a polarized dichotomy in which the *bakla* identity of the Philippine traditions is feudal and pathologically underdeveloped, while the gay identity of the international cultural network is "modern" and liberated. Like the ILGA constituency for which he writes, Fleras unwittingly prioritizes a Eurocentric model of liberation.

Of the three, Garcia is the only one who reflects on the exigencies of *bakla* culture *vis-à-vis* the emerging politicized gay culture. His essay appears in an anthology called *Ladlad* (Unfurling), which he coedited. In a close reading of a play by another Filipino author, Orlando Nadres, *Hangang Dito na Lamang at Maraming Salamat* (Up to this point and thank you very much), Garcia focuses on the two main characters, the seemingly masculine, respectable Fidel, and Julie, the screaming vulgar queen – the stereotypical *bakla*. He points out that the author has Fidel identify with Julie, and he demonstrates the startling realization that it is Julie who rises up from the chaotic world he lives in. Garcia writes, "Nadres then depicts the political and strategic desirability of using Julie for the gay movement, when he makes Julie emerge from the floor of Fidel's childish rage and frustration, in tatters yet brimming with pride. For this short and noble moment . . . [the play] is finally a celebration of gay resistance and pride, pure and simple."[18]

Garcia articulates the need to look beyond one monolithic construction of a "gay" community. He writes, "The urgency of forming a community that embraces all kinds of homosexuals – be they the selectively out Fidel or the unabashedly and uncompromisingly out Julie – is clear in *Ladlad*, where themes on *kabaklaan* [being *bakla*] intersect if not merge with the homo-erotic self-avowals of those 'other gays' whose primary anguish concerns their desire and the difficulty of pursuing it to fulfillment."[19] Garcia's multi-vocal conception of a "gay" community is an attempt to nuance the types of practices that emerge from sites characterized by hybridity, sites in which local traditions, attitudes, and practices are historically fused with "outside" influences owing to colonialism and foreign capital. Instead of uncritically "transferring or buying the technology" of gay and lesbian politics from the outside, Garcia proposes a syncretic move: a notion of a multiply determined subject and a possibility of coalitions between different identities and political agendas.

However, what is missing is a critical examination of notions such as coming out, visibility, and the closet. What kind of conceptual space is the closet, such that it confines people who seem neither highly politicized nor self-reflexively "gay"? In the next section I juxtapose the words of three Filipino gay immigrants living in the United States and examine how their resistance to the highly spectacular images of mainstream US gay culture, particularly the story of Stonewall, represents a different kind of engagement from that of Perez, Fleras, and Garcia.

Oppositions at the Sidelines: The Words/Worlds of Diasporic Gay Men

The two extracts that follow are from ethnographic fieldwork on Filipino gay men in New York that I have been conducting for three years. The first is from a life narrative interview with Mama Rene,[20] who participated in the riots at the Stonewall Inn. The other is from a conversation between two Filipino gay men, Rodel and Ron. In both texts, the meaning of Stonewall is translated and configured by the life narratives of these men.

I met Mama Rene in the summer of 1992, when I was told by my other Filipino gay men informants that he was one of the few remaining Filipinos who took part in the Stonewall Rebellion. As one of my informants told me, Mama Rene is one of the "pioneers" among Filipino gay men in New York. Mama Rene is an affable man of about fifty to sixty years (he refused to state his age). He emigrated to the United States in the mid-1960s to study at New York University. We talked for about two hours before he even mentioned being arrested in 1969. When I asked him to narrate that moment, Mama Rene nonchalantly said:

> It was one of those nights. It was so hot. I was wearing white slacks – dungarees, I think you call them – and I was really sweating. I knew that there had been a police raid several nights before, but I didn't want to be cooped up in my apartment so I went there – to the Stonewall Bar. Anyway, I was standing there – trying to look masculine – it was the thing then. All of a sudden the lights went on and the police barged in. They told us that they were arresting everybody there – I don't know why – I guess I forgot why they were doing that. Of course it was harassment, but anyway. So . . . we were led out of the building to the streets. And you know what? There were lights, huge spotlights, and all these gay men clapping. I felt like a celebrity. The police took us in, booked us, and then we were released. We were supposed to appear a week later, I think to be arraigned or tried, but the charges were dropped.

When I asked him how he felt about being part of that historic event, Mama Rene just shrugged and said, "They say it is a historic event, I just thought it was funny. Do I feel like I made history? People always ask me that. I say no. I am a quiet man, just like how my mom raised me in the Philippines. With dignity."

Mama Rene rarely goes out to watch gay pride parades. He said, "Too many people and quite chaotic." He insisted that he was not an "activist" like most of the white gay men he knew. He had nothing to say to the public, nor was he particularly interested in doing so.

In their disengagement from the originary event of Stonewall, Ron's and Rodel's attitudes are not dissimilar from those of Mama Rene. Both Ron and Rodel emigrated in the early 1980s and are now in their thirties. We were comparing our plans for the following several weeks when the conversation turned to the Stonewall anniversary celebrations and took a curious turn. I moved to the backseat, a listener. The following is a transcription of what transpired. (I have translated the Tagalog words and phrases; the interchange was conducted in both English and Tagalog.)

RODEL: The march is on June 23. Are you going to watch or maybe join a float in drag?

RON: Oh please, why would I do that? Besides, why do people do it? What do they [these gay men] have to prove?

RODEL: Yes, that is true. It is too much. All these drag queens in floats and macho muscle men wearing almost nothing. It is like the carnival.

RON: Every year we have these celebrations – won't it stop?

RODEL: Hey, aren't you the one who likes to go around in drag?

RON: It isn't the drag part that is awful, it is the spectacle. It is a different thing if I go to clubs and cruise in drag, but it is another thing to parade on Fifth Avenue in high heels – you lose your mystique, your mystery.

RODEL: That is so true. It would seem like you are a *baklang karnabal* [*bakla* of the carnival].

For some Filipino gay men, public spaces such as the "streets" (as in the Stonewall slogan, "Out of the bars and into the street") are not spaces of pride, but, to the contrary, are potential arenas of shame and degradation. These informants' views are not the result of homophobia, but are racialized and classed readings of the gay world. The kinds of exclusions and boundaries involved in the immigrant experience form the parameters for these ideas. The term *baklang karnabal* carries over meanings from Filipino traditions that illustrate the differences these three Filipino gay men perceive between American gays and themselves. For these men and some other Filipino gay men I have interviewed, American gay men practice the kind of spectacular and scandalous cross-dressing of the *bakla* in the carnival sideshows, unlike their own mode that attempts verisimilitude. In other words, these informants apprehend this public display of identity to be inappropriate, reminiscent of the kind of carnivalesque vulgarity of a particular type of *bakla*.

While class elements partially underlie these attitudes toward Stonewall, further conversation with these three informants indicates that class issues (they all come from different class backgrounds in the Philippines) are subordinated to the immigrant experience. For Ron and Rodel, the experience of coming to the United States to start a new life was both exciting and traumatic. When I asked Ron and Rodel about the symbolic meaning of Stonewall, Ron answered, "I am an ordinary *bakla*. I have no anger. I have no special joys. Other gay men have so much anguish. I came here to America to seek a new life. I have been successful. I don't have too much *drama*."[21]

Rodel's recuperation of the idiom *baklang karnabal* is not only an instance of his understanding of certain practices as vulgar and carnivalesque, it also implicitly suggests that there are different, multiple ways in which to perform "*bakla*ness." Ron differentiated himself from other gay men by calling himself an "ordinary *bakla*." In doing so, he unwittingly exposes a specific mode of *bakla* self-fashioning that resists and renounces the inelegant and churlish public performance of gay identity. Ron's words in fact exemplify the kinds of translations and transvaluations of the closet and the process of coming out by Filipino gay men.

Public visibility, canonized in the mainstream gay community, is questioned and held at bay by these men. In my conversations with many Filipino gay men, coming out, or, more properly, the public avowal of identity, is not necessary for their own self-fashioning. In a discussion group that involved members of Kambal sa Lusog, a Filipino gay and lesbian organization based in New York, several individuals expressed their concern about the usefulness of coming out narratives based on their experiences as immigrants or children of immigrants. One person in the group actually declared: "coming out" is a "foreign thing – totally American and not at all Filipino."

For my immigrant informants who self-identify as gay, narratives of the "closet" and "coming out" fragment and are subordinated in relation to the more highly fraught arena of the law and citizenship. I asked one informant whether he felt that coming out as a gay man was an important issue for him; he reminded me that until very recently to publicly declare oneself as a homosexual or as a gay man was a cause for the denial of entry visas, permanent residency, or citizenship. Until the late 1980s, US immigration laws categorized homosexuality, together with membership in the Communist Party and being convicted of a crime, as grounds for barring individuals from entering the country. However, he went on to say, "When you are an illegal alien, you have other things to hide apart from being gay. It is actually the least of your problems." Another informant said that he would rather declare he was gay than say he was a Filipino, since he was here illegally. He said, "I had no qualms about acting like a queen, but I would lie and tell people I was Hawaiian since there would not be any questions about citizenship."

The closet and the process of coming out are not culturally constituted by Filipino gay men in the same way as the mainstream gay community. As one informant said, "I know who I am, and most people, including my family, know about me – without any declaration." Filipino gay men argue that identities are not just proclaimed verbally, but are also "felt" (*paki-ramdaman*) or intuited. The swardspeak term *ladlad ng kapa* (which literally means "unfurling the cape" and has been unproblematically translated as "coming out") belies how identity is something "worn" and not always "declared." It is this act of "wearing" identity that makes public arenas for gay identity articulation superfluous for many of my informants. This idea of identity is what spurred Ron to declare himself as one "ordinary *bakla*." This particular phrase is echoed by the opinions of several other informants about how their identities go against the simplistic movement from the private domain to the public realm implied by the ideas of the closet and coming out. One informant, Joe, encapsulated their opinions: "Here in

America, people always talk about everything, including those things that you really don't need to or necessarily want to divulge . . . isn't it all obvious anyway? Talking is a luxury. A lot of us [Filipinos] don't have that luxury. Besides, I don't think we need it [talking about sexual identities]. When I see another *bakla* he does not need to say anything. I don't have to say anything. Instantly, we know. Or, with my friends and family, they know . . . they have known way before my cape [*kapa*] ever unraveled or I mistakenly stepped all over it. I have been wearing it all my life!"

Informants who came here as immigrants considered narratives about success and "making it" in the United States to be more important than coming out. Here class and its translation in a diasporic setting is very telling. Many of my informants who came here illegally, but were well-educated and hailed from privileged backgrounds, were forced to take working-class or low-wage jobs such as janitors, sales clerks, and domestics. As one informant would say, "That is part of coming to America." This sublimation of class runs parallel with Americans' discomfort with notions of class and the rhetoric of equal opportunity. Many of these Filipinos imply that to survive in the United States it is necessary, at least provisionally, to relegate class to the background. This does not mean, however, that class does not figure into their narratives. Rather, class loses its central location in identity articulation and is implicated and inflected by other important nodes of identity, such as race.

Race and racial difference, which is not a popular or highly visible discourse in the Philippines, acquired a greater importance for many of my informants once they had immigrated to the United States. While only a few of them reported direct discrimination, they recognized that not all gay spaces were open to them. Some informants told me of how they were ostracized in several gay establishments that catered to particular racial and class groupings. One informant said, "I may be a doctor, wear expensive clothes, but when I go to [a predominantly white, upper-class bar on the Upper East Side of Manhattan], I feel left out. Like I do not belong." Some reported being hounded out of predominantly white or black gay bars. Others have complained about how the gay media do not consistently have many images of "people who look like me." The crucial markers of difference among *bakla* in the Philippines do not readily cross the borders to the United States.

Amid the realization of racial tensions and differences, there have been attempts by Filipino gay men to create ties and establish affinities with other groups of gay men. Close affinities have been established with other Asian gay men. While racial stereotypes about the Chinese and Japanese and an aversion to being called "Asian" still exist among Filipinos, the situation in the gay community that lumps them into "Orientals" and ghettoizes them into "rice" bars has encouraged the creation of groups such as the Gay Asian Pacific Islander Men of New York (GAPIMNY). Hector, another informant, said, "I know we are very different from the other APIS [Asian and Pacific Islanders], but we're always placed in situations where we are together and, in fact, whether we like it or not, are oppressed together. Remember, we are the gooks, chinks, and brown-skinned fags – even other fags can't seem to stand us. So, I think that if we are to survive in the gay world, we need to connect with other Asians. I used to think, what for? Now, I realize, there are a lot of things we can do if we band together."

Cross-dressing has provided a kind of anchor for the creation of affinities with other Asian men, Latinos, and African-Americans.[22] One informant suggested that cross-dressing among "minorities" or "people of color" contrasts sharply with "white" notions of drag.[23] Vogueing or culture houses, which are composed predominantly of Latino and African-American gays are notorious for excluding or being particularly unfriendly to Caucasians, but have in many cases been welcoming of Asians, specifically Filipinos.[24] I witnessed a competition where a Caucasian was dissed and booed while he/she was on the runway, while in the same category, a Filipino gay man who was a member of the house was wildly applauded. This Filipino voguer or house member rationalized the disparate reactions this way: "We know all too well that there are very few places where people like us can really feel at home. I know that some of my Filipino friends think that associating with Latinos and African Americans is kinda tacky, but tell me, where can you find better cross-dressers than these guys? And where else can our skills as *bakla* be better appreciated than in those fabulous balls? White men are not really skilled. They are too big and too 'unreal.' "

The myth of Stonewall that founds US gay politics is often incongruous with the forms and practices of the gay men in the Filipino diaspora who are my informants. For Mama Rene, his greatest achievement was eventually getting his green card and being legalized after almost fifteen years of living illegally in the United States. The identity politics of American gays therefore becomes just another new local "custom" for Filipino men, as they face racism and encounter the other vicissitudes of immigrant life.

The narratives of these diasporic Filipino gay men demonstrate that the closet is not a monolithic space, and that "coming out" or becoming publicly visible is not a uniform process that can be generalized across different national cultures. Filipino gay men in the diaspora have, to use their own rhetoric, a different drama, that is, a particular performance of coming out and identity articulation, that is emblematic of both their experiences of the gay community in the United States and of *bakla* culture. While Fenella Cannell argued that the *bakla* in a rural area of the Philippines negotiate their identities with images of the United States, I suggest that Filipino gay immigrants like Ron make sense of their existence in the United States by utilizing experiences in and symbolic practices from the Philippines. This particular performance, afforded by the diasporic experience, enables the contestation of long-held beliefs about the translation and transferal of modern gay technologies. For example, Mama Rene's refusal to valorize Stonewall displaces it as an originary event and contests the model of "coming out" for which Stonewall has become the emblem.

The writings of Filipino gay men in the Philippines represent various engagements with "gay culture" through "native" lenses. In these cases the liberatory rhetoric often constructs a shift from *bakla* to gay in both political organizing and cultural production (gay film festivals, parades, and books). With the exception of one or two authors, these writers uncritically echo the modern global rhetoric of the international gay and lesbian movement. On the other hand, Filipino diasporic gay men reinterpret the *bakla* and articulate it in terms of being in excess of the modern gay subject. The words of Mama Rene, Ron, and Rodel rewrite the public, visible, and verbalized gay identity against the grain of the *bakla*. However, it must be noted that the comparison between gay writers in the Philippines and gay Filipinos in New York is a leap between genres. Nevertheless, both instances provide particular articulations and engagements with gay identity and gay political culture.

I have attempted to clarify and analyze the practices of gay transnational politics. Gay "technologies," in the Foucauldian sense, resurrect the images of "uneven development" and first world and third world economic relationships. However, by juxtaposing the globalizing rhetoric with which various individuals, agencies, and institutions speak of Stonewall and gay/lesbian identity against the multiple "localized" articulations of Filipino gay men in different sites, we find that implications and connections do not follow a single axis from center to periphery. As Arjun Appadurai has suggested, disjunctive lines and boundaries form as borders break down.[25] Focusing on global gay culture, Ken Plummer warned against suggesting a convergence of homosexual lifestyles across the world, against "one true universal gayness." Plummer writes that each national and local culture brings its own richness, its own political strategies, its own uniqueness: "Along with globalization comes an intensification of the local. Indeed, with the process of globalization comes a tendency towards tribalism: a fundamentalism winning over difference, a politics that separates rather than unites."[26] Likewise, A. Ferguson advocates a view that promotes a sensitivity to the processes of self-determination of local and national movements within the global gay and lesbian movement.[27] However, Ferguson's dialectical approach suggests a kind of bifurcation of spaces and, as I have argued above, the articulations of *bakla* and gay involve diverse engagements from different locations. The local and national are inflected and implicated in manifold ways with each other and with the international/transnational on the level of the everyday and political mobilization.

In the shadows of Stonewall's history lie multiple engagements and negotiations. Conversations about globalizing tendencies of gay identity, politics, and culture are accompanied by disruptive local dialogues from people who speak from the margins. Such eruptions need to be heard. I conclude with a particular voice, of Ted Nierras, a young Filipino gay man educated in the United States, who articulates a strategy for Philippine gay politics:

> Thus, our perspectives are always partial, always interested. When we say to straight people or more rarely, to Western gay people, "We are like you," we must also remember to add "only different." When we say "we are different," that our difference at the margin creates their sameness, already bifurcated into a violently oppressive hierarchy of gender at the straight Western center and replicated and transformed into another oppressive hierarchy of gender here ... We need yet to listen more carefully and more seriously to narratives of global and interconnected sexual and racial dominance and subordination, to narratives of our poor and unjustly inequitable national social reality, to narratives of the women in our society, whether they attempt to destroy or to affirm our "humanity." We need yet to speak our different desires, we need to speak our name.[28]

Notes

An earlier version of this essay was presented at the sixth North American Conference on Lesbian, Gay and Bisexual Studies at the University of Iowa, November 17–20, 1994. The author would like to express appreciation to Lisa Lowe and David Lloyd for their comments. Special thanks to Victor Bascara and Chandan Reddy for their critical reading of earlier drafts.

1   The literature on diaspora and transnationalism indicates varied modes of dispersal and settlement as well as divergent ways of apprehending movement and travel of people and technologies; see the following contending views: Gillian Bottomley, *From Another Place: Migration and the Politics of Culture* (Melbourne: Cambridge University Press, 1992); Linda Basch, Nina Glick Schiller, and Cristina Szanton Blanc, *Nations Unbound: Transnational Projects, Postcolonial Predicaments and Deterritorialized Nation States* (New York: Gordon and Breach, 1994); James Clifford, "Traveling Cultures," in *Cultural Studies*, ed. L. Grossberg, C. Nelson, and P. Treichler (New York: Routledge, 1992), pp. 96–116, and "Diasporas," *Cultural Anthropology* 9.3. (1994): 302–38; Stuart

Hall, "Cultural Identity and Diaspora," in *Identity: Community, Culture, Difference*, ed. J. Rutherford (London: Lawrence & Wishart, 1990), pp. 222–37. In this essay I have developed these two concepts in terms of syncretic dynamics (Kobena Mercer, "Diaspora Culture and the Dialogic Imagination," in *Blackframes: Critical Perspectives on Black Independent Cinema*, ed. M. Cham and C. Watkins (Cambridge, MA: MIT Press, 1988), pp. 50–61) and creolizing dynamics (Ulf Hannerz, *Cultural Complexity: Studies in the Social Organization of Meaning* (New York: Columbia University Press, 1992)).

2   See Chandra Talpade Mohanty, "Under Western Eyes: Feminist Scholarship and Colonial Discourses," *Feminist Review* 30 (1988): 65–88.

3   Stonewall 25 Committee, *New York Pride Guide* (New York: Pride Publishing, 1994), p. 19.

4   For a travelogue-type of "gay" journalism, see Neil Miller's *Out in the World: Gay and Lesbian Life from Buenos Aires to Bangkok* (New York: Random House, 1992), where he maintains that "the spread of Western notions of sexuality and relationships appeared inevitable," at the same time "the creation of a universal gay and lesbian identity, culture, and movement [was] difficult at best" (p. 360).

5   Stephan Likosky, *Coming Out: An Anthology of International Gay and Lesbian Writing* (New York: Pantheon Books, 1992), p. xvi.

6   Likosky oversimplified Adam's argument. In the later chapters Adam problematized the issues of the gay and lesbian movement in the 1980s by looking at political organizing in different parts of the world. However, by limiting his conception of the global conditions of the gay and lesbian movement to the establishment of organizations and acquisition of rights, Adam did not consider the various cultural engagements with gay and lesbian subjection. In the end, he implicitly presented a teleological view of the gay and lesbian movement.

7   Likosky, *Coming Out*, p. xvii.

8   A. Hendriks, R. Tielman, and E. van der Veen, eds., *The Third Pink Book: A Global View of Lesbian/Gay Liberation and Oppression* (Buffalo, NY: Prometheus Books, 1993).

9   John Clark, Aart Hendriks, Lisa Power, Rob Tielman, and Evert van der Veen, introduction, in Hendriks, Tielman, and van der Veen *Third Pink Book*, p. 17; emphases mine.

10   See Martin Manalansan, "Speaking of AIDS: Language and the Filipino Gay Experience in America," in *Discrepant Histories: Translocal Essays on Filipino Cultures*, ed. Vicente Rafael (Philadelphia, PA: Temple University Press, 1995), pp. 193–220, for an extended discussion on the social construction of the *bakla*.

11   Michael L. Tan, "From *Bakla* to Gay: Shifting Gender Identities and Sexual Behaviours in the Philippines," in *Conceiving Sexuality: Approaches to Sex Research in a Postmodern World*, ed. John Gagnon and Richard Parker (New York: Routledge, 1995). Men who have sex with men, or MSM, is an epidemiological category of a particular "risk group" that attempts to encompass various configurations of sexual identities.

12   Fenella Cannell, "The Power of Appearances: Beauty, Mimicry and Transformation in Bicol," in *Discrepant Histories: Translocal Essays on Filipino Cultures*, ed. Vicente Rafael (Philadelphia, PA: Temple University Press, 1995).

13 Tony Perez, *Cubao 1980 at iba pang katha: Unang Sigaw ng Gay Liberation Movement sa Pilipinas* [Cubao 1980 and other works: The first cry of the Gay Liberation Movement in the Philippines] (Manila: Cacho Publishing House, 1992). Cubao is a commercial district in Quezon City which is part of metropolitan Manila and is known for (among other things) male hustlers who dot the area.

14 Ibid, p. xvii; translation mine.

15 Jomar Fleras, "Reclaiming Our Historic Rights: Gays and Lesbians in the Philippines," in *The Third Pink Book: A Global View or Lesbian/Gay Liberation and Oppression*, ed. A. Hendriks, R. Tielman, and E. van der Veen (Buffalo, NY: Prometheus Books, 1993), p. 74.

16 Ibid, p. 76.

17 Ibid, p. 78. Danton Remoto, *Seduction and Solitude: Essays* (Manila: Anvil Press, 1995), chronicled the first Philippine Gay Pride March on June 26, 1994 amid what he termed "gay bashing in the local media" (pp. 183–99).

18 J. Neil C. Garcia, "Unfurling Lives: An Introduction," in *Ladlad: An Anthology of Philippine Gay Writings*, ed. J. N. C. Garcia and D. Remoto (Manila: Anvil Press, 1993), p. xvi.

19 Ibid, p. xviii.

20 All names of informants and other identifying situations and facts have been changed to protect their identities.

21 In Filipino gay argot, or swardspeak, *drama* can mean personhood, occupation, health, sexual role, sadness, fate, or plans.

22 According to reports from Asian AIDS Project staff members, transvestite sex workers in the Tenderloin District, which has a significant number of Filipino *bakla*, were exhibiting interesting cultural alignments that ran across racial and ethnic lines. Apparently, Latino and African-American transvestite sex workers were utilizing Filipino swardspeak as coded speech to protect themselves in risky situations. For example, one report indicated that the sex workers would warn each other when the police were in the area by shouting "Kagang" (swardspeak for "police") to each other.

23 I discuss this issue of cross-dressing among Filipinos, other gay men of color, and white mainstream gay men in a manuscript on a religious pageant transformed and performed by Filipino gay men in Manhattan.

24 These informal groups are named after fashion labels or designers such as Mizrahi, Revlon, and Armani. They hold balls or competitions for cross-dressing individuals. In these balls, which are patterned after fashion shows, there are categories that promote the notion of "realness" or the attempt to look like the opposite sex.

25 Arjun Appadurai, "Global Ethnoscapes: Notes and Queries for a Transnational Anthropology," in *Recapturing Anthropology*, ed. R. Fox (Santa Fe, NM: School of American Research Press, 1991). See also Inderpal Grewal and Caren Kaplan, eds., *Scattered Hegemonies: Postmodernity and Transnational Feminist Practices* (Minneapolis: University of Minnesota Press, 1994).

26 Ken Plummer, "Speaking Its Name: Inventing a Gay and Lesbian Studies," in *Modern Homosexualities: Fragments of Lesbian and Gay Experience*, ed. K. Plummer (London: Routledge, 1992), p. 17.

27 A. Ferguson, "Is There a Lesbian Culture?" in *Lesbian Philosophies and Cultures*, ed. J. Allen (Albany: State University of New York Press, 1990).

28 Eduardo R. Nierras, "This Risky Business of Desire: Theoretical Notes For and Against Filipino Gay Male Identity Politics," in *Ladlad: An Anthology of Philippine Gay Writings*, ed. J. N. C. Garcia and D. Remoto (Manila: Anvil Press, 1994).

Additional Readings on Sexuality, Gender, and Diaspora

Acosta-Belen, Edna. "Beyond Island Boundaries: Ethnicity, Gender and Cultural Revitalization." *Callaloo* 15.4 (1992): 979–98.

Bhabha, Jacqueline. "Embodied Rights: Gender Persecution, State Sovereignty and Refugees." *Public Culture* 9.1 (1996): 3–32.

Blackwood, Evelyn and Saskia E. Wieringa, eds. *Female Desires: Same-Sex Relations and Transgender Practices Across Cultures.* New York: Columbia University Press, 1999.

Brinker-Gabler, Gisela and Sidonie Smith, eds. *Writing New Identities: Gender, Nation, and Immigration in Contemporary Europe.* Minneapolis: University of Minnesota Press, 1997.

Charles, Carolle. "Gender and Politics in Contemporary Haiti: The Duvalierist State, Transnationalism, and the Emergence of a New Feminism (1980–1990)." *Feminist Studies* 21.1 (1995): 135–64.

Chow, Rey. "Between Colonizers: Hong Kong's Postcolonial Self-Writing in the 1990s." *Diaspora* 2.2 (1992): 151–70.

—— *Writing Diaspora: Tactics of Intervention on Contemporary Cultural Studies.* Bloomington: Indiana University Press, 1993.

DeCosmo, Janet L. "Crossing Gendered Space: An Analysis of Trinidad's Carnival from a Feminist and African-Centered Perspective." *Wadabagei: A Journal of the Caribbean and Its Diaspora* 3.1 (2000): 1–48.

DeLoughrey, Elizabeth. "Gendering the Oceanic Voyage: Trespassing the (Black) Atlantic and Caribbean." *Thamyris* 5.2 (1998): 205–31.

Duggan, Lisa. "Queering the State." *Social Text* 39 (1994): 1–14.

Elmhirst, Rebecca. "A Javanese Diaspora? Gender and Identity Politics in Indonesia's Transmigration Resettlement Program." *Women's Studies International Forum* 23.4 (2000): 487–500.

Eng, David L. "Out Here and Over There: Queerness and Diaspora in Asian American Studies." *Social Text* 15.3–4 (1997): 31–52.

—— *Racial Castration: Managing Masculinity in Asian America.* Durham, NC: Duke University Press, 2001.

Eng, David L. and Alice Y. Hom, eds., *Q&A: Queer in Asian America.* Philadelphia, PA: Temple University Press, 1998.

Espin, Oliva. *Women Crossing Boundaries: A Psychology of Immigration and Transformations of Sexuality.* London: Routledge, 1999.

Geschwender, James. "Ethnicity and the Social Construction of Gender in the Chinese Diaspora." *Gender and Society* 6.3 (1992): 480–507.

Gold, Steven J. "Gender and Social Capital Among Israeli Immigrants in Los Angeles." *Diaspora* 4.3 (1995): 267–301.

Gopinath, Gayatri. "'Bombay, UK, Yuba City': Bhangra Music and the Engendering of Diaspora." *Diaspora* 4.3 (1995): 303–22.

—— "Funny Boys and Girls: Notes on a Queer South Asian Planet." *Asian American Sexualities: Dimensions of the Gay and Lesbian Experience.* Ed. Russell Leong. New York: Routledge, 1996. 119–27.

—— "Nostalgia, Desire, Diaspora: South Asian Sexualities in Motion." *positions* 5.2 (1997): 467–89.

—— "Homo-Economics: Queer Sexualities in a Transnational Frame." *Burning Down The House: Recycling Domesticity.* Ed. Rosemary Marangoly George. Boulder, CO: Westview Press, 1998. 102–24.

Gray, Breda. "Irish Women in London: National or Hybrid Diasporic Identities?" *NWSA Journal* 8.1 (1996): 85–109.

—— "Longings and Belongings: Gendered Spatialities of Irishness." *Irish Studies Review* 7.2 (1999): 193–210.

—— "Gendering the Irish Diaspora: Questions of Enrichment, Hybridization and Return." *Women's Studies International Forum* 23.2 (2000): 167–85.

Grossman, Andrew, ed. *Queer Asian Cinema: Shadows in the Shade.* New York: Harrington Park Press, 2000.

Holland, Sharon Patricia. "Bill T. Jones, Tupac Shakur and the (Queer) Art of Death." *Callaloo* 23.1 (2000): 384–93.

Huang, Shirlena, Peggy Teo, and Brenda S. Yeoh. "Diasporic Subjects and Identity Negotiations: Women in and from Asia." *Women's Studies International Forum* 23.4 (2000): 391–98.

Ifekuwingwe, Jayne O. "Diaspora's Daughters, Africa's Orphans?: On Lineage, Authenticity and 'Mixed Race' Identity." *Black British Feminism.* Ed. Heidi Safia Mirza. London: Routledge, 1997. 127–52.

—— *Scattered Belongings: Cultural Paradoxes of "Race", Nation and Gender.* London: Routledge, 1999.

Kauanui, Kehaulani J. "Off-Island Hawaiians 'Making' Ourselves at 'Home': A (Gendered) Contradiction in Terms?" *Women's Studies International Forum* 21.6 (1998): 681–93.

Kempadoo, Kamala and Jo Doezema, eds. *Global Sex Workers: Rights, Resistance and Redefinition.* London: Routledge, 1998.

Koshy, Susan. "The Geography of Female Subjectivity: Ethnicity, Gender, and Diaspora." *Diaspora* 3.1 (1994): 69–84.

Leong, Russell, ed. *Asian American Sexualities: Dimensions of the Gay and Lesbian Experience.* New York: Routledge, 1996.

Lu, Sheldon Hsiao-peng. *Transnational Chinese Cinemas: Identity, Nationhood, Gender.* Honolulu: University of Hawaii Press, 1997.

Moghissi, Haideh and Mark J. Goodman. "'Cultures of Violence' and Diaspora: Dislocation and Gendered Conflict in Iranian-Canadian Communities." *Humanity and Society* 23.4 (1999): 297–318.

Muñoz, José Esteban. "The Autoethnographic Performance: Reading Richard Fung's Queer Hybridity." *Screen* 36.2 (1995): 83–99.

Nassy Brown, Jacqueline. "Black Liverpool, Black America and the Gendering of Diasporic Space." *Cultural Anthropology* 13.3 (1998): 291–325.

Parker, Andrew, Mary Russo, Dorris Sommer, and Patricia Yaeger, eds. *Nationalisms and Sexualities*. New York: Routledge, 1992.

Patton, Cindy and Benigno Sanchez Eppler, eds. *Queer Diasporas*. Durham, NC: Duke University Press, 2000.

Paxson, Heather. "Demographics and Diaspora, Gender and Genealogy: Anthropological Notes on Greek Population Policy." *South European Society and Politics* 2.2 (1997): 34–56.

Puar, Jasbir K. "Writing My Way 'Home': Travelling South Asian Bodies and Diasporic Journeys." *Socialist Review* 24.4 (1994): 75–108.

—— "Resituating Discourse of 'Whiteness' and 'Asianness' in Northern England: Second Generation Sikh Women and Construction of Identity." *Socialist Review* 24.1–2 (1995): 21–53.

—— "Transnational Sexualities: South Asian (Trans)nation(alism)s and Queer Diasporas." *Q&A: Queer in Asian America*. Ed. David L. Eng and Alice V. Hom. Philadelphia, PA: Temple University Press, 1998. 405–22.

Robin, Diana and Ira Jaffe, eds. *Redirecting the Gaze: Gender, Theory, and Cinema in the Third World*. Albany: State University of New York Press, 1999.

Rosello, Mireille. "Interpreting Immigration Laws: 'Crimes of Homosexuality' or 'Crimes Against Hospitality'." *Diaspora* 8.3 (1999): 209–24.

Shukla, Sandhya R. "Feminisms of the Diaspora Both Local and Global: The Politics of South Asian Women Against Domestic Violence." *Women Transforming Politics: An Alternative Reader*. Ed. Cathy J. Cohen, Kathleen B. Jones, and Joan C. Tronto. New York: New York University Press, 1997.

Silvey, Rachel M. "Diasporic Subjects: Gender and Mobility in South Sulawesi." *Women's Studies International Forum* 23.4 (2000): 501–15.

Sinfield, Alan. "Diaspora and Hybridity: Queer Identities and the Ethnicity Model." *Textual Practice* 10.2 (1996): 271–93.

Sweet, James H. "Male Homosexuality and Spiritism in the African Diaspora: The Legacies of a Link." *Journal of the History of Sexuality* 7.2 (1996): 184–202.

Watney, Simon. "AIDS and the Politics of Queer Diaspora." *Negotiating Lesbian and Gay Subjects*. Ed. Monica Dorenkamp and Richard Henke. New York: Routledge, 1995.

Wekker, Gloria. "Mati-ism and Black Lesbianism: Two Ideal Typical Expressions of Female Homosexuality in Black Communities of the Diaspora." *Journal of Homosexuality* 24.3–4 (1993): 145–58.

Yeoh, Brenda and Katie Willis. "'Heart' and 'Wing', Nation and Diaspora: Gendered Discourses in Singapore's Regionalisation Process." *Gender, Place and Culture* 6.4 (1999): 355–72.

Part IV

Cultural Production and Diaspora

9

Cultural Identity and Diaspora

Stuart Hall

In this essay Stuart Hall begins with a discussion of Caribbean and "Third Cinema" using this discussion as a springboard for addressing questions about identity, cultural practices, and cultural production. Hall theorizes two ways of reflecting on "cultural identity": first, identity understood as a collective, shared history among individuals affiliated by race or ethnicity that is considered to be fixed or stable; and second, identity understood as unstable, metamorphic, and even contradictory – an identity marked by multiple points of similarities as well as differences.

From this second, more complex understanding of identity, Hall proceeds to theorize the multiple presences and absences that are constitutive of cultural identities in the Caribbean. Utilizing Jacques Derrida's theoretical play of *différance*, Hall posits Caribbean cultural identities – heterogeneous composites defined in relation to first world terrains and in relation to the different heritages of the Caribbean islands – as the play of three dominant presences: *Présence Africaine*, *Présence Européene*, and *Présence Américaine*. In Hall's configuration, *Présence Africaine* is the "site of the repressed"; *Présence Européene* is the site of colonialist, hegemonic construction of knowledges; and *Présence Américaine* is the "New World" site of cultural confrontation, possibility for creolization and points of new becomings.

A new cinema of the Caribbean is emerging, joining the company of the other "Third Cinemas." It is related to, but different from, the vibrant film and other forms of visual representation of the Afro-Caribbean (and Asian) "blacks" of the diasporas of the West – the new postcolonial subjects. All these cultural practices and forms of representation have the black subject at their center, putting the issue of cultural identity in question. Who is this emergent, new subject of the cinema? From where does he/she speak? Practices of representation always implicate the positions from which we speak or write – the positions of *enunciation*. What recent theories of enunciation suggest is that, though we speak, so to say "in our own name," of ourselves and from our own experience, nevertheless who speaks, and the subject who is spoken of, are never identical, never exactly in the same place. Identity is not as transparent or unproblematic as we think. Perhaps instead of thinking of identity as an already accomplished fact, which the new cultural practices then represent, we should think, instead, of identity as a "production" which is never complete, always in process, and always constituted within, not outside, representation. This view problematizes the very authority and authenticity to which the term "cultural identity" lays claim.

We seek, here, to open a dialogue, an investigation, on the subject of cultural identity and representation. Of course, the "I" who writes here must also be thought of as, itself, "enunciated." We all write and speak from a particular place and time, from a history and a culture which is specific. What we say is always "in context," *positioned*. I was born into and spent my childhood and adolescence in a lower-middle-class family in Jamaica. I have lived all my adult life in England, in the shadow of the black diaspora – "in the belly of the beast." I write against the background of a lifetime's work in cultural studies. If the chapter seems preoccupied with the diaspora experience and its narratives of displacement, it is worth remembering that all discourse is "placed," and the heart has its reasons.

There are at least two different ways of thinking about "cultural identity." The first position defines "cultural identity" in terms of one, shared culture, a sort of collective "one true self," hiding inside the many other, more superficial or artificially imposed "selves," which people with a shared history and ancestry hold in common. Within the terms of this definition, our cultural identities reflect the common historical experiences and shared cultural codes which provide us, as "one people," with stable, unchanging, and continuous frames of reference and meaning, beneath the shifting divisions and vicissitudes of our actual history. This "oneness," underlying all the other, more superficial differences, is the truth, the essence, of "Caribbeanness," of the black experience. It is this identity which a Caribbean or black diaspora must discover, excavate, bring to light, and express through cinematic representation.

Such a conception of cultural identity played a critical role in all postcolonial struggles which have so profoundly reshaped our world. It lay at the center of the vision of the poets of "Negritude," like Aimé Césaire and Leopold Senghor, and of the Pan-African political project, earlier in the century. It continues to be a very powerful and creative force in emergent forms of representation among hitherto marginalized peoples. In postcolonial societies the rediscovery of this identity is often the object of what Frantz Fanon once called a passionate research . . . directed by the secret hope of discovering beyond the misery of today, beyond self-contempt, resignation and abjuration, some very beautiful and splendid era whose existence rehabilitates us both in regard to ourselves and in regard to others.

New forms of cultural practice in these societies address themselves to this project for the very good reason that, as Fanon puts it, in the recent past,

Colonization is not satisfied merely with holding a people in its grip and emptying the native's brain of all form and content. By a kind of perverted logic, it turns to the past of oppressed people, and distorts, disfigures and destroys it.[1]

The question that Fanon's observation poses is, what is the nature of this "profound research" which drives the new forms of visual and cinematic representation? Is it only a matter of unearthing that which the colonial experience buried and overlaid, bringing to light the hidden continuities it suppressed? Or is a quite different practice entailed – not the rediscovery but the *production* of identity? Not an identity grounded in the archeology, but in the *retelling* of the past?

We should not, for a moment, underestimate or neglect the importance of the act of imaginative rediscovery that this conception of a rediscovered, essential identity entails. "Hidden histories" have played a critical role in the emergence of many of the most important social movements of our time – feminist, anti-colonial and anti-racist. The photographic work of a generation of Jamaican and Rastafarian artists, or of a visual artist like Armet Francis (a Jamaican-born photographer who has lived in Britain since the age of eight) is a testimony to the continuing creative power of this conception of identity within the emerging practices of representation. Francis's photographs of the peoples of the Black Triangle, taken in Africa, the Caribbean, the USA, and the UK, attempt to reconstruct in visual terms "the underlying unity of the black people whom colonization and slavery distributed across the African diaspora." His text is an act of imaginary reunification.

Crucially, such images offer a way of imposing an imaginary coherence on the experience of dispersal and fragmentation, which is the history of all enforced diasporas. They do this by representing or "figuring" Africa as the mother of these different civilizations. This Triangle is, after all, "centered" in Africa. Africa is the name of the missing term, the great aporia, which lies at the center of our cultural identity and gives it a meaning which, until recently, it lacked. No one who looks at these textural images now, in the light of the history of transportation, slavery, and migration, can fail to understand how the rift of separation, the "loss of identity," which has been integral to the Caribbean experience only begins to be healed when these forgotten connections are once more set in place. Such texts restore an imaginary fullness or plenitude to set against the broken rubric of our past. They are resources of resistance and identity, with which to confront the fragmented and pathological ways in which that experience has been reconstructed within the dominant regimes of cinematic and visual representation of the West.

There is, however, a second, related but different view of cultural identity. This second position recognizes that, as well as the many points of similarity, there are also critical points of deep and significant *difference* which constitute "what we really are"; or rather – since history has intervened – "what we have become." We cannot speak for very long, with any exactness, about "one experience, one identity," without acknowledging its other side – the ruptures and discontinuities which constitute, precisely, the Caribbean's "uniqueness." Cultural identity, in this second sense, is a matter of "becoming" as well as of "being." It belongs to the future as much as to the past. It is not something which already exists, transcending place, time, history, and culture. Cultural identities come from somewhere, have histories. But, like everything which is historical, they undergo constant transformation. Far from being eternally fixed in some essentialized past, they are subject to the continuous "play" of history, culture, and power. Far from being grounded in mere "recovery" of the past, which is waiting to be found, and which when found, will secure our sense of ourselves into eternity, identities are the names we give to the different ways we are positioned by, and position ourselves within, the narratives of the past.

It is only from this second position that we can properly understand the traumatic character of "the colonial experience." The ways in which black people, black experiences, were positioned and subject-ed in the dominant regimes of representation were the effects of a critical exercise of cultural power and normalization. Not only, in Said's "Orientalist" sense, were we constructed as different and other within the categories of knowledge of the West by those regimes. They had the power to make us see and experience *ourselves* as "Other." Every regime of representation is a regime of power formed, as Foucault reminds us, by the fatal couplet "power/knowledge." But this kind of knowledge is internal, not external. It is one thing to position a subject or set of peoples as the Other of a dominant discourse. It is quite another thing to subject them to that "knowledge," not only as a matter of imposed will and domination, by the power of inner compulsion and subjective conformation to the norm. That is the lesson – the somber majesty – of Fanon's insight into the colonizing experience in *Black Skin, White Masks*.

This inner expropriation of cultural identity cripples and deforms. If its silences are not resisted, they produce, in Fanon's vivid phrase, "individuals without an anchor, without horizon, colorless, stateless, rootless – a race of angels."[2] Nevertheless, this idea of otherness as an inner compulsion changes our conception of "cultural identity." In this perspective, cultural identity is not a fixed essence at all, lying unchanged outside history and culture. It is not some universal and transcendental spirit inside us on which history has made no fundamental mark. It is not once-and-for-all. It is not a fixed origin to which we can make some final and absolute return. Of course, it is not a mere phantasm either. It is *something* – not a mere trick of the imagination. It has its histories – and histories have their real, material, and symbolic effects. The past continues to speak to us. But it no longer addresses us as a simple, factual "past," since our relation to it, like the child's relation to the mother, is always-already "after the break." It is always constructed through memory, fantasy, narrative, and myth. Cultural identities are the points of identification, the unstable points of identification or suture, which are made, within the discourses of history and culture. Not an essence but a *positioning*. Hence, there is always a politics of identity, a politics of position, which has no absolute guarantee in an unproblematic, transcendental "law of origin."

This second view of cultural identity is much less familiar, and more unsettling. If identity does not proceed in a straight unbroken line from some fixed origin, how are we to understand its formation? We might think of black Caribbean identities as "framed" by two axes or vectors, simultaneously operative: the vector of similarity and continuity; and the vector of difference and rupture. Caribbean identities always have to be thought of in terms of the dialogic relationship between these two axes. The one gives us some grounding in, some continuity with, the past. The second reminds us that what we share is precisely the experience of a profound discontinuity: the peoples dragged into slavery, transportation, colonization, migration, came predominantly from Africa – and when that supply ended, it was temporarily refreshed by indentured labor from the Asian subcontinent. (This neglected fact explains why, when you visit Guyana or Trinidad, you see, symbolically inscribed in the faces of their peoples, the paradoxical "truth" of Christopher Columbus's mistake: you *can* find "Asia" by sailing west, if you know where to look!) In the history of the modern world, there are few more traumatic ruptures to match these enforced separations from Africa – already figured, in the European imaginary, as "the Dark Continent." But the slaves were also from different countries, tribal communities, villages, languages, and gods. African religion, which has been so profoundly formative in Caribbean spiritual life, is precisely *different* from Christian monotheism in believing that God is so powerful that he can only be known through a proliferation of spiritual manifestations, present everywhere in the natural and social world. These gods live on, in an underground existence, in the hybridized religious universe of Haitian voodoo, pocomania, Native pentecostalism, Black baptism, Rastafarianism, and the black *Saints of Latin American* Catholicism. The paradox is that it was the uprooting of slavery and transportation and the insertion into the plantation economy (as well as the symbolic economy) of the Western world that "unified" these peoples across their differences, in the same moment as it cut them off from direct access to their past.

Difference, therefore, persists – in and alongside continuity. To return to the Caribbean after any long absence is to experience again the shock of the "doubleness" of similarity and difference. Visiting the French Caribbean for the first time, I also saw at once how different Martinique is from, say, Jamaica: and this is no mere difference of topography or climate. It is a profound difference of culture and history. And the difference *matters*. It positions Martiniquains and Jamaicans as *both* the same *and* different. Moreover, the boundaries of difference are continually repositioned in relation to different points of reference. *Vis-à-vis* the developed West, we are very much "the same." We belong to the marginal, the underdeveloped, the periphery, the "Other." We are at the outer edge, the "rim," of the metropolitan world – always "South" to someone else's *El Norte*.

At the same time, we do not stand in the same relation of the "otherness" to the metropolitan centers. Each has negotiated its economic, political, and cultural dependency differently. And this "difference," whether we like it or not, is already inscribed in our cultural identities. In turn, it is this negotiation of identity which makes us, *vis-à-vis* other Latin American people, with a very similar history, different – Caribbeans, *les Antilliennes* ("islanders" to their mainland). And yet, *vis-à-vis* one another, Jamaican, Haitian, Cuban, Guadeloupean, Barbadian, etc. . . .

How, then, to describe this play of "difference" within identity? The common history – transportation, slavery, colonization – has been profoundly formative. For all these societies, unifying us across our differences. But it does not constitute a common *origin*, since it was, metaphorically as well as literally, a translation. The inscription of difference is also specific and critical. I use the word "play" because the double meaning of the metaphor is important. It suggests, on the one hand, the instability, the permanent unsettlement, the lack of any final resolution. On the other hand, it reminds us that the place where this "doubleness" is most powerfully to be heard is "playing" within the varieties of Caribbean musics. This cultural "play" could not therefore be represented, cinematically, as a simple, binary opposition – "past/present," "them/us." Its complexity exceeds this binary structure of representation. At different places, times, in relation to different questions, the boundaries are resited. They become, not only what they have, at times, certainly been – mutually excluding categories, but also what they sometimes are – differential points along a sliding scale.

One trivial example is the way Martinique both *is* and *is not* "French." It is, of course, a *department* of France, and this is reflected in its standard and style of life: Fort de France is a much richer, more "fashionable" place than Kingston – which is not only visibly poorer, but itself at a point of transition between being "in fashion" in an Anglo-African and Afro-American way – for those who can afford to be in any sort of fashion at all. Yet, what is distinctively "Martiniquais" can only be described in terms of that special and peculiar supplement which the black and mulatto skin adds to the "refinement" and sophistication of a Parisian-derived *haute couture*: that is, a sophistication which, because it is black, is always transgressive.

To capture this sense of difference which is not pure "otherness," we need to deploy the play on words of a theorist like Jacques Derrida. Derrida uses the anomalous "a" in his way of writing "difference" – *différance* – as a marker which sets up a disturbance in our settled understanding or translation of the word/concept. It sets the word in motion to new meanings without erasing the *trace* of its other meanings. His sense of *différance*, as Christopher Norris puts it, thus

> remains suspended between the two French verbs "to differ" and "to defer" (postpone), both of which contribute to its textual force but neither of which can fully capture its meaning. Language depends on difference, as Saussure showed . . . the structure of distinctive propositions which make up its basic economy. Where Derrida breaks new ground . . . is in the extent to which "differ" shades into "defer" . . . the idea that meaning is always deferred, perhaps to this point of an endless supplementarity, by the play of signification.[3]

This second sense of difference challenges the fixed binaries that stabilize meaning and representation and show how meaning is never finished or completed, but keeps on moving to encompass other, additional, or supplementary meanings, which, as Norris puts it elsewhere,[4] "disturb the classical economy of language and representation." Without relations of difference, no representation could occur. But what is then constituted within representation is always open to being deferred, staggered, serialized.

Where, then, does identity come into this infinite postponement of meaning? Derrida does not help us as much as he might here, though the notion of the "trace" goes some way toward it. This is where it sometimes seems as if Derrida has permitted his profound theoretical insights to be reappropriated by his disciples into a celebration of formal "playfulness," which evacuates them of their political meaning. For if signification depends upon the endless repositioning of its differential terms, meaning, in any specific instance, depends on the contingent and arbitrary stop – the necessary and temporary "break" in the infinite semiosis of language. This does not detract from the original insight. It only threatens to do so if we mistake this "cut" of identity – this *positioning*, which makes meaning possible – as a natural and permanent, rather than an arbitrary and contingent "ending" – whereas I understand every such position as "strategic" and arbitrary, in the sense that there is no permanent equivalence between the particular sentence we close, and its true meaning, as such. Meaning continues to unfold, so to speak, beyond the arbitrary closure that makes it, at any moment, possible. It is always either over- or underdetermined, either an excess or a supplement. There is always something "left over."

It is possible, with this conception of "difference," to rethink the positioning and repositioning of Caribbean cultural identities in relation to at least three "presences," to borrow Aimé Césaire's and Leopold Senghor's metaphor: *Présence Africaine, Présence Européenne*, and the third, most ambiguous, presence of all – the sliding term, *Présence Américaine*. Of course, I am collapsing, for the moment, the many other cultural "presences" that constitute the complexity of Caribbean identity (Indian, Chinese, Lebanese, etc.). I mean America, here not in its "first-world" sense – the big cousin to the North whose "rim" we occupy – but in the second, broader sense: America, the "New World," *Terra Incognita*.

Présence Africaine is the site of the repressed. Apparently silenced beyond memory by the power of the experience of slavery, Africa was, in fact, present everywhere: in the everyday life and customs of the slave quarters, in the languages and patois of the plantations, in names and words, often disconnected from their taxonomies, in the secret syntactical structures through which other languages were spoken, in the stories and tales told to children, in religious practices and beliefs in the spiritual life, the arts, crafts, musics, and rhythms of slave and post-emancipation society. Africa, the signified which could not be represented directly in slavery, remained and remains the unspoken unspeakable "presence" in Caribbean culture. It is "hiding" behind every verbal inflection, every narrative twist of Caribbean cultural life. It is the secret code with which every Western text was "reread." It is the groundbass of every rhythm and bodily movement. *This* was – is – the "Africa" that "is alive and well in the diaspora."[5]

When I was growing up in the 1940s and 1950s as a child in Kingston, I was surrounded by the signs, music, and rhythms of this Africa of the diaspora, which only existed as a result of a long and discontinuous series of transformations. But, although almost everyone around me was some shade of brown or black (Africa "speaks"!), I never once heard a single person refer to themselves or to others as, in some way, or as having been at some time in the past, "African." It was only in the 1970s that this Afro-Caribbean identity became historically available to the great majority of Jamaican people, at home and abroad. In this historic moment, Jamaicans discovered themselves to be "black" – just as, in the same moment, they discovered themselves to be the sons and daughters of "slavery."

This profound cultural discovery, however, was not, and could not be, made directly, without "mediation." It could only be made *through* the impact on popular life of the postcolonial revolution, the civil rights struggles, the culture of Rastafarianism, and the music of reggae – the metaphors, the figures or signifiers of a new construction of "Jamaican-ness." These signified a "new" Africa of the New World, grounded in an "old" Africa: a spiritual journey of discovery that led, in the Caribbean, to an indigenous cultural revolution; this is Africa, as we might say, necessarily "deferred" – as a spiritual, cultural, and political metaphor.

It is the presence/absence of Africa, in this form, which has made it the privileged signifier of new conceptions of Caribbean identity. Everyone in the Caribbean, of whatever ethnic background, must sooner or later come to terms with this African presence. Black, brown, mulatto, white – all must look *Présence Africaine* in the face, speak its name. But whether it is, in this sense, an *origin* of our identities, unchanged by four hundred years of displacement, dismemberment, transportation, to which we could in any final or literal sense return, is more open to doubt. The original "Africa" is no longer there. It too has been transformed. History is, in that sense, irreversible. We must not collude with the West which, precisely, normalizes and appropriates Africa by freezing it into some timeless zone of the primitive, unchanging past. Africa must at last be reckoned with by Caribbean people, but it cannot in any simple sense be merely recovered.

It belongs irrevocably, for us, to what Edward Said once called an "imaginative geography and history," which helps "the mind to intensify its own sense of itself by dramatizing the difference between what is close to it and what is far away."[6] It "has acquired an imaginative or figurative value we can name and feel."[7] Our belongingness to it constitutes what Benedict Anderson calls "an imagined community."[8] To *this* "Africa," which is a necessary part of the Caribbean imaginary, we can't literally go home again.

The character of this displaced "homeward" journey – its length and complexity – comes across vividly, in a variety of texts. Tony Sewell's documentary archival photographs, "Garvey's Children: the Legacy of Marcus Garvey," tell the story of a "return" to an African identity which went, necessarily, by the long route through London and the United States. It "ends," not in Ethiopia, but with Garvey's statue in front of the St. Ann Parish Library in Jamaica: not with a traditional tribal chant but with the music of Burning Spear and Bob Marley's "Redemption Song." This is our "long journey" home. Derek Bishton's courageous visual and written text, *Black Heart Man* – the story of the journey of a *white* photographer "on the trail of the promised land" – starts in England, and goes, through Shashemene, the place in Ethiopia to which many Jamaican people have found their way on their search for the Promised Land, and slavery; but it ends in Pinnacle, Jamaica, where the first Rastafarian settlements were established, and "beyond" – among the dispossessed of twentieth-century Kingston and the streets of Handsworth, where Bishton's voyage of discovery first began. These symbolic journeys are necessary for us all – and necessarily circular. This is the Africa we must return to – but "by another route": what Africa has *become* in the New World, what we have made of "Africa": "Africa" – as we retell it through politics, memory, and desire.

What of the second, troubling, term in the identity equation – the European presence? For many of us, this is a matter not of too little but of too much. Where Africa was a case of the unspoken, Europe was a case of that which is endlessly speaking – and endlessly speaking *us*. The European presence interrupts the innocence of the whole discourse of "difference" in the Caribbean by introducing the question of power. "Europe" belongs irrevocably to the "play" of power, to the lines of force and consent, to the role of the *dominant* in Caribbean culture. In terms of colonialism, under-development, poverty, and the racism of color, the European presence is that which, in visual representation, has positioned the black subject within its dominant regimes of representation: the colonial discourse, the literatures of adventure and exploration, the romance of the exotic, the ethnographic and traveling eye, the tropical languages of tourism, travel brochure and Hollywood, and the violent, pornographic languages of *ganja* and urban violence.

Because *Présence Européenne* is about exclusion, imposition, and expro-priation, we are often tempted to locate that power as wholly external to us – an extrinsic force, whose influence can be thrown off like the serpent sheds its skin. What Frantz Fanon reminds us, in *Black Skin, White Masks*, is how this power has become a constitutive element in our own identities.

> The movements, the attitudes, the glances of the Other fixed me there in the sense in which a chemical solution is fixed by a dye. I was indignant; I demanded an explanation. Nothing happened. I burst apart. Now the frag-ments have been put together again by another self.[9]

This "look," from – so to speak – the place of the Other, fixes us, not only in its violence, hostility, and aggression, but in the ambivalence of its desire. This brings us face to face with the dominating European presence not simply as the site or "scene" of integration where those other presences that it had actively disaggregated were recomposed – reframed, put together in a new way; but as the site of a profound splitting and doubling – what Homi Bhabha has called "this ambivalent identification of the racist world . . . the 'Otherness' of the Self inscribed in the perverse palimpsest of colonial identity."[10]

The dialogue of power and resistance, of refusal and recognition, with and against *Présence Européenne* is almost as complex as the "dialogue" with Africa. In terms of popular cultural life, it is nowhere to be found in its pure, pristine state. It is always-already fused, syncretized, with other cultural elements. It is always-already creolized – not lost beyond the Middle Passage, but ever-present: from the harmonics in our musics to the ground-bass of Africa, traversing and intersecting our lives at every point. How can we stage this dialogue so that, finally, we can place it, without terror or violence, rather than being forever placed by it? Can we ever recognize its irreversible influence, while resisting its imperializing eye? The enigma is impossible, so far, to resolve. It requires the most complex of cultural strategies. Think, for example, of the dialogue of every Caribbean filmmaker or writer, one way or another, with the dominant cinemas and literature of the West – the complex relationship of young black British filmmakers with the "avant-gardes" of European and American filmmaking. Who could describe this tense and tortured dialogue as a "one way trip"?

The Third, "New World" presence, is not so much power, as ground, place, territory. It is the juncture-point where the many cultural tributaries meet, the "empty" land (the European colonizers emptied it) where strangers from every other part of the globe collided. None of the people who now occupy the islands – black, brown, white, African, European, American, Spanish, French, East Indian, Chinese, Portuguese, Jew, Dutch – originally "belonged" there. It is the space where the creolizations and assimilations and syncretisms were negotiated. The New World is the third term – the primal scene – where the fateful/fatal encounter was staged between Africa and the West. It also has to be understood as the place of many, continuous displacements: of the original pre-Columbian inhabitants, the Arawaks, Caribs, and Amerindians, permanently displaced from their homelands and decimated; of other peoples displaced in different ways from Africa, Asia, and Europe; the displacements of slavery, colonization, and conquest. It stands for the endless ways in which Caribbean people have been destined to "migrate"; it is the signifier of migration itself – of traveling, voyaging, and return as fate, as destiny; of the Antillean as the prototype of the modern or postmodern New World nomad, continually moving between center and periphery. This preoccupation with movement and migration Caribbean cinema shares with many other "Third Cinemas," but it is one of our defining themes, and it is destined to cross the narrative of every film script or cinematic image.

Présence Américaine continues to have its silences, its suppressions. Peter Hulme, in his essay on "Islands of enchantment,"[11] reminds us that the word "Jamaica" is the Hispanic form of the indigenous Arawak name – "land of wood and water" – which Columbus's renaming ("Santiago") never replaced. The Arawak presence remains today a ghostly one, visible in the islands mainly in museums and archeological sites, part of the barely knowable or usable "past." Hulme notes that it is not represented in the emblem of the Jamaican National Heritage Trust, for example, which chose instead the figure of Diego Pimienta, "an African who fought for his Spanish masters against the English invasion of the island in 1655" – a deferred, metonymic, sly, and sliding representation of Jamaican identity if ever there was one! He recounts the story of how Prime Minister Edward Seaga tried to alter the Jamaican coat-of-arms, which consists of two Arawak figures holding a shield with five pineapples, surmounted by an alligator. "Can the crushed and extinct Arawaks represent the dauntless character of Jamaicans? Does the low-slung, near extinct crocodile, a cold-blooded reptile, symbolize the warm, soaring spirit of Jamaicans?" Prime Minister Seaga asked rhetorically.[12] There can be few political statements which so eloquently testify to the complexities entailed in the process of trying to represent a diverse people with a diverse history through a single, hegemonic "identity." Fortunately, Mr. Seaga's invitation to the Jamaican people, who are overwhelmingly of African descent, to start their "remembering" by first "forgetting" something else, got the comeuppance it so richly deserved.

The "New World" presence – America, *Terra Incognita* – is therefore itself the beginning of diaspora, of diversity, of hybridity and difference, what makes Afro-Caribbean people already people of a diaspora. I use this term here metaphorically, not literally: diaspora does not refer us to those scattered tribes whose identity can only be secured in relation to some sacred homeland to which they must at all costs return, even if it means pushing other people into the sea. This is the old, the imperializing, the hegemonizing, form of "ethnicity." We have seen the fate of the people of Palestine at the hands of this backward-looking conception of diaspora – and the complicity of the West with it. The diaspora experience as I intend it here is defined, not by essence or purity, but by the recognition of a necessary heterogeneity and diversity; by a conception of "identity" which lives with and through, not despite, difference; by *hybridity*. Diaspora identities are those which are constantly producing and reproducing themselves anew, through transformation and difference. One can only think here of what is uniquely – "essentially" – Caribbean: precisely the mixes of color, pigmentation, physiognomic type; the "blends" of tastes that is Caribbean cuisine; the aesthetics of the "cross-overs," of "cut-and-mix," to borrow Dick Hebdige's telling phrase, which is the heart and soul of black music. Young black cultural practitioners and critics in Britain are increasingly coming to acknowledge and explore in their work this "diaspora aesthetic" and its formations in the post-colonial experience:

> Across a whole range of cultural forms there is a "syncretic" dynamic which critically appropriates elements from the master-codes of the dominant culture and "creolizes" them, disarticulating given signs and rearticulating their symbolic meaning. The subversive force of this hybridizing tendency is most apparent at the level of language itself where creoles, patois and black English decenter, destabilize and carnivalize the linguistic domination of "English" – the nation-language of master-discourse – through strategic inflections, reaccentuations and other performative moves in semantic, syntactic and lexical codes.[13]

It is because this New World is constituted for us as place, a narrative of displacement, that it gives rise so profoundly to a certain imaginary plenitude, recreating the endless desire to return to "lost origins," to be one again with the mother, to go back to the beginning. Who can ever forget, when once seen rising up out of that blue-green Caribbean, those islands of enchantment? Who has not known, at this moment, the surge of an overwhelming nostalgia for lost origins, for "times past"? And yet, this "return to the beginning" is like the imaginary in Lacan – it can neither be fulfilled nor requited, and hence is the beginning of the symbolic, of representation, the infinitely renewable source of desire, memory, myth, search, discovery – in short, the reservoir of our cinematic narratives.

We have been trying, in a series of metaphors, to put in play a different sense of our relationship to the past, and thus a different way of thinking about cultural identity, which might constitute new points of recognition in the discourses of the emerging Caribbean cinema and black British cinemas. We have been trying to theorize identity as constituted not outside but within representation; and hence of cinema, not as a second-order mirror held up to reflect what already exists, but as that form of representation which is able to constitute us as new kinds of subjects, and thereby enable us to discover places from which to speak. Communities, Benedict Anderson argues in *Imagined Communities*, are to be distinguished, not by their falsity/genuineness, but by the style in which they are imagined.[14] This is the vocation of modern black cinemas: by allowing us to see and recognize the different parts and histories of ourselves, to construct those points of identification, those positionalities we call in retrospect our "cultural identities."

> We must not therefore be content with delving into the past of a people in order to find coherent elements which will counteract colonialism's attempts to falsify and harm . . . A national culture is not a folk-lore, nor an abstract

populism that believes it can discover a people's true nature. A national culture is the whole body of efforts made by a people in the sphere of thought to describe, justify and praise the action through which that people has created itself and keeps itself in existence.[15]

Notes

1   Frantz Fanon, "On National Culture," in *The Wretched of the Earth* (London, 1963), p. 170.
2   Ibid, p. 176.
3   Christopher Norris, *Deconstruction: Theory and Practice* (London, 1982), p. 32.
4   Christopher Norris, *Jacques Derrida* (London, 1987), p. 15.
5   Stuart Hall, *Resistance Through Rituals* (London), 1976.
6   Edward Said, *Orientalism* (London, 1985), p. 55.
7   Ibid.
8   Benedict Anderson, *Imagined Communities: Reflections on the Origin and Rise of Nationalism* (London, 1982).
9   Frantz Fanon, *Black Skin, White Masks* (London, 1986), p. 109.
10   Homi Bhabha, "Foreword" to Fanon, *Black Skin, White Masks*, pp. xiv–xv.
11   Peter Hulme, "Islands of Enchantment," *New Formations* 3, winter 1987.
12   *Jamaica Hansard* 9, 1983–4, p. 363. Quoted in Hulme, "Islands of Enchantment."
13   Kobena Mercer, "Diaspora Culture and the Dialogic Imagination," in M. Cham and C. Watkins (eds.), *Blackframes: Critical Perspectives on Black Independent Cinema* (Cambridge, MA, 1988), p. 57.
14   Anderson, *Imagined Communities*, p. 15.
15   Fanon, *Black Skin, White Masks*, p. 188.

10

Diaspora Culture and the Dialogic Imagination: The Aesthetics of Black Independent Film in Britain

Kobena Mercer

In this essay Kobena Mercer examines the emergence of avant-garde black cinema in the 1980s. Mercer contrasts these experimental films (concerned with representation itself) with earlier black British films that emphasized political content and relied on a "realist aesthetics" to create counter-realities adequate to contest Britain's racist ideologies. Mercer argues that contemporary black British films do not reify a black essence that may be realistically represented in film, but rather, they expose how identity itself is heterogeneous, contradictory, and hybrid.

He does so by analyzing these films within the historical frames of diaspora cultures, everyday black practices, and within the theoretical frame of Bahktin's notion of *dialogism* (a subversion of dominant linguistic and cultural codes through local appropriation and creolization of those codes). Mercer argues, finally, that black cultural criticism should also open itself to dialogic models that encourage contradiction and polysemy, rather than rely upon monologic models that privilege authority over plurality, and thus, homogenize black experiences. Critical dialogism, Mercer explains, offers more diverse sites from which to contest neo-conservative political forces.

> *Our imaginations processed reality and dream, like maniacal editors turned loose in some frantic film cutting room . . . we were dream serious in our efforts.*
>
> *Ralph Ellison*[1]

The question of aesthetics arises today as a crucial issue for black filmmak-ing practices in Britain for two important reasons. First, significant changes in the material conditions of black politics since the early 1980s have enabled a prolific upsurge in black filmmaking activity in recent years. The emergence of a new generation of cinematic activists – Ceddo, Sankofa, Retake, Black Audio Film Collective – symbolizes a new threshold of cultural struggle in the domain of image-making. Their work deepens and extends the narrative and documentary frameworks established by Horace Ove, Lionel Ngakane, and Menelik Shabazz in the 1960s and 1970s. The emergence of a new experimental approach has also widened the parameters of black independ-ent film practice, bringing a new quality of diversity to black cinema.

Until now, black film in Britain has emphasized the radical content of its political message over the politics of representation inherent in the medium. Certain aesthetic qualities generated by self-consciously cinematic strategies at work in new forms of black filmmaking today, however, indicate signifi-cant shifts and critical differences in attitudes to the means of representation. In this context it becomes necessary to think through the political implica-tions of choices and decisions made at the level of film form. If such shifts and changes may be momentarily grasped as an accentuation of the expres-sive over the referential, or as an emphasis on the complexity rather than homogeneity of black experiences in Britain, then what is at stake is not a categorical break with the past but the embryonic articulation of something new which does not fit a pregiven category.

Second, insofar as aesthetics concerns conceptual criteria for evaluating artistic and cultural practices, it now becomes necessary to reflect more rig-orously on the role of critics and criticism. This need arises with urgency not simply because the increase in quantity at the point of production neces-sitates clarification of qualitative distinctions at the point of reception, but more importantly because of the bewildering range of conflicting responses provoked by new work such as *Handsworth Songs* (Black Audio Film Col-lective, 1986) and *Passion of Remembrance* (Sankofa, 1986).

I would like to be able to use a word like *modernist* to describe "the shock of the new" here, as responses among audiences, critics, and institutions have ranged from hostile impatience to the awarding of prestigious prizes. It is precisely this dissensus that indicates something important is going on! It would be useful to note the terms of dissensus in order to grasp what is at issue. White audiences and critics have commented on the influence of Euro-American avant-garde cinema and film theory, which is not in itself a criti-cism, but which nevertheless suggests an underlying anxiety to pin down and categorize a practice that upsets and disrupts fixed expectations and norma-tive assumptions about what black films should look like.[2] Black audiences and critics have been similarly bemused by the originality of a practice that explicitly draws on a dual inheritance from both Third World and First World film cultures, but it is important to note that the most vociferous critiques here concern a dispute over the political content of the films.

In particular, I want to highlight the brief debate initiated by Salman Rushdie's singularly unconstructive criticism of *Handsworth Songs*, as it implicitly reveals a crisis of criticism in black cultural politics.[3] Rushdie's disdainful and dismissive response – "There's more to life in Handsworth than race riots [*sic*] and police brutality" – betrays a closed mind which assumes, as Stuart Hall pointed out in reply, that "*his* [Rushdie's] songs are not only different but better." What makes Rushdie's position all the more worrying is not merely that the conservative literary-humanist criteria he adopts are so at odds with the open-ended textual strategies performed in his own work, but that he uses his literary authority to delegitimate the film's discourse and disqualify its right to speak.

As with the unfavorable review in *Race Today*,[4] Rushdie enacts an authoritarian practice of "interpretation" which assumes *a priori* that one version of reality, his political analysis of Handsworth, has more validity, legitimacy, and authority than another, the version put forward in the film. What is at stake here is the fact that there is no shared framework for a viable practice of black cultural criticism, something both acknowledged and disavowed by Darcus Howe's defense of Rushdie's polemic, which claimed that it "[lays] the foundations of a critical tradition." To argue that a few columns of newsprint "lay the foundations" for black film criticism is to recognize that such a tradition does not yet exist, which itself could be read as a partial indictment of the kind of legitimating authority Howe arrogates to himself as "an activist in the black movement for over twenty years, organizing political, cultural, and artistic thrusts . . . from our black communities."

At one level, the lack of an ongoing discourse of radical black film criticism is one unhappy legacy of the marginalization and underdevelopment of black filmmaking in Britain. This must be understood as a consequence of material conditions. Previously we had to wait so long to see a black-made film that we did not really criticize; there was not enough space to theorize aesthetics; we were simply "thankful" the film got made in the first place. Moreover, we encounter a double absence here, as the professionalization of critical film theory in journals like *Screen* in the 1970s effectively screened out black and Third World film practices, confining itself to a narrowly Eurocentric canon. At this critical conjuncture we cannot afford to merely "celebrate" the achievements of black filmmakers or act as cheerleaders for the so-called ethnic arts. As Stuart Hall remarks on black British cultural production generally, "we have come out of the age of innocence [which] says, as it were, 'It's good if it's there'," and are now entering the next phase, in which "we actually begin to recognize the extraordinary complexity of ethnic and cultural differences."[5]

In the thick of this difficult transition, my concern is to explore whether a more adequate model of criticism might not be derived from the critical practice performed in the films themselves. To the extent that what is at issue is not a struggle between one person and another but between different ways of thinking and talking about black filmmaking, a more useful and viable criterion for criticism comes from the concept of "interruption," which "seeks not to impose a language of its own [as does the practice of "interpretation"], but to enter critically into existing configurations [of discourse] to reopen the closed structures into which they have ossified."[6]

> To articulate the past historically does not mean to recognize it "the way it really was." It means to seize hold of a memory as it flashes up at a moment of danger . . . Only that historian will have the gift of fanning the spark of hope in the past who is firmly convinced that *even the dead* will not be safe from the enemy if he wins. (Walter Benjamin)[7]

A cursory survey of the work of black filmmakers in Britain will reveal the preponderance of a realist aesthetic across both documentary and narrative genres. This insistent emphasis on the real must be understood as the prevailing mode in which black independent film has performed a critical function in providing a counter-discourse against those versions of reality produced by dominant voices and discourses in British film and media. Thus the substantive concern with the politicizing experience of black youth in films such as *Pressure* (director Horace Ove, 1975) and *Step Forward Youth* (director Menelik Shabazz, 1977) demonstrates a counter-reply to the criminalizing stereotypes generated and amplified by media-led moral panics on race and crime in the 1970s.[8] Similarly, *Blacks Britannica* (director David Kopff, 1979, US) – although not a black British film, it is read, used, and circulated as such – gives voice to those silenced and excluded by the discourse of media racism. This oral testimony combines with the political analysis advanced by activists and intellectuals featured in the film to present an alternative definition of the situation. As *Struggles for the Black Community* (director Colin Prescod, 1983) shows, the historicizing emphasis in such critical counter-discourse is an overdetermined necessity in order to counteract the dehistoricizing logic of racist ideologies.

There is significant continuity at the level of thematic concern with the politics of racism in new documentaries such as *Handsworth Songs* (director John Akomfrah, 1986) and *Territories* (director Isaac Julien, 1984). Yet important differences in the articulation of a counter-discourse reveal distinct approaches to the politics of representation. Certain aesthetic strategies in these recent films question the limitations of documentary realism.

The reality effect produced by realist methods depends on the operation of four characteristic values – transparency, immediacy, authority, and authenticity – which are in fact aesthetic values central to the dominant film and media culture itself. By adopting a neutral or instrumental relation to the means of representation, this mode of black film practice seeks to redefine referential realities of race through the same codes and forms as the prevailing film language whose discourse of racism it aims to contest. Clearly we need to clarify the contradictions involved in this paradox.

By presenting themselves as transparent "windows on the world" of racism and resistance, black films in the documentary realist mode emphasize the urgency, immediacy, and "nowness" of their message. In the case of campaigning interventions, such as *The People's Account* (director Milton Bryan, 1986), this is a contextual necessity, as such films perform a critical function by providing an alternative version of events so as to inform, agitate, and mobilize political action. However, such communicative efficacy in providing counter-information exhausts itself once the political terrain changes. Further, although it is always necessary to document and validate the authority of experience ("who feels it, knows it"), the selection of *who* is given the right to speak may also exclude Others: the voices and viewpoints of black women, for example, are notable by their absence from films such as *Blacks Britannica*. Finally, the issue of authenticity, the aspiration to be "true to life" in drama especially, is deeply problematic, as a given *type* of black person or experience is made to speak for black people as a whole. Not only does this reduce the diversity of black experiences and opinions to a single perspective assumed to be typical, it may also reinforce the tokenistic idea that a single film can be regarded as *representative* of every black person's perception of reality.

In short, black film practices which incorporate these filmic values are committed to a mimetic conception of representation which assumes that reality has an objective existence "out there" and that the process of representation simply aims to correspond to or reflect it. Certain limitations inherent in this view become apparent once we contrast it to the semiotic conception of signification at work in new modes of black film discourse. My aim is not to polarize different approaches in black filmmaking, but to argue that this latter mode offers new perspectives on the *realpolitik* of race by entering into a struggle with the means of representation itself. Foregrounding an awareness of the decisions and choices made in the selection and combination of signifying elements in sound and image, the new films are conscious of the fact that the reality effect of documentary realism is itself *constructed* by the formal tendency to regulate, fix, contain, and impose closure on the chain of signification. By intervening at the level of cinematic codes of narration and communication, the new films interrupt the ideological purpose of naturalistic illusion and perform a critical function by liberating the imaginative and expressive dimension of the filmic signifier as a material reality in its own right.

Territories is not "about" Notting Hill Carnival[9] so much as it documents the problems of trying to "represent" the complex multifaceted aesthetic and political meanings of this particular phenomenon of diaspora culture. Its fragmentary collage of archival and original material interrupts the transparency necessary for an "objective" account to achieve a quality of *critical reverie*. By this I mean that the openness of the film text hollows out a cognitive and affective space for critical reflection on the polyvocal dimension of Carnival – an event/process in which social boundaries and hierarchical power relations are momentarily dissolved and upended. So, rather than passively reflect this (which risks neutralizing the subversive potential of Carnival), the text enacts or embodies the critical spirit of Carnival with "the sense of the gay relativity of prevailing truth and authority" (Bakhtin) that itself *carnivalizes* codes and conventions such as space-time continuity in editing. In this way the film destabilizes fixed boundaries, which is precisely what happened in Carnival 1976 (when black youth massively reveled in the pleasures of political resistance to the policing of black culture) when the state attempted to literally impose closure and containment.

Carnival breaks down barriers between active performer and passive audience. *Territories* does something similar by emphasizing its performative and reflexive mode of address in order to enlist the participation of the spectator. Discontinuous gaps between sound and image tracks create a rhythmic homology between the jump-cut montage principle and the deconstructive aesthetic of dub-versioning – which distances and lays bare the musical anatomy of the original song through skillful reediting which sculpts out aural space for the DJ's talk-over.[10]

The phatic mode of enunciation in *Territories*, highlighted by images showing two women examining footage on an editing machine, also questions the univocal captioning role of the voice-over within the documentary realist tradition. The choral refrain – "we are struggling to tell a story/a history, a herstory" – underlines the fact that its story does not arrive at a point of closure, and this deferral of any authoritative resolution to the issues it raises implies that the spectator shares active responsibility for making semantic connections between the multi-accentuated elements of the image flow. This is important because by pluralizing the denotative value of given signs, such as the Union Jack flag, the surplus of connotations engendered by multiple layering of imagery does not lead to the "infinite regression" of formalism. Of the many readings the film allows, it can be said that *Territories* is a film about black identity, or "self-image," because the ambivalence of its images – such as the two men entwined in an intimate embrace while the flag burns behind them – is directional; its multi-accentuality is strategically anchored to a sense of location in order to raise questions about the dialectics of race, class, and especially, gender and sexuality, as vectors of power that cut across the public/private division in which social identities are constructed in the first place.

Handsworth Songs engages similar carnivalizing techniques at the level of montage and dissonant reverberation between sound and image. The juxtaposition of actuality footage of civil disorder, on the one hand, and images drawn from official archive sources and "family album" photographs, on the other, interrupts the amnesia of media representations of the 1985 conflicts between the police and the black communities in Handsworth and Tottenham. Instead of "nowness," the film reaches for historical depth, creating a space of critical reverie which counteracts the active ideological forgetting of England's colonial past in media discourses on Handsworth, in order to articulate an alternative, archeological account of the contemporary crisis of race and nation.

A female narrator tells of a journalist pestering a black woman on Lozell's Road for a news story: in the poetry of resistance she replies, "There are no stories in the riots, only the ghosts of other stories." This reflexive comment on the intertextual logic of the film marks out its struggle to reclaim and excavate a creole counter-memory of black struggle in Britain, itself always repressed, erased, and made invisible in the "popular memory" of dominant film and media discourse. Against divisive binary oppositions between Asian and Afro-Caribbean, and between first and third generations, the film's interweaving of the past-in-the-present through oral testimony and poetic re-encoding of archive imagery seeks to recover a "sense of intimacy"; the film itself struggles to "seize hold of a memory as it Hashes up at a moment of danger." It talks back to the disparaging view of our foreparents as naive or innocent by invoking the dreams and desires that motivated migrations from the Caribbean and the Indian subcontinent. In this way, it "rescues the dead" from the amnesia and structured forgetfulness which haunt the English collective consciousness whenever it thinks of its crisis-ridden "race relations" in the here and now.

History is not depicted in a linear novelistic narrative – which would imply that our stories of struggle are "over." Rather, the presence of the past in the absences of popular memory is invoked through multiple chains of association. Retinted images of chains in an iron foundry, overlaid by the eerie intonation of an English workingmen's song, powerfully evoke not only the connection with the chains of slavery that made the industrial revolution possible, but the legacy of the imperial past in England's contemporary decline. Again, the spectator is enlisted as an active discursive partner, sharing subjective responsibility for making cognitive connections between the latent nuclei of meanings inscribed beneath the manifest racial forms of social antagonism. What *Handsworth Songs* does is activate the psychic reality of social phantasy in shaping our cognition of the real world: the metaphorical and metonymic logics that cut across the signifying chain of the film-work operate at an unconscious level along the lines of condensation and displacement which Freud identified in the symbolic mechanisms of the dream-work.

"In dreams begin responsibilities," wrote Delmore Schwartz. It seems to me to be crucially important to recognize the multi-accentuated character of the voices that speak in these new modes of black filmmaking because, as Volosinov/Bakhtin pointed out,

> The social *multi-accentuality* of the ideological sign is a very crucial aspect [of class struggle in language] . . . Each living ideological sign has two faces, like Janus . . . This *inner dialectical quality* of the sign comes out fully into the open only in times of social crisis or revolutionary changes.[11]

To the extent that this view echoes Frantz Fanon's insight that the ideological fixity of the signs of colonial authority become increasingly unstable, uncertain, and ambivalent at the point where struggles for national liberation reach a new threshold of intensity,[12] the emergence of this quality in black film discourse today implies a qualitative intensification of the cultural struggle to decolonize and deterritorialize cinema as a site of political intervention. The liberation of the imagination is a precondition of revolution, or so the Surrealists used to say. Carnival is *not* "the revolution," but in the carnivalesque aesthetic emerging here we may discern the mobility of what Bakhtin called "the dialogic principle in which the possibility of social change is prefigured in collective consciousness by the multiplication of critical dialogues.[13] What is at issue can be characterized as the critical difference between a *monologic* tendency in black film which tends to homogenize and totalize the black experience in Britain, and a *dialogic* tendency which is responsive to the diverse and complex qualities of our black Britishness and British blackness – our differentiated specificity as a diaspora people.

> They will be intimately related to the British people, but they cannot be fully part of the English environment because they are black. Now that is not a negative statement . . . Those people who are in Western civilization, who have grown up in it, but made to feel and themselves feeling that they are outside, have a unique insight into their society. (C. L. R. James)[14]

It has been said that the films of Sankofa and the Black Audio Film Collective are influenced and informed by ideas from European artistic practices. Indeed they are, but then so are those films made on the implicit premise of a mimetic theory of representation, whose neutral aesthetic dimension bears traces of the prevailing codes and professional ideology of the capital-ist film industry which, of course, is centered in the West. There is no escape from the fact that, as a diaspora people blasted out of one history into another by the "commercial deportation of slavery" (George Lamming) and its enforced displacement, our blackness is thoroughly imbricated in Western modes and codes to which we arrived as the disseminated masses of migrant dispersal. What is in question is not the expression of some lost origin or some uncontaminated essence in black film language, but the adoption of a critical voice that promotes consciousness of the collision of cultures and his-tories that constitute our very conditions of existence.

We return therefore to confront the paradox, which is that the mimetic mode as of cinematic expression can be seen as a form of cultural mimicry which demonstrates a neocolonized dependency on the codes, which val-orize film as a commodity of cultural imperialism.[15] The problem of imita-tion and domination was confronted in literary debates around aesthetics and politics in the African, Caribbean, and Afro-American novel in the 1940s and 1950s, which highlighted the existential dilemma of dependent expres-sivity: how can the "colonized" express an authentic self in an alien language imposed by the imperial power of the "colonizer"?[16]

There is, however, another response to this problematic, inscribed in aes-thetic practices of everyday life among black peoples of the African diaspora located in the new world of the capitalist West, which explores and exploits the creative contradictions of the clash of cultures. Across a whole range of cultural forms there is a powerfully *syncretic* dynamic which critically appro-priates elements from the master-codes of the dominant culture and *creolizes* them, disarticulating the given signs and rearticulating their symbolic meaning otherwise. The subversive force of this hybridizing tendency is most apparent at the level of language itself where creoles, patois, and Black English decenter, destabilize, and carnivalize the linguistic domination of "English" – the nation-language of master discourse – through strategic inflections, reaccentuations, and other performative moves in semantic and lexical codes. Such patterns of linguistic subversion in Caribbean practices of interculturation have been rigorously examined by Edward Brathwaite.[17] Creolizing practices of counter-appropriation exemplify the critical process of *dialogism* as such practices are self-consciously aware that, in Bakhtin's terms,

> The word in language is half someone else's. It becomes "one's own" only when . . . the speaker appropriates the word, adapting it to his own semantic and expressive intention. Prior to this moment of appropriation the word does not exist in a neutral or impersonal language . . . but rather it exists in other people's mouths, serving other people's intentions: it is from there that one must take the word and make it one's own.[18]

Today, the emergence of this dialogic tendency in black film practice is important as it has the potential to renew the critical function of "independent" cinema. Since former generations of black intelligentsia have now entered the media marketplace and broadcasting institutions, and some appear to have happily embraced commonsense notions of "artistic excellence,"[19] I would argue that the creole versioning and critical dialogue with selective elements from Euro-American modernism is infinitely preferable to the collusion with the cultural conservatism inherent in such conformist positions (which continue the great British tradition of anti-intellectualism).

There is, on the other hand, a powerful resonance between the aspirations of the new work, which seeks to find a film language adequate to the articulation of our realities as third-generation black people in Britain, and the critical goals advocated by the concept of Third Cinema, which seeks to combat the values of both commercialism and auteurism.[20] Aware of the pernicious ethnologocentric force which Clyde Taylor has shown to be inherent in the very concept of "aesthetics" within the dominant European philosophical tradition,[21] my aim has been precisely to avoid setting up a monolithic system of evaluative criteria (itself neither useful nor desirable). Rather, by appropriating elements of Bakhtin's theory of discursive struggle I have tried to differentiate *relational* tendencies in the way black films perform their critical function. Evaluating this function is always context-dependent. The lucid immediacy of *We Are the Elephant* (Ceddo, 1987), for example, not only articulates an incisive account of South African realities of repression and resistance, but in doing so it strikes a dialogic blow against the censorship and control of image and information flows imposed by apartheid and by the alienating spectacle of epics like *Cry Freedom* (director Richard Attenborough, 1986). Which is to say that if there are dialogic moments within films conceived in a conventional documentary realist mode, there are also a few profoundly monologic moments in some of the new work, such as the "speaker's drama" in Sankofa's *Passion of Remembrance* and the remorseless repetition of Black Audio's earlier tape-slide *Signs of Empire* (1984). We are dealing, then, not with categorical absolutes but the relative efficacy of strategic choices made in specific conjunctures and contexts of production and reception.

I would argue that new modes of black British filmmaking are instances of "imperfect cinema," in Julio Garcia Espinosa's phrase:[22] conducting research and experiments, adopting an improvisational approach, and hopefully learning from active mistakes through trial and error. In this sense, Stuart Hall's comment that the originality of the new work is "precisely that it retells the black experience as an *English* experience" must be amplified. In place of reductionist tendencies in the monologic single-issue approach – which often creates a binary "frontier effect" in its political analysis of reality, as if black subjects confront white society as our monolithic Other – critical dialogism gestures towards a counter-hegemonic perspective which assumes that questions of race cannot be isolated from wider social politics. In Hall's terms,

> The fact of the matter is that it is no longer possible to fight racism as if it had its own, autonomous dynamic, located between white people or the police on the one hand and blacks on the other. The problem of racism arises from *every single political development* which has taken place since the New Right emerged.[23]

Critical dialogism has the potential to overturn the binaristic relations of hegemonic boundary maintenance by multiplying critical dialogues *within* particular communities and *between* the various constituencies that make up the "imagined community" of the nation. At once articulating the personal and the political, such dialogism shows that our "other" is already inside each of us, that black identities are plural and heterogeneous, and that political divisions of gender and sexual identity are to be transformed as much as those of race and class. Moreover, critical dialogism questions the monologic exclusivity on which the dominant version of national identity and collective belonging are based. Paul Gilroy has shown how the sense of mutual exclusivity or logical incompatibility between the two terms *black* and *British* is one essential condition for the hegemony of racism over the English collective consciousness.[24] New ways of interrupting this hegemonic logic are suggested by the dialogic movement of creolizing appropriation.

Fully aware of the creative contradictions, and the cost, of our outside-in relation to England, cultural work based on this strategy gives rise to the thought that it is possible to turn dominant versions of Englishness inside out. Gramsci argued that a political struggle enters its hegemonic phase when it goes beyond particular economic interests to forge alliances among different classes of the people so as to redirect the collective will of the nation ("state + civil society"). On this view, counter-hegemonic strategy depends on the struggle to appropriate given elements of the common sense of the people and to rearticulate these elements out of the discourse of the dominant bloc and into a radical democratic direction, which used to be called "equality." At a microlevel, the textual work of creolizing appropriation activated in new forms of black cultural practice awakens the thought that such strategies of disarticulation and rearticulation may be capable of transforming the democratic imaginary at a macrolevel by "othering" inherited discourses of British identity.

Aware that "there is a Third World in every First World and vice versa" (Trinh T. Minh-ha), the diaspora perspective has the potential to expose and illuminate the sheer heterogeneity of the diverse social forces always repressed into the margin by the monologism of dominant discourses – discourses of domination. In a situation where neo-conservative forces have deepened their hold on our ability to apprehend reality, and would have us believe that "It's great to be Great again" (1987 Tory election slogan), we must encourage and develop this critical potential. It might enable us to overcome reality.

Notes

1 Ralph Ellison, Introduction, *Shadow and Act* (New York: Vintage/Random House, 1964), p. xvi.
2 Reviewing *Passion*, Judith Williamson discerned the influence of Godard, Duras, Mulvey, and Wollen (*New Statesman*, December 5, 1986). On *Territories*, Colin McCabe found its "visual flair . . . limited by its adherence to the bankrupt aesthetics of that narrow modernism advocated by much of the film theory of the '70s" (*Guardian*, December 4, 1986). Problems of "Eurocentrics" in contemporary English critical film theory are discussed in Robert Cruz, "Black Cinemas, Film Theory and Dependent Knowledge," *Screen* ("Other Cinemas, Other Criticisms"), vol. 26, no. 3–4, May–August 1985.
3 Novelist Salman Rushdie, born in India and living in Britain, is the author of *Midnight's Children* (winner of the 1981 Booker Prize) and *Shame*. Rushdie's polemic, "Songs doesn't know the score," *Guardian*, January 12, 1987, was followed by letters from Stuart Hall (January 15) and Darcus Howe (January 19).
4 See Michael Cadette, "Contrived Passions and False Memories," *Race Today Review '87* (London: vol. 17, no. 4, March 1987).
5 Cited in David A. Bailey, Introduction, *Ten.8*, no. 22, "Black Experiences" (summer 1986), p. 2.
6 David Silverman and Brian Torode, *The Material Word: Some Theories of Language and Its Limits* (London: Routledge, Kegan and Paul, 1980), p. 6.
7 Walter Benjamin, "Theses on the Philosophy of History," *Illuminations* (London: Fontana, 1973), p. 257.
8 See Stuart Hall and others, *Policing the Crisis* (London: Macmillan, 1979) and Stuart Hall, "The Whites of their Eyes: Racist Ideologies and the Media," in George Bridges and Rosalind Brunt (eds.) *Silver Linings* (London: Lawrence & Wishart, 1981).
9 The Notting Hill Gate neighborhood in the London borough of Kensington was an area of mass Caribbean settlement in the 1940s and 1950s; scene of the white-initiated "race-riots" of 1958, the first carnival was organized by activist Claudia Jones, and the event has subsequently developed as one of the largest street festivals in Britain, held annually on August Bank Holiday weekend.
10 See Paul Gilroy, "Stepping Out of Babylon – Race, Class and Autonomy," in Centre for Contemporary Cultural Studies, *The Empire Strikes Back* (London: Hutchinson, 1982), p. 300.

11   V. N. Volosinov, *Marxism and the Philosophy of Language* (New York: Seminar Press, 1973). p. 19.

12   See Frantz Fanon, "On National Liberation," in *The Wretched of the Earth* (Harmondsworth: Penguin Books, 1967), and see also Homi Bhabha's introduction, "Remembering Fanon," in the reprint of *Black Skin/White Masks* (London: Pluto Press, 1986).

13   See M. Bakhtin, "Discourse in the Novel," *The Dialogic Imagination* (Austin: University of Texas Press, 1981, trans. C. Emerson and M. Holquist), and see also Tvetzan Todorov, *Mikhail Bakhtin: The Dialogical Principle* (Manchester: Manchester University Press, 1984).

14   C. L. R. James, "Africans and Afro-Caribbeans: A Personal View," *Ten.8*, no. 14, "Black Image/Slaying On" (spring 1984).

15   The imitation of Hollywood form in initial developmental phases of various "national" cinemas is discussed in Roy Armes, *Third World Film-making and the West* (Berkeley: University of California Press, 1987). The transfer of professional ideology is discussed in Peter Golding, "Media Professionalism in the Third World" in James Curran and others (eds.), *Mass Communication and Society* (London: Edward Arnold, 1977).

16   See Homi K. Bhabha, "Representation and the Colonial Text" in Frank Gloversmith, *The Theory of Reading* (Brighton: Harvester Press, 1984). These debates have been recently revived in Ngugi wa Thiong'o, *Decolonising the Mind: The Politics of Language in African Literature* (London: John Currey/Heinemann, 1986).

17   On creolization and interculturation, see Edward K. Brathwaite, *The Development of Creole Society in Jamaica* (Oxford: Oxford University Press, 1971), *Contradictory Omens* (Mona, Jamaica: Savacou Publications, 1974), and on linguistic subversion in the formation of "nation-language," *The Story of the Voice* (London: New Beacon Publications, 1983).

18   Bakhtin, *The Dialogic Imagination*, pp. 293–4.

19   Farrukh Dondy (Commissioning Editor for Multicultural Programming, Channel Four Television) on UBC "ethnic minority" magazine *Ebony*, transmitted November 1986. Darcus Howe and Tariq Ali edit *The Bandung File*, a black/Third World current affairs programme, Channel Four.

20   The concept of Third Cinema proposed by Latin American independent film practice in the 1960s – see F. Solanas and O. Getino, "Towards a Third Cinema," in Bill Nichols (ed.) *Movies and Methods* (Berkeley: University of California Press, 1976) – and subsequently developed with reference to African cinema by Teshome Gabriel, *Third Cinema in the Third World: The Aesthetics of Liberation* (Ann Arbor: University of Michigan Research Press, 1982), was the focus of the conference held at the 40th Edinburgh International Film Festival (EIFF), 1986. For two versions of this real event see my reflections on "Third Cinema at Edinburgh," *Screen* vol. 27, no. 6, 1986, and David Will's account in *Framework*, no. 32/33, 1986.

21   Clyde Taylor's paper "Black Cinema/White Aesthetics" was presented at the EIFF conference "Third Cinema: Theories and Practices" (organized by Jim Pines, Paul Willemen, and June Givanni). Dialogic elucidation of Taylor's

argument is provided in his counter-reply to Will in "Eurocentrics VS, New Thought at Edinburgh," *Framework*, no. 34, 1987.

22   See Julio Garcia Espinosa, "Meditations on Imperfect Cinema . . . Fifteen Years Later," *Screen*, vol. 26, no. 3–4, May–August 1985.

23   Stuart Hall, "Cold Comfort Farm" (on Tottenham and Handsworth "riots"), *New Socialist*, no. 32, November 1985.

24   See Paul Gilroy, *There Ain't No Black in the Union Jack* (London: Hutchinson, 1987), especially ch 2. Ch. 5, "Diaspora, utopia and the critique of capitalism," provides further clarification of Bakhtin's relevance for thinking a diasporan aesthetic.

11

Nostalgia, Desire, Diaspora: South Asian Sexualities in Motion

Gayatri Gopinath

In this essay Gayatri Gopinath reads three diasporic South Asian texts about sexuality – the novel *Funny Boy* by Sri Lankan–Canadian author Shyam Selvadurai, the film *Fire* directed by Indian-Canadian Deepa Mehta, and a mainstream Hindi film, *Hum aapke hain koun* – alongside each other as a way to elaborate on the connections between nostalgia, home, and desire. Specifically, Gopinath is interested in thinking about how desire to belong to a home or nation is inflected by gender and sexuality. Building on important scholarship about the place of women in critical discourse that explores how heterosexual women come to embody the idea of the pure and traditional home, Gopinath's essay inquires into the role of sexuality and same-sex desire within the domestic space.

Gopinath thinks through how ideas of the nation and diaspora – where the home is read as an emblem of the nation – are reimagined within a queer framework. She argues that queer subjects who are traditionally rendered invisible in the nation, or are even seen to not exist in the nation, might negotiate alternative ways to belong to the nation. She argues that queer diasporic subjects strategically deploy modes of nostalgia to imagine a form of belonging to spaces such as the home and nation that have traditionally denied their existence.

Gopinath aims to dispel the myths that desire and modes of queer organizing and cultural production in South Asia and its diaspora are always inferior to and less complex than forms of queer organizing and cultural production in the West. The essay makes an important intervention in contemporary gay and lesbian discourse, suggesting that questions of belonging to a nation-state and the desire to belong to a home are complicated for queer South Asian subjects who must continually think about how same-sex sexual practices and identity intersect with their identities as diasporic national subjects.

In *Funny Boy*, Sri Lankan–Canadian writer Shyam Selvadurai's 1994 novel in six stories, the upper-middle-class Sri Lankan Tamil narrator traces a seven-year period of his childhood and adolescence that preceded the Tamil–Sinhalese riots of 1983 and his family's subsequent migration to Canada.[1] This experience of migration is the ground upon which the narrative unfolds; the novel is structured in terms of remembrance, with the narrator, Arjie, recalling a "remembered innocence of childhood . . . now colored in the hues of a twilight sky" (p. 5). Such a phrase, coming early on in the novel, seems to signal that the text can be comfortably contained within a conventional genre of exile literature, one that evokes from the vantage point of exile an idyllic, coherent, preexilic past shattered by war and dislocation. Similarly, the novel's parallel narrative of Arjie's sexual awakening initially locates the text within an established genre of "coming out" stories, where the protagonist grows into an awareness of his "true" homosexual identity. Yet while *Funny Boy* references the familiar narratives of exile and "coming out," it reworks the conventions of these genres as well as the very notions of exile and sexual subjectivity. In this essay I will read Selvadurai's novel alongside two other South Asian diasporic narratives of sexuality[2] – Indian–Canadian filmmaker Deepa Mehta's 1996 film *Fire*, and a scene from the popular 1993 Hindi film *Hum aapke hain koun* – to interrogate our understandings of nostalgia, "home," and desire in a transnational frame.

Non-heteronormative Sexuality and the Nation

An important body of feminist criticism has emerged in the past decade that examines the complicity of nationalist discourses with gender hierarchies and demonstrates how the figure of the woman in nationalist discourse acts as a primary marker of an essential, inviolable communal identity or tradition.[3] Anne McClintock and others have argued that a gender critique of nationalism reveals the ways in which the nation is construed in terms of familial and domestic metaphors, where "the woman" is enshrined as both the symbolic center and boundary marker of the nation as "home" and "family."[4] Deniz Kandiyoti, following Benedict Anderson, further explicates this conflation of "woman," "home," "family," and "nation" by pointing out that "nationalism describes its object using either the vocabulary of kinship (motherland, *patria*) or home (*heimat*) in order to denote something to which one is 'naturally' tied . . . The association of women with the private domain reinforces the merging of the nation/community with the selfless mother/devout wife."[5] The nation (as many critics have asserted) is a nostalgic construction, one that evokes an archaic past and authentic communal identity to assert and legitimize its project of modernization.[6] Women's bodies, then, become crucial to nationalist discourse in that they serve not only as the site of biological reproduction of national collectivities,[7] but as the very embodiment of this nostalgically evoked communal past and tradition.

If recent work on gender and nationalism has enabled us to see the ways in which women become emblematic of the concept of "home" as nation, as feminized domestic space, and as a site of pure and sacred spirituality,[8] much less attention has been paid to the production and deployment of non-heteronormative, or "queer," sexuality within colonial, anti-colonial nationalist, and contemporary nationalist discourses.[9] Given the increasing recognition that sexuality historically secures the grounds for the production of gendered colonial and bourgeois nationalist subjects,[10] it is somewhat surprising that some recent attempts to consider the imbrication of discourses of nationalism and women's sexuality still presume the heterosexuality of the female subject.[11] By failing to examine the existence and workings of alterior sexualities within dominant nationalisms, such analyses leave intact hegemonic constructions of the nation as essentially heterosexual. Whereas "the woman" carries a powerful symbolic freight in the constitution of the nation, a non-heteronormative subject necessarily has a very different relation to the constructions of "home" and "family" upon which nationalism depends.

Within the familial and domestic space of the nation as imagined community, non-heteronormative sexuality is either criminalized,[12] or disavowed and elided; it is seen both as a threat to national integrity and as perpetually outside the boundaries of nation, home, and family. As M. Jacqui Alexander states in an important essay discussing the 1991 Sexual Offenses and Domestic Violence Act in the Bahamas:

> The nation has always been conceived in heterosexuality, since biology and reproduction are at the heart of its impulse. The citizenship machinery is also located here, in the sense that the prerequisites of good citizenship and loyalty to the nation are simultaneously sexualized and hierarchized into a class of good, loyal, reproducing heterosexual citizens, and a subordinated, marginalized class of non-citizens.[13]

Alexander's comment is instructive because it makes explicit the fact that the nation demands heterosexuality as a prerequisite of "good citizenship," since it depends on the family as a reproductive unit through which the stability of gender roles and hierarchies is preserved. Heterosexuality, in other words, is fundamental to the way in which the nation imagines itself. Alexander goes on to elaborate upon the interplay of nation and nostalgia as understood by other critics by noting that the archaic past produced within nationalism is one of "sexual 'purity' . . . imagined within a geography (and a home) that only heterosexuals inhabit" (p. 85). If women under nationalism, as I noted earlier, are figured as "inherently atavistic – the conservative repository of the national archaic"[14] – non-heteronormative subjects, conversely, are written out of national memory entirely. Thus, within a nationalist logic where women embody the past and that past is figured as heterosexual, the non-heterosexual female in particular is multiply excluded from the terms of national belonging and "good citizenship."

It is true that, as Alexander points out, the charge of sexual "impurity" or "perversion" is not leveled solely against lesbians and gay men but extends to all those who cannot be located within the strict confines of middle-class heteronormativity: prostitutes, those who are HIV infected, and working-class and single women, for instance.[15] "Perversion," then, may most clearly mark the figure of the homosexual, but it is certainly not contained by or exclusive to it. Nevertheless, it is worth specifying the different forms of violence and disciplinary mechanisms that mark the various bodies within this "marginalized class of non-citizens," as each subject position engenders its own highly particular forms of resistance to, and at times accommodation with, nationalist logic. This essay, then, is a small part of a much larger project that begins the work of identifying the ways in which those who occupy one "perverse" subject position – a "queer South Asian diasporic subjectivity" – reimagine and reconstitute their particular, fraught relation to multiple national sites, and as such, demand a rethinking of the very notions of "home" and nostalgia.[16] My contention here is that a consideration of a queer diasporic subject prompts a different understanding of the mechanisms by which national belonging is internalized in the constitution of "modern" national subjects. More specifically, I want to point to some of the ways in which queer diasporic subjects – especially those who are women – negotiate their elision from national memory, as well as their function both as threat to home/family/nation and as perennially outside the confines of these entities. I stress queer female subjectivity in the diaspora because dominant diasporic articulations of community and identity intersect with patriarchal nationalist logic in its figuring of "woman" as bearer and guardian of communal tradition.[17]

Queer Sexuality and the Diaspora

As Anannya Bhattacharjee has shown in her work on domestic violence within Indian immigrant communities in the United States, immigrant women are positioned by an immigrant male bourgeoisie as repositories of an essential "Indianness." Thus, any form of transgression on the part of women may result in their literal and symbolic exclusion from the multiple "homes" that they as immigrant women inhabit: the patriarchal, hetero-sexual household, the extended "family" made up of an immigrant com-munity, and the national spaces of both India and the United States.[18] Within the patriarchal logic of an Indian immigrant bourgeoisie, then, a "non-heterosexual Indian woman" occupies a space of impossibility, in that not only is she excluded from these various "home" spaces but, quite literally, she simply cannot be imagined.

The impossibility of imagining such a subject within dominant diasporic and nationalist logics has been made all too apparent by the ongoing battle in New York City between the South Asian Lesbian and Gay Association (SALGA) and a group of Indian immigrant businessmen known as the Federation of Indian Associations (FIA) over SALGA's inclusion in the FIA-sponsored annual India Day Parade. The parade, which ostensibly cele-brates India's independence day, makes explicit the ways in which an Indian immigrant male bourgeoisie (embodied by the FIA) reconstitutes anti-colonial and contemporary nationalist discourses of communal belonging by positioning "India" as Hindu, patriarchal, middle class, and free of homo-sexuals. In 1995 the FIA denied both SALGA and Sakhi for South Asian Women (an anti-domestic violence women's group) the right to march in the parade on the grounds that both groups were, in essence, "anti-national."[19] In 1996, however, the FIA allowed Sakhi to participate while continuing to deny SALGA the right to march. The FIA, as self-styled arbiter of communal and national belonging, thus deemed it appropriate for women to march as "Indian women" – even, perhaps, as "feminist Indian women" – but it could not envision women marching as "Indian queers" or "Indian lesbians"; clearly, the probability that lesbians may indeed exist within Sakhi was not allowed for by the FIA.

I mention the controversy surrounding the India Day Parade here because it highlights how hegemonic nationalist discourses, reproduced in the dias-pora, position "woman" and "lesbian" as mutually exclusive categories to be disciplined in different ways. Within patriarchal diasporic logic, the "lesbian" can only exist outside the "home" (as household, community, and nation of origin), whereas the "woman" can only exist within it. Indeed, the "lesbian" is seen as "foreign," as a product of "being too long in the West," and she is therefore annexed to the "host" nation where she may be further elided – particularly if undocumented – as a non-white immigrant within both a mainstream (white) lesbian and gay movement and the larger body of the nation-state.

Given the illegibility and unrepresentability of a non-heteronormative (female) subject within patriarchal and heterosexual configurations of both nation and diaspora, the project of locating a queer South Asian diasporic subject – and a queer female subject in particular – may begin to challenge the dominance of such configurations. To this end, I want to suggest here some reading strategies by which to render queer subjects intelligible and to mark the presence of what Alexander terms an "insurgent sexuality" that works within and against hegemonic nationalist and diasporic logic. Indeed, the representations of non-heteronormative desire within the three texts that I consider here call for an alternative set of reading practices, a "queer diasporic" reading that juxtaposes wildly disparate texts and traces the cross-pollination between the various sites of non-normative desires that emerge within them. On the one hand, such a reading renders intelligible the particularities of same-sex desiring relations within spaces of homosociality and presumed heterosexuality, and, on the other hand, it deliberately wrenches particular scenes and moments out of context and extends them further than they would want to go. It would exploit the tension in the texts between the staging of female homoerotic desire as simply a supplement to a totalizing heterosexuality and the potentiality that they raise for a different logic and organization of female homoerotic desire. A queer diasporic reading and viewing practice conceptualizes a viewing public as located within multiple diasporic sites and the text itself as accruing multiple, sometimes contradictory meanings within these various locations. In other words, I place these texts within a framework of a queer South Asian diaspora, one that allows us to conceive of both the text and the viewer in motion; scenes and moments in popular culture that in their "originary" locations simply reiterate conventional nationalist and gender ideologies may, in a South Asian diasporic context, become the very foundation of queer culture. Furthermore, as I hope to demonstrate, queer diasporic readings within such a framework allow us to read non-heteronormative arrangements within rigidly heterosexual structures and to recognize the ways in which queer articulations of desire and pleasure both draw from and infiltrate popular culture. While queer reading practices alone cannot prevent the violences of heteronormativity, they do intervene in formulations of "home" and diaspora that – in their elision and disavowal of the particularities of queer subjectivities – inevitably reproduce the heteronormative family as central to national identity.

This framework of a queer South Asian diaspora produces linkages between the various representations of queer desire and cultural practices among South Asians in migrancy. It enables us to consider formations of queer desire and pleasure in radically particular sites, as well as in the context of movement and migration. Reading these texts as both constituting and constituted by a queer South Asian diaspora also resituates the conventions by which homosexuality has traditionally been encoded in an Anglo-American context. Queer sexualities as articulated by the texts I consider here reference familiar tropes and signifiers of Anglo-American homosexuality – such as the coming-out narrative and its attendant markers, secrecy and disclosure, as well as gender inversion and cross-dressing – while investing them with radically different and distinct significations. It is through a particular deployment of South Asian popular culture that this defamiliarization of conventional markers of homosexuality takes place, and that alternative strategies for signifying non-heteronormative desire are subsequently produced. These alternative strategies suggest a mode of reading and "seeing" same-sex eroticism that challenges modern epistemologies of visibility, revelation, and sexual subjectivity. Indeed, the notion of a queer South Asian diaspora can be seen as a conceptual apparatus that poses a critique of modernity and its various narratives of progress and development.[20] A queer South Asian diasporic geography of desire and pleasure stages this critique on multiple levels: it rewrites colonial constructions of Asian sexualities as anterior, premodern, and in need of Western political development – constructions that are recirculated by contemporary gay and lesbian transnational politics[21] – while simultaneously interrogating different South Asian nationalist narratives that imagine and consolidate the nation in terms of organic heterosexuality.

Pigs Can't Fly

"Pigs Can't Fly," the first story in Selvadurai's novel *Funny Boy*, lays out the complex system of prohibition, punishment, and compulsion that governs and structures gender differentiation. The story tells of the childhood game Bride-Bride that Arjie and his girl cousins play in the house of their grandparents, and which entails an elaborate performance of a marriage ceremony. For Arjie, dressing up as the bride – complete with shimmering white sari, flowers, and jewelry – is a way of accessing a particular mode of hyperbolic femininity embodied both by his mother and by the popular Sri Lankan female film stars of the day. The pleasure Arjie takes in this activity causes intense embarrassment and consternation on the part of the adults, who decree that henceforth Arjie is to play with the boys. Arjie's eventual traumatic banishment from the world of the girls and his forced entry into proper gender identification are figured in terms of geography and spacialization, of leaving one carefully inscribed space of gender play and entering another of gender conformity: Arjie is compelled to leave the inner section of the compound inhabited by the girls and enter the outer area where the boys congregate. Similarly, he is barred from watching his mother dress in her room, which throughout his childhood has been the site of his most intense spectatorial pleasure.[22]

The game itself, brilliantly titled Bride-Bride (not Bride-Groom), offers a reconfiguration of the contractual obligations of heterosexuality and gender conformity. Arjie installs himself in the most coveted role – that of bride – and makes it abundantly clear that the part of groom occupies the lowest rung of the game's hierarchy. Indeed, the game is predicated on the apparent non-performativity of masculinity,[23] as opposed to the hyperbolic feminine performance of Arjie as bride. The game's title then references both the unimportance of the groom and the pleasure derived from Arjie's performance of hyperfemininity, as well as the potentiality of a female same-sex eroticism that dispenses with the groom altogether. Arjie thus sutures himself into the scene of marriage, radically displacing it from the scene of heterosexuality and calling into question the very logic and authority of heteronormativity. "Pigs Can't Fly," then, encodes gender differentiation within multiple narratives, not all of which are necessarily pathologizing. While Arjie's father reads Arjie's cross-gender identification as unnatural and perverse, his mother is unable to come up with a viable explanation for the logic of gender conformity. When pushed by Arjie to explain why he can no longer watch her dress or play with the girls, she resorts to a childhood nursery rhyme, stating, "Because the sky is so high and pigs can't fly, that's why" (p. 19). Her answer attempts to grant to the fixity of gender roles the status of universally recognized natural law and to root it in "common sense"; however, such an explanation fails to satisfy Arjie, and his mother seems equally unconvinced but unable to imagine an alternative "order of things." Thus, gender conformity and nonconformity are narrativized through competing discourses in the story, where the rhetoric of nonconformity as perversion is undercut by Arjie's mother making apparent the nonsensical nature of gender codification, as well as by the anti-normative performance of gender in Bride-Bride.

Arjie's sexual encounters with a Sinhalese classmate, Shehan, and his realization that such homoerotic sex has pushed him outside the purview of "family," as he has known it, can initially be read within the narrative tradition of the coming-out story. Such narratives can be characterized as journeys toward an essential wholeness, toward the discovery of a true, gay identity through a teleological process of individuation that is granted representative status. Indeed, the novel's title, *Funny Boy*, can be read as a reference to Edmund White's 1982 narrative of gay coming-of-age in the 1950s, *A Boy's Own Story*.[24] However, unlike White's text, where sexuality is privileged as the singular site of radical difference and the narrator's sole claim to alterity, sexuality in *Funny Boy* is but one of many discourses, such as ethnic identity and forced migration, that speak to multiple displacements and exiles. Thus, gender inversion in "Pigs Can't Fly" is not really a primary marker of Arjie's latent homosexuality, a childhood signifier of adult homosexuality as charted along a linear narrative of sexual development that ends with a fully realized "gay" subject. Rather, cross-gender identification in the story takes on numerous complex valences, given the novel's engagement with questions of loss and memory in the context of diasporic displacement. It is from the vantage point of "a new home . . . in Canada" that the narrator remembers the intense pleasure derived from the ritual of becoming "like the goddesses of the Sinhalese and Tamil cinema, larger than life" (p. 5) and of watching his mother dress. Thus the narrator's evocation of these remembered instances of cross-gender identificatory practices and pleasures becomes a means of negotiating the loss of "home" as a fantasied site of geographic rootedness, belonging, and gender and erotic play. Indeed, if "home," as Dorinne Kondo states, is, for "peoples in diaspora," that which "we cannot not want,"[25] home for a queer diasporic subject becomes not only that which "we cannot not want" but also that which we cannot and could never have. Home in the queer fantasy of the past is the space of violent (familial and national) disowning.

Cross-Gender Identification and Queer Diasporic Memory

Cross-gender identification – through the game of Bride-Bride and in his mother's dressing room – allows Arjie to momentarily lay claim to domestic space and its gendered arrangements. The remembrance of such moments, then, mediates the multiple alienations of the queer diasporic subject from "home" as familial, domestic, and national space. Sri Lankan popular culture – the images of "the Malini Fonsekas and the Geeta Kumarasinghes" – acts as the vehicle through which "home" is conjured into being, mourned, and reimagined. The various meanings that the novel ascribes to Arjie's cross-dressing echoes anthropologist Martin Manalansan's depiction of the uses of drag within contemporary gay Filipino communities in New York City. Manalansan finds that for diasporic Filipino gay men, drag is inextricably intertwined with nostalgia, in that it evokes "the image and memory of the Filipino homeland while at the same time acknowledging being settled in a 'new home' here in the US."[26] Similarly, the narrator's memory of cross-dressing in *Funny Boy* negotiates multiple cultural and geographic sites while suggesting the uses of nostalgia for queer diasporic subjects.

Indeed, Arjie's performance of what we can term "queer femininity" radically reconfigures hegemonic nationalist and diasporic logic, which depends on the figure of the "woman" as a stable signifier of "tradition." Within a queer diasporic imaginary, the "lost homeland" is represented not by the pure and self-sacrificing wife and mother, but rather by a queer boy in a sari. The project of reterritorializing national space, and the uses of drag in such a project, are explicitly articulated within South Asian queer activism and popular culture in various diasporic sites. For instance, at the 1995 India Day Parade, where SALGA was literally positioned at the sidelines of the official spectacle of national reconstitution, one cross-dressed SALGA member held up a banner that read "Long Live Queer India." The banner, alongside the SALGA member's gender presentation, references not a utopic future space of national belonging, but rather an already existing queer diasporic space of insurgent sexualities and gender identities. In another example of queer diasporic popular cultural reconfigurations of the nation, a SALGA flyer for a party celebrating the publication of Selvadurai's novel depicts a sari-clad figure exclaiming: "Shyam was right! I look better in Mummy ki sari!" On the one hand, the flyer makes apparent the ways in which popular cultural practices (parties and drag performances) and literary texts such as *Funny Boy* inform and produce each other, and by so doing, call into existence a queer South Asian diaspora. The flyer also replaces the woman-in-sari figure that typically stands for "India" with a gay male/transgendered performance of queer femininity that references and remembers non-heteronormative childhoods in other national sites.[27]

The novel's final section makes all the more evident the ways in which "home" is reconfigured in queer diasporic memory. Here, Arjie has sex with Shehan for the last time before leaving with his family for Canada after the 1983 riots. The smell of Shehan's body lingering on his clothes becomes "a final memento," not only of a remembered scene of homoerotic desire but of Sri Lanka, of "home," itself. The text thus "queers" the space of Sri Lanka as "home" by disrupting the logic of nationalism, which consolidates "the nation" through normative hierarchical sexual and gender arrangements that coalesce around the privatized, bourgeois domestic space of "home" as a site of sanitized heterosexuality. The mapping of homoeroticism onto the national space of "Sri Lanka" also reverses the standard notion of a "gay" subject having to leave a "third world" site of gender and sexual oppression in order to "come out" into the more liberated West. As such, it disorganizes the conventional coming-out narrative that "begins with an unliberated, 'prepolitical' homosexual practice and that culminates in a liberated, 'out,' politicized, 'modern' 'gay' subjectivity."[28] This moment in the narrative encapsulates the text's deployment of what I would call a generative or enabling nostalgia and homesickness, where the "home" that is evoked signifies multiply: as both national space and domestic space, it is the site of homoerotic desire and cross-gender identification and pleasure, of intense gender conformity and horrific violence, of multiple leave-takings and exiles. Thus, the text also complicates the axes of a conventional exilic novel with fixed points of origin and departure. Instead, the stories detail the layered crises and multiple losses, the leave-takings and exiles that occur within the site of "home" itself.

Female Homosociality, Queer Femininity

Arjie's game of Bride-Bride not only references a particular mode of hyperbolic femininity and cross-gender identificatory pleasure, it also suggests the possibility of a female homoeroticism located within the home and working through the absence and irrelevance of the groom. Since the moments of cross-dressing that I have thus far discussed tend to privilege a gay male diasporic subject, I want to detach Arjie's performance of queer femininity from a narrative of queer boyhood and instead use it to locate a queer female subject within multiple "home" spaces. For a staging of the game of Bride-Bride within a female homosocial context, then, we can turn to the recent independent film *Fire*, which depicts the relationship between two brides, that is, two sisters-in-law in the North Indian urban home of a middle-class extended family. Filmmaker Deepa Mehta quickly establishes the familiar familial violences and compulsions that underlie this space of home: both women (ironically named Radha and Sita)[29] do most of the labor for the family business while their husbands alternately abuse or ignore them; this eventually precipitates their turning to each other for sex and emotional sustenance.

The film renders explicit the female homoerotic desire hinted at in Arjie's game of Bride-Bride by producing a complicated relay between female homosociality and female homoerotic practices. In one scene, for instance, Sita massages Radha's feet at a family picnic, transforming a daily female homosocial activity into an intensely homoerotic one while the other members of the family unwittingly look on. The slide from female homosociality into female homoeroticism in this scene, as well as in another where Radha rubs oil into Sita's hair, serves to locate female same-sex desire and pleasure firmly within the confines of the home and "the domestic" rather than occurring safely "elsewhere."[30] This emergence of female homoeroticism at the interstices of heterosexuality interrupts, as Geeta Patel phrases it, the "apparently necessary slide from marriage into heterosexuality," and denaturalizes the linkages between heterosexuality and the domestic.[31] This articulation of female same-sex desire within the space of the domestic directly confronts and disrupts contemporary nationalist constructions of the bourgeois Hindu home as the reservoir of essential national cultural values, embodied in the figure of the Hindu woman as chaste, demure, and self-sacrificing.[32]

Furthermore, the erotic interplay between Radha and Sita speaks to a specific modality of South Asian femininity through which – in a middle-class context – lesbian desire is articulated within sites of extreme heteronormativity. The trope of dressing and undressing that threads through *Funny Boy* marks *Fire* as well: in the absence of their husbands, the two women indulge not only in dressing each other but in dressing for each other, donning heavy silk saris, makeup, and gold jewelry in a performance of the hyperbolic femininity that Selvadurai's narrator also references. Their eroticization of a particular aesthetic of Indian femininity brings to mind the problematic sketched out by Kaushalya Bannerji in the South Asian lesbian and gay anthology *A Lotus of Another Color.*[33] Bannerji remarks upon her alienation from a white lesbian aesthetic of androgyny, given her "fondness for bright colors, long hair, jewelry" – bodily signs that have multiple meanings for her as an Indian – Canadian woman but read within a white lesbian context simply as markers of a transparent "femme" identity. Bannerji's presentation of a South Asian femininity elicits fetishistic responses from white lesbians, whereas for her, this particular aesthetic is a means of negotiating and reconciling categories of both ethnic and sexual identity. Similarly, the two protagonists in *Fire* derive pleasure from a particular, middle-class version of South Asian (and specifically North Indian) femininity that sometimes slips into an equally class-marked articulation of female homoerotic desire.[34]

Clearly, then, the "mythic mannish lesbian" (to use Esther Newton's term)[35] that haunts Euramerican discourses of twentieth-century lesbian sexuality is not the dominant modality through which female same-sex desire can be read here; rather, within the context of the middle-class home in the film, it is Radha and Sita's performance of queer femininity that emerges as the dominant mode or aesthetic through which female same-sex desire is rendered intelligible. As such, the film suggests an alternative trajectory of representing female homoeroticism in a South Asian context – one that is at odds with conventional Euramerican "lesbian" histories that chart a developmental narrative from a nineteenth-century model of asexual "romantic friendship" between bourgeois women in privatized, domestic, gender-segregated spaces to a contemporary modern, autonomous, "lesbian" identity, sexuality, and community.[36] The film's depiction of the ways in which this privatized, seemingly sanitized "domestic" space can simultaneously function as a site of intense female homoerotic pleasure and practices calls into question a narrative of "lesbian" sexuality as needing to emerge from a private, domestic sphere into a public, visible, "lesbian" subjectivity.[37] *Fire* then, like *Funny Boy*, refuses to subscribe to the notion that the proper manifestation of same-sex eroticism is within a "politics of visibility" in the public sphere. Rather, it suggests that in a South Asian context, what constitutes "lesbian" desire may both look and function differently than it does within Euramerican social and historical formations, and draw from alternative modes of masculinity and femininity. In other words, the film makes explicit the ways in which not all female same-sex desire culminates in an autonomous "lesbianism," and not all "lesbianism" is at odds with domestic marital arrangements.

The film in a sense references this problematic of visuality and identity in its opening scene, which recurs throughout the film. The scene is that of Radha's dreamscape: a wide, open field of yellow flowers, where Radha's mother exhorts a young Radha to "see the ocean" lying at the limits of the landlocked field. This exhortation to "see" differently, to "see" without literally seeing, speaks to the need for a particular strategy of reading sexuality outside dominant configurations of visibility, desire, and identity. I am not asserting here that the film depicts an authentic, autonomous, or indigenous form of lesbian desire; rather, it suggests an alternative mode of reading and "seeing" non-normative erotic and gender configurations as they erupt within sites of extreme heteronormativity. The film thus enacts the critique articulated by Manalansan of transnational gay and lesbian globalizing discourse, which in its privileging of Western definitions of same-sex sexual practices "risks duplicating an imperial gaze in relation to non-Western non-metropolitan, sexual practices and collectivities."[38]

Insofar as the two women come together because of the failures of their respective marriages, however, *Fire* recenters heterosexuality by relying on a conventional framing of "lesbian" desire as the result of failed heteronormative arrangements. Yet one particular scene in the film hints at an alternative organization of female same-sex desire, and perhaps exceeds the film's narrative framing of "lesbian" desire as simply an auxiliary to heterosexuality. In it, Sita (dressed in a suit with her hair slicked back) and Radha (as a Hindi film heroine) engage in a playful lip-synching duet that both inhabits and ironizes the genre of popular Hindi film songs. Whereas Radha's fantasy space is that of the field that gives way to the ocean, this evocation of popular Hindi film becomes Sita's fantasied site of erotic and gender play. This scene of cross-gender identification stands apart from an earlier scene of playful cross-dressing where Sita discards her sari and dons her husband's jeans and smokes his cigarettes as a way of temporarily laying claim to male authority, freedom, and privilege. In the later scene, cross-dressing is not a means for claiming male privilege but rather functions as an articulation of same-sex desire; echoing *Funny Boy*, the film suggests that if one mode for making lust between women intelligible is through the representation of hyperbolic femininity, another is through the appropriation of popular culture and its particular gender dynamics.

Female Same-Sex Desire and South Asian Popular Culture

We can read this scene in *Fire* as referencing a strikingly similar female cross-dressing scene in the immensely popular 1993 mainstream Hindi film *Hum aapke hain koun*. This sequence takes place during a woman-only celebration of an upcoming marriage, around which the film's entire plot revolves. Into this space of female homosociality enters a woman cross-dressed as the film's male hero, in an identical white suit, who proceeds to dance suggestively with the heroine (played by Madhuri Dixit) and with various other women in the room. What follows is an elaborate dance sequence where the cross-dressed woman and Dixit engage in a teasing, sexualized exchange that parodies the trappings of conventional middle-class Hindu family arrangements (that is marriage, heterosexuality, domesticity, and motherhood). Halfway through the song, however, order is apparently restored as the cross-dressed interloper is chased out of the room by the "real" hero (Salman Khan). The cross-dressed woman disappears from both the scene and indeed the entire film, and Salman Khan proceeds to claim his rightful place opposite Dixit. What meanings, then, can we ascribe to these instances in both *Fire* and *Hum aapke* of an explicitly gendered erotics between women? Clearly, neither scene is purely transgressive of conventional gender and sexual hierarchies: in *Fire*, the gendered erotic interplay of the two women can be seen as simply an articulation of their desire for each other in the absence of "real" men, while in *Hum aapke* the cross-dressed woman seems merely to hold the place of the "real" hero until he can make his entrance, that is, to hold in place the hierarchical gendered relations in the scene.[39] Indeed, the film can afford such a transparent rendering of female–female desire precisely because it remains so thoroughly convinced of the hegemonic power of its own heterosexuality. However, the fact that gender reversal in *Hum aapke* occurs within a space of female homosociality renders the implied homoeroticism of the scene explicit to both the characters and to the film's audience, and by doing so, makes it eminently available for a queer diasporic viewership. For a queer South Asian viewing subject, then, the scene foregrounds the ways in which South Asian popular culture acts as a repository of queer desiring relations; it also marks the simultaneous illegibility of those relations to a heterosexual viewing public and their legibility in a queer South Asian diasporic context.[40]

It is critical to note that upon *Hum aapke*'s release, the popular press attributed its tremendous and sustained popularity to its return to "family values," a phrase that apparently referred to the film's rejection of the sex and violence formulas of other popular Hindi movies. However, this phrase speaks more to the ways in which the film works within Hindu nationalist discourses of the nation by articulating a desire for a nostalgic "return" to an impossible ideal, that of supposedly "traditional" Hindu family and kinship arrangements that are staunchly middle class and heterosexual. The incursion of female homoerotic desire into this ultraconventional Hindu marriage plot – both suggested and contained by the scene between Dixit and her cross-dressed partner – threatens the presumed seamlessness of both familial and nationalist narratives by calling into question the functionality and imperviousness of heterosexual bonds.

Pigs with Wings

The nostalgia evoked by the film is quite unlike the longing in *Funny Boy* for a space of "home" that is permanently and already ruptured, rent by colliding and colluding discourses around class, sexuality, and ethnic identity. *Funny Boy* lays claim to both the space of "home" and the nation by making both the site of non-heteronormative desire and pleasure in a nostalgic diasporic imaginary. Such a move disrupts nationalist logic by forestalling any notion of queer or non-heteronormative desire as insufficiently authentic. *Funny Boy* thus refuses to subsume sexuality within a larger narrative of ethnic, class, or national identity, or to subsume these other conflicting trajectories within an overarching narrative of "gay" sexuality. Within *Funny Boy* as well as in *Fire* and *Hum aapke*, sexuality functions not as an autonomous narrative but instead as enmeshed and immersed within multiple discourses. Clearly, none of these texts allows for a purely redemptive recuperation of same-sex desire, conscribed and implicated as it is within class, religious, and gender hierarchies. Indeed, it is precisely in the friction between these various competing discourses that queer pleasure and desire emerge. In both *Fire* and *Hum aapke*, for instance, female homoerotic pleasure is generated and produced by the very prohibitions around class, religion, and gender that govern and discipline the behavior of middle-class women.

Throughout this essay I have attempted to gesture toward the ways in which nation and diaspora are refigured within a queer diasporic imaginary. Nostalgia as deployed by queer diasporic subjects is a means for imagining oneself within those spaces from which one is perpetually excluded or denied existence. If the nation is "the modern Janus," a figure that gazes at a primordial, ideal past while at the same time facing a modern future,[41] a queer diaspora instead recognizes the past as a site of intense violence as well as pleasure; it acknowledges the spaces of impossibility within the nation and their translation within the diaspora into new logics of affiliation. The logic of "pigs can't fly" becomes transformed, in the diaspora, into the alternative queer diasporic logic that allows for two brides in bed together, a marriage without a groom, pigs with wings. In other words, a queer diasporic logic displaces heteronormativity from the realm of natural law and instead launches its critique of hegemonic constructions of both nation and diaspora from the vantage point of an "impossible" subject.

Notes

I would like to thank Lisa Lowe, Chandan Reddy, and two anonymous readers from *positions* for their valuable comments on an earlier draft of this essay. Special gratitude goes to Judith Halberstam, to whom this essay is dedicated.

1   Shyam Selvadurai, *Funny Boy* (Toronto: McClelland and Stewart, 1995). Subsequent references to this work will be given in parentheses in the text.
2   I use the term "South Asian" throughout this essay to reference a particular diasporic political formation that locates itself outside the national boundaries of any one national site (such as Bangladesh, Bhutan, India, Nepal, Pakistan, or Sri Lanka). However, I am also aware of the regional hierarchies that may be resurrected within the term. For a cogent explication of the oppositional uses and limits of the term "South Asian" among activists in the United States, see Anannya Bhattacharjee, "The Public/Private Mirage: Mapping Homes and Undomesticating Violence Work in the South Asian Immigrant Community," in *Feminist Genealogies, Colonial Legacies, Democratic Futures*, ed. M. Jacqui Alexander and Chandra T. Mohanty (New York: Routledge, 1997), p. 309.
3   A few examples of such work include Partha Chatterjee, *The Nation and Its Fragments* (Princeton, NJ: Princeton University Press, 1993); Anne McClintock, *Imperial Leather: Race, Gender, and Sexuality in the Colonial Contest* (New York: Routledge, 1993); Floya Anthias and Nira Yuval Davis, eds., *Women-Nation-State* (London: Macmillan, 1989); and Deniz Kandiyoti, "Identity and Its Discontents: Women and the Nation," in *Colonial Discourse and Post-colonial Theory*, ed. Patrick Williams and Laura Chrisman (New York: Columbia University Press, 1994), pp. 376–91.
4   McClintock, *Imperial Leather*, p. 354.
5   Kandiyoti, "Identity and Its Discontents," p. 382.
6   See, for instance, Tom Nairn, *The Break-up of Britain: Crisis and Neo-nationalism* (London: Verso, 1981); Homi K. Bhabha, ed., *Nation and Narration* (New York: Routledge, 1991); Benedict Anderson, *Imagined Communities* (London: Verso, 1991); and Kandiyoti, "Identity and Its Discontents."
7   Anthias and Yuval Davis, *Women-Nation-State*, p. 7.
8   Inderpal Grewal, *Home and Harem: Nation, Gender, Empire, and the Cultures of Travel* (Durham, NC: Duke University Press, 1996), p. 7.
9   I use the term "queer" throughout this essay to suggest a range of non-heteronormative sexual practices and desires that may not necessarily coalesce around categories of identity.
10   For an exemplary study of sexuality and colonialism see Mrinalini Sinha, *Colonial Masculinity: The "Manly Englishman" and the "Effeminate Bengali" in the Late Nineteenth Century* (Manchester: Manchester University Press, 1995).
11   For one recent instance of this particular blindspot in feminist critiques of nationalism see Kumari Jayawardena and Malathi de Alwis, eds., *Embodied Violence: Communalising Women's Sexuality in South Asia* (New Delhi: Kali for Women, 1996).

12   In India, for instance, Section 377 of the Indian Penal Code bans same-sex sexual relations as "unnatural offences." The law was initially instituted under British colonial rule in the 1830s, which makes explicit the complicity of colonial and anti-colonial nationalist framings of sexuality.

13   M. Jacqui Alexander, "Erotic Autonomy As a Politics of Decolonization: An Anatomy of State Practice in the Bahamas Tourist Economy," in Alexander and Mohanty, *Feminist Genealogies*, p. 84.

14   McClintock, *Imperial Leather*, p. 359.

15   Alexander, "Erotic Autonomy," p. 97.

16   For work that begins to trace the contours of queer South Asian subjectivity see, for instance, Geeta Patel, "Homely Housewives Run Amok: Lesbians in Marital Fixes," *Public Culture* (forthcoming); Gayatri Gopinath, "Homo-Economics: Queer Sexualities in a Transnational Frame," in *Burning Down the House: Recycling Domesticity*, ed. Rosemary M. George (New York: Westview/Harper Collins, 1998); and Rakesh Ratti, ed., *A Lotus of Another Color: An Unfolding of the South Asian Gay and Lesbian Experience* (Boston, MA: Alyson, 1993).

17   For further discussion of how diasporic articulations of community and identity both replicate and challenge the masculinist logic of conventional nationalisms, see Gayatri Gopinath, "Bombay, U.K., Yuba City: Bhangra Music and the Engendering of Diaspora," *Diaspora* 4, no. 3 (winter 1995): 303–22.

18   Bhattacharjee, "The Public/Private Mirage," pp. 308–29. See also Anannya Bhattacharjee, "The Habit of Ex-nomination: Nation, Woman, and the Indian Immigrant Bourgeoisie," *Public Culture* 5, no. 1 (fall 1992): 19–46.

19   The official grounds for denying Sakhi and SALGA the right to march were ostensibly the fact that both groups called themselves not "Indian" but "South Asian"; the possibility of Pakistanis, Bangladeshis, or Sri Lankans marching in an "Indian" parade was apparently too much of an affront to FIA members.

20   The imbrication of narratives of "progress," "modernity," and "visibility" is made obvious in what Alexander terms "prevalent metropolitan impulses that explain the absence of visible lesbian and gay movements [in non-Western locations] as a defect in political consciousness and maturity, using evidence of publicly organized lesbian and gay movements in the US . . . as evidence of their originary status (in the West) and superior political maturity" (Alexander, "Erotic Autonomy," p. 69).

21   See Martin Manalansan, "In the Shadows of Stonewall: Gay Transnational Politics and the Diasporic Dilemma," in *The Politics of Culture in the Shadow of Capital*, ed. Lisa Lowe and David Lloyd (Durham, NC: Duke University Press, 1997), for an important interrogation of contemporary gay transnational politics.

22   In its depiction of the "inner" as a female site but also a site of gender play and reversal, the story refigures in interesting ways anti-colonial nationalist framings of space that posit the "inner" as a space of essential spirituality and tradition, embodied by "woman," as opposed to the "outer," male sphere of progress, materiality, and modernity. For an analysis of the creation of "inner" and "outer" spheres in anti-colonial nationalist discourse see Partha Chatterjee, "The Nationalist Resolution to the Woman's Question," in *Recasting Women:*

Essays in Colonial History, ed. Kumkum Sangari and Sudesh Vaid (New Delhi: Kali for Women, 1989), pp. 233–54.

23 See Judith Halberstam, *Female Masculinity* (Durham, NC: Duke University Press, 1998), for a discussion of masculine non-performativity in the context of female "drag king" performances.

24 See Robert McRuer, "Boys' Own Stories and New Spellings of My Name: Coming Out and Other Myths of Queer Positionality," *Genders* 2, no. 1 (1994): 260–83, for a critique of the coming-out narrative as "necessary for under-standing one's (essential) gay identity" (p. 267) and of Edmund White's novel in particular.

25 Dorinne Kondo suggests this formulation of "home" in her essay on Asian-American negotiations of community and identity, "The Narrative Production of 'Home,' Community and Political Identity in Asian American Theater," in *Displacement, Diaspora, and Geographies of Identity*, ed. Smadar Lavie and Ted Swedenburg (Durham, NC: Duke University Press, 1996), p. 97.

26 Martin Manalansan, "Diasporic Deviants/Divas: How Filipino Gay Transmigrants 'Play with the World,'" in *Homosexuality in Motion: Gay Diasporas and Queer Peregrinations*, ed. Cindy Patton and Benigno Sanchez-Eppler (Durham, NC: Duke University Press, in press). [*Editors' note:* the volume was actually published in 2000 under the title *Queer Diasporas*.]

27 However, the flyer's use of Hindi (rather than Tamil or Sinhala), even when referencing a Sri Lankan text, points to the ways in which (North) Indian hegemony within South Asia may be replicated within queer South Asian spaces in the diaspora.

28 Manalansan, "Diasporic Deviants/Divas," p. 3.

29 In Hindu mythology, Sita proves her chastity to her husband, Ram, by immersing herself in fire; she thereby embodies the ideals of womanly virtue and self-sacrifice. Radha, similarly, is the devoted consort of the god Krishna, who is famous for his womanizing. The irony in the film's naming of the two female protagonists lies in their refusal to inhabit these overdetermined roles of woman as devoted, chaste, and self-denying.

30 I have further explored this particular relation between female homoeroticism and female homosociality in a South Asian context in a discussion of Ismat Chughtai's short story "The Quilt." See Gopinath, "Homo-Economics."

31 See Patel, "Homely Housewives," p. 7.

32 See Charterjee, "Nationalist Resolution," for an analysis of the ways in which anti-colonial nationalism used the figure of the woman as a bearer of inviolate tradition in order to imagine the independent nation.

33 Kaushalya Bannerji, "No Apologies," in Ratti, *Lotus of Another Color*, pp. 59–64.

34 Outside the confines of the middle-class North Indian home depicted in *Fire*, female homoerotic desire may manifest itself in forms other than that of hyper-bolic or queer femininity. As Geeta Patel has noted in her discussion of the controversy around the 1987 "marriage" of two policewomen in central India, the police barracks in which the two women lived constituted a site of complicated and explicitly gendered erotic relations between women. See Patel, "Homely Housewives," pp. 14–22.

35 Esther Newton, "The Mythic Mannish Lesbian: Radclyffe Hall and the New Woman," in *Hidden from History: Reclaiming the Gay and Lesbian Past*, ed. Martin Duberman et al. (New York: Meridian, 1989), pp. 281–93.

36 See ibid. for a critique of nineteenth-century "romantic friendships" as protolesbian/feminist relationships.

37 Clearly, a Euramerican bourgeois space of "home" is not akin to the domestic space represented in *Fire*, given that the latter is marked by a history of British colonialism, anti-colonial nationalism, and contemporary Indian (and Hindu) nationalist politics.

38 Manalansan, "Under the Shadows," p. 6.

39 *Hum aapke*'s brief interlude of gender reversal and implied female homoeroticism seems to locate the film within Chris Straayar's definition of the "temporary transvestite film," those that "offer spectators a momentary, vicarious trespassing of society's accepted boundaries for gender and sexual behavior. Yet one can relax confidently in the orderly [heterosexual] demarcations reconstituted by the films' endings." See Chris Straayar, *Deviant Eyes, Deviant Bodies: Sexual Reorientations in Film and Video* (New York: Columbia University Press, 1996), p. 44.

40 These scenes of cross-dressing and gender reversal can also be read as gesturing toward the gendered arrangements of female same-sex desire that Patel details, and that shadow the middle-class domestic locations of both *Fire* and *Hum aapke*.

41 McClintock, *Imperial Leather*, p. 358.

Additional Readings on Cultural Production and Diaspora

Alvarez, Sonia E., Evelina Dagnino, and Arturo Escobar, eds. *Cultures of Politics/ Politics of Cultures: Re-visioning Latin American Social Movements*. Boulder, CO: Westview Press, 1998.

Amit-Talai, Vered and Helena Wulff, eds. *Youth Cultures: A Cross Cultural Perspective*. London: Routledge, 1995.

Ang, Ien and Jon Stratton. "Asianising Australia: Notes Towards A Critical Transnationalism in Cultural Studies." *Cultural Studies* 10.1 (1996): 16–36.

Anwar, Muhammad. *Between Cultures: Continuity and Change in the Lives of Young Asians*. London: Routledge, 1998.

Appadurai, Arjun. *Modernity at Large: Cultural Dimensions of Globalization*. Minneapolis: University of Minnesota Press, 1996.

Averill, Gage. "'*Mezanmi, Kouman Nou Ye*? My Friends, How Are You?': Musical Constructions of the Haitian Transnation." *Diaspora* 3: 3 (1994): 253–69.

Baily, John. "The Role of Music in Three British Muslim Communities." *Diaspora* 4.1 (1995): 77–87.

Baumann, Gerd. *Contesting Culture: Discourses of Identity in Multi-Ethnic London*. Cambridge: Cambridge University Press, 1996.

Best, Curwen. "Ideology, Sound, Image and Caribbean Music Videos." *Wadabagei: A Journal of the Caribbean and Its Diaspora* 3.1 (2000): 77–109.

Boscagli, Maurizia. "The Resisting Screen: Multicultural Politics in a Global Perspective." *Diaspora* 5.3 (1996): 497–508.

Bowser, Pearl. "Testing the Waters: African Diaspora Filmmaking and Identity." *Wide Angle – A Quarterly Journal of Film History Theory & Criticism* 17.1–4 (1995): 193–6.

Cheah, Pheng. "Given Culture: Rethinking Cosmopolitan Freedom and Trans-Nationalism." *Boundary 2*. 24.2 (1997): 157–97.

Ciecko, Anne. "Representing the Spaces of Diaspora in Contemporary British Films by Women Directors." *Cinema Journal* 38.3 (1999): 67–90.

Clifford, James. "Traveling Cultures." *Cultural Studies*. Ed. Lawrence Grossberg, Cary Nelson and P. Treichler. New York: Routledge, 1992. 96–116.

Cultural Studies. Special issue on "Chicana/o Latina/o Cultural Studies: Transnational and Transdisciplinary Movements." 13.2 (1999).

Delgado, Guillermo. *Diaspora and Heterocultures: Spanish-Speaking Peoples in the US.* Santa Cruz, CA: CLRC, University of California at Santa Cruz, 1997.

Diawara, Manthia. *African Cinema: Politics and Culture.* Bloomington: Indiana University Press, 1992.

——ed. *Black African Cinema.* London: Routledge, 1993.

——"The 'I' Narrator in Black Diaspora Documentary." *Struggles for Representation: African American Documentary Film and Video.* Ed. Phyllis R. Klotman and Janet K. Cutler. Bloomington: Indiana University Press, 1999. 315–28.

Diawara, Manthia, Houston A. Baker, and Ruth H. Lindenborg, eds. *Black British Cultural Studies.* Chicago, IL: University of Chicago Press, 1996.

Foster, Gwendolyn Audrey. *Women Filmmakers of the African and Asian Diaspora: Decolonizing the Gaze, Locating Subjectivity.* Carbondale, IL: Southern Illinois University Press, 1997.

Gilman, Sander L. *The Visibility of the Jew in the Diaspora: Body Imagery and Its Cultural Context.* Syracuse, NY: Syracuse University Press, 1992.

Gilroy, Paul. *Small Acts: Thoughts on the Politics of Black Cultures.* London: Serpent's Tail, 1993.

Gopinath, Gayatri. "'Bombay, UK, Yuba City': Bhangra Music and the Engendering of Diaspora." *Diaspora* 4.3 (1995): 303–22.

Grenier, Line, and Jocelyne Guilbautt. "*Créolité* and *Francophonie* in Music: Sociomusical Repositioning Where it Matters." *Cultural Studies* 11.2 (1997): 207–34.

Hammarlund, Anders. "Migrancy and Syncretism: A Turkish Musician in Stockholm." *Diaspora* 3.3 (1994): 305–23.

Harney, Stefano. *Nationalism and Identity: Culture and the Imagination in a Caribbean Diaspora.* Atlantic Highlands, NJ: Zed Books, 1996.

Kun, Josh. "Against Easy Listening: Audiotopic Readings and Transnational Soundings." *Everynight Life: Culture and Dance in Latin/o America.* Ed. Celeste Delgado and José Esteban Muñoz. Durham, NC: Duke University Press, 1997.

Lowe, Lisa. *Immigrant Acts: On Asian American Cultural Politics.* Durham, NC: Duke University Press, 1996.

Maira, Sunaina. "Desis reprazent: Bhangra Remix and Hip Hop in New York City." *Postcolonial Studies* 1.3 (1998): 357–70.

——"Identity Dub: The Paradoxes of an Indian American Youth Subculture." *Cultural Anthropology* 14.1 (1999): 29–60.

——"The Politics of 'Cool': Indian American Youth Culture in New York City." *Encounters: People of Asian Descent in the Americas.* Ed. Roshni Rustomji Kerns, Rajini Srikanth, and Leny Mendoza Strobel. Lanham, MD: Rowman and Littlefield, 1999. 177–93.

Meadows, Eddie S. "African Americans and 'Lites Out Jazz' in San Diego: Marketing, Impact, and Criticism." *California Soul: Music of African Americans in the West.* Ed. Jacqueline DjeDje and Eddie S. Meadows. Berkeley: University of California Press, 1998. 244–74.

Mercer, Kobena. *Welcome to the Jungle.* London: Routledge, 1994.

Mirzoeff, Nicholas, ed. *Diaspora and Visual Culture.* London: Routledge, 1999.

Monson, Ingrid. "Doubleness and Jazz Improvisation: Irony, Parody and Ethno-musicology." *Critical Inquiry* 20.2 (1994): 283–313.

Morley, David, and Kuan-Hsing Chen, eds. *Stuart Hall: Critical Dialogues in Cultural Studies*. London: Routledge, 1996.

Mukuna, Kazadi wa. "Creative Practice in African Music: New Perspectives in the Scrutiny of Africanisms in Diaspora." *Black Music Research Journal* 17.2 (1997): 239–50.

Myers, Helen. *Music of Hindu Trinidad: Songs from the India Diaspora*. Chicago, IL: University of Chicago Press, 1998.

Nurse, Keith. "Globalization and Trinidad Carnival: Diaspora, Hybridity and Identity in Global Culture." *Cultural Studies* 13.4 (1999): 661–90.

Owusu, Kwesi, ed. *Black British Culture and Society*. London: Routledge, 1999.

Pacini Hernandez, Deborah. "Sound Systems, World Beat and the Diasporan Identity in Cartagena, Colombia." *Diaspora* 5.3 (1996): 429–66.

Price, Sally. *Maroon Arts: Cultural Vitality in the African Diaspora*. Boston, MA: Beacon Press, 1999.

Regev, Motti. "Present Absentee: Arab Music in Israeli Culture." *Public Culture* 7.2 (1995): 433–45.

Remtulla, Aly, ed. *Memory, (Re)presentation, Fusion: Popular Culture in South Asian Diasporic Communities*. In press.

Roberts, Martin. " 'World Music' and the Global Cultural Economy." *Diaspora* 2.2 (1992): 229–42.

Rutherford, Jonathan, ed. *Identity: Community, Culture, Difference*. London: Lawrence and Wishart, 1990.

Salamone, Frank A., ed. *Art and Culture in Nigeria and the Diaspora*. Williamsburg, VA: Deptartment of Anthropology, College of William and Mary, 1991.

Sharma, Sanjay, John Hutnyk, and Ashwani Sharma, eds. *The Politics of New Asian Dance Music*. London: Zed Press, 1996.

Skrbis, Zlatko. "Making It Tradeable: Videotapes, Cultural Technologies and Diasporas." *Cultural Studies* 12.2 (1998): 265–73.

Slobin, Mark. "Music in Diaspora: The View From Euro-America." *Diaspora* 3.3 (1994): 243–51.

Ukadike, N. Frank. "Reclaiming Images of Women in Films from Africa and the Black Diaspora." *Frontiers – A Journal of Women Studies* 15.1 (1994): 102–22.

Walcott, Rinaldo. "Caribbean Pop Culture in Canada: Or, the Impossibility of Belonging to the Nation." *Small Axe* 5.1 (2000): 123–39.

Winders, James A. "African Musicians in Contemporary Paris: Post-Colonial Culture in Exile." *Contemporary French Civilization* 20.2 (1996): 220–30.

Zheng, Su. "Music Making in Cultural Displacement: The Chinese American Odyssey." *Diaspora* 3.3 (1994): 273–88.

Postscript: Cyberscapes and the Interfacing of Diasporas

Anita Mannur

In this transnational moment it is crucial to examine national constructions of "diaspora," diasporic constructions of "nation," and the often mediating and contradictory boundaries of the two. We are in an era of technospheric space, where dislocated geographical points merge and re-pollinate one another in virtual realms (such as online bulletin boards). As we move from paradigms of geosphere to infosphere,[1] the boundaries of nation and diaspora begin to traverse, re-traverse, inform, and deform one another. Ultimately, the movement of capital across diasporic/national divides creates a liminal territory that is neither *here* nor *there* but not exactly separate from either domain. But how is diaspora, and theorizations thereof, connected with the virtual realm of Web-based interfacing? Specifically, how will national and ethnic communities and affiliations – virtual and physical – be reconfigured by the presence of cyberscapes and the World Wide Web? And more importantly, how will class-based distinctions create new divides? Much talk in recent times about the digital divide and how access to digital media and technologies separates the "haves" from the "have-nots" acquires a certain urgency in this context. Clearly, some of these ways we understand nation and diaspora are already mediated through cyber and digital scapes.

In the weeks leading up to the World Cup Cricket Tournament[2] hosted in England in June 1999, several news publications distributed to South Asian communities in North America regularly ran feature articles on the various cricketers, pending games, speculations as to who would win, by what margins, and so forth. While cricket fans everywhere know that the fervor surrounding the World Cup is by no means a new phenomenon, the interfacing of cricket and the World Wide Web significantly altered the tenor of World Cup mania. Several Internet websites,[3] devoted exclusively to the coverage of World Cup '99, provided 24-hour access to the latest information about the games. Like the various print publications, these internet websites provided information about each game, team profiles and statistics, but they were also able to provide information about each player, histories of each team's performance, and commemorative memorabilia on sale; most importantly, some of the Web pages provided live coverage of selected cricket matches, including the all-important matches between India and Pakistan,[4] and the final matches.

For diasporic South Asian, West Indian, and African (as well as many other) viewers, particularly those located in non-metropolitan centers in North America,[5] it became possible to watch cricket games live and uninterrupted from a library in Amherst, Massachusetts, at home in Madison, Wisconsin, or in cyber-cafés around the world – assuming that one could actually log on to the Websites that were inundated and over-extended by cricket fans – simply by logging on to one's computer. For those among us with less than state-of-the-art Web browsers, it was possible to follow the games "live" by watching the cyber-scoreboards that would be instantly updated simply by clicking on the "Refresh" option on the Web browser. Access to the World Wide Web allowed certain diasporic communities – middle- to upper-middle class – to connect with the homeland's[6] activity, albeit in a virtual sense, in ways that have not been possible in the past. The example of the World Cup cricket phenomenon on the Web is (but one in a list of many examples) symptomatic of a growing trend of middle-class diasporic communities turning to cyber-technology in order to connect with the homeland, or activities associated with the homeland.

In my own example as a multiply located person of middle-class background – I am born of Indian parents, lived in Malaysia, Papua New Guinea, and Australia before moving to the United States – access to the World Wide Web has "centered" my life. Having spent my formative childhood and adolescent years in Port Moresby, Papua New Guinea, I took it as given that leaving my "home" in Moresby would be permanent; the faces I had grown up loving and hating would eventually fade into memories. But as a good friend from New York recently remarked to me, it is amazing how I, who had gone to school thousands of miles away in Papua New Guinea, have been able to maintain such a close connection with multiple friends from high school, whereas he has barely run across any of his friends from his childhood and adolescence in Florida. In part, it is the sense of unbridgeable distance that binds those of us away from Papua New Guinea. In my years in the United States I rarely meet people who have heard of Port Moresby, the city where I was raised, let alone been there. There is thus perhaps more of a sense of urgency for those of us who lived in PNG to keep those bonds alive. I grew up amid rather unique circumstances – most of my friends at my international school (privileged though we were) came to PNG from somewhere else. While there were a few Papua New Guinean students in my graduating class of 63 persons, there were also people who identified as Finnish, British, American, Indian, Kiwi, Australian, Fijian, Samoan, Ghanaian, Zambian, Filipino, Taiwanese, Thai, Sri Lankan, Indonesian, Dutch, German, Japanese, Korean, Iranian, Bangladeshi, Canadian, and Guyanese, and yet more than half of them had never lived in their "nation of origin." Even today, many are not in their "home nation," living instead in Boston, Amherst, Manila, Colombo, Atlanta, Pittsburgh, Sydney, Surabaya, Auckland, Kuala Lumpur, Perth, New York, London. Many of us have ended up in the "West" – it seemed the "natural" endpoint. But in many ways it is also true that these spaces are diasporic switching points for many of us. We have always been in movement, and for many of us it is extremely difficult to understand what is meant by the question, "but where are you from?" and "where are you going?"

One way for many of us to keep track of our multiple border crossings has been through an Internet forum (http://www.5logic.com/personal/nik/pomhi/). With a current membership base of about 734, the members range in age from fifty to eighteen and live in all corners of the world. The only thing we have in common is having lived in Port Moresby. In many ways, Port Moresby was a place where strands of Asian, African, and Middle Eastern diasporas converged; through the possibilities of cyber-interfacing, it has become apparent that many of us constitute a new diaspora – a Papua New Guinean diaspora. For many of us the dream of "returning" exists, but for most it is only a dream and does not seem likely to ever become a reality. For this group of individuals the World Wide Web has served as a way to keep those webs of affiliation spinning. We can feel that we were part of a community that is not in danger of becoming an ossified memory. The World Wide Web in this example has legitimized a generation of memories of a particular place – Port Moresby – and a particular time – the 1980s and early 1990s. It has allowed people who never dreamed of being connected with each other after embarking on a flight out of Jackson's International Airport in Moresby to feel part of a community that is alive and well – albeit in cyberspace.

Diasporic zones of alliance (sexual, gender, and otherwise) abound in virtual terrains accessible to middle- and upper-class communities. A notable example is the Malaysian Gay and Lesbian organization *Suara, the Malaysian Gay and Lesbian Voice*, a San Francisco-based organization. A note about their mission reads: "[Suara] is reaching many Malaysian gays and lesbians everywhere and uniting them with us. It is truly a feeling of belonging and connecting with our own kind, not only being Malaysian but being homosexual too."[7] "Everywhere," however, is not restricted to communities of diasporic Malaysians; message boards and chat rooms linked to this website made it possible for queer Malaysians within the geographic borders of

Malaysia to build communities through this website. Through the networks created by diasporic affiliations, like-minded queers located within the geopolitical borders of Malaysia are able to forge communal links in new and exciting ways. Within an economy of state surveillance of sexuality, and an aggressive state-sanctioned insistence on heteronormativity, queer Malaysians are afforded new possibilities to explore same-sex desire without necessarily having to leave home *per se*. This attempt to build community in diasporic (if also virtual) zones also leads to changes within the nation-state and demands a rethinking of the explicitly heteromasculinist hierarchization that always subordinates diaspora to the nation-state within gendered and sexuated terms.

The important role that diasporic communities play in reconfiguring feminist and queer political movements in the "homeland" is not a recent development. For example, Pratibha Parmar's influential film about South Asian gay and lesbian communities in Britain, North America, and South Asia, *Khush*, addresses how diasporic South Asian gay and lesbian movements in North America and Britain reconfigure the contours of gay and lesbian subjectivities in India. One gay South Asian male interviewed in the film notes that North American-based queer publications such as *Trikone* magazine intervene in vitally constitutive ways into the articulation of a queer Indian-based identity. This is not to suggest that the West is the liberatory space that allows for a freer celebration of non-heteronormative sexualities,[8] but rather to add to a critical conversation that scrutinizes how and where diasporic interventions mobilize movements "at home" in significant ways.

Scholars such as Gopinath and Manalansan are concerned with understanding the complex relations of nation-state, diaspora, home, homeland, and queerness. How nostalgia for the "homeland" – real or imagined – signifies for queer individuals and communities is a question increasingly asked by theorists working on issues of queerness and diaspora. Queer diasporic subjects grapple with this question by examining the myriad significations and contestations of queer diaspora among different ethnic affiliations – Korean, South Asian, Chinese, Southeast Asian, for example. As literary critic David Eng remarks, "issues of home are particularly vexing" for queer diasporic subjects, as many are literally ejected from such spaces.[9] Such subjects experience deep ambivalence towards the notion of home, rather than experiencing it in nostalgic terms as a safe space of refuge or shelter and desiring return. What happens when the space of the home intersects in vital ways with the notion of a homeland elsewhere? In the context of supposed nostalgia for the homeland, what are the different ways in which this nostalgia can be, and indeed should be, rethought in the context of queer diasporic subjectivity? How can we begin to understand the layering of multiple subjectivities that tenuously link queer diasporic individuals here and communities with a homeland over there? Clearly, or *queerly* as the case may be, thinking about home and (post)memories of homeland is an arduous, complicated, and ambivalent process for queer individuals and communities. In contexts where the site/sight of home does not allow for an easy entry into a comfortably safe zone of sexual alterity, romanticized metaphors of looking back to a past over "there" and to a future "here" need to be interrogated.

In analyzing the possibilities to forge cyber-alliances, however, I would caution against a premature celebration of what technospheres can offer. At the same time that it allows people such as myself to stay connected with places and peoples, it is also available to me because I can afford to own a PC and because I live in an area that gives me easy access to the World Wide Web and other forms of digital technology. I am on the "correct" side of the digital divide and have the luxury of indulging my nostalgia for childhood and adolescence.[10] There are many others, including persons in Papua New Guinea – the place that we all miss – who do not have the option of indulging in this type of activity because Internet access is exceedingly difficult to come by. While there are many contexts in which technospheric space is used for positive ends to promote a better, more inclusive version of the nation and its constituent parts, it is also true that such space can be deployed for markedly different political ends. At the same time that the Web is used by progressive diasporic groups that challenge concepts of nationhood and identity based on state-endorsed heterosexualities, such as Suara or the San Francisco-based South Asian group Trikone, to disseminate information about their organizations and to build community within specific diasporic settings,[11] cyberspace can also be used to forge links among politically reactionary, or even chauvinistic groups.[12] Both the Hindu Student Council and Global Hindu Electronic Network endorse the website www.freeindia.org that posits a notion of Indianness that symmetrically aligns itself with Hinduism, excluding Christian, Muslim, Sikh, Jain, and Parsi-based religio-ethnic affiliations from their vision of Indianness. That this website is created to consolidate and reaffirm communal links among diasporic Hindu Indians is obvious. The problem inheres in the fact that they posit this communal link by alluding to a "shared" concept of Indianness that is rigidly Hindu and patriarchal.

The Eelam website, for example, focuses on disseminating information about the anti-Tamil atrocities committed by the Sri Lankan government. Focused on creating a homeland (Eelam) for Tamils, located on the northeastern part of the Sri Lankan island,[13] this website overtly seeks the financial and ideological endorsement of the Tamil diaspora – Sri Lankan or otherwise. A section titled "Eelamweb: Our People Around the World Towards Tamil Eelam!" explains that "the freedom struggle of Tamil Eelam is not limited to Tamil Eelam alone. Without the help of Tamils spread out around the world, it would become an uphill task for the Tamils in Eelam to overcome the oppression of the Sri Lankan government. It is the responsibility of each Tamil worldwide to ensure that the rights of the Tamils in Tamil Eelam are won."[14] Note the repeated appeal to Tamils: Tamils worldwide, not just the Tamils in Sri Lanka, are asked to join in the struggle to reconfigure the geographic parameters of Sri Lanka. As but one instance of many, the strategic deployment of cyberspace by this group demands that we must thoroughly interrogate how and why cyberspace articulates specific – if at times chauvinistic and masculinist – notions of nationhood and patriotism.

These comments are not intended to be exhaustive – rather they are tentative musings on how and why we need to think about the era of technosphere and cyberscapes when thinking about diaspora and its relation to the national politic. As the world economy becomes increasingly linked with digital economies, and as companies like WorldCom glibly assert that "Generation D^{SM}" is one that is "totally at ease with the electronic flow of modern life" and in contrast to preceding generations – Baby Boomers, Gen X and Gen Y – Generation D^{SM} is "not characterized by one's age, but by one's attitude,"[15] it becomes incumbent on us to think how the parameters of nationhood will be altered by new configurations of global capital, the creation of new types of niche marketing, and how new class divides will emerge and how this might challenge basic assumptions about "home" and national belonging.

Notes

1   Paul Virilio, *The Virilio Reader*, ed. James Der Derian; trans. Michael Degener, Lauren Osepchuk, and James Der Derian (Oxford: Blackwell, 1998).
2   Held approximately every four years, the World Cup Cricket Tournament is the most highly anticipated event for cricket fans worldwide. Unlike many other international sports gatherings, only a select group of nations (notably, former "possessions" of the British empire) are invited to participate in the tournament. In 1999 a record twelve nations participated in the tournament – Australia, Bangladesh, England, Kenya, India, New Zealand, Pakistan, Scotland, South Africa, Sri Lanka, West Indies, Zimbabwe – with Australia winning the World Cup for the second time.
3   See http://www.khel.com (Khel in Hindi means sport/game) and http://www.cybercricket.com (August 1, 1999).
4   A symptom and legacy of the colonial history emanating from the Partition of 1947 that divided India and Pakistan into two separate nations, the Indian and Pakistani cricket teams have been rivals for many years.
5   This formulation applies less to diasporic South Asians in Australia and Britain

who would have access to the games via television coverage; communities in Toronto, New York City, and Los Angeles had greater access, as public screenings of select games were made possible in these cities.

6   I evoke the term "homeland" not to argue for an essentialized, binary definition of identity that would clearly separate between a home (there) and an away (here); in this use, it is deployed strategically to comment on the way cricket is consumed so as to engender these feelings of a *here* and a *there*. For critical work that analyzes the intersections of race, nationalism, and cricket, see the following: C. L. R. James, *Beyond A Boundary* (New York: Pantheon, 1983); Manthia Diawara, "Englishness and Blackness: Cricket as Discourse on Colonialism," *Callaloo* 13.4 (1990); Arjun Appadurai, "Playing with Modernity: The Decolonization of Indian Cricket," in *Modernity at Large: Cultural Dimensions of Globalization* (Minneapolis: University of Minnesota Press, 1996), pp. 89–113; Grant Farred, "The Nation in White: Cricket in a Post-Apartheid South Africa," *Social Text* 15.1 (spring 1997): 9–32; and also by Farred, "The Maple Man: How Cricket Made A Postcolonial Intellectual," *Rethinking C. L. R. James*, ed. Farred (Oxford: Blackwell, 1996), pp. 165–86; Qadri Ismail, "Batting Against the Break: On Cricket, Nationalism, and the Swashbuckling Sri Lankans," *Social Text* 15.1 (spring 1997): 33–56; Neil Lazarus, "Cricket, Modernism, National Culture: The Case of C. L. R. James," *Nationalism and Cultural Practice in the Postcolonial World* (Cambridge: Cambridge University Press, 1999), pp. 144–95. An interesting take on cricket emerges in the recent Bollywood hit, *Lagaan* (director Ashutosh Gowarkiar, 2001).

7   *Suara, the Malaysian Gay and Lesbian Voice*, http://www.best.com/~aloha/mglc.

8   On similar cautionary critiques, see Gayatri Gopinath, "On Fire," *GLQ* 4.4 (1998): 631–6 and "Homo-Economics: Queer Sexualities in a Transnational Frame," in *Burning Down the House: Recycling Domesticity*, ed. Rosemary Marangoly George (Boulder, CO: Westview/Harper Collins, 1998), pp. 117, 122 n. 29.

9   David Eng, "Out Here and Over There: Queerness and Diaspora in Asian American Studies," *Social Text* 52–3 (1997): 31.

10 See, for instance, *Technicolor: Race, Technology and Everyday Life*. Ed. Alondra Nelson and Thuy Linh N. Tu. New York: New York University Press, 2001.

11 Nayan Shah's essay, "Sexuality, Identity and the Uses of History," in *Q&A: Queer in Asian America* (David L. Eng and Alice V. Hom, eds.; Philadelphia, PA: Temple University Press, 1998) describes how various South Asian queer organizations disseminate information in a global context (see pp. 150–1). Note also the numerous bulletin boards and e-groups, such as Khushnet and SAWNET. On the latter, see the online publication by Radhika Gajjala, "Cyborg Diaspora and Virtual Imagined Community: Studying SAWNET," published in *Cybersociology* 6 (August 1999) ⟨http://ernie.bgsu.edu/%7Eradhik/sanov/html⟩.

12 Amit Rai, "India On-line: Electronic Bulletin Boards and the Construction of a Diasporic Hindu Identity," *Diaspora* 4.1 (1995): 31–57.

13 For a salient discussion of eelamweb.com, and other Web pages slated to engender a connection between "lived-space" and "web-space" in the context of the Tamil demand for a separate homeland, see Pradeep Jaganath "eelam.com:

Place, Nation and Imagi-Nation in Cyberspace," *Public Culture* 10.3 (1998): 515–28. See also Amit Rai, "Indian On-line: Electronic Bulletin Boards and the Construction of a Diasporic Hindu Identity," *Diaspora* 4.1 (1995): 31–57.

14   Eelam webpage, http://www.eelamweb.com/people. Date accessed: February 8, 2002.

15   Worldcom webpage, http://www.worldcom.com/about/generation_D. Date accessed: February 8, 2002.

Additional Readings
on Diaspora
and Cyberelectronics

Gajjala, Radhika. "Cyborg Diaspora and Virtual Imagined Community: Studying SAWNET." *Cybersociology* 6 (1999): 1–16.

Jain, Ravindra K. "Reality and Representation: Aspects of the Electronic Media in Contemporary Indian Society and Diaspora." *Sociological Bulletin* 47.2 (1998): 167–84.

Jeganathan, Pradeep. "eelam.com: Place, Nation and Imagi-Nation in Cyberspace." *Public Culture* 10.3 (1998): 515–28.

Kadende, Rose Marie. "Interpreting Language and Cultural Discourse: Internet Communication Among Burundians in the Diaspora." *Africa Today* 47.2 (2000): 121–48.

Lal, Vinay. "The Politics of History on the Internet: Cyber-Diasporic Hinduism and the North American Hindu Diaspora." *Diaspora* 8.2 (1999): 137–72.

Nelson, Diane M. "Maya Hackers and the Cyberspatialized Nation-State: Modernity, Ethnostalgia and a Lizard Queen in Guatemala." *Cultural Anthropology* 11.3 (1996): 287–308.

Rai, Amit. "India On-line: Electronic Bulletin Boards and the Construction of a Diasporic Hindu Identity." *Diaspora* 4.1 (1995): 31–57.

Select Bibliography of Works on Diaspora

Compiled by Anita Mannur

This is only a partial bibliography and by no means an exhaustive list of all the work on diaspora. It comprise titles of selected works published after 1990. Although some of these titles are indexed in the most recent version of the MLA Bibliography and Sociofile, many are not on either database. I found many of the items here by sifting manually through indexes and volumes of several journals, including *Public Culture*, *GLQ*, *Diaspora*, *genders*, *positions*, *Social Text*, *Critical Inquiry*, *Cultural Studies*, *Cultural Anthropology*, *Cultural Critique*, *Socialist Review*, *Boundary 2*, *Transition*, *Amerasia Journal*, *Quebec Studies*, *MELUS*, *Textual Practice*, and *Callaloo*. Literary studies of specific novels, doctoral dissertations, book reviews, and films are generally not included here. I thank Jana Evans Braziel, Elizabeth Fitzpatrick, and Shobana Mannur for helping to compile this bibliography.

Abodunrin, Femi. "Ayi Kwei Armah and the Origins of the African Diaspora." *Journal of Humanities* 14 (2000): 63–98.

Abu Duhou, Ibtisam. "Writing the Palestinian Diaspora through Poetry." *Span: Journal of the South Pacific Association for Commonwealth Literature & Language Studies* 34–5 (1992–3): 71–81.

Acosta-Belen, Edna. "Beyond Island Boundaries: Ethnicity, Gender and Cultural Revitalization." *Callaloo* 15.4 (1992): 979–98.

Adeleke, Tunde. "Black Americans, Africa and History: A Reassessment of the Pan-African and Identity Paradigms." *Western Journal of Black Studies* 22.3 (1998): 182–94.

Aguilar-San Juan, Karin, ed. *The State of Asian America: Activism and Resistance in the 1990s*. Boston, MA: South End Press, 1994.

Akenson, Donald Harman. "The Historiography of English-speaking Canada and the Concept of Diaspora: A Skeptical Appreciation." *Canadian Historical Review* 76 (1995): 377–409.

—— *The Irish Diaspora: A Primer*. Belfast: University of Belfast Press, 1998.

Akyeampong, Emmanuel. "Africans in the Diaspora: The Diaspora and Africa." *African Affairs* 99 (2000): 183–215.

Allahar, Anton L. "Popular Culture and Racialisation of Political Consciousness in Trinidad & Tobago." *Wadabagei: A Journal of the Caribbean and Its Diaspora* 1.2 (1998): 1–41.

Alpers, Edward. "The African Diaspora in the Northwestern Indian Ocean: Reconsideration of an Old Problem, New Directions for Research." *Comparative Studies of South Asia, Africa and the Middle East* 17.2 (1997): 62–81.

Altman, Dennis. "Rupture or Continuity? The Internationalization of Gay Identities." *Social Text* 48 (1996): 77–94.

Altman, Patrick and Nancy L. Green. *Jewish Workers in the Modern Diaspora.* Berkeley: University of California Press, 1998.

Alvarez, Sonia E., Evelina Dagnino, and Arturo Escobar, eds. *Cultures of Politics/ Politics of Cultures: Re-visioning Latin American Social Movements.* Boulder, CO: Westview Press, 1998.

Amit-Talai, Vered and Helena Wulff, eds. *Youth Cultures: A Cross Cultural Perspective.* London: Routledge, 1995.

Anagnostu, Georgios. "Anthropological Constructions of Greek American Ethnicity." *Journal of the Hellenic Diaspora* 23.2 (1997): 61–83.

Anderson, A. *Caribbean Immigrants: A Socio-Demographic Profile.* Toronto: Canadian Scholars Press, 1993.

Anderson, Benedict. "Exodus." *Critical Inquiry* 20.2 (1994): 314–27.

Andrews, David R. *Sociocultural Perspectives on Language Change in Diaspora: Soviet Immigrants in the United States.* Amsterdam: Benjamins, 1999.

Ang, Ien. "To Be or Not to Be Chinese: Diaspora, Culture and Postmodern Ethnicity." *Southeast Asian Journal of Social Science* 21.1 (1993): 1–17.

——"The Differential Politics of Chineseness." *Southeast Asian Journal of Social Science* 22.1 (1994): 72–9.

Ang, Ien and Jon Stratton. "Asianising Australia: Notes Towards A Critical Transnationalism in Cultural Studies." *Cultural Studies* 10.1 (1996): 16–36.

——"Can One Say No To Chineseness? Pushing the Limits of the Diasporic Paradigm." *Boundary 2.* 25.3 (1998): 223–42.

Ang-Lygate, Magdalene. "Charting the Space of (Un)location: On Theorizing Diaspora." *Black British Feminism.* Ed. Heidi Safia Mirza. London: Routledge, 1997.

Angelo, Michael. *The Sikh Diaspora: Tradition and Change in an Immigrant Community.* New York: Garland Press, 1997.

Anthias, Flora. "Evaluating 'Diaspora': Beyond Ethnicity?" *Sociology* 32.3 (1998): 557–80.

——"Beyond Unities of Identity in High Modernity." *Identities: Global Studies in Culture and Power* 6.1 (1999): 121–44.

Anwar, Muhammad. *Between Cultures: Continuity and Change in the Lives of Young Asians.* London: Routledge, 1998.

Anzaldúa, Gloria. *Borderlands: La Frontera The New Mestiza.* San Francisco, CA: Aunt Lute Books, 1987.

Appadurai, Arjun. *Modernity at Large: Cultural Dimensions of Globalization.* Minneapolis: University of Minnesota Press, 1996.

Appiah, Kwame Anthony. "Cosmopolitan Patriots." *Critical Inquiry* 23.3 (1997): 617–39.

Apter, Andrew. "Herskovits's Heritage: Rethinking Syncretism in the African Diaspora." *Diaspora* 1.3 (1991): 235–60.

Apter, Emily. *Continental Drift: From National Characters to Virtual Subjects.* Chicago, IL: University of Chicago Press, 1999.

Ards, Angela. "The Diaspora Comes to Dartmouth." *American Theatre* 15.5 (1998): 50–2.

Aronowitz, Stanley. "The Double Bind: America and the African Diaspora." *Transition* 6.1 (1996): 222–35.

Arrighi, Giovanni. "The Rise of East Asia: World Systemic and Regional Aspects." *International Journal of Sociology and Social Policy* 16.7–8 (1996): 6–44.

Arrowsmith, Aidan. "Debating Diasporic Identity: Nostalgia, (Post) Nationalism, 'Critical Traditionalism.' " *Irish Studies Review* 7.2 (1999): 173–81.

Arthur, John A. *Invisible Sojourners: African Immigrant Diaspora in the United States.* Westport, CT: Praeger, 2000.

Arthur, Paul. "Diasporan Intervention in International Affairs: Irish America as a Case Study." *Diaspora* 1.2 (1991): 143–62.

Asher, Mukul G. "The Indian Diaspora: Strengthening the Economic Base." *Population Review* 40.1–2 (1996): 34–42.

Averill, Gage. " '*Mezanmi, Kouman Nou Ye?* My Friends, How Are You?': Musical Constructions of the Haitian Transnation." *Diaspora* 3.3 (1994): 253–69.

Azevedo, Mario. *Africana Studies: A Survey of Africa and the African Diaspora.* Durham, NC: Carolina Academic Press, 1993.

Azria, Regine. "The Diaspora-Community – Tradition Paradigms of Jewish Identity: A Reappraisal." *Sociological Papers* 6 (1998): 21–32.

Bacon, Jean. *Lifelines: Community, Family and Assimilation Among Asian Indian Immigrants.* New York: Oxford University Press, 1996.

Baily, John. "The Role of Music in Three British Muslim Communities." *Diaspora* 4.1 (1995): 77–87.

Bakalian, Anny. *Armenian-Americans: From Being to Feeling Armenian.* New Brunswick, NJ: Transaction Publishers, 1993.

Balakrishnan, Gopal, ed. *Mapping the Nation.* London: Verso, 1996.

Baldock, Cora Vellekoop. "Migrants and Their Parents: Caregiving from a Distance." *Journal of Family Issues* 21.2 (2000): 205–24.

Balibar, Etienne. "Is European Citizenship Possible?" *Public Culture* 8.2 (1996): 355–76.

Ballal, Prateeti Punja. "Illiberal Masala: The Diasporic Distortions of Mira Nair and Dinesh D'Souza." *Weber Studies* 15.1 (1998): 95–104.

Ballard, Roger, ed. *Desh Pardesh.* London: Hurst, 1994.

Banerjea, Koushik. "Sonic Diaspora and Its Dissident Footfalls." *Postcolonial Studies* 1.3 (1998): 389–400.

—— "Sounds of Whose Underground? The Fine Tuning of Diaspora in an Age of Mechanical Reproduction." *Theory, Culture and Society* 17.3 (2000): 64–79.

Bar-Kochva, Bezalel. *Pseudo-Hecataeus, On the Jews: Legitimizing the Jewish Diaspora.* Berkeley: University of California Press, 1996.

Barber, Pauline Gardner. "Transnationalism and the Politics of 'Home' for Philippine Domestic Workers." *Anthropologica* 39.1–2 (1997): 39–52.

—— "Agency in Philippine Women's Labour Migration and Provisional Diaspora." *Women's Studies International Forum* 23.4 (2000): 399–411.

Barbieri, William A. "Group Rights and the Muslim Diaspora." *Human Rights Quarterly* 21.4 (1999): 907–26.

Barkan, Elazar and Marie-Denise Shelton, eds. *Borders, Exiles, Diasporas.* Stanford, CA: Stanford University Press, 1998.

Basch, Linda, Nina Glick Schiller, and Christina Szanton Blanc, eds. *Nations Unbound: Transnational Projects, Postcolonial Predicaments and Deterritiorialized Nation-States.* New York: Gordon and Breach, 1994.

Batra, Roger. "South of the Border: Mexican Reflections on Distorted Images." *Telos* 103 (1995): 143–8.

Baubock, Rainer. "Sharing History and Future? Time Horizons of Democratic Membership in an Age of Migration." *Constellations* 4.3 (1998): 320–45.

Baucom, Ian. "Charting the 'Black Atlantic'." *Postmodern Culture* 8.1 (1997).

Baumann, Gerd. *Contesting Culture: Discourses of Identity in Multi-Ethnic London.* Cambridge: Cambridge University Press, 1996.

Baumann, Martin. "Conceptualizing Diaspora: The Preservation of Religious Identity in Foreign Parts, Exemplified by Hindu Communities Outside India." *Temenos* 31.19–35 (1995).

—— "Diaspora: Genealogies of Semantics and Transcultural Comparison." *Numen – International Review for the History of Religions* 47.3 (2000): 313–37.

Beauchamp-Byrd, Myra J. and M. Franklin Sirmans, eds. *Transforming the Crown: African, Asian and Caribbean Artists in Britain, 1966–1996.* New York: Franklin H. Williams Caribbean Cultural Center/African Diaspora Institute, 1997.

Beevi, Mariam. "The Passing of Literary Traditions: The Figure of the Woman From Vietnamese Nationalism to Vietnamese American Transnationalism." *Amerasia Journal* 23.2 (1997): 27–53.

Behdad, Ali. "Nationalism and Immigration to the United States." *Diaspora* 6.2 (1997): 155–78.

Beinin, Joel. "Exile and Political Activism: The Egyptian–Jewish Communists in Paris, 1950–59." *Diaspora* 2.1 (1992): 73–94.

—— *The Dispersion of Egyptian Jewry: Culture, Politics and the Formation of a Modern Diaspora.* Berkeley: University of California Press, 1998.

Beit-Hallahmi, Benjamin. "Naming Norms and Identity Choices in Israel." *Sociological Papers* 6 (1998): 191–205.

Berlant, Lauren. "The Theory of Infantile Citizenship." *Public Culture* 5.3 (1993): 395–410.

Berrouet-Oriol, Robert and Rober Fournier. "L'Émergence des écritures migrantes et métisses au Québec." *Quebec Studies* 14 (1992): 7–22.

Best, Curwen. "Ideology, Sound, Image and Caribbean Music Videos." *Wadabagei: A Journal of the Caribbean and Its Diaspora* 3.1 (2000): 77–109.

Bethel, Elizabeth Rauh. "Images of Haiti: The Construction of an Afro-American *Lieu de Mémoire*." *Callaloo* 15.3 (1992): 827–41.

Beyer, Peter. "The City and Beyond as Dialogue: Negotiating Religious Authenticity in Global Society." *Social Compass* 45.1 (1998): 67–79.

Bhabha, Jacqueline. "Embodied Rights: Gender Persecution, State Sovereignty and Refugees." *Public Culture* 9.1 (1996): 3–32.

Bhana, Hershini. "Splitting Open Wide: Letters of Exile." *Socialist Review* 24.4 (1994): 109–49.

Bhatia, Nandi. "Women, Homelands, and the Indian Diaspora." *Centennial Review* 42.3 (1998): 511–26.

Bhatt, Chetan and Parita Mukta. "Hindutva in the West: Mapping the Antinomies of Diaspora Nationalism." *Ethnic and Racial Studies* 23.3 (2000): 407–41.

Bhattacharjee, Anannya. "The Habit of Ex-Nomination: Nation, Woman and the Indian Immigrant Bourgeoise." *Public Culture* 5.1 (1992): 19–44.

Birbalsingh, Frank. *From Pillar to Post: The Indo Caribbean Diaspora*. Toronto: Tsar, 1997.

Bjorklund, Ulf. "Armenia Remembered and Remade: Evolving Issues in a Diaspora." *Ethnos* 58.3–4 (1993): 335–60.

Black, Michael and Dick Hebdige. "Women's Soccer and the Irish Diaspora." *Peace Review* 11.4 (1999): 531–7.

Blackwood, Evelyn and Saskia E. Wieringa, eds. *Female Desires: Same-Sex Relations and Transgender Practices Across Cultures*. New York: Columbia University Press, 1999.

Blakely, Allison. *Blacks in the Dutch World: The Evolution of Racial Imagery in a Modern Society*. Bloomington: Indiana University Press, 1993.

—— "Historical Ties Among Suriname, the Netherlands Antilles, Aruba and the Netherlands." *Callaloo* 21.3 (1998): 472–8.

Bolt, Paul J. "Looking to the Diaspora: The Overseas Chinese and China's Economic Development 1978–1994." *Diaspora* 5.3 (1996): 476–96.

Boscagli, Maurizia. "The Resisting Screen: Multicultural Politics in a Global Perspective." *Diaspora* 5.3 (1996): 497–508.

Bottomley, Gillian. "Culture, Ethnicity and the Politics/Poetics of Representation." *Diaspora* 1.3 (1991): 303–20.

—— "Anthropologists and the Rhizomatic Study of Migration." *Australian Journal of Anthropology* 9.1 (1998): 31–44.

Bowser, Pearl. "Testing the Waters: African Diaspora Filmmaking and Identity." *Wide Angle – A Quarterly Journal of Film History, Theory & Criticism* 17.1–4 (1995): 193–6.

Boyarin, Daniel and Jonathan Boyarin. "Diaspora: Generational Ground of Jewish Identity." *Critical Inquiry* 19.4 (1993): 693–725.

Boyce Davies, Carole, Savory Fido, eds. *Out of the Kumbla: Caribbean Women and Literature*. Trenton, NJ: Africa World Press, 1990.

Boyce Davies, Carole and Savory Fido, and Molara Ogundipe-Leslie, eds. *Black Women's Diasporas, Writing New Worlds*. London: Pluto Press, 1994.

—— eds. *Moving Beyond Boundaries*. Washington Square: New York University Press, 1995.

Boym, Svetlana. "On Diasporic Intimacy: Ilya Kabakov's Installations and Immigrant Homes." *Critical Inquiry* 24.2 (1998): 498–524.

Bracks, Lean'tin L. *Writings on Black Women of the Diaspora: History, Language, and Identity*. New York: Garland, 1998.

Bradley, Joseph. "Facets of the Irish Diaspora: 'Irishness' in 20th Century Scotland." *Irish Journal of Sociology* 6 (1996): 79–100.

Brah, Avtar. *Cartographies of Diaspora*. London: Routledge, 1996.

—— "The Scent of Memory: Strangers, Our Own, and Others." *Feminist Review* 61 (1999): 4–26.

Brandon, George. *Santería From Africa to the New World: The Dead Sell Memories*. Bloomington: Indiana University Press, 1993.

Braziel, Jana Evans. " 'Becoming-Woman-dog-goldfish-flower-molecular' and the 'non-becoming-Québécois': Dissolution and Other Deleuzian Traversals in Flora Balzano's *Soigne ta chute*." *Tessera: Feminist Interventions on Writing and Culture* 24 (1998): 125–34.

—— "Islam, Individualism and *Dévoilement* in the Works of Out El Kouloub and Assia Djebar." *Journal of North African Studies* 4.5 (1999): 81–101.

—— "Jamaica Kincaid's 'In the Night' – Jablesse, Obeah, and Diasporic Alterrains in *At the Bottom of the River*." *Re-Thinking Postcoloniality*. Special Issue of *Journal X: A Journal in Culture and Criticism* 5.2 (2002): 79–104.

—— "Jamaica Kincaid's *Alterbiographic* Transmutations of Genre in Diaspora: Reading 'Biography of a Dress' and *Autobiography of My Mother*." *A/B: Auto/Biography Studies*, forthcoming.

Brennan, Timothy. "Controlling Terms: Originality in African Diasporic Studies." *College Literature* 24.3 (1997): 152–7.

Brinker-Gabler, Gisela and Sidonie Smith, eds. *Writing New Identities: Gender, Nation, and Immigration in Contemporary Europe*. Minneapolis: University of Minnesota Press, 1997.

Browning, Barbara. *Infectious Rhythm: Metaphor of Contagion and the Spread of African Culture*. London: Routledge, 1998.

Bun, Chan-Kwok and Tong Chee Kiong. "Modelling Culture Contact and Chinese Ethnicity in Thailand." *Southeast Asian Journal of Social Science* 23.1 (1995): 1–12.

Burlet, Stacey and Helen Reid. "Cooperation and Conflict: The South Asian Diaspora after Ayodhya." *New Community* 21.4 (1995): 587–97.

Bush, Barbara. "History, Memory, Myth? Reconstructing the History (or Histories) of Black Women in the African Diaspora." *Nature, Society, and Thought* 9.4 (1996): 419–45.

Byron, M. *The Unfinished Cycle: Post-War Migration from the Caribbean to Britain*. Avebury: Aldershot, 1994.

Byron, M. and Condon, S. "A Comparative Study of Caribbean Migration to Britain and France Towards a Context-Dependent Explanation." *Transactions of the Institute of British Geographers* 21.1 (1996): 91–104.

Calliste, A. "Women of 'Exceptional Merit': Immigration of Caribbean Nurses to Canada." *Canadian Journal of Women and the Law* 6 (1993): 85–102.

Campa, Ramón de la. "The Latino Diaspora in the United States: Sojourns from a Cuban Past." *Public Culture* 6.2 (1994): 293–317.

Campbell, D. *National Deconstruction: Violence, Identity and Justice in Bosnia*. Minneapolis: University of Minnesota Press, 1998.

Captain-Hidalgo, Yvonne. *Writing the Diaspora Experience*. Boston, MA: William Monroe Trotter Institute, University of Massachusetts, 1993.

Carter, Marina. *Voices From Indenture: Experiences of Indian Migrants in the British Empire.* London: Leicester University Press, 1996.

Castles, Stephen. "Italians in Australia: Building a Multicultural Society on the Pacific Rim." *Diaspora* 1.1 (1991): 45–66.

Castronovo, Russ. "'As to Nation, I Belong to None': Ambivalence, Diaspora, and Frederick Douglass." *ATQ* 9 (1995): 245–60.

Catanese, Anthony. *Haitians: Migration and Diaspora.* Boulder, CO: Westview Press, 1999.

Caucci, Frank. "Topoi de la transculture dans l'imaginaire italo-québécois." *Quebec Studies* 15 (1993): 41–50.

Cha-Jua, Sundiata-Keita. "C. L. R. James, Blackness, and the Making of a Neo-Marxist Diasporan Historiography." *Nature, Society and Thought* 11.1 (1998): 53–89.

Chakraborty, Dipesh. "Reconstructing Liberalism? Notes Toward A Conversation Between Area Studies and Diaspora Studies." *Public Culture* 10.3 (1998): 457–81.

Chambers, Iain. "A Stranger in the House." *Communal/Plural* 6.1 (1998): 33–49.

Chan, Kwok Bun. "A Family Affair: Migration, Dispersal, and the Emergent Identity of the Chinese Cosmopolitan." *Diaspora* 6.2 (1997): 195–213.

Chan, Kwok Bun and Louis Jacques Dorais. "Family, Identity, and the Vietnamese Diaspora: The Quebec Experience." *Sojourn: Journal of Social Issues in Southeast Asia* 13.2 (1998): 285–308.

Chan, Stephen. "What is This Thing Called a Chinese Diaspora?" *Contemporary Review* 274.1597 (1999): 81–3.

Chapin, Wesley D. "The Turkish Diaspora in Germany." *Diaspora* 5.2 (fall 1996): 275–301.

Charles, Carolle. "Gender and Politics in Contemporary Haiti: The Duvalierist State, Transnationalism, and the Emergence of a New Feminism (1980–1990)." *Feminist Studies* 21.1 (1995): 135–64.

Charme, Stuart L. "Varieties of Authenticity in Contemporary Jewish Identity." *Jewish Social Studies* 6.2 (2000): 133–55.

Cheah, Pheng. "Given Culture: Rethinking Cosmopolitan Freedom and Trans-Nationalism." *Boundary 2.* 24.2 (1997): 157–97.

Chernaik, Laura. "Spatial Displacements: Transnationalism and the New Social Movements." *Gender, Place and Culture* 3.3 (1996): 251–75.

Cheyette, Bryan. "'Ineffable and Usable': Towards a Diasporic British–Jewish Writing." *Textual Practice* 10.2 (1996): 295–313.

Chomsky, Aviva. "'Barbados or Canada?' Race, Immigration and Nation in Early Twentieth Century Cuba." *Hispanic American Historical Review* 80.3 (2000): 415–62.

Chow, Rey. "Between Colonizers: Hong Kong's Postcolonial Self-Writing in the 1990s." *Diaspora* 2.2 (1992): 151–70.

—— *Writing Diaspora: Tactics of Intervention on Contemporary Cultural Studies.* Bloomington: Indiana University Press, 1993.

Chu, Patricia. "'The Invisible World the Emigrants Built': Cultural Self-Inscription and the Anti-Romantic Plots of the *Woman Warrior*." *Diaspora* 2.1 (1992): 95–115.

Chuh, Kandice. "Transnationalism and Its Pasts." *Public Culture* 9.1 (1996): 93–112.

Ciecko, Anne. "Representing the Spaces of Diaspora in Contemporary British Films by Women Directors." *Cinema Journal* 38.3 (1999): 67–90.

——"Superhit Hunk Heroes for Sale: Globalization and Bollywood's Gender Politics." *Asian Journal of Communication*, forthcoming.

Cizmic, Ivan. "Political Activities of Croatian Immigrants in the USA and the Creation of an Independent Croatia." *Drustvena Istrazivanja* 7.1 (1998): 5–25.

Clark Hine, Darlene and Jacqueline McLeod, eds. *Crossing Boundaries: Comparative History of Black People in Diaspora*. Bloomington: Indiana University Press, 1999.

Clifford, James. "Traveling Cultures." *Cultural Studies*. Ed. Lawrence Grossberg, Cary Nelson, and P. Treichler. New York: Routledge, 1992. 96–116.

——"Diasporas." *Cultural Anthropology* 9.3 (1994): 302–38.

Cochran, Terry. "The Emergence of Global Contemporaneity." *Diaspora* 5.1 (1996): 119–40.

Cohen, Eric. "Israel as a Post-Zionist Society." *Israel Affairs* 1.3 (1995): 203–14.

Cohen, Phil. "Rethinking the Diasporama." *Patterns of Prejudice* 33.1 (1999): 3–22.

Cohen, Rina. "From Ethnonational Enclave to Diasporic Community: The Mainstreaming of Israeli Jewish Migrants in Toronto." *Diaspora* 8.2 (1999): 121–36.

Cohen, Robin. "The Diaspora of a Diaspora: The Case of the Caribbean." *Social Science Information* 31.1 (1992): 159–69.

—— *The Cambridge Survey of World Migration*. Cambridge: Cambridge University Press, 1995.

——"Rethinking 'Babylon': Iconoclastic Conceptions of the Diasporic Experience." *New Community* 21.1 (1995): 5–18.

—— *Global Diasporas: An Introduction*. Seattle: University of Washington Press, 1997.

Cohen, Steven M. and Charles S. Liebman. "American Jewish Liberalism: Unraveling the Strands." *Public Opinion Quarterly* 61.3 (1997): 405–30.

Conniff, Michael L. and Thomas J. Davis. *Africans in the Americas: A History of the Black Diaspora*. New York: St. Martin's Press, 1994.

Constable, Nancy. "At Home But Not at Home: Filipina Narratives of Ambivalent Returns." *Cultural Anthropology* 14.2 (1999): 203–28.

Cultural Studies. Special issue on "Chicana/o Latina/o Cultural Studies: Transnational and Transdisciplinary Movements." 13.2 (1999).

Cunningham, Stuart and John Sinclair. *Floating Lives: The Media and Asian Diasporas*. Brisbane: University of Queensland Press, 2000.

Cusack, Igor. "Hispanic and Bantu Inheritance, Trauma, Dispersal and Return: Some Contributions to a Sense of National Identity in Equatorial Guinea." *Nations and Nationalism* 5.2 (1999): 207–36.

Dabydeen, David and Brinsley Samaroo, eds. *Across the Dark Waters: Ethnicity and Indian Identity in the Caribbean*. Basingstoke: Macmillan, 1996.

D'Agostino, Peter R. "The Triad of Roman Authority: Fascism, the Vatican, and Italian Religious Clergy in the Italian Emigrant Church." *Journal of American Ethnic History* 17.3 (1998): 3–37.

Danforth, Loring M. "National Conflict in a Transnational World: Greeks and Macedonians at the Conference on Security and Cooperation in Europe." *Diaspora* 3.3 (1994): 325–47.

Danticat, Edwidge, ed. *The Butterfly's Way: Voices from the Haitian Dyaspora in the United States*. New York: SoHo, 2001.

Dayal, Samir. "Postcolonialism's Possibilities: Subcontinental Diasporic Intervention." *Cultural Critique* 33 (1996): 113–49.

Davis, Angela Y. "Afro Images: Politics, Fashion and Nostalgia." *Critical Inquiry* 21.1 (1994): 37–45.

DeCosmo, Janet L. "Crossing Gendered Space: An Analysis of Trinidad's Carnival from a Feminist and African-Centered Perspective." *Wadabagei: A Journal of the Caribbean and Its Diaspora* 3.1 (2000): 1–48.

Dei, George J. "Interrogating 'African Development' and the Diasporan Reality." *Journal of Black Studies* 29.2 (1998): 141–53.

Delgado, Guillermo. *Diaspora and Heterocultures: Spanish-speaking Peoples in the US*. Santa Cruz, CA: CLRC, University of California, 1997.

DeLoughrey, Elizabeth. "Gendering the Oceanic Voyage: Trespassing the (Black) Atlantic and Caribbean." *Thamyris* 5.2 (1998): 205–31.

Dhaliwal, Amarpal K. "Reading Diaspora: Self Representational Practices and the Politics of Representation" *Socialist Review* 24.4 (1994): 13–44.

Dharwadker, Aparna. "Diaspora, Nation and the Failure of Home: Two Contemporary Indian Plays." *Theatre Journal* 50.1 (1998): 71–94.

Diawara, Manthia. "Englishness and Blackness: Cricket as Discourse on Colonialism." *Callaloo* 13.4 (1990): 830–43.

—— *African Cinema: Politics and Culture*. Bloomington: Indiana University Press, 1992.

—— ed. *Black African Cinema*. London: Routledge, 1993.

—— *In Search of Africa*. Cambridge, MA: Harvard University Press, 1995.

—— "The 'I' Narrator in Black Diaspora Documentary." *Struggles for Representation: African American Documentary Film and Video*. Ed. Phyllis R. Klotman and Janet K. Cutler. Bloomington: Indiana University Press, 1999. 315–28.

Diawara, Manthia, Houston A. Baker, and Ruth H. Lindenborg, eds. *Black British Cultural Studies*. Chicago, IL: University of Chicago Press, 1996.

Diedrich, Maria, Henry Louis Gates Jr., and Carl Pedersen, eds. *Black Imagination and the Middle Passage*. Oxford: Oxford University Press, 1999. 255–70.

Dingwaney Needham, Anuradha. "Inhabiting the Metropole: C. L. R. James and the Postcolonial Intellectual of the African Diaspora." *Diaspora* 2.3 (1993): 281–303.

—— "Fictions of National Belonging." *Socialist Review* 24.4 (1994): 173–183.

Diouf, Mamadou. "The Senegalese Murid Trade Diaspora and the Making of a Vernacular Cosmopolitanism." Trans. Steven Rendall. *Public Culture* 12.13 (2000): 679–702.

Dirlik, Arif. " 'Like A Song Gone Silent': The Political Ecology of Barbarism and Civilization in *Waiting For the Barbarians* and *The Legend of the Thousand Bulls*." *Diaspora* 1.3 (1991): 321–52.

—— "The Postcolonial Aura: Third World Criticism in the Age of Global Capitalism." *Critical Inquiry* 20.2 (1994): 328–56.

Don-Yehiya, Eliezer. *Israel and Diaspora Jewry: Ideological and Political Perspectives.* Ramat-Gan: Bar-Ilan University Press, 1991.

Donnelly, James S., Jr. "The Construction of the Memory of the Famine in Ireland and the Irish Diaspora, 1850–1900." *Eire-Ireland* 31.1–2 (1996): 26–61.

Dossa, Parin. "(Re)imagining Aging Lives: Ethnographic Narratives of Muslim Women in Diaspora." *Journal of Cross Cultural Gerontology* 14.3 (1999): 245–72.

Duggan, Lisa. "Queering the State." *Social Text* 39 (1994): 1–14.

Dusenberry, Verne A. "Diasporic Imagings and the Conditions of Possibility: Sikhs and the State in Southeast Asia." *Sojourn: Journal of Social Issues in Southeast Asia* 12.2 (1997): 226–60.

Dwyer, Claire. "Negotiating Diasporic Identities: Young British South Asian Muslim Women." *Women's Studies International Forum* 23.4 (2000): 475–86.

Dyatlov, Viktor I., Dimid Dorohov, Dmitri G. Lyustritski, and Yelena V. Palyutina. "The New Chinese Diaspora in Irkutsk and the Receiving Society." *Migration* 29–31 (1998): 63–82.

Ebron, Paula and Anna Lowenhauot Tsing. "From Allegories of Identity to Sites of Dialogue." *Diaspora* 4.2 (1995): 125–51.

Elazar, Daniel J. and Morton Weinfeld, eds. *Still Moving: Recent Jewish Migration in Comparative Perspective.* New Brunswick, NJ: Transaction, 2000.

Eldridge, Michael. " 'Why Did You Leave There?': Lillian Allen's *Geography Lesson.*" *Diaspora* 3.2 (1994): 169–83.

Ellis, Patricia and Zafar Khan. "Diasporic Mobilization and the Kashmir Issue in British Politics." *Journal of Ethnic and Migration Studies* 24.3 (1998): 471–88.

Elmhirst, Rebecca. "A Javanese Diaspora? Gender and Identity Politics in Indonesia's Transmigration Resettlement Program." *Women's Studies International Forum* 23.4 (2000): 487–500.

Endelman, Todd M., ed. *Comparing Jewish Societies.* Ann Arbor: University of Michigan Press, 1997.

Eng, David L. "Out Here and Over There: Queerness and Diaspora in Asian American Studies." *Social Text* 15.3–4 (1997): 31–52.

—— *Racial Castration: Managing Masculinity in Asian America.* Durham, NC: Duke University Press, 2001.

Eng, David L. and Alice Y. Hom, eds. *Q&A: Queer in Asian America.* Philadelphia, PA: Temple University Press, 1998.

England, Sarah. "Negotiating Race and Place in the Garifuna Diaspora: Identity Formation and Transnational Grassroots Politics in New York City and Honduras." *Identities: Global Studies in Culture and Power* 6.1 (1999): 5–53.

Enwezor, Okwui. "Between Localism and Worldliness." *Art Journal* 57.4 (1998): 32–6.

Eriksen, Thomas Hylland. "Indians in New Worlds: Mauritius and Trinidad." *Social and Economic Studies* 41.1 (1992): 157–87.

—— *Us and Them in Modern Societies: Ethnicity and Nationalism in Mauritius, Trinidad and Beyond.* Stockholm: Scandinavian University Press, 1992.

Esman, Milton J. "The Political Fallout of International Migration." *Diaspora* 2.1 (1992): 3–41.

Espin, Oliva. *Women Crossing Boundaries: A Psychology of Immigration and Transformations of Sexuality*. London: Routledge, 1999.

Fabricant, Carole. "Riding the Waves of (Post) Colonial Migrancy: Are We All Really in the Same Boat?" *Diaspora* 7.1 (1998): 25–52.

Faist, Thomas. "Transnationalization in International Migration: Implications for the Study of Citizenship and Culture." *Ethnic and Racial Studies* 23.2 (2000): 189–222.

Fanning, Charles, ed. *New Perspectives on the Irish Diaspora*. Carbondale: Southern Illinois University Press, 2000.

Farred, Grant. "You Can Go Home Again, You Just Can't Stay: Stuart Hall and the Caribbean Diaspora." *Research in African Literatures* 27.4 (1996): 28–48.

—— "Endgame Identity? Mapping the New Left Roots of Identity Politics." *New Literary History* 31.4 (2000) 627–49.

Feldman, Allen. "'Gaelic Gotham': Decontextualizing the Diaspora." *Eire-Ireland* 31.1–2 (1996): 189–201.

Fleras, A. *Multiculturalism in Canada: The Challenge of Diversity*. Toronto: Nelson Canada, 1992.

Fletcher, John. "The Huguenot Diaspora." *Diaspora* 2.2 (1992): 251–60.

Foner, Nancy. "What's New About Transnationalism? New York Immigrants Today and at the Turn of the Century." *Diaspora* 6.3 (1997): 355–75.

—— "West Indian Identity in the Diaspora: Comparative and Historical Perspectives." *Latin American Perspectives* 25.3 (1998): 173–88.

Fortier, Anne Marie. "The Politics of 'Italians Abroad': Nation, Diaspora, and New Geographies of Identity." *Diaspora* 7.2 (1998): 197–224.

Foster, Gwendolyn Audrey. *Women Filmmakers of the African and Asian Diaspora: Decolonizing the Gaze, Locating Subjectivity*. Carbondale: Southern Illinois University Press, 1997.

Fromm, Annette. "Greek Jewry in the Twentieth Century, 1913–1983: Patterns of Jewish Survival in the Greek Provinces Before and After the Holocaust." *Journal of the Hellenic Diaspora* 23.1 (1997): 132–35.

Fuglerud, Oivind. *Life on the Outside: The Tamil Diaspora and Long Distance Nationalism*. Sterling, VA: Pluto Press, 1999.

Gabaccia, Donna R. and Frase Ottanelli. "Diaspora or International Proletariat? Italian Labor, Labor Migration, and the Making of Multiethnic States, 1815–1939." *Diaspora* 6.1 (1997): 61–84.

Gafni, Isaiah. *Land, Center and Diaspora: Jewish Constructs in Late Antiquity*. Sheffield: Sheffield University Press, 1997.

Gaillard, Jacques and Anne-Marie Gaillard. "The International Mobility of Brains: Exodus or Circulation?" *Science, Technology and Society* 2.2 (1997): 195–228.

Gaines, Kevin Kelly. "Revisiting Richard Wright in Ghana: Black Radicalism and the Dialectics of Diaspora." *Social Text* 19.2 (2001): 75–101.

Gajjala, Radhika. "Cyborg Diaspora and Virtual Imagined Community: Studying SAWNET." *Cybersociology* 6 (1999): 1–16.

Ganguly, Keya. "Migrant Identities, Personal Memory and the Construction of Selfhood." *Cultural Studies* 6.1 (1992): 27–50.

Garrett, Paul Michael. "Notes from the Diaspora: Anti-Discriminatory Social Work
    Practice, Irish People and the Practice Curriculum." *Social Work Education* 17.4
    (1998): 435–48.
Garvey, Johanna X. K. "Passages to Identity: Re-Membering the Diaspora." *Black
    Imagination and the Middle Passage.* Ed. Henry Louis Gates Jr., Maria Diedrich
    and Carl Pedersen. Oxford: Oxford University Press, 1999. 255–70.
Gavaki, Efie. "Greek Immigration to Quebec: The Process and the Settlement."
    Journal of the Hellenic Diaspora 17.1 (1991): 69–89.
George, Rosemary Marangoly. "'At a Slight Angle To Reality': Reading Indian
    Diaspora Literature." *MELUS* 21.3 (1996): 179–93.
—— "'From Expatriate Immigrant to Immigrant Nobody': South Asian Racial
    Strategies in the Southern Californian Context." *Diaspora* 6.1 (1997): 31–60.
Gerber, David A. "The Political Dilemmas and Opportunities of Diaspora Jewry."
    Journal of Policy History 8.2 (1996): 260–6.
Geschwender, James. "Ethnicity and the Social Construction of Gender in the
    Chinese Diaspora." *Gender and Society* 6.3 (1992): 480–507.
Gibb, Camilla. "Religious Identification in Transnational Contexts: Being and
    Becoming Muslim in Ethiopia and Canada." *Diaspora* 7.2 (1998): 247–69.
Gilbert, Helen, Tseen Khoo, and Jacqueline Lo, eds. *Diaspora: Negotiating Asian
    Australia.* St. Lucia: Queensland University Press, 2000.
Gilman, Sander L. *The Visibility of the Jew in the Diaspora: Body Imagery and its
    Cultural Context.* Syracuse, NY: Syracuse University Press, 1992.
Gilman, Sander L. and Milton Shain. *Jewries at the Frontier: Accommodation,
    Identity, Conflict.* Bloomington: Indiana University Press, 1999.
Gilroy, Paul. "It Ain't Where You're From, It's Where You're At: The Dialectics of
    Diasporic Identification." *Third Text* 13 (winter 1991): 3–16.
—— *The Black Atlantic: Modernity and Double Consciousness.* Cambridge, MA:
    Harvard University Press, 1993.
—— *Small Acts: Thoughts on the Politics of Black Cultures.* London: Serpent's Tail,
    1993.
—— "'After the Love Has Gone': Bio-Politics and Etho-Poetics in the Black Public
    Sphere." *Public Culture* 7.1 (1994): 49–76.
—— "Diaspora." *Paragraph* 17.1 (March 1994): 207–12.
Gitelman, Zvi. "The Decline of the Diaspora Jewish Nation: Boundaries, Content,
    and Jewish Identity." *Jewish Social Studies* 4.2 (1998): 112–32.
Glick-Schiller, Nina and Georges Fouron. "Transnational Lives and National Identi-
    ties: The Identity Politics of Haitian Immigrants." *Comparative Urban and Com-
    munity Research* 6 (1998): 130–61.
—— *Georges Woke Up Laughing: Long-Distance Nationalism and the Search for Home.*
    Durham, NC: Duke University Press, 2001.
Gmelch, G. *Double Passage: The Lives of Caribbean Migrants Abroad and Back Home.*
    Ann Arbor: University of Michigan Press, 1992.
Godden, Richard. "Bourgeois Diaspora 1979–1992." *Critical Survey* 10.2 (1998):
    68–9.
Goekijan, Gregory F. "Diaspora and Denial: The Holocaust and the 'Question' of
    the Armenian Genocide." *Diaspora* 7.1 (1998): 3–24.

Gold, Steven J. "Gender and Social Capital Among Israeli Immigrants in Los Angeles." *Diaspora* 4.3 (1995): 267–301.

Goldschmidt, Henry. " 'Crown Heights is the Center of the World': Reterritorializing a Jewish Diaspora." *Diaspora* 9.1 (2000): 83–106.

Gomez, Michael A. "African Identity and Slavery in the Americas." *Radical History Review* 75 (1999): 111–20.

Goodman, James. "National Multiculturalism and Transnational Migrant Politics: Australian and East Timorese." *Asian and Pacific Migration Journal* 6.3–4 (1997): 457–80.

—— "Marginalisation and Empowerment: East Timorese Diaspora Politics in Australia." *Communal/Plural* 8.1 (2000): 25–46.

Gopinath, Gayatri. " 'Bombay, UK, Yuba City': Bhangra Music and the Engendering of Diaspora." *Diaspora* 4.3 (1995): 303–22.

—— "Funny Boys and Girls: Notes on a Queer South Asian Planet." *Asian American Sexualities: Dimensions of the Gay and Lesbian Experience.* Ed. Russell Leong. New York: Routledge, 1996. 119–27.

—— "Nostalgia, Desire, Diaspora: South Asian Sexualities in Motion." *positions* 5.2 (1997): 467–89.

—— "Homo-Economics: Queer Sexualities in a Transnational Frame." *Burning Down The House: Recycling Domesticity.* Ed. Rosemary Marangoly George. Boulder, CO: Westview Press, 1998. 102–24.

—— "Local Sites, Global Contexts: The Transnational Trajectories of Deepa Mehta's *Fire.*" *Queer Globalization/Local Homosexualities: Citizenship, Sexualities, and the Afterlife of Colonialism.* Ed. Arnaldo Cruz Malave and Martin Manalansan. New York: New York University Press, forthcoming.

Gordon, April. "The New Diaspora: African Immigration to the United States." *Journal of Third World Studies* 15.1 (1998): 79–103.

Gordon, Edmund Taylor. *Disparate Diasporas: Identity and Politics in an African Nicaraguan Community.* Austin: University of Texas Press, Institute of Latin American Studies, 1998.

Gordon, Edmund Taylor, and Mark Anderson. "The African Diaspora: Toward an Ethnography of Diasporic Identification." *Journal of American Folklore* 112.445 (1999): 282–96.

Gosine, Mahin. *The East Indian Odyssey: Dilemmas of a Migrant People.* New York: Windsor Press, 1990.

Gourgouris, Stathis. "Nationalism and Oneirocriticism: Of Modern Hellenes in Europe." *Diaspora* 2.1 (1992): 43–71.

Graham, Mark and Shahram Khosravi. "Home Is Where You Make It: Repatriation and Diaspora Culture among Iranians in Sweden." *Journal of Refugee Studies* 10.2 (1997): 115–33.

Gray, Breda. "Irish Women in London: National or Hybrid Diasporic Identities?" *NWSA Journal* 8.1 (1996): 85–109.

—— "Longings and Belongings: Gendered Spatialities of Irishness." *Irish Studies Review* 7.2 (1999): 193–210.

—— "Gendering the Irish Diaspora: Questions of Enrichment, Hybridization and Return." *Women's Studies International Forum* 23.2 (2000): 167–85.

Gray, Victor. "Beyond Bosnia: Ethno-National Diasporas and Security in Europe." *Contemporary Security Policy* 17.1 (1996): 146–73.

Green, Charles. *Globalization and Survival in the Black Diaspora: The New Urban Challenge*. Albany: State University of New York Press, 1997.

Gregory, Lucille H. "Children of the Diaspora: Four Novels About the African-Caribbean Journey." *African-American Voices in Young Adult Literature: Tradition, Transition, Transformation*. Ed. Karen Patricia Smith. Metuchen, NJ: Scarecrow, 1994.

Grenier, Line and Jocelyne Guilbautt. "*Créolité* and *Francophonie* in Music: Sociomusical Repositioning Where it Matters." *Cultural Studies* 11.2 (1997): 207–34.

Grewal, Inderpal. "The Postcolonial, Ethnic Studies and the Diaspora: The Contexts of Ethnic Immigrant/Migrant Cultural Studies in the US." *Socialist Review* 24.4 (1994): 45–74.

—— *Transnational America: South Asians, Immigration and Diaspora*. Durham, NC: Duke University Press, forthcoming.

Grewal, Inderpal and Caren Kaplan, eds. *Scattered Hegemonies: Postmodernity and Transnational Feminist Practices*. Minneapolis: University of Minnesota Press, 1994.

Gribben, Arthur, ed. *The Great Famine and the Irish Diaspora in America*. Amherst: University of Massachusetts Press, 1999.

Grofoguel, R. "Colonial Caribbean Migration to France, the Netherlands, Great Britain and the United States." *Ethnic and Racial Studies* 20.3 (1997): 594–612.

Grosfoguel, R. and Hector Cordero-Guzman. "International Migration in a Global Context: Recent Approaches to Migration Theory." *Diaspora* 7.3 (1998): 351–68.

Grosfoguel, R. and Chloe S. Georas. "'Coloniality of Power' and Racial Dynamics: Notes toward a Reinterpretation of Latino Caribbeans in New York City." *Identities: Global Studies in Culture and Power* 7.1 (2000): 85–125.

Gross, Joan, David McMurray, and Ted Swedenburg. "Arab Noise and Ramadan Nights: Rai, Rap and Franco-Maghrebi Identity." *Diaspora* 3.1 (1994): 3–39.

Grossman, Andrew, ed. *Queer Asian Cinema: Shadows in the Shade*. New York: Harrington Park Press, 2000.

Grossman, Jeffrey. "Herder and the Language of Diaspora Jewry." *Monatshefte* 86.1 (1994): 59–79.

Guarnizo, Luis Eduardo. "The Rise of Transnational Social Formations: Mexican and Dominican State Responses to Transnational Migration." *Political Power and Social Theory* 12 (1998): 45–94.

Guarnizo, Luis Eduardo and Michael Peter Smith. "The Locations of Transnationalism." *Comparative Urban and Community Research* 6 (1998): 3–34.

Guha, Ranajit. "Not at Home in Empire." *Critical Inquiry* 23.3 (1997): 482–93.

Gundaker, Grey. *Signs of Diaspora, Diaspora of Signs: Literacies, Creolization and Vernacular Practice in African America*. New York: Oxford University Press, 1998.

Gunew, Sneja. "Diaspora and Exile: Translation and Community." *International Journal of Canadian Studies/Revue Internationale D'Études Canadiennes* 18 (1998): 193–9.

Gunning, Sandra. "Nancy Prince and the Politics of Mobility, Home and Diasporic (Mis)Identification." *American Quarterly* 53.1 (2001): 32–69.

Gupta, Akhil and James Ferguson. "Beyond 'Culture': Space, Identity and the
Politics of Difference." *Cultural Anthropology* 7.1 (1992): 6–23.
—— "The Song of the Nonaligned World: Transnational Identities and the Rein-
scription of Space in Late Capitalism." *Cultural Anthropology* 7.1 (1992): 63–79.
Habermas, Jürgen. "The European Nation-State: On The Past and Future of
Sovereignty and Citizenship." Trans. Ciaran Cronin. *Public Culture*. 10.2 (1998):
397–416.
Hall, Stuart. "Cultural Identity and Diaspora." *Identity: Community, Culture,
Difference.* Ed. Jonathan Rutherford. London: Lawrence and Wishart, 1990. 222–
37.
Hammarlund, Anders. "Migrancy and Syncretism: A Turkish Musician in Stock-
holm." *Diaspora* 3.3 (1994): 305–23.
Hanchard, Michael. "Identity, Meaning and the African-American." *Social Text* 24
(1990): 31–42.
—— "Racial Consciousness and Afro-Diasporic Experiences: Antonio Gramsci
Reconsidered." *Socialism and Democracy* 3 (1991): 83–106.
—— "Afro-Modernity: Temporality, Politics and the African Diaspora." *Public
Culture* 11.1 (1999): 245–68.
Hannerz, Ulf. *Transnational Connections: Culture, People, Places.* London:
Routledge, 1996.
Hargreaves, Alex G. *Immigration, Race and Ethnicity in Contemporary France.*
London: Routledge, 1995.
Harney, Stefano. *Nationalism and Identity: Culture and the Imagination in a
Caribbean Diaspora.* Atlantic Highlands, NJ: Zed Books, 1996.
Harper, Philip Brian. "Take Me Home: Location, Identity, Transnational Exchange."
Callaloo 23.1 (2000): 461–78.
Harper, T. N. "Globalism and the Pursuit of Authenticity: The Making of a Dias-
poric Public Sphere in Singapore." *Sojourn: Journal of Social Issues in Southeast
Asia* 12.2 (1997): 261–92.
Harris, Joseph E., Alusine Jalloh, and Stephen E. Maizlish, eds. *Global Dimensions
of the African Diaspora* (2nd edition). Washington, DC: Howard University Press,
1993.
—— eds. *The African Diaspora.* College Station: Texas A&M University Press, 1996.
Hathaway, Heather. *Caribbean Waves.* Bloomington: Indiana University Press, 1999.
Helmreich, Stefan. "Kinship, Nation and Paul Gilroy's Concept of Diaspora." *Dias-
pora* 2.2. (1992): 243–9.
Helton, Arthur C. "Forced Migration, Humanitarian Intervention and Sovereignty."
SAIS Review 20.1 (2000): 61–80.
Henry, Frances. *The Caribbean Diaspora in Toronto: Learning to Live With Racism.*
Toronto: University of Toronto Press, 1994.
Hertzberg, Arthur. "Israel and the Diaspora: A Relationship Reexamined." *Israel
Affairs* 2.3–4 (1996): 169–83.
—— "The Meaning of Zionism for the Diaspora." *Cross Currents* 48.4 (1998–9):
500–9.
Hilal, Jamil M. "The PLO: Crisis in Legitimacy." *Race and Class* 37.2 (1995): 1–18.
Hill, Kulu. "The Estonian Diaspora." *Trames* 1.3 (1997): 277–86.

Hirsch, Marianne. *Family Frames: Photography, Narrative and Postmemory*. Cambridge, MA: Harvard University Press, 1997.

Ho, C. *Saltwater Trinnies: Afro-Trinidadian Immigrant Network and Non-Assimilation in Los Angeles*. New York: AMS, 1991.

Holland, Sharon Patricia. "Bill T. Jones, Tupac Shakur and the (Queer) Art of Death." *Callaloo* 23.1 (2000): 384–93.

Holston, James and Appadurai, Arjun. "Cities and Citizenship." *Public Culture* 8 (1996): 187–204.

Hondagneu-Sotelo, Pierrette. "Women and Children First: New Directions in Anti-Immigrant Politics." *Socialist Review* 25.1 (1995): 169–90.

Howell, Sally. "Cultural Interventions: Arab American Aesthetics between the Transnational and the Ethnic." *Diaspora* 9.1 (2000): 59–82.

Hsu, Ruth. " 'Will the Model Minority Please Identify Itself?' American Ethnic Identity and its Discontents." *Diaspora* 5.1 (1996): 37–63.

Huang, Shirlena, Peggy Teo, and Brenda S. Yeoh. "Diasporic Subjects and Identity Negotiations: Women in and from Asia." *Women's Studies International Forum* 23.4 (2000): 391–8.

Huang, Yunte. "Writing against the Chinese Diaspora." *Boundary 2.* 26.1 (1999): 145–6.

Humphrey, Michael. "Globalization and Arab Diasporic Identities: The Australian Arab Case." *Bulletin of the Royal Institute for Inter Faith Studies* 2.1 (2000): 141–58.

Hune, Shirley, ed. *Asian Americans: Comparative and Global Perspectives*. Pullman: Washington State University Press, 1991.

Ifekuwingwe, Jayne O. "Diaspora's Daughters, Africa's Orphans?: On Lineage, Authenticity and 'Mixed Race' Identity." *Black British Feminism*. Ed. Heidi Safia Mirza. London: Routledge, 1997. 127–52.

—— *Scattered Belongings: Cultural Paradoxes of "Race", Nation and Gender*. London: Routledge, 1999.

Ignacio, Emily Noelle. "Ain't I a Filipino (Woman)?: An Analysis of Authorship/Authority through the Construction of 'Filipina' on the Net." *Sociological Quarterly* 41.4 (2000): 551–72.

Inglis, Christine. "The Chinese of Papua New Guinea: From Settlers to Sojourners." *Asian and Pacific Migration Journal* 6.3–4 (1997): 317–41.

Iordanova, Dina. "The New Russians: Nostalgia for the Occupier, Commiseration for the Immigrant." *Canadian Slavonic Papers–Revue Canadienne des Slavistes* 42.1–2 (2000): 113–29.

Ip, David. "Reluctant Entrepreneurs: Professionally Qualified Asian Migrants in Small Businesses in Australia." *Asian and Pacific Migration Journal* 2.1 (1993): 57–74.

Isenberg, Noah. " 'Critical Post-Judaism': or, Reinventing a Yiddish Sensibility in a Postmodern Age." *Diaspora* 6.1 (1997): 85–96.

Jacobson, Matthew Frye. *Special Sorrows: The Diasporic Imagination of Irish, Polish, and Jewish Immigrants in the United States*. Cambridge, MA: Harvard University Press, 1995.

Jacquemet, Marco. "From the Atlas to the Alps: Chronicle of a Moroccan Migration." *Public Culture* 8.2 (1996): 377–88.

Jain, Ravindra K. "Indian Diaspora, Globalisation and Multiculturalism: A Cultural Analysis." *Contributions to Indian Sociology* 32.2 (1998): 337–60.

—— "Reality and Representation: Aspects of the Electronic Media in Contemporary Indian Society and Diaspora." *Sociological Bulletin* 47.2 (1998): 167–84.

James, Winston and Clive Harris, eds. *Inside Babylon: The Caribbean Diaspora in Britain*. London: Verso, 1993.

Jeganathan, Pradeep. "eelam.com: Place, Nation and Imagi-Nation in Cyberspace." *Public Culture* 10.3 (1998): 515–28.

Jolly, Margaret. " 'Our Part of the World': Indigenous and Diasporic Differences and Feminist Anthropology in America and the Antipodes." *Communal/Plural* 7.2 (1999): 195–212.

Joseph, May. *Nomadic Identities: The Performance of Citizenship*. Minneapolis: University of Minnesota Press, 1999.

Joseph, May and Jennifer Natalya Fink, eds. *Performing Hybridity*. Minneapolis: University of Minnesota Press, 1999.

Jules-Rosette, Benneta. "Identity Discourses and Diasporic Aesthetic in Black Paris: Community Formation and the Translation of Culture." *Diaspora* 9.1 (2000): 39–48.

Jusdanis, Gregory. "Culture, Culture, Everywhere: The Swell of Globalization Theory." *Diaspora* 5.1 (1996): 141–61.

Kadende, Rose Marie. "Interpreting Language and Cultural Discourse: Internet Communication Among Burundians in the Diaspora." *Africa Today* 47.2 (2000): 121–48.

Kaiwar, Vasant and Sucheta Mazumdar, eds. *South Asia and the New Globalization*. Boulder, CO: Westview Press, in press.

Kalra, Virinder S. "Vilayeti Rhythms: Beyond Bhangra's Emblematic Status to a Translation of Lyrical Texts." *Theory, Culture and Society* 17.3 (2000): 80–102.

Kaminsky, Amy K. *After Exile: Writing the Latin American Diaspora*. Minneapolis: University of Minnesota Press, 1999.

Kang, Laura Hyun-Yi. "Si(gh)ting Asian/American Women as Transnational Labor." *positions* 5.2 (1997): 403–37.

Kaplan, Amy and Donald Pease, eds. *Cultures of United States Imperialism*. Durham, NC: Duke University Press, 1993.

Kaplan, Caren. "Deterritorializations: The Rewritings of Home and Exile in Western Feminist Discourse." *The Nature and Context of Minority Discourse*. Ed. Abdul JanMohamed and David Lloyd. New York: Oxford University Press, 1990. 357–68.

—— *Questions of Travel*. Durham, NC: Duke University Press, 1996.

Kaplan, David E. "Reversing the Brain Drain: The Case for Utilising South Africa's Unique Intellectual Diaspora." *Science, Technology and Society* 2.2 (1997): 387–406.

Kardases, Vasiles A. *Diaspora Merchants in the Black Sea: The Greeks in Southern Russia, 1775–1861*. Lanham, MD: Lexington Books, 2001.

Karpathakis, Anna. " 'Whose Church Is It Anyway?' Greek Immigrants of Astoria, New York, and Their Church." *Journal of the Hellenic Diaspora* 20.1 (1994): 97–122.

Karran, Kampta. "Trinidad and Tobago's Parang, Calypso and Chutney." *Indo Caribbean Review* 3.1 (1996): 47–66.

Karsten, Peter. "Cows in the Corn, Pigs in the Garden, and 'the Problem of Social Costs': 'High' and 'Low' Legal Cultures of the British Diaspora Lands in the 17th, 18th, and 19th Centuries." *Law and Society Review* 32.1 (1998): 63–92.

Kasinitz, Philip. *Caribbean New York: Black Immigrants and the Politics of Race.* Ithaca, NY: Cornell University Press, 1992.

Kassabian, Anahid and David Kazanjian. "Melancholic Memories and Manic Politics: Feminism, Documentary, and the Armenian Diaspora." *Feminism and Documentary.* Ed. Diane Waldman, Diane Walker, and Janet Walker. Minneapolis: University of Minnesota Press, 1999. 202–23.

Kastoryano, Riva. "Settlement, Transnational Communities and Citizenship." *International Social Science Journal* 52.3 (2000): 307–12.

Katriel, Tamar. "Remaking Place: Cultural Production in Israeli Pioneer Settlement Museums." *Grasping Land: Space and Place in Contemporary Israeli Discourse and Experience.* Ed. Eyal Ben-Ari and Yoram Bilu. Albany: State University of New York Press, 1997. 147–75.

Kauanui, Kehaulani J. "Off-Island Hawaiians 'Making' Ourselves at 'Home': A (Gendered) Contradiction in Terms?" *Women's Studies International Forum* 21.6 (1998): 681–93.

Kawash, Samira. "The Homeless Body." *Public Culture* 10.2 (1998): 319–39.

Kaya, Ayhan. "Multicultural Clientelism and Alevi Resurgence in the Turkish Diaspora: Berlin Alevis." *New Perspectives on Turkey* 18 (1998): 23–49.

Kearney, M. "The Local and the Global: The Anthropology of Globalization and Transnationalism." *Annual Review of Anthropology* 24 (1995): 547–65.

Keaton, Trica Danielle. "Muslim Girls and the 'Other France': An Examination of Identity Construction." *Social Identities* 5.1 (1999): 47–64.

Kelley, Robin D. G. "The World the Diaspora Made: C. L. R. James and the Politics of History." *Rethinking C. L. R. James.* Ed. Grant Farred. Oxford: Blackwell, 1996. 103–30.

——"'House Negroes on the Loose': Malcolm X and the Black Bourgeoisie." *Callaloo* 21.2 (1998): 419–43.

Kelly, John D. "Diaspora and World War, Blood and Nation in Fiji and Hawai'i." *Public Culture* 7.3 (spring 1995): 475–97.

Kempadoo, Kamala and Jo Doezema, eds. *Global Sex Workers: Rights, Resistance and Redefinition.* London: Routledge, 1998.

Keng, Chua-Siew. "Sunless Days: Questions of Identity and Exile." *Southeast Asian Journal of Social Science* 22.1 (1994): 80–91.

Khan, Aisha. "Migration Narratives and Moral Imperatives: Local and Global in the Muslim Caribbean." *Comparative Studies of South Asia, Africa and the Middle East* 17.1 (1997): 127–44.

Khan, Shahnaz. "Muslim Women: Negotiations in the Third Space." *Signs* 23.2 (1998): 463–94.

Khan, Zafar. "Muslim Presence in Europe: The British Dimension – Identity, Integration and Community Activism." *Current Sociology/Sociologie Contemporaine* 48.4 (2000): 29–43.

Khorana, Meena G., ed. "Diasporic Children: Assimilation or Deracination?" *Book-bird: A Journal of International Children's Literature* 37.2 (1999).

King, Charles and Neil J. Melvin, eds. *Nations Abroad: Diaspora Politics and International Relations in the Former Soviet Union*. Boulder, CO: Westview Press, 1998.

Kirshenblatt-Gimblett, Barbara. "Spaces of Dispersal." *Cultural Anthropology* 9.3 (1994): 339–44.

Kirss, Tiina. "Branches of the Cleft Oak: Homeland–Diaspora Literary Relations in Estonia." *World Literature Today* 72.2 (1998): 317–24.

Kitson, Thomas J. "Tempering Race and Nation: Recent Debates in Diaspora Identity." *Research in African Literatures* 30.2 (1999): 88–95.

Klimt, Andrea. "Enacting National Selves: Authenticity, Adventure, and Disaffection in the Portuguese Diaspora." *Identities: Global Studies in Culture and Power* 6.4 (2000): 513–50.

Kolar-Panov, Dona. "Video and the Diasporic Imagination of Selfhood: A Case Study of the Croatians in Australia." *Cultural Studies* 10.2 (1996): 288–314.

Kolsto, Pal. "The New Russian Diaspora: An Identity of Its Own? Possible Identity Trajectories for Russians in the Former Soviet Republic." *Ethnic and Racial Studies* 19.3 (1996): 609–39.

—— "Territorialising Diasporas: The Case of Russians in the Former Soviet Republics." *Millennium* 28.3 (1999): 607–31.

Kondo, Dorinne. *About Face: Performing Race in Fashion and Theater*. London: Routledge, 1997.

Korom, Frank J. "Memory, Innovation and Emergent Ethnicity: The Creolization of an Indo-Trinidadian Performance." *Diaspora* 3.2 (1994): 135–55.

Koshy, Susan. "The Geography of Female Subjectivity: Ethnicity, Gender, and Diaspora." *Diaspora* 3.1 (1994): 69–84.

—— "Category Crisis: South Asian Americans and Questions of Race and Ethnicity." *Diaspora* 7.3 (1998): 285–320.

Kosmarskaya, Natalya. "Russian Women in Kyrgyzstan: Coping with New Realities." *Women's Studies International Forum* 19.1–2 (1996): 125–32.

Kourvetaris, George A. "Conflicts and Identity Crises among Greek-Americans and Greeks of the Diaspora." *International Journal of Contemporary Sociology* 27.3–4 (1990): 137–53.

Kruger, Loren. "Apartheid on Display: South Africa Performs for New York." *Diaspora* 1.2 (1991): 191–208.

Kulu, Hill and Tiit Tammaru. "Ethnic Return Migration from the East and the West: The Case of Estonia in the 1990s." *Europe Asia Studies* 52.2 (2000): 349–69.

Kumar, Amitava. *Passport Photos*. Berkeley: University of California Press, 2000.

Kun, Josh. "Against Easy Listening: Audiotopic Readings and Transnational Soundings." *Everynight Life: Culture and Dance in Latin/o America*. Ed. Celeste Delgado and José Esteban Muñoz. Durham, NC: Duke University Press, 1997.

—— "The Yiddish Are Coming: Mickey Katz, Anti Semitism and the Sounds of Jewish Difference." *American Jewish History* 87.4 (1999): 343–74.

Kyle, David. "The Otavalo Trade Diaspora: Social Capital and Transnational Entrepreneurship." *Ethnic and Racial Studies*. 22.2 (1999): 422–46.

Labelle, Micheline and Franklin Midy. "Re-Reading Citizenship and the Transnational Practices of Immigrants." *Journal of Ethnic and Migration Studies* 25.2 (1999): 213–32.

Laguerre, Michel S. *Diasporic Citizenship: Haitian Americans in Transnational America*. New York: St. Martin's Press, 1998.

—— "State, Diaspora, and Transnational Politics: Haiti Reconceptualised." *Millennium* 28.3 (1999): 633–51.

Laitin, David D. "Identity in Formation: The Russian-Speaking Nationality in the Post-Soviet Diaspora." *Archives Européennes de Sociologie* 36.2 (1995): 281–316.

Lake, Obiagele. "Toward a Pan-African Identity: Diaspora African Repatriates in Ghana." *Anthropological Quarterly* 68.1 (1995): 21–36.

Lal, Brij. "The Odyssey of Indenture: Fragmentation and Reconstitution in the Indian Diaspora." *Diaspora* 5.2 (1996): 167–88.

Lal, Vinay. "The Politics of History on the Internet: Cyber-Diasporic Hinduism and the North American Hindu Diaspora." *Diaspora* 8.2 (1999): 137–72.

Lao-Montes, Agustin and Arlene Davila. *Mambo Montage: The Latinization of New York*. New York: Columbia University Press, 2001.

Larson, Pier M. "Reconsidering Trauma, Identity, and the African Diaspora: Enslavement and Historical Memory in Nineteenth-Century Highland Madagascar." *William and Mary Quarterly* 56.2 (1999): 335–62.

Lavie, Smadar and Ted Swedenburg, eds. *Displacement, Diaspora and Geographies of Identity*. Durham, NC: Duke University Press, 1996.

Law, Robin, ed. *Source Material For Studying the Slave Trade and the African Diaspora*. Stirling: University of Stirling Press, 1997.

Lazarus, Neil. "Is Counterculture of Modernity a Theory of Modernity?" *Diaspora* 4.3 (1995): 323–39.

Lemelle, Sidney J. and Robin D. G. Kelley, eds. *Imagining Home: Class, Culture, and Nationalism in the African Diaspora*. London: Verso, 1998.

Lentin, Ronit. "A Yiddishe Mame Desperately Seeking a Mame Loshn: Toward a Theory of the Feminisation of Stigma in the Relations between Israelis and Holocaust Survivors." *Women's Studies International Forum* 19.1–2 (1996): 87–97.

Leonard, Karen Isaksen. *Making Ethnic Choices: California's Punjabi Mexican Americans*. Philadelphia, PA: Temple University Press, 1992.

—— "State Culture and Religion: Political Action and Representation among South Asians in North America." *Diaspora* 9.1 (2000): 21–38.

Leong, Russell, ed. *Asian American Sexualities: Dimensions of the Gay and Lesbian Experience*. New York: Routledge, 1996.

Leontis, Artemis. "Beyond Hellenicity: Can We Find Another Topos?" *Journal of Greek Studies* 15.2 (1997): 217–37.

—— "Mediterranean Topographies before Balkanization: On Greek *Emporion*, Revolution and Diaspora." *Diaspora* 6.2 (1997): 179–94.

Lever-Tracy, Constance, David Ip, and Noel Tracy. *The Chinese Diaspora and Mainland China: An Emerging Economic Synergy*. New York: St. Martin's Press, 1996.

—— "Diaspora Capitalism and the Homeland: Australian Chinese Networks into China." *Diaspora* 5.2 (1996): 239–73.

Levine, Robert M. *Tropical Diaspora: The Jewish Experience in Cuba*. Gainesville: University of Florida Press, 1993.

Levy, Andre. "Diasporas through Anthropological Lenses: Contexts of Postmodernity." *Diaspora* 9.1 (2000): 137–58.

Lewis, Marvin A. *Afro-Argentine Discourse: Another Dimension of the Black Diaspora*. Columbia: University of Missouri Press, 1996.

Lie, John. "From International Migration to Transnational Diaspora." *Contemporary Sociology* 24.4 (1995): 303–6.

Lim, Shirley Geok-Lin. "Immigration and Diaspora." *An Interethnic Companion to Asian American Literature*. Ed. King-kok Cheung. Cambridge: Cambridge University Press, 1997. 289–311.

Lim, Shirley Geok-Lin and Amy Ling. *Reading the Literatures of Asian America*. Philadelphia, PA: Temple University Press, 1992.

Lindberg-Seyersted, Brita. *Black and Female: Essays on Writings by Black Women in the Diaspora*. Oslo: Scandinavian University Press, 1994.

Liss, Julia E. "Diasporic Identities: The Science and Politics of Race in the Work of Franz Boas and W. E. B. Dubois, 1894–1919." *Cultural Anthropology* 13.2 (1998): 127–66.

Lomsky-Feder, Edna. "Homecoming, Immigration and the National Ethos: Russian–Jewish Homecomers Reading Zionism." *Anthropological Quarterly* 74.1 (2001): 1–14.

Lowe, Lisa. *Immigrant Acts: On Asian American Cultural Politics*. Durham, NC: Duke University Press, 1996.

Lowenthal, William F. and Karina Burgess, eds. *The California–Mexico Connection*. Stanford, CA: Stanford University Press, 1993.

Lu, Sheldon Hsiao-peng. *Transnational Chinese Cinemas: Identity, Nationhood, Gender*. Honolulu: University of Hawaii Press, 1997.

Lui, Toming Jun. "At an Intercultural Frontier: Concept-Metaphors for the Chinese Diaspora." *The Image of the Frontier in Literature, the Media and Society*. Ed. Will Wright and Steven Kaplan. Pueblo, CO: Society for the Interdisciplinary Study of Social Imagery, University of Southern Colorado, 1997. 72–9.

Lynn, Martin. "Technology, Trade and 'A Race of Native Capitalists': The Krio Diaspora of West Africa and the Steamship, 1852–95." *Journal of African History* 33.3 (1992): 421–40.

Ma, Sheng-mei. *Immigrant Subjectivities in Asian American and Asian Diaspora Literatures*. Albany: State University of New York Press, 1998.

McCaffrey, Lawrence John. *The Irish Catholic Diaspora in America*. Washington, DC: Catholic University of America Press, 1997.

McClintock, Anne, Aamir Mufti, and Ella Shohat, eds. *Dangerous Liaisons: Gender, Nation and Postcolonial Perspectives*. Minneapolis: University of Minnesota Press, 1997.

McDowell, Chris. *A Tamil Asylum Diaspora: Sri Lankan Migration, Settlement and Politics in Switzerland*. Providence, RI: Berghan Books, 1996.

Mac Laughlin, Jim. *Location and Dislocation in Contemporary Irish Society: Emigration and Irish Identities*. Notre Dame, IN: Notre Dame University Press, 1997.

McRoberts, Kenneth. "Diaspora and Exile/La Diaspora et l'exil." Special issue of *International Journal of Canadian Studies/Revue Internationale D'Études Canadiennes* 18 (1998).

Madan, Manu. "'It's Not Just Cricket!' World Series Cricket: Race, Nation, and Diasporic Indian Identity." *Journal of Sport and Social Issues* 24.1 (2000): 24–35.

Mahony, Christina Hunty. "Memory and Belonging: Irish Writers, Radio and the Nation." *New Hibernia Review* 5.1 (2001): 10–19.

Maira, Sunaina. "Desis reprazent: Bhangra Remix and Hip Hop in New York City." *Postcolonial Studies* 1.3 (1998): 357–70.

—— "Identity Dub: The Paradoxes of an Indian American Youth Subculture." *Cultural Anthropology* 14.1 (1999): 29–60.

—— "The Politics of 'Cool': Indian American Youth Culture in New York City." *Encounters: People of Asian Descent in the Americas.* Ed. Roshni Rustomji Kerns, Rajini Srikanth, and Leny Mendoza Strobel. Lanham, MD: Rowman and Littlefield, 1999. 177–93.

—— *Desis in the House: Indian American Culture in New York City.* Philadelphia, PA: Temple University Press, 2002.

Malkki, Liisa. "Citizens of Humanity: Internationalism and the Imagined Community of Nations." *Diaspora* 3.1 (1994): 41–68.

—— "Refugees and Exile: From 'Refugee Studies' to the National Order of Things." *Annual Review of Anthropology* 24 (1995): 495–523.

Manalansan IV, Martin F. "In the Shadows of Stonewall: Examining Gay/Lesbian Transnational Politics and the Diasporic Dilemma. " *GLQ* 2 (1995): 1–14.

Mann, Barbara. "Modernism and the Zionist Uncanny: Reading the Old Cemetery in Tel Aviv." *Representations* 69 (2000): 63–95.

Mann, Coramae Richey. *Unequal Justice: A Question of Color.* Bloomington: Indiana University Press, 1993.

Mannur, Anita. "'At Home in an Indian World': Constructions of Ethnicity in the Works of Farrukh Dhondy and Malcolm Bosse." *Bookbird: A Journal of International Children's Literature* 37.2 (1999): 18–23.

—— "'The Glorious Heritage of India': Notes on the Politics of *Amar Chitra Katha.*" *Bookbird: A Journal of International Children's Literature* 38.4 (2000): 32–3.

—— "Padma's Easy Exoticism: Consuming Alterity in the Melting Pot." *Cultural Studies* forthcoming.

Markowitz, Fran. "Criss-Crossing Identities: The Russian Jewish Diaspora and the Jewish Diaspora in Russia." *Diaspora* 4.2 (1995): 201–10.

—— "Living in Limbo: Bosnian Muslim Refugees in Israel." *Human Organisation* 5.2 (1996): 127–32

—— "Diaspora With A Difference: Jewish and Georgian Teenagers; Ethnic Identity in the Russian Federation." *Diaspora* 6.3 (1997): 331–53.

Marks, Laura U. "A Deleuzian Politics of Hybrid Cinema." *Screen* 35.3 (1994): 244–64.

Martin, Michael T. *Cinemas of the Black Diaspora: Diversity, Dependence and Oppositionality.* Detroit, MI: Wayne State University Press, 1995.

Martinez-Echazabal, Lourdes. "Mestizaje and the Discourse of National/Cultural Identity in Latin America, 1845–1959." *Latin American Perspectives* 25.3 (1998): 21–42.

Mascarenhas-Keyes, Stella. "Language and Diaspora: The Use of Portuguese, English and Konkani by Catholic Goan Women." *Bilingual Women: Anthropological Approaches to Second-Language Use*. Ed. Pauline Burton, Ketaki Kushari Dyson, and Shirley Ardener. Oxford: Oxford University Press, 1994. 149–66.

Mathew, Biju and Vijay Prashad. "The Protean Forms of Yankee Hindutva." *Ethnic and Racial Studies* 23.3 (2000): 516–34.

Matory, Lorand. "The English Professors of Brazil: On the Diasporic Roots of the Yoruba Nation." *Comparative Studies in Society and History* 41.1 (1999): 72–103.

Mavratsas, Caesar. "Approaches to Nationalism: Basic Theoretical Considerations in the Study of the Greek-Cypriot Case and a Historical Overview." *Journal of the Hellenic Diaspora* 22.1 (1996): 77–102.

Meadows, Eddie S. "African Americans and 'Lites Out Jazz' in San Diego: Marketing, Impact, and Criticism." *California Soul: Music of African Americans in the West*. Ed. Jacqueline DjeDje and Eddie S. Meadows. Berkeley: University of California Press, 1998. 244–74.

Mercer, Kobena. "Diaspora Culture and the Dialogic Imagination." *Blackframes: Critical Perspectives on Black Independent Cinema*. Ed. M. Cham and C. Watkins. Cambridge, MA: MIT Press, 1988. 50–61.

—— *Welcome to the Jungle*. London: Routledge, 1994.

Metaferia, Getachew. "The Ethiopian Connection to the Pan-African Movement." *Journal of Third World Studies* 12.2 (1995): 300–25.

Miles, William and Gabriel Sheffer. "Francophonie and Zionism: A Comparative Study in Transnationalism and Trans-Statism." *Diaspora* 7.2 (1998): 119–48.

Mirza, Heidi Safia, ed. *Black British Feminism*. London: Routledge, 1997.

Mirzoeff, Nicholas, ed. *Diaspora and Visual Culture*. London: Routledge, 1999.

Mishra, Vijay. "(B)ordering Naipaul: Indenture History and Diasporic Poetics." *Diaspora* 5.2 (1996): 189–237.

—— "The Diasporic Imaginary: Theorizing the Indian Diaspora." *Textual Practice* 10.3 (1996): 421–7.

—— "New Lamps for Old: Diasporas Migrancy Border." *Interrogating Post-Colonialism: Theory, Text and Context*. Ed. Harish Trivedi and Meenakshi Mukherjee. Rashtrapati Indian Institute of Advanced Study Nivas: 1996.

Mitra, Ananda. "Diasporic Web Sites: Ingroup and Outgroup Discourse." *Critical Studies in Mass Communication* 14.2 (1997): 158–81.

Miyoshi, Masao. "A Borderless World? From Colonialism to Transnationalism and the Decline of the Nation-State." *Critical Inquiry* 19.4 (1993): 726–51.

Moghissi, Haideh. "Away from Home: Iranian Women, Displacement, Cultural Resistance and Change." *Journal of Comparative Family Studies* 30.2 (1999): 207–17.

Moghissi, Haideh and Goodman, Mark J. "'Cultures of Violence' and Diaspora: Dislocation and Gendered Conflict in Iranian–Canadian Communities." *Humanity and Society* 23.4 (1999): 297–318.

Molho, Anthony. "The Jewish Community of Salonika: The End of a Long History." *Diaspora* 1.2 (1991): 100–22.

Monson, Ingrid. "Doubleness and Jazz Improvisation: Irony, Parody and Ethnomusicology." *Critical Inquiry* 20.2 (1994): 283–313.

Moore, David Chioni. "African Philosophy vs. Philosophy of Africa: Continental Identities and Traveling Names for Self." *Diaspora* 7.3 (1998): 321–50.

Morley, David and Kuan-Hsing Chen, eds. *Stuart Hall: Critical Dialogues in Cultural Studies*. London: Routledge, 1996.

Morris, Rosalind C. "Educating Desire: Thailand, Transnationalism and Transgression." *Social Text* 15.3–4 (1997): 53–74.

Mountz, Alison and Richard A. Wright. "Daily Life in the Transnational Migrant Community of Agustin, Oaxaca and Poughkeepsie, New York." *Diaspora* 5.3 (1996): 403–28.

Mudimbe, V. Y. and Chungmoo Choi. *Diaspora and Immigration*. Durham, NC: Duke University Press, 1997.

Mukta, Parita. "The Public Face of Hindu Nationalism." *Ethnic and Racial Studies* 23.3 (2000): 42–466.

Mukuna, Kazadi wa. "Creative Practice in African Music: New Perspectives in the Scrutiny of Africanisms in Diaspora." *Black Music Research Journal* 17.2 (1997): 239–50.

Muñoz, José Esteban. "The Autoethnographic Performance: Reading Richard Fung's Queer Hybridity." *Screen* 36.2 (1995): 83–99.

Murphy, Joseph M. *Working the Spirit: Ceremonies of the African Diaspora*. Boston, MA: Beacon Press, 1994.

Murphy, Peter. "The Seven Pillars of Nationalism." *Diaspora* 7.3 (1998): 369–415.

Murshid, Tazeen M. "Bengali Diaspora Within a UK Context: Examining Some Issues of Ethnicity, Identity and Education." *Contributing to Bengal Studies: An Interdisciplinary and International Approach*. Ed. Enyatur Rahim and Henry Schwarz. Dhaka: Beximco, 1998. 130–9.

Muthyale, John. "Reworlding America: The Globalization of American Studies." *Cultural Critique* 47.1 (2001): 99–122.

Myers, Helen. *Music of Hindu Trinidad: Songs from the India Diaspora*. Chicago: University of Chicago Press, 1998.

Naficy, Hamid. "The Poetics and Practice of Iranian Nostalgia in Exile." *Diaspora* 1.3 (1991): 285–302.

—— "Narrowcasting in Diaspora: Middle Eastern Television in Los Angeles." *Living Color: Race and Television in the United States*. Ed. Sasha Torres. Durham, NC: Duke University Press, 1998. 82–96.

Nagar, Richa. "The South Asian Diaspora in Tanzania: A History Retold." *Comparative Studies of South Asia, Africa and the Middle East* 16.2 (1996): 62–80.

Nandan, Satendra. "Exilic Explorations: Diaspora and Dispossession in Fiji." *Nationalism vs. Internationalism: (Inter)National Dimensions of Literature in English*. Ed. Wolfgang Zach and Ken L. Goodwin. Tubingen: Stauffenberg, 1996.

Nassy Brown, Jacqueline. "Black Liverpool, Black America and the Gendering of Diasporic Space." *Cultural Anthropology* 13.3 (1998): 291–325.

Nelson, Alondra and Thuy Linh N. Tu, eds. *Technicolor: Race, Technology and Everyday Life.* New York: New York University Press, 2001.

Nelson, Cary. "Cohorts: The Diaspora of the Teachers." *Journal of the Midwest Modern Language Association* 32.2–3 (1999): 19–29.

Nelson, Diane M. "Maya Hackers and the Cyberspatialized Nation-State: Modernity, Ethnostalgia and a Lizard Queen in Guatemala." *Cultural Anthropology* 11.3 (1996): 287–308.

Nelson, Emmanuel S., ed. *Reworlding: The Literature of the Indian Diaspora.* Westport, CT: Greenwood Press, 1992.

——ed. *Writers of the Indian Diaspora: A Bio-Bibliographical Critical Sourcebook.* Westport, CT: Greenwood Press, 1993.

Newell, Stephanie, ed. *Images of African and Caribbean Women: Migration, Displacement, Diaspora.* Stirling: University of Stirling Press, 1996.

Newsome, Yvonne. "International Issues and Domestic Ethnic Relations: African Americans, American Jews, and the Israel–South Africa Debate." *International Journal of Politics, Culture and Society* 5.1 (1991): 19–48.

Ng, Franklin, ed. *Adaptation, Acculturation, and Transnational Ties Among Asian Americans.* New York: Garland, 1998.

Nnaemeka, Obioma, ed. *Sisterhood, Feminisms and Power: From Africa to the Diaspora.* Trenton, NJ: Africa World Press, 1998.

Nonini, Donald M. "'Chinese Society,' Coffee-Shop Talk, Possessing Gods: The Politics of Public Space Among Diasporic Chinese in Malaysia." *positions* 6.2 (1998): 439–73.

Nurse, Keith. "Globalization and Trinidad Carnival: Diaspora, Hybridity and Identity in Global Culture." *Cultural Studies* 13.4 (1999): 661–90.

Okafor, Victor Oguejiofor. "The Functional Implications of Afrocentrism." *Western Journal of Black Studies* 18.4 (1994): 185–94.

Okamura, Jonathan Y. "Writing the Filipino Diaspora: Roman R. Cariaga's *The Filipinos in Hawaii.*" *Social Process in Hawaii* 37 (1996): 36–56.

—— *Imagining the Filipino American Diaspora: Transnational Relations, Identities and Communities.* New York: Garland, 1998.

Okpewho, Isidore, Carole Boyce Davies, and Ali A. Mazrui, eds. *The African Diaspora: African Origins and New World Identities.* Bloomington: Indiana University Press, 1999.

Olwig, Karen Fog. "Defining the National in the Transnational: Cultural Identity in the Afro-Caribbean Diaspora." *Ethnos* 58.3–4 (1993): 361–76.

Ong, Aihwa. "On the Edge of Empires: Flexible Citizenship Among Chinese in Diaspora." *positions* 1.3 (1993): 745–78.

—— "Southeast Asian Refugees and Investors in Our Midst." *positions* 3.3 (1995): 806–13.

—— "'A Better Tomorrow'? The Struggle for Global Visibility." *Sojourn: Journal of Social Issues in Southeast Asia* 12.2 (1997): 192–225.

—— *Flexible Citizenship: The Cultural Logics of Transnationality.* Durham, NC: Duke University Press, 1999.

Ong, Aihwa and Donald M. Nonini, eds. *Ungrounded Empires: The Cultural Politics of Modern Chinese Transnationalism.* New York: Routledge, 1997.

Ortiz, Ricardo. "Café, Culpa and Capital: Nostalgia Addictions of Cuban Exile." *Yale Journal of Criticism* 10.1 (1997): 63–84.

Ostergaard-Nielsen, Eva. "Trans-State Loyalties and the Politics of Turks and Kurds in Western Europe." *SAIS Review* 20.1 (2000): 61–80.

Owusu, Kwesi, ed. *Black British Culture and Society.* London: Routledge, 1999.

Pacini Hernandez, Deborah. "Sound Systems, World Beat and the Diasporan Identity in Cartagena, Colombia." *Diaspora* 5.3 (1996): 429–66.

Page, Helan Enoch. "No Black Public Sphere in White Public Space: Racialized Information and Hi-Tech Diffusion in the Global African Diaspora." *Transforming Anthropology* 8.1–2 (1999): 111–28.

Paine, Robert. "Topophilia, Zionism and 'Certainty': Making a Place Out of the Space That Became Israel Again." *The Pursuit of Certainty: Religious and Cultural Formations.* Ed. Wendy James. London: Routledge, 1995. 61–192.

Palmer, R, ed. *In Search of a Better Life: Perspectives on Migration from the Caribbean.* New York: Praeger, 1990.

Pan, Lynn. *Sons of the Yellow Emperor: A History of the Chinese Diaspora.* Boston, MA: Little, Brown, 1990.

Panagakos, Anastasia N. "Citizens of the Trans-Nation: Political Mobilization, Multiculturalism and Nationalism in the Greek Diaspora." *Diaspora* 7.1 (1998): 53–73.

Panford, Kwamina. "Pan-Africanism, Africans in the Diaspora and the OAU." *Western Journal of Black Studies* 20.3 (1996): 140–50.

Panossian, Razmik. "Ambivalence and Intrusion: Politics and Identity in Armenia-Diaspora Relations." *Diaspora* 7.2 (1998): 149–96.

Panov, Dona Kolar. "Video and the Diasporic Imagination of Selfhood: A Case Study of the Croatians in Australia." *Cultural Studies* 10.2 (1996): 288–314.

Parker, Andrew, Mary Russo, Dorris Sommer, and Patricia Yaeger, eds. *Nationalisms and Sexualities.* New York: Routledge, 1992.

Patton, Adell. *Physicians, Colonial Racism and Diaspora in West Africa.* Gainesville: University of Florida Press, 1996.

Patton, Cindy and Benigno Sanchez Eppler, eds. *Queer Diasporas.* Durham, NC: Duke University Press, 2000.

Paul, Heike. "Not 'On the Backs of Blacks': US American (Im)Migration and Jewish Diaspora in the German-Language Writings of Jeannette Lander." *Multilingual America: Transnationalism, Ethnicity, and the Languages of American Literature.* Ed. Werner Sollors. New York: New York University Press, 1998. 281–96.

Paul, Rachel Anderson. "Grassroots Mobilization and Diaspora Politics: Armenian Interest Groups and the Role of Collective Memory." *Nationalism and Ethnic Politics* 6.1 (2000): 24–47.

Paxson, Heather. "Demographics and Diaspora, Gender and Genealogy: Anthropological Notes on Greek Population Policy." *South European Society and Politics* 2.2 (1997): 34–56.

Pease, Donald. "National Identity, Postmodern Artifacts and Postnational Narratives." *Boundary 2* 19.1 (1992): 1–13.

Pedraza, Silvia. "Assimilation or Diasporic Citizenship?" *Contemporary Sociology* 28.4 (1999): 377–81.

Perez-Torres, Rafael. "Nomads and Migrants: Negotiating a Multicultural Post-modernism." *Cultural Critique* 26 (1993–4): 161–89.

Pitner, Julia. "The Palestinian in Diaspora." *Mid American Review of Sociology* 16.1 (1992): 61–88.

Pitts, Walter F. *Old Ship of Zion: The Afro-Baptist Ritual in the African Diaspora.* New York: Oxford University Press, 1993.

Pizanias, Caterina. "(Re)Thinking the Ethnic Body: Performing 'Greekness' in Canada." *Journal of the Hellenic Diaspora* 22.1 (1996): 7–60.

—— "Graph(t)ing the Visual." *Modern Greek Studies in the Diaspora* 15.2 (1997): 268–73.

Plaut, Gunther W. "Jewish Ethics and International Migration." *International Migration Review* 30.1 (1996): 18–26.

Portuges, Catherine. "Accenting LA: Central Europeans in Diasporan Hollywood in the 1940s." *Borders, Exiles, Diasporas.* Ed. Elazar Barkan and Marie-Denise Shelton. Stanford, CA: Stanford University Press, 1998. 46–57.

positions: east asia cultural critique. Special issue on "Asian Transnationalities." 7.3 (1999).

Potts, Lydia. *The World Labour Market: A History of Migration.* London: Zed Books, 1990.

Povinelli, Elizabeth A. "The State of Shame: Australian Multiculturalism and the Crisis of Indigenous Citizenship." *Critical Inquiry* 24.2 (1998): 575–610.

Prakash, Gyan. "The Modern Nation's Return to the Archaic." *Critical Inquiry* 23.3 (1997): 536–56.

Prashad, Vijay. *The Karma of Brown Folk.* Minneapolis: University of Minnesota Press, 2000.

—— *Everybody Was Kung Fu Fighting: Afro-Asian Connections and the Myth of Cultural Purity.* Boston, MA: Beacon Press, 2001.

Premnath, Gautam. "Remembering Fanon, Decolonizing Diaspora." *Postcolonial Theory and Criticism.* Ed. Laura Chrisman and Benita Parry. Cambridge: Brewer, 1999. 57–73.

Price, Sally. *Maroon Arts: Cultural Vitality in the African Diaspora.* Boston, MA: Beacon Press, 1999.

Puar, Jasbir K. "Writing My Way 'Home': Travelling South Asian Bodies and Diasporic Journeys." *Socialist Review* 24.4 (1994): 75–108.

—— "Resituating Discourse of 'Whiteness' and 'Asianness' in Northern England: Second Generation Sikh Women and Construction of Identity." *Socialist Review* 24.1–2 (1995): 21–53.

—— "Transnational Sexualities: South Asian (Trans)nation(alism)s and Queer Diasporas." *Q&A: Queer in Asian America.* Ed. David L. Eng and Alice V. Hom. Philadelphia, PA: Temple University Press, 1998. 405–22.

Pulis, John W. *Moving On: Black Loyalists in the Afro-Atlantic World.* New York: Garland, 1999.

Qureshi, Karen and Shaun Moores. "Identity Remix: Tradition and Translation in the Lives of Young Pakistani Scots." *European Journal of Cultural Studies* 2.3 (1999): 311–30.

Rabin, Elliott. " 'Hebrew' Culture: The Shared Foundations of Ratosh's Ideology and Poetry." *Modern Judaism* 19.2 (May 1999): 119–32.

Radhakrishnan, Rajagopalan. "Towards an Eccentric Cosmopolitanism." *positions* 3.3 (1995): 814–21.

—— *Diasporic Mediations: Between Home and Location.* Minneapolis: University of Minnesota Press, 1996.

—— "Adjudicating Hybridity, Co-ordinating Betweenness." *Jouvert: A Journal of Postcolonial Studies* 5.1 (2000).

Rafael, Vicente. "Nationalism, Imagery and the Filipino Intelligentsia in the Nineteenth Century." *Critical Inquiry* 16.3 (1990): 591–611.

—— "Anticipating Nationhood: Collaboration and Rumor in the Japanese Occupation of Manila." *Diaspora* 1.1 (1991): 67–82.

—— " 'Your Grief is Our Gossip': Overseas Filipinos and Other Spectral Presences." *Public Culture* 9.2 (1997): 267–91.

Rai, Amit. "India On-line: Electronic Bulletin Boards and the Construction of a Diasporic Hindu Identity." *Diaspora* 4.1 (1995): 31–57.

Raj, Dhooleka Sarhadi. "Partition and Diaspora: Memories and Identities of Punjabi Hindus in London." *International Journal of Punjab Studies* 4.1 (1997): 101–27.

Ralston, Helen. "South Asian Immigrant Women Organize for Social Change in the Diaspora: A Comparative Study." *Asian and Pacific Migration Journal* 7.4 (1998): 453–82.

Ram, Kalpana. "Migratory Women, Travelling Feminisms." *Women's Studies International Forum* 21.6 (1998): 571–9.

Rando, Gaetano. "Italian Diaspora Literature and the Social Sphere: Some Theoretical Considerations." *Canadian Ethnic Studies* 28.3 (1996): 95–9.

Rassool, Naz. "Fractured or Flexible Identities? Life Histories of 'Black' Diasporic Women in Britain." *Black British Feminism.* Ed. Heidi Safia Mirza. London: Routledge, 1997. 187–204.

Rath, Sura P. "Home(s) Abroad: Diasporic Identities in Third Spaces." *Jouvert: A Journal of Postcolonial Studies* 4.3 (2000).

Rayaprol, Aparna. *Negotiating Identities: Women in the Indian Diaspora.* Delhi: Oxford University Press, 1997.

Regev, Motti. "Present Absentee: Arab Music in Israeli Culture." *Public Culture* 7.2 (1995): 433–45.

Remtulla, Aly, ed. *Memory, (Re)presentation, Fusion: Popular Culture in South Asian Diasporic Communities.* In press.

Renaz, Celina. "Neither Here Nor There . . . Yet." *Callaloo* 15.4 (1992): 1034–8.

Research in African Literatures. Special issue on "The 'Black Atlantic'." 27.4 (1996).

—— Special issue on "The African Diaspora and its Origins." 29.4 (1998).

Ribeiro, Gustavo Lins. "Transnational Virtual Community? Exploring Implications for Culture, Power and Language." *Organization* 4.4 (1997): 496–505.

Ribenmayor, R. and A. Skotes, eds. *Migration and Identity.* Oxford: Oxford University Press, 1994.

Richmond, Anthony. "Citizens, Denizens and Exiles." *Citizenship Studies* 3.1 (1999): 151–5.

Roach, Joseph. "Barnumizing Diaspora: The 'Irish Skylark' Does New Orleans." *Theatre Journal* 50.1 (1998): 39–51.

Robbins, Bruce. "Some Versions of US Internationalism." *Social Text* 45 (1995): 97–123.

—— *Feeling Global: Internationalism in Distress*. New York: New York University Press, 1999.

Roberts, Martin. "'World Music' and the Global Cultural Economy." *Diaspora* 2.2 (1992): 229–42.

Robin, Diana and Ira Jaffe, eds. *Redirecting the Gaze: Gender, Theory, and Cinema in the Third World*. Albany: State University of New York Press, 1999.

Rosello, Mireille. "Interpreting Immigration Laws: 'Crimes of Homosexuality' or 'Crimes Against Hospitality'." *Diaspora* 8.3 (1999): 209–24.

Rosen, Philip. "Nation and Anti-Nation: Concepts of National Cinema in the 'New' Media Era." *Diaspora* 5.3 (1996): 375–402.

Rothenberg, Celia. "Proximity and Distance: Palestinian Women's Social Lives in Diaspora." *Diaspora* 8.1 (1999): 23–50.

—— "Ties That Bind: The Gulf Palestinian Community in Toronto." *Communal/Plural* 8.2 (2000): 237–55.

Rouner, Leroy S, ed. *The Longing For Home*. Notre Dame, IN: Notre Dame University Press, 1997.

Rouse, Roger. "Mexican Migration and the Social Space of Postmodernism." *Diaspora* 1.1 (1991): 8–23.

—— "Thinking Through Transnationalism: Notes on the Cultural Politics of Class Relations in the Contemporary United States." *Public Culture* 7.2 (1995): 353–402.

Roy, Anindyo. "Postcoloniality and the Politics of Identity in the Diaspora: Figuring 'Home,' Locating Histories." *Postcolonial Discourse and Changing Cultural Contexts: Theory and Criticism*. Ed. Gita Rajan and Radhika Mohanram. Westport, CT: Greenwood Press, 1995.

Roy-Fequiere, Magali. "Contested Territory: Puerto Rican Women, Creole Identity and Intellectual Life in the Early Twentieth Century." *Callaloo* 17.3 (1994): 916–24.

Rubchak, Marian J. "Dancing with the Bones: A Comparative Study of Two Ukrainian Exilic Societies." *Diaspora* 2.3 (1993): 337–71.

Rustomji-Kerns, Roshni, Rajini Srikanth, and Leny Mendoza Strobel, eds. *Encounters: People of Asian Descent in the Americas*. Lanham, MD: Rowman and Littlefield, 1999.

Rutherford, Jonathan, ed. *Identity: Community, Culture, Difference*. London: Lawrence and Wishart, 1990.

Ryang, Sonia. "Nationalist Inclusion or Emancipatory Identity? North Korean Women in Japan." *Women's Studies International Forum* 21.6 (1998): 581–97.

Sadowski-Smith, Claudia. "US Border Theory, Globalization, and Ethnonationalisms in Post-Wall Eastern Europe." *Diaspora* 8.1 (1999): 3–22.

Safran, William. "Diasporas in Modern Societies: Myths of Homeland and Return." *Diaspora* 1.1 (1991): 83–9.

Salamone, Frank. A., ed. *Art and Culture in Nigeria and the Diaspora*. Williams-burg, VA: Department of Anthropology, College of William and Mary, 1991.

Salgado, Maria A. "Women Poets of the Cuban Diaspora: Exile and the Self." *The Americas Review: A Review of Hispanic Literature & Art of the USA* 18.3–4 (1990): 227–34.

Samers, Michael. "The Production of Diaspora: Algerian Emigration from Colonial-ism to Neo-Colonialism (1840–1970)." *Antipode* 29.1 (1997): 32–64.

San Juan Jr., E. "Configuring the Filipino Diaspora in the United States." *Diaspora* 3.2 (1994): 117–33.

——*From Exile to Diaspora: Versions of the Filipino Experience in the United States*. Boulder, CO: Westview Press, 1998.

Sanadijan, Manuchehr. "'They Got Game' Asylum Rights and Marginality in the Diaspora: The World-Cup and Iranian Exiles." *Social Identities* 6.2 (2000): 143–64.

Sanasarian, Eliz. "State Dominance and the Communal Perseverance: The Armenian Diaspora in the Islamic Republic of Iran, 1979–1989." *Diaspora* 4.3 (1995): 243–65.

Sanchez-Gonzalez, Lisa. "Reclaiming Salsa." *Cultural Studies* 13.2 (1999): 237–50.

Sanders, Leslie. "American Scripts, Canadian Realities: Toronto's *Showboat*." *Diaspora* 5.1 (1996): 99–117.

Sansone, Livio. "The Making of a Black Youth Culture: Lower-Class Young Men of Surinamese Origin in Amsterdam." *Youth Cultures: A Cross Cultural Perspective*. Ed. Vered Amit-Talai and Helena Wuff. London: Routledge, 1995. 114–43.

Sayigh, Rosemary. "Palestinian Camp Women as Tellers of History." *Journal of Palestine Studies* 27.2 (1998): 42–58.

Schein, Louisa. "Diaspora Politics, Homeland Erotics, and the Materializing of Memory." *positions: east asia cultural critiques* 7.3 (1999): 697–729.

Schiller, Nina Glick, Linda Basch, and Cristina Blanc-Szanton, eds. *Towards a Transnational Perspective on Migration: Race, Class, Ethnicity and Nationalism Reconsidered*. New York: New York Academy of Sciences, 1992.

Schnapper, Dominique Aron. "A Host Country of Immigrants That Does Not Know Itself." Trans. Lorne Shirinian. *Diaspora* 1.3 (1991): 353–63.

——"From the Nation-State to the Transnational World: On the Meaning and Usefulness of Diaspora as a Concept." Trans. Denise L. Davis. *Diaspora* 8.3 (1999): 225–54.

Schulze, Kirsten E., Martin Stokes, and Colm Campbell, eds. *Nationalism, Minori-ties and Diasporas: Identities and Rights in the Middle East*. New York: Tauris Academic Studies, 1996.

Scott, David. "That Event, This Memory: Notes on the Anthropology of African Diasporas in the New World." *Diaspora* 1.3 (1991): 261–84.

Scourby, Alice. "Ethnicity at the Crossroads: The Case of Greek America." *Journal of the Hellenic Diaspora* 20.1 (1994): 123–33.

Segal, Ronald. *The Black Diaspora*. New York: Farrar, Straus and Giroux, 1995.

Shain, Yossi. "Marketing the Democratic Creed Abroad: US Diasporic Politics in the Era of Multiculturalism." *Diaspora* 3.1 (1994): 84–111.

——"Arab-Americans at a Crossroads." *Journal of Palestine Studies* 25.3 (1996): 46–59.

———— *Marketing the American Creed Abroad: Diasporas in the US and Their Homelands.* Cambridge: Cambridge University Press, 1999.

Shain, Yossi, and Martin Sherman. "Dynamics of Disintegration: Diaspora, Secession and the Paradox of Nation-States." *Nations and Nationalism* 4.3 (1998): 321–46.

Shami, Seteney. "Transnationalism and Refugee Studies: Rethinking Forced Migration and Identity in the Middle East." *Journal of Refugee Studies* 9.1 (1996): 3–26.

Shanes, Joshua. "Yiddish and Jewish Diaspora Nationalism." *Monatshefte* 90.2 (1998): 178–88.

Sharma, Sanjay, John Hutnyk, and Ashwani Sharma, eds. *The Politics of New Asian Dance Music.* London: Zed Press, 1996.

Sharman, Russell Leigh. "Carnival in Costa Rica: Ideology and Phenomenological Experience in Puerto Limon." *Wadabagei: A Journal of the Caribbean and Its Diaspora* 3.1 (2000): 43–62.

Sharot, Stephen. "Judaism and Jewish Ethnicity: Changing Interrelationships and Differentiations in the Diaspora and Israel." *Sociological Papers* 6 (1998): 87–105.

Sharpe, Jenny. "Is the United States Postcolonial? Transnationalism, Immigration and Race." *Diaspora* 4.2 (1995): 181–99.

Sharrad, Paul. "Blackbirding: Diaspora Narratives and the Invasion of the Bodysnatchers." *Span: Journal of the South Pacific Association for Commonwealth Literature & Language Studies* 34–5 (1992–3): 141–52.

Sheinein, David and Lois Baer Barr, eds. *The Jewish Diaspora in Latin America: New Studies on History and Literature.* New York: Garland, 1996.

Shiblak, Abbas. "Residency Status and Civil Rights of Palestinian Refugees in Arab Countries." *Journal of Palestine Studies* 25.3 (1996): 36–45.

Shlapentokh, Vladimir, Munir Sendich, and Emil Payin. *The New Russian Diaspora: Russian Minorities in the Former Soviet Republics.* Armonk, NY: M. E. Sharpe, 1994.

Shofar: Interdisciplinary Journal of Jewish Studies. Special issue on "Jewish Diaspora of Latin America." 19.3 (2001).

Shohat, Ella. "Dislocated Identities: Reflections of an Arab-Jew." *Movement Research: Performance Journal* 5 (1992).

———— "Taboo Memories and Diasporic Visions: Columbus, Palestine, and Arab-Jews." *Performing Hybridity.* Ed. May Joseph and Jennifer Natalya Fink. Minneapolis: University of Minnesota Press, 1999. 131–56.

Shohat, Ella and Robert Stam, eds. *Unthinking Eurocentrism: Multiculturalism and the Media.* London: Routledge, 1994.

Shokeid, Moshe. "My Poly-Ethnic Park: Some Thoughts on Israeli-Jewish Ethnicity." *Diaspora* 7.2 (1998): 225–46.

Shreiber, Maeera Y. "The End of Exile: Jewish Identity and Its Diasporic Poetics." *PMLA: Publications of the Modern Language Association of America* 113.2 (1998): 273–87.

Shukla, Sandhya R. "Building Diaspora and Nation: The 1991 'Cultural Festival of India'." *Cultural Studies* 11.2 (1997): 296–315.

———— "Feminisms of the Diaspora Both Local and Global: The Politics of South Asian Women Against Domestic Violence." *Women Transforming Politics: An*

Alternative Reader. Ed. Cathy J. Cohen, Kathleen B. Jones, and Joan C. Tronto. New York: New York University Press, 1997.

Shuval, Judith. "Migration to Israel: The Mythology of 'Uniqueness'." *International Migration/Migrations-Internationales/Migraciones Internationales* 36.1 (1998): 3–26.

Sicher, Efraim, ed. *Breaking Crystal: Writing and Memory after Auschwitz.* Urbana: University of Illinois Press, 1998.

Siegel, Richard and Tamar Sofer, eds. *The Writer in the Jewish Community: An Israeli–North American Dialogue.* Rutherford, NJ: Fairleigh Dickinson University Press, 1993.

Silvey, Rachel M. "Diasporic Subjects: Gender and Mobility in South Sulawesi." *Women's Studies International Forum* 23.4 (2000): 501–15.

Simon, Jonathan. "Refugees in a Carceral Age: The Rebirth of Immigration Prisons in the United States." *Public Culture* 10.3 (1998): 577–607.

Sinfield, Alan. "Diaspora and Hybridity: Queer Identities and the Ethnicity Model." *Textual Practice* 10.2 (1996): 271–93.

Singh, Anand. "Contradictions in Consciousness or Variations in Tradition: Hindu Women in the South African Diaspora." *Guru Nanak Journal of Sociology* 16.2 (1995): 95–126.

Singh, Darshan Tatla. *The Sikh Diaspora: The Search for Statehood.* Seattle: University of Washington Press, 1999.

Sinn, Elizabeth. "Xin Xi Guxiang: A Study of Regional Associations as a Bonding Mechanism in the Chinese Diaspora. The Hong Kong Experience." *Modern Asian Studies* 31.2 (1997): 375–97.

Siraganian, Lisa. " 'Is This My Mother's Grave?' Genocide and Diaspora in Atom Egoyan's *Family Viewing.*" *Diaspora* 6.2 (1997): 127–54.

Siu, Lok. "Diasporic Cultural Citizenship: Chineseness and Belonging in Central America and Panama." *Social Text* 19.4 (2001): 7–28.

Skrbis, Zlatko. "The Distant Observers? Towards the Politics of Diasporic Identification." *Nationalities Papers* 25.3 (1997): 601–10.

—— "Homeland–Diaspora Relations: From Passive to Active Interactions." *Asian and Pacific Migration Journal* 6.3–4 (1997): 439–55.

—— "Making It Tradeable: Videotapes, Cultural Technologies and Diasporas." *Cultural Studies* 12.2 (1998): 265–73.

Slobin, Mark. "Music in Diaspora: The View From Euro-America." *Diaspora* 3.3 (1994): 243–51.

Slyomovics, Susan. "The Memory of Place: Rebuilding the Pre-1948 Palestinian Village." *Diaspora* 3.2 (1994): 157–68.

Small, Cathy A. *From Tongan Villages to American Suburbs.* Ithaca, NY: Cornell University Press, 1997.

Smith, Anthony. "Chosen Peoples: Why Ethnic Groups Survive." *Ethnic and Racial Studies* 15.3 (1992): 436–56.

—— "Zionism and Diaspora Nationalism." *Israel Affairs* 2.2 (1995): 1–19.

Smith, Graham. "Transnational Politics and the Politics of the Russian Diaspora." *Ethnic and Racial Studies* 22.3 (1999): 500–23.

Smith, Graham and Andrew Wilson. "Rethinking Russia's Post-Soviet Diaspora: The Potential for Political Mobilisation in Eastern Ukraine and North-East Estonia." *Europe Asia Studies* 49.5 (1997): 845–64.

Smith, Michael Pete. "Transnational Migration and the Globalization of Grassroots Movements." *Social Text* 39 (1994): 15–34.

Smith, M. van Wyk. "Writing the African Diaspora in the Eighteenth Century." *Diaspora* 1.2 (1991): 127–42.

Smith-Hefner, Nancy Joan. *Khmer American: Identity and Moral Education in a Diasporic Community.* Berkeley: University of California Press, 1999.

Social Text. Special issue on "Politics of Sport." 14.3 (1996).

Sollors, Werner, ed. *Multilingual America: Transnationalism, Ethnicity, and the Languages of American Literature.* New York: New York University Press, 1998.

Sorensen, Diana. "From Diaspora to Agora: Cortazar's Reconfiguration of Exile." *MLN* 114.2 (1999): 57–88.

Sorenson, John. "Essence and Contingency in the Construction of Nationhood: Transformations of Identity in Ethiopia and Its Diasporas." *Diaspora* 2.2 (1992): 201–28.

—— "Learning to Be Oromo: Nationalist Discourse in the Diaspora." *Social Identities* 2.3 (1996): 439–67.

Soyer, Daniel. "Back to the Future: American Jews Visit the Soviet Union in the 20s and 30s." *Jewish Social Studies* 6.3 (2000): 124–59.

Soysal, Yasemin Nuhoglu. "Citizenship and Identity: Living in Diasporas in Post-War Europe?" *Ethnic and Racial Studies* 23.1 (2000): 1–15.

Spitzer, Leo. "Invisible Baggage in a Refuge From Nazism." *Diaspora* 2.3 (1993): 305–36.

Spivak, Gayatri Chakravorty. "Diasporas, Old and New: Women in the Transnational World." *Textual Practice* 10.12 (1996): 346–59.

Stavans, Ilan. "Introduction to the Hispanic Diaspora." *Massachusetts Review* 37.3 (1996): 317–22.

Stephens, Michelle A. "Black Transnationalism and the Politics of National Identity: West Indian Intellectuals on Harlem in the Age of War and Revolution." *American Quarterly* 50.3 (1998): 592–608.

Stepputat, Finn. "Repatriation and the Politics of Space: The Case of the Mayan Diaspora and Return Movement." *Journal of Refugee Studies* 7.2–3 (1994): 175–85.

Stevens, Christine A. "The Illusion of Social Inclusion: Cambodian Youth in South Australia." *Diaspora* 4.1 (1995): 59–76.

Stillman, Yedida K. and Norman A. Stillman, eds. *From Iberia to Diaspora: Studies in Sephardic History and Culture.* Leiden: E. J. Brill, 1999.

Stratton, Jon. "The Impossible Ethnic: Jews and Multiculturalism in Australia." *Diaspora* 5.3 (1996): 339–73.

—— "(Dis)placing the Jews: Historicizing the Idea of Diaspora." *Diaspora* 6.3 (1997): 301–29.

Suarez, Virgil. "The Culture of Leaving: Balsero Dreams." *Hopscotch: A Cultural Review* 2.2 (2000): 2–13.

Subramani. "The Oceanic Imaginary." *Contemporary Pacific* 13.1 (2001): 149–62.

Sundiata, Ibrahim K. "Puerto Rico and Africa: The Ambiguity of Diaspora." *21st Century Afro Review* 3.1 (1997): 1–36.

Suzuki, Nobue. "Between Two Shores: Transformational Projects and Filipina Wives in/from Japan." *Women's Studies International Forum* 23.4 (2000): 431–44.

Sweet, James H. "Male Homosexuality and Spiritism in the African Diaspora: The Legacies of a Link." *Journal of the History of Sexuality* 7.2 (1996): 184–202.

Swierenga, Robert P. *The Forerunners: Dutch Jewry in the North American Diaspora.* Detroit, MI: Wayne State University Press, 1994.

Szanton-Blanc, Cristina, Linda Basch, and Nina Glick-Schiller. "Transnationalism, Nation-States, and Culture." *Current Anthropology* 36.4 (1995): 683–6.

Tadiar, Neferti Xina M. "Domestic Bodies of the Philippines." *Sojourn: Journal of Social Issues in Southeast Asia* 12.2 (1997): 153–91.

Tagliamonte, Sali and Jennifer Smith. "Roots of English in the African American Diaspora." *Links & Letters* 5 (1998): 147–65.

Takenaka, Ayumi. "Transnational Community and Its Ethnic Consequences: The Return Migration and the Transformation of Ethnicity of Japanese Peruvians." *American Behavioral Scientist* 42.9 (1999): 1459–74.

Tannock, Stuart. "Nostalgia Critique." *Cultural Studies* 9.3 (1995): 453–64.

Taylor, Clarence. "A Glorious Age for African-American Religion." *Journal of American Ethnic History* 15.2 (1996): 79–87.

Temple, Bogusia. "Diaspora, Diaspora Space and Polish Women." *Women's Studies International Forum* 22.1 (1999): 17–24.

Terborg-Penn, Rosalyn, Sharon Harley, and Andrea Benton Rushing, eds. *Women in Africa and the African Diaspora: A Reader,* 2nd edition. Washington, DC: Howard University Press, 1996.

Thomas, Bert. "Caribbean Carnival in the Diaspora: Labor Day in Brooklyn." *Wadabagei: A Journal of the Caribbean and Its Diaspora* 3.1 (2000): 49–75.

Thomas, Mandy. "Crossing Over: The Relationship between Overseas Vietnamese and Their Homeland." *Journal of Intercultural Studies* 18.2 (1997): 153–76.

—— *Place, Memory and Identity in the Vietnamese Diaspora.* New York: Allen and Unwin, 1998.

Threadgold, Terry. "When Home Is Always a Foreign Place: Diaspora, Dialogue, Translations." *Communal/Plural* 8.2 (2000): 193–217.

Todorov, Nikolay. "Politics and Contemporary Bulgaria." *Journal of the Hellenic Diaspora* 19.2 (1993): 109–20.

Tolentino, Roland B. "Bodies, Letters, Catalogs: Filipinas in Transnational Space." *Social Text* 14.3 (1996): 49–76.

Tölölyan, Khachig. "The Nation-State and Its Others: In Lieu of a Preface." *Diaspora* 1.1 (1991): 3–7.

—— "Rethinking Diaspora(s): Stateless Power in the Transnational Moment." *Diaspora* 5.1 (1996): 3–35.

—— "Elites and Institutions in the Armenian Transnation." *Diaspora* 9.1 (2000): 107–36.

Torres, Andres and Jose E. Velazquez, eds. *The Puerto Rican Movement: Voices From the Diaspora.* Philadelphia, PA: Temple University Press, 1998.

Torres, Maria de los Angeles. "*Encuentros y Encontronazos*: Homeland in the Politics and Identity of the Cuban Diaspora." *Diaspora* 4.2 (1995): 211–38.

Torres-Saillant, Silvio. "Diaspora and National Identity: Dominican Migration in the Postmodern Society." *Migration World Magazine* 25.3 (1997): 18–22.

Trinh T. Minh-ha. *When the Moon Waxes Red: Representation, Gender, and Cultural Politics*. New York: Routledge, 1991.

—— *Framer/Framed*. London: Routledge, 1992.

Tsur, Yaron. "Jewish 'Sectional Societies' in France and Algeria on the Eve of the Colonial Encounter." *Journal of Mediterranean Studies* 4.2 (1994): 263–77.

Uberoi, Patricia. "The Diaspora Comes Home: Disciplining Desire in DDLJ." *Contributions to Indian Sociology* 32.2 (1998): 305–36.

Ukadike, N. Frank. "Reclaiming Images of Women in Films from Africa and the Black Diaspora." *Frontiers – A Journal of Women Studies* 15.1 (1994): 102–22.

Van der Veer, Peter T. *Nation and Migration: The Politics of Space in the South Asian Diaspora*. Philadelphia, PA: University of Philadelphia Press, 1995.

Van der Veer, Peter T. and Steven Vertovec. "Brahmanism Abroad: On Caribbean Hinduism as an Ethnic Religion." *Ethnology* 30.2 (1991): 149–66.

Van Hear, Nicholas. *New Diasporas: The Mass Exodus, Dispersal and Regrouping of Migrant Communities*. Seattle: University of Washington Press, 1998.

Van Reenan, Antanas J. *Lithuanian Diaspora: Konigsburg to Chicago*. Lanham, MD: University Press of America, 1990.

Van Wyk Smith, M. "Writing the African Diaspora in the Eighteenth Century." *Diaspora* 1.2 (1991): 127–42.

Varadarajan, Tunku. "Differential Creolization: East Indians in Trinidad and Guyana." *Indo Caribbean Review* 1.2 (1994): 123–40.

Vasile, Elizabeth. "Re-Turning Home: Transnational Movements and the Transformation of Landscape and Culture in the Marginal Communities of Tunis." *Antipode* 29.2 (1997): 177–96.

Velez, Maria Teresa. "*Eya, Arnala*: Overlapping Perspectives on a Santería Group." *Diaspora* 3.3 (1994): 289–303.

Venturino, Steven. "Translating Tibet's Cultural Dispersion: Solzhenitsyn, Paine and Orwell in Dharmasala." *Diaspora* 4.2 (1995): 153–80.

—— "Reading Negotiations in the Tibetan Diaspora." *Constructing Tibetan Culture: Contemporary Perspectives*. Ed. Frank J. Korom. Quebec: World Heritage Press, 1997. 98–121.

Verdicchio, Pasquale. *Bound By Distance: Rethinking Nationalism Through the Italian Diaspora*. Madison, NJ: Farleigh Dickinson University Press, 1997.

Vertovec, Steven. "Community and Congregation in London Hindu Temples: Divergent Trends." *New Community* 18.2 (1992): 251–64.

—— "Three Meanings of 'Diaspora,' Exemplified Among South Asian Religions." *Diaspora* 6.3 (1997): 277–99.

Visweswaran, Kamala. "Diaspora by Design: Flexible Citizenship and South Asians in US Racial Formations." *Diaspora* 6.1 (1997): 5–29.

Walcott, Rinaldo. "Caribbean Pop Culture in Canada: Or, the Impossibility of Belonging to the Nation." *Small Axe* 5.1 (2000): 123–39.

Walters, Ronald W. *Pan Africanism in the African Diaspora: An Analysis of Modern Afrocentric Political Movements.* Detroit, MI: Wayne State University Press, 1993.

Walvin, James. *Making the Black Atlantic: Britain and the African Diaspora.* London: Cassell Academic Press, 2000.

Wang, L. Ling-chi. "The Structure of Dual Domination: Toward a Paradigm for the Study of the Chinese Diaspora in the United States." *Amerasia Journal* 21.1–2 (1995): 149–69.

Wang, L. Ling-chi and Wang Gungwu. *The Chinese Diaspora: Selected Essays.* Singapore: Times Academic Press, 1998.

Warner, Stephen R. and Judith G. Wittner. *Gatherings in Diaspora: Religious Communities and the New Immigration.* Philadelphia, PA: Temple University Press, 1998.

Warren, Kenneth W. "Appeals for (Mis) Recognition: Theorizing the Diaspora." *Cultures of United States Imperialism.* Ed. Amy Kaplan and Donald Pease. Durham, NC: Duke University Press, 1993. 392–406.

Wasserstein, Bernard. *Vanishing Diaspora: The Jews in Europe Since 1945.* Cambridge, MA: Harvard University Press, 1996.

Waters, M. C. "Ethnic and Racial Identities of Second-Generation Black Immigrants in New York City." *International Migration Review* 28.4 (1991): 795–830.

Watkins-Owen, Irma. *Blood Relations: Caribbean Immigrants and the Harlem Community 1900–1930.* Bloomington: Indiana University Press, 1996.

Watney, Simon. "AIDS and the Politics of Queer Diaspora." *Negotiating Lesbian and Gay Subjects.* Ed. Monica Dorenkamp and Richard Henke. New York: Routledge, 1995.

Webb, James L. "The Evolution of the Idaw al-Hajj Commercial Diaspora." *Cahiers d'Études Africaines* 35.2 (1995): 455–75.

Weik, Terry. "The Archaeology of Maroon Societies in the Americas: Resistance, Cultural Continuity, and Transformation in the African Diaspora" *Historical Archaeology* 31.2 (1997): 81–92.

Weinstein, Norman C. *A Night in Tunisia: Imaginings of Africa in Jazz.* Metuchen, NJ: Scarecrow Press, 1992.

Wekker, Gloria. "Mati-ism and Black Lesbianism: Two Ideal Typical Expressions of Female Homosexuality in Black Communities of the Diaspora." *Journal of Homosexuality* 24.3–4 (1993): 145–58.

Wellmeier, Nancy J. *Ritual, Identity and the Mayan Diaspora.* New York: Garland, 1998.

Werbner, Pnina. "Diasporic Political Imaginaries: A Sphere of Freedom or a Sphere of Illusions?" *Communal/Plural* 6.1 (1998): 11–31.

—— "Global Pathways: Working Class Cosmopolitans and the Creation of Transnational Ethnic Worlds." *Social Anthropology* 7.1 (1999): 17–35.

—— "The Materiality of Diaspora – Between Aesthetic and 'Real' Politics." *Diaspora* 9.1 (2000): 5–20.

West, Cornell. "The New Cultural Politics of Difference." *The Identity in Question.* Ed. John Rajchman. New York: Routledge, 1995. 147–71.

Whitten Norman E. and Arlene Torres, eds. *Blackness in Latin America and the Caribbean: Social Dynamics and Cultural Transformations.* Bloomington: Indiana University Press, 1998.

Wickramagamage, Carmen. "Relocation as Positive Act: The Immigrant Experience in Bharati Mukherjee's Novels." *Diaspora* 2.2 (1992): 171–200.

Wieviorka, Michel. "Racism and Diasporas." *Thesis Eleven* 52–5 (1998): 69–81.

Wilentz, Gay. *Binding Cultures: Black Women Writers in Africa and the Diaspora.* Bloomington: Indiana University Press, 1992.

Williams, Bronwyn. "A State of Perpetual Wandering: Diaspora and Black British Writers." *Jouvert: A Journal of Postcolonial Studies* 3.3 (1999).

Wilson, Carlton. "Conceptualizing the African Diaspora." *Comparative Studies of South Asia, Africa and the Middle East* 17.2 (1997): 118–22.

Winders, James A. "African Musicians in Contemporary Paris: Post-Colonial Culture in Exile." *Contemporary French Civilization* 20.2 (1996): 220–30.

Winland, Daphne N. "'We Are Now an Actual Nation': The Impact of Independence on the Croatian Diaspora in Canada." *Diaspora* 4.1 (1995): 3–29.

—— "Contingent Selves: The Croatian Diaspora and the Politics of Desire." *Revija za Sociologiju* 1–2 (1998): 49–57.

—— "Our Home and Native Land'? Canadian Ethnic Scholarship and the Challenge of Transnationalism." *Canadian Review of Sociology and Anthropology* 35.4 (1998): 555–77.

Wolf, Diane. "Family Secrets: Transnational Struggles Among Children of Filipino Immigrants." *Sociological Perspectives* 40.3 (1997): 457–82.

Wong, Lloyd L. "Globalization and Transnational Migration: A Study of Recent Chinese Capitalist Migration from the Asian Pacific to Canada." *International Sociology* 12.3 (1997): 329–51.

Wragg, Sue. "After-Image: Holocaust and Diaspora." *The Image of the Twentieth Century in Literature, Media, and Society.* Ed. Will Wright and Steve Kaplan. Pueblo: University of Southern Colorado, 2000.

Wright, Donald. "Out of Africa in Body and Mind: The Black Diaspora and Pan-Africanism." *Journal of American Ethnic History* 17.1 (1997): 71–5.

Wright, Thomas C. "Legacy of Dictatorship: Works on the Chilean Diaspora." *Latin American Research Review* 30.3 (1995): 198–209.

Xiaoping, Li. "New Chinese Art in Exile." *Border/Lines* 29–30 (1993): 40–4.

Yamanaka, Keiko. "Return Migration of Japanese-Brazilians to Japan: The *Nikkeijin* as Ethnic Minority and Political Construct." *Diaspora* 5.1 (1996): 65–97.

Yang, Mayfair Mei-Hui, ed. *Spaces of Their Own: Women's Public Sphere in Transnational China.* Minneapolis: University of Minnesota Press, 1999.

Yeager, Jack A. "Bach Mai's Francophone Eurasian Voice: Remapping Margins and Center." *Quebec Studies* 14 (1992): 49–64.

Yeoh, Brenda and Shirlena Huang. "'Home' and 'Away': Foreign Domestic Workers and Negotiations of Diasporic Identity in Singapore." *Women's Studies International Forum* 23.4 (2000): 413–29.

Yeoh, Brenda and Katie Willis. "'Heart' and 'Wing', Nation and Diaspora: Gendered Discourses in Singapore's Regionalisation Process." *Gender, Place and Culture* 6.4 (1999): 355–72.

Young, James. "The Holocaust as Vicarious Past: Art Spiegelman's *Maus* and the Afterimages of History." *Critical Inquiry* 24 (1998): 669–99.

Young, Robert J. C. *Colonial Desire: Hybridity in Theory, Culture and Race*. London: Routledge, 1995.

Yue, Ming Bao. "On Not Looking German: Ethnicity, Diaspora and the Politics of Vision." *European Journal of Cultural Studies* 3.2 (2000): 173–94.

Yun, Lisa and Ricardo Rene Laremont. "Chinese Coolies and Afro Slaves in Cuba 1847–74." *Journal of Asian American Studies* 4.2 (2001): 32–69.

Zack-Williams, Alfred D. "African Diaspora Conditioning: The Case of Liverpool." *Journal of Black Studies* 27.4 (1997): 528–42.

Zheng, Su. "Music Making in Cultural Displacement: The Chinese American Odyssey." *Diaspora* 3.3 (1994): 273–88.

Index